ERRORS

IN

ENGLISH COMPOSITION

Owing to the antiquity and rarity of this book, certain pages are regrettably absent, and readability is compromised due to the blurring of the original text. If you possess any insights regarding the availability of these missing sections, kindly inform us. Your assistance is crucial in ensuring the completion of this significant work for the benefit of future generations.

ERRORS

IN

ENGLISH COMPOSITION

IN TWO PARTS

BY

J. C. NESFIELD, M.A.

Published by

Gyan Publishing House
5, Ansari Road
Daryaganj, New Delhi-110002
Phone: 011-47034999, 9811692060
E-mail: books@gyanbooks.com

Distribution Network
gyanbooks.com
India, USA, Canada, UK, Australia

ISBN: 978-93-6208-440-8 (HB)
First Published, 1903

2nd Impression 2024

Printed at: Gyan Press, Delhi.

ERRORS IN ENGLISH COMPOSITION
Author: J. C. NESFIELD

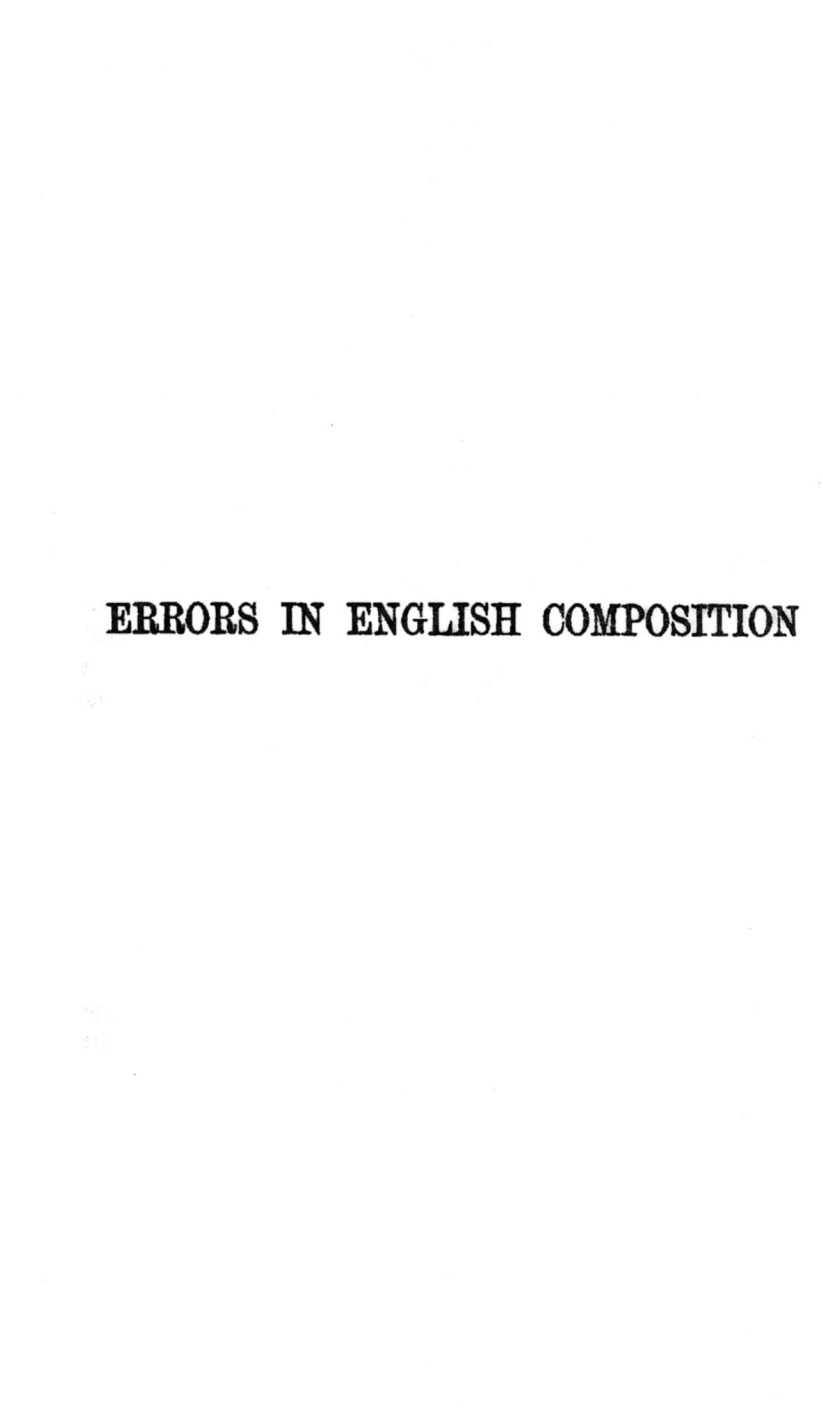

ERRORS IN ENGLISH COMPOSITION

ERRORS

IN

ENGLISH COMPOSITION

IN TWO PARTS

PART I.—SENTENCES TO BE CORRECTED OR JUSTIFIED
II.—SOLUTIONS OF EXAMPLES IN PART I

BY

J. C. NESFIELD, M.A.

AUTHOR OF 'ENGLISH GRAMMAR PAST AND PRESENT,' 'HISTORICAL
ENGLISH AND DERIVATION,' ETC.

MACMILLAN AND CO., LIMITED
ST. MARTIN'S STREET, LONDON, W.C.
NEW YORK : THE MACMILLAN COMPANY

1903

PREFACE

THIS book is called "Errors in English Composition," because it chiefly consists of examples in which some error in Grammar, Construction, or Order occurs. The sentences, which the student is asked to "correct, improve, or justify," have been taken both from literature and from journalism, mainly, however, from the latter, and mainly from very recent journalism. They are likely, therefore, to show the kinds of inaccuracies which (if my views on such matters are sound) are most prevalent at the present day, and against which a writer who desires to be accurate has most need to be on his guard.

Certain books, or rather certain portions of books, having the same object in view have been published already, viz. the section on "Solecisms" in Campbell's *Philosophy of Rhetoric*; the long chapter on "Composition" in Breen's *Modern English Literature, Its Blemishes and Defects;* and Part II., dealing with "Accidence," together with Part III., on "Syntax," in Hodgson's *Errors in the Use of English*,—the most complete book of the three.

In each of these books the solution of every sentence that is quoted for correction is given immediately under the sentence itself. My own plan is different. I have given the solutions at the end of the book quite apart from the sentences themselves (just as "Answers to Examples" are given at the end of a book on Arithmetic), so that the student may have the profitable labour of examining and, if necessary, correcting each sentence himself, before he refers to the answer for verification.

Most students, even those who have made some progress in original composition, find it necessary to revise the first draft of an essay before making a fair copy. Practice in working out the examples given in this book will, it is hoped, be an aid to such revision, by showing the student what kinds of mistakes

v

he is likely to make, and in what way or ways such mistakes can be put right As the book contains a key to all the examples that it contains, it can be used privately by any one who desires to study its contents without the help of a teacher. If it should be used in class, I advise that the students be required to give their answers orally and at sight, so that greater facility may be acquired in the detection and avoidance of error, and time may not be wasted either in preparation or in writing.

At the head of each set of examples I have given a few notes explaining the principles involved.

There are some points in English Grammar and Construction about which no final settlement equally satisfactory to all has yet been reached. On all such points I have given my own view and the reasons for it. But no one, as I need scarcely add, is obliged to endorse what I say, if he sees reason to dissent, and can substitute something which he considers better.

J. C. NESFIELD.

April 1903.

CONTENTS

PART II.—SOLUTIONS OF EXAMPLES IN PART I.

PART I.—SENTENCES TO BE CORRECTED OR JUSTIFIED.

CHAPTER I.—ERRORS OF GRAMMAR.

By errors of grammar are meant errors in Accidence, Concord, and Government. The present chapter consists mainly of sentences involving such errors. The student is asked to examine these sentences, and where he sees reason, to correct them. The answers will be found in Part II. But he is advised not to refer to these answers, until he has studied each sentence himself, and decided what correction, if any, is needed.

It has been found convenient to subdivide the sentences contained in this chapter into two main classes—(a) those involving questions of Verb and Subject, in which errors are more likely to be made than in any others ; (b) those involving questions of any other kind, and therefore headed "miscellaneous." At the head of each section I have given a few notes calling attention to certain salient points in which errors are most commonly met with, or about which the student may feel some uncertainty.

(a) Verb and Subject.

1. Two Singular subjects followed by a Singular verb. —Three different cases arise :—

(a) When the two Singular nouns refer to the same person or thing, and have but one article or other qualifying word in front of them, the verb is Singular. In such a case the plurality is apparent, not real.

> The poet and statesman *is* dead.

This is equivalent to saying, "The man who was both poet and statesmen is dead." If different persons had been intended, the sentence would have been, "The poet and *the* statesmen *are* dead." Here observe the article is repeated.

When the Duke died, his son and namesake and successor *was* an infant.

Here observe *son*, *namesake*, and *successor* all refer to the same person, and have a single qualifying word, "his," placed before them.

(*b*) When the two Singular nouns are practically synonymous, one being added to the other for the sake of emphasis or elucidation, the verb may be Singular. No plurality is felt to exist in such a case.

His power and influence *is* quite as much their creation as *it is that* of the Unionists.—*Spectator*, p. 209, Aug. 17, 1901.

Wherein *doth* sit the fear and dread of kings.—SHAKESPEARE.

The peace and good order of society *was* not promoted by the feudal system.—HALLAM.

The very scheme and plan of his life differed from *that* of other men.—SEELY.

(*c*) When the two Singular nouns, though not synonymous, are intended to express jointly a single idea or a single whole, the verb may be Singular :—

Bread and butter *is* what they usually have for breakfast.

The ebb and flow of the tides *is* now understood.

The style of a man should be the image of his mind, but the choice and command of language *is* the fruit of experience.—GIBBON's *Autobiography*.

"The choice and command" means "facility in the choice and command." Choice of words necessarily depends on one's having a corresponding command of words. Hence plurality is not felt.

The language and history of the Lithuanians *is* closely connected with *that* of the Greeks.—FREEMAN.

This last example is more doubtful than the three preceding.[1] The language of a nation is often quite independent of its history ; hence two such nouns might correctly be followed by a Plural verb. Observe, however, that the author mentions the article only once,—which shows that he intended language and history to be combined in thought as representing a single fact :—"The character of the language and history," etc.

Both minister and magistrate *is* compelled to choose between his duty and his reputation.—JUNIUS, *Preface to Letters*.

This is obviously indefensible, since "minister" and "magistrate"

---

[1] According to Breen (*Modern English Literature*) this kind of construction is under all circumstances indefensible. The example of some of our best authors is, however, in its favour. Bain, in *Companion to Higher English Grammar*, p. 285, justifies the use of a Singular verb, where the combination of nouns suggest unity or collectiveness.

refer to two entirely distinct persons. Say, "The minister no less than the magistrate is," etc.

2. Singular subject followed by a Plural verb.—Two different cases arise :—

(*a*) When the same Singular noun is qualified by two contrasted adjectives, so that two separate persons or things are thereby denoted, the verb is Plural :—

> The logical and the historical analysis of a language generally *coincide.*—BAIN.

This construction, though grammatically defensible, has an awkward sound, and is not recommended for imitation. Its admissibility depends entirely on the article being repeated before the second adjective. It would sound better, if the noun were made Plural instead of Singular, or if the Singular noun were mentioned twice :—

> The logical and historical analyses of a language generally coincide. (The repetition of the article is not necessary, when the noun is pluralised.)
> The logical analysis and the historical analysis of a language generally coincide.

When there is no article before the two adjectives, the noun must certainly be mentioned twice :—

> Logical analysis and historical analysis generally coincide.
> Linguistic science and mental science are not one and the same thing.—WHITNEY, *Oriental and Linguistic Studies,* p. 261.
> Roman Catholic Europe and reformed Europe *were* struggling for death or life.—MACAULAY, *Hist. England.*

(*b*) When the Singular noun is a noun of Multitude, *i.e.* a Collective noun used in a Distributive or plural sense, the verb is Plural. Here plurality, though not represented by the form of the noun, is felt to exist.

> The Cape Ministry *are* much divided regarding the Imperial policy. —*Daily Telegraph,* p. 10, April 25, 1900.

Here "Ministry" is equivalent to "Ministers." To the same class belong such words as "poultry," "cattle," "vermin," "gentry," "people," all of which express individuals acting singly and apart, and are therefore followed by Plural verbs. ("People," in the sense of nation, as "a people," has a Singular verb.)

Care must be taken that the Collective noun is really used in a distributive sense. Otherwise it is wrong, as in the following example, to make the verb plural :—

> The whole group *do* not as a body wage war on another alien.— ANDREW LANG, *Making of Religion,* p. 289.

It is possible (though the possibility is of very rare occurrence) to use the noun collectively with one verb and distributively with another in the same sentence :—

> The Megarean sect *was* founded by Euclid (not the mathematician), and *were* the happy *inventors* of logical syllogism or the art of quibbling.—TYTLER.   (The sect as a whole was founded by Euclid.   Individuals of the sect were inventors, etc.)

3. Plural Subject followed by a Singular verb.—When the Plural noun is a proper name for some collective unit or some single object, the verb is Singular :—

> Thomson's *Seasons is* studied in class this year, and a noble poem *it is.*
> The *Characteristics* (of Shaftesbury) *consists* of a collection of disquisitions.—CRAIK, ii. 251.
> In Europe the United States *has* no friend except Great Britain. — *Spectator*, p. 649, Nov. 10, 1900.
> The United States easily *take* the lead in the production of pig-iron and steel.—*Review of Reviews*, p. 181, Aug. 1900.   (Change *take* to *takes*, since reference is not made to individual states, but to the United States as one power or nationality competing with all other powers.)

Similarly where a Plural noun denotes some specific quantity considered as a whole, the verb can be Singular, and is generally so in fact :—

> Twenty-four pence *is* equal to two shillings.
> Forty yards *is* a good distance.—SHERIDAN.
> Nine-tenths of the miseries and vices of mankind *proceed* from idleness.—CARLYLE.   (Here the Plural is correct, since number is prominent rather than quantity.)

We have a few nouns which, though Plural in form, are Singular in meaning.   With such nouns a Singular verb is generally preferred.

> *Politics* is not a game any more than is war.—*Daily Telegraph*, p. 8, March 28, 1903.
> Your *amends has* been accepted.   (Never used in the Singular, except in the foreign form, *amende*, which is French, not English.)
> The *wages* of sin *is* death.—*New Testament*.   (We can speak of "a living wage," but it is against idiom to say, "The wage of sin is death.")
> The *news* that you bring *is* most encouraging.   (Always Plural in form.   To express plurality of meaning say, "Items of news.")
> The *means* employed by you *is* sufficient.   (Always Plural in form. To express plurality of meaning say, "The different or several or various means.")

All possible means *have* been adopted. (This may stand, since plurality is expressed by "all.")

4. Exceptional Singulars.—We have a few nouns which, when used in the Singular number, can be followed by a Plural verb :—

> Once more the cannon *have* begun to speak in earnest.—*Daily Telegraph*, p. 9, May 15, 1900.
> The enemy *are* still withdrawing guns and waggons.—*Times Weekly*, p. 274, May 4, 1900.
> From Pretoria there *come* a number of interesting rumours.—*Daily Telegraph*, p. 9, May 22, 1900.
> There *are* plenty of men who would work and not mind the hours. —*Spectator*, p. 408, Sept. 29, 1900.
> A variety of improvements *are* suggested, and some few are actually tried.—*Ibid.* p. 488, April 6, 1901.

Note.—The propriety of placing a Plural verb after such nouns as "number," "plenty," and "variety," depends entirely on the context. Unless the context shows that these nouns are used in a Distributive sense so as to imply plurality, the verb must be Singular.

5. Attraction, or the Error of Proximity.—"Attraction" is the name given to that kind of blunder, in which some violation of Concord or Agreement is produced by the greater nearness of some outside word or words. This is called by Dr. Abbott "the Error of Proximity." There is no kind of Concord in which this error is more frequently exemplified than in the Concord of Verb and Subject.

(*a*) If a Plural noun happens to come between a Singular subject and its Verb, writers are apt to make the verb Plural instead of Singular for no better reason than that the nearest noun is Plural :—

> The Church of England never declared that every one of her articles *are* fundamental in the faith.—ARCHBISHOP LAUD, quoted in *Social England*, p. 144, vol. iv.
> The usual litter of new books *remind* me that, etc.—*Harmsworth's Magazine*, p. 102, Sept. 1901.
> The end was come, as the end of such matters generally *come*, by gradual decay.—KINGSLEY, *Westward Ho!* ch. xxxi.
> All but the very foundation of manners *are* learnt by young people in the hard school of experience.—*Spectator*, p. 366, March 7, 1903.

(*b*) If a Singular noun happens to come between a Plural subject and its Verb, writers are apt to make the verb Singular instead of Plural :—

> Few, if any town or village, in the south of England *has* a name ending in -*by*.—HARRISON, *English Language*.

Few political conspiracies, whenever religion forms a pretext, *is* without a woman.—D'ISRAELI, *Quarrels of Authors.*

(c) If two Singular nouns connected by *and* come between a Singular subject and its Verb, writers are apt to make the verb Plural instead of Singular :—

It is in such moments of gloom and depression that the immortal superiority of genius and virtue most strongly *appear.*—ALISON, *Essay on Chateaubriand.*

It has already been stated that the difference between the new and the old German, the Dutch and the Frisian, the Italian and the Latin, the Roman and the Greek, *are* precisely similar. — LATHAM, *The English Language.*

6. Subject followed by "with."—Another snare, against which the writer should be on his guard, is when a Singular subject is joined to some other noun by the preposition *with.* The use of *with* after a Singular subject does not make the verb Plural.

The farm with all its buildings and live-stock *were* sold for £4000. (Say *was.*)

Instances, however, arise in which a Singular verb, though grammatically correct, does not suit the sense. In such a case *with* must be changed to *and.*

The commander with all his forces *was* destroyed. (Change *with* to *and,* and *was* to *were.*)

Your poor gamekeeper with all his large family *have* been perishing.—FIELDING, *Tom Jones,* ch. iii. (The sense is better than the grammar. Change *with* to *and.*)

7. Subject followed by "as well as."—Another snare is when the Subject is connected with some other noun by *as well as.* The verb must take the number and person of its Subject, *i.e.* of the noun or pronoun preceding *as well as,* whatever may be the number and the person of the noun following : [1]—

The temper as well as the knowledge of a modern historian *require*

---

[1] On this point I find myself at variance with Bain, who in *Higher English Grammar,* p. 306, ed. 1896, justifies such a sentence as the following :—

Pompey as well as Cæsar *were* great men.

He does so on the ground that, if the predicate is meant to be affirmed of both, *as well as* is a synonym of *and.* But *as well as* is not and never can be a synonym of *and.* Bain himself in p. 102 of the same book lays down the fact, universally admitted, that *as well as* gives more emphasis to the first subject than to the second, and that hence the verb belongs to the first and is understood for the second. If no such emphasis is intended, the proper conjunction to use is *and,* not *as well as.*

a more sober and accurate language.—GIBBON, *Decline and Fall.* (Say *requires.*)

Homer as well as Virgil *were* transcribed and studied on the banks of the Rhine and Danube.—*Ibid.*

8. Subjects connected by "either . . . or," "neither . . . nor."—Two or more Singular nouns connected by these conjunctions require a Singular verb. If the subjects differ in number or in person, the verb follows the number and person of that subject which stands nearest to it. Attraction or proximity is here a safe guide.

> It is a speculation upon which neither his works nor his life throws any light.—*Review of Reviews*, p. 440, May 1901. (Correct. But when one of the subjects is Plural, it sounds better to place it last and make the verb Plural.)
>
> Although the bullets were ploughing up all around, neither I nor my pony *was* touched.—WARREN, *Life of Prince Christian Victor.* (Correct.)
>
> To Catherine and Lydia neither the letter nor its writer *was* in any degree interesting.—JANE AUSTEN, *Pride and Prejudice*, ch. xiii. (Correct.)
>
> No action or institution can be stable which *are* not based on reason and the will of God.—M. ARNOLD, *Culture and Anarchy*, p. 9. (Wrong. Change *are* to *is.*)

When two Singular pronouns of different persons are connected by a disjunctive, the verb according to rule should agree with the one nearest to it :—

> Either you or I *am* in the wrong.
> Either he or you *are* in the wrong.
> Either you or he *is* in the wrong.

Such is the rule. But the construction has an awkward sound, which can be obviated by mentioning the verb in its proper form with each Subject :[1]—

> Either you are in the wrong, or I am.
> Either he is in the wrong, or you are.
> Either you are in the wrong, or he is.

9. "Either," "neither," as Distributives. — These, whether they are used as nouns or as adjectives, must be followed by Singular verbs :—

---

[1] I am unable to agree with Hodgson, who, in *Errors in the Use of English*, p. 143, sums up as follows :—"On the whole, the latter (the pluralising of the verb) seems the least objectionable form." This is not consistent with the rule given by the same author that the Disjunctive or alternative conjunctions, when they stand between two Singular subjects, have no pluralising effect on the verb that follows, p. 142.

Homer, you know, has employed many verses in the description of
the arms of Achilles, as Virgil also has in those of Æneas ; yet
neither of them are prolix, because they each keep within the
limits of their original design.—MELMOTH'S *Pliny*, **v.** 6 (H).[1]
(Change *are* to *is*, *they each keep* to *each keeps*, and *their* to *his*.)

Neither of my brothers *do* anything to make this place amusing.—
THACKERAY.   (Change *do* to *does*.)

10. Nouns qualified by "each," "every."—Any noun
qualified by such adjectives must be followed by a Singular
verb.   Even if two nouns so qualified are connected by *and*, the
verb must still be Singular : a Singular verb is demanded by
the decisively Singular effect of "every."

Every trade and (every) industry of men or women *has* its technical
school with advanced and research work.—*School World*, p.
41, Feb. 1901.   (Correct.)

That night every man of the boat's crew save Amyas *were* down
with raging fever.— KINGSLEY, *Westward Ho!* ch. **xxi.**
(Change *were* to *was*.)

The whole book and every component part of it *is* on a large scale.
—MACAULAY.   (This is equivalent to saying—"The whole book
is on a large scale ; and so is every part of it.")

Every emotion and every operation of the mind *has* a corresponding
expression of the countenance.—BAIN.   (Correct.)

11. Pendent Nominative (Nominative without a verb).—
A Nominative (unless it is a Nominative of address) cannot stand
alone, unconnected with some Finite verb as subject or as
complement, or with some participle in the absolute construction,
or with some other Nominative to which it stands in apposition.
A Nominative thus isolated is said to be "pendent" or hanging, *i.e.* hanging loose and detached from the rest of the construction.   (See Note on *than whom* at the close of this section.)

Our revenue system is somewhat inelastic, and I am afraid the
complaint that denudation of forest lands, affecting it may
be the rainfall, is partially true.—CURRIE, *Below the Surface*,
p. 72.   (There is no verb, expressed or understood, to which
denudation is the subject.)

The reason assigned for the revival of this long dormant right,
which was to increase the number of law-lords, by whom
appeals were heard.—MOLESWORTH, *Hist. of Eng.* iii. p. 73.
(In order to give "reason" a predicate-verb cancel the comma
after *right* and cancel *which*.)

He who needs any other lesson on this subject than the whole
course of history affords, let him read Cicero, *De Officiis*—J. S.
MILL, *Essays on Religion*, p. 107.   (In order to give a verb, for
which *he* can be the subject, change *let him* to *should*.   Also

---

[1] The letter *H* here and elsewhere signifies that the example quoted in
the text has been selected from Hodgson's *Errors in the Use of English*.

insert *what* after *than;* otherwise there is no object to the verb "affords.")

12. The verb in a Compound Sentence.—In a Compound sentence a single Predicate is sometimes made to do duty for two Subjects, one of which may be Singular and the other Plural. Provided the verb has the same form in the Singular as in the Plural, such abridgment is admissible. But if the verb has one form in the Singular and another in the Plural, both forms of the verb should be given,—the Singular form for the Singular subject, and the Plural form for the Plural one.

> At which last Amyas shook his head, and said that friars were liars and seeing believing.—KINGSLEY, *Westward Ho!* ch. xi. (Insert *was* between "seeing" and "believing.")

13. The Relative as Subject.—When the Subject of the verb is a Relative pronoun, care must be taken to refer the Relative to its true antecedent or antecedents and to regulate the number and person of the verb accordingly :—

> This is the epoch of one of the most singular discoveries that has been made amongst men.—HUME. (Change *has* to *have*, since "discoveries" is the antecedent.)
>
> Sully bought of Monsieur de la Roche Guyon one of the finest Spanish horses that ever was seen.—SOUTHEY, *The Doctor.* (Change *was* to *were.*)
>
> It is the scent and the beauty of the rose which makes it the prince of flowers. (Change *makes* to *make*, since "which" has two antecedents, "scent" and "beauty.")
>
> Thou art the God that doest wonders.—*Old Testament.* (Change *doest* to *doeth*, as it is actually given in the English Prayer Book. The antecedent is "God," not "thou.")

Note.—As regards the principle involved in the example last given, some latitude is allowed. The verb in the Relative clause is sometimes made to agree in Person with the preceding pronoun, when the said pronoun is connected in sense by the verb *to be* with a noun following :—

> Art not thou that Egyptian which before these days *madest* an uproar."—*Acts* xxi. 38. (The real antecedent is "that Egyptian,' which is in the Third person. But *madest* has been written for *made* through the influence of "thou.")

14. Omission of "that of" after "and."—In consequence of omissions of this kind writers are apt to make a verb Singular which ought to be Plural. Even when the verb is correctly made Plural, the subject should not be expressed elliptically :—

> A rise in rents and wages has been found to go together.—*Spectator,* p. 850, July 3, 1875 (H). (Say, "a rise in rents and *a rise in* wages *have* been found to go together.")

The same line of proof would show that the stature of a man and
boy were identical.—*Contemporary Review*, p. 895, vol. xxiv.
1876 (H). (Say, "the stature of a man and *that of a* boy.")

15. "None," "not one."—*None*, though properly a Singular,
being a compound formed of "not one," is followed by a Plural
verb, when plurality is implied by the sense :—

None of the original characters *survive.*—*Literature*, p. 299, April
14, 1900.

None but the brave *deserves* the fair.—DRYDEN, *Ode on Alexander's
Feast*. (Yet, because plurality is implied by the words "the
brave," *deserves* is almost always misquoted as *deserve*.)

There are times, however, when plurality is not implied by
the sense. In such a case the verb should be Singular :—

I should like to say that *none* (= no one) *admires* the engineers as
a body more than I.—Quoted in *Spectator*, p. 331, Feb. 28,
1903. (Here the Singular, as implied by the sense, is preferable to the Plural. Let the pro-verb *do* be placed after "I.")

16. Singular verb caused by ellipse.—Two kinds of cases
arise :—

(*a*) When the verb precedes its subject, it may agree with
the first only, and be understood of the rest :—

Such *was* the intelligence, the gravity, and the self-command of
Cromwell's warriors.—MACAULAY, *Hist. Eng.* vol. i.

(*b*) When the verb separates its subjects, it may agree with
the first only and be understood of the rest :—

The earth *is* the Lord's, and the fulness thereof.—*Psalm* xxiv. 1.

Ah! then and there *was* hurrying to and fro,
And gathering tears, and tremblings of distress.

BYRON, *Childe Harold*.

17. Pendent Verb (verb without a Nominative).—A Finite
verb must not be left to stand alone, without any Nominative
or other form of subject to which it can be referred :—

Wherein then is to consist the freedom of his heart? We answer,
in self-government on a large scale,—in so dealing with his
years and months *as* shall impart a certain orderly liberty
to his days and hours.—TAYLOR, *Notes from Books*.

There is no Subject to "shall impart"; for *as* preceded by *so* is a
conjunction, not a Relative. Say, "in dealing with his years and
months in such a way as shall impart," etc. *As* is now a Relative,
having "way" for its antecedent.

18. Superfluous Nominative.—If a Nominative has been
already given, it should not be repeated in another form in the
same sentence :—

> The conduct of the King and Cabinet evinced that vacillation *which*, as it is the invariable mark of weakness in presence of danger, so *it* is the usual precursor of the greatest public calamities. —ALISON, *Hist. of Europe from Fall of Napoleon.*

The latter part of the sentence must be rewritten : "which is not only the invariable mark, etc., but the usual precursor," etc.

19. "Much," "more," "little," "less."—When these adjectives are used as nouns, they must be followed by a Singular verb :—

> From every eye and soul *have* disappeared much of the beauty and glory both of nature and life.—WILSON, *Recreations of Christopher North.* (Wrong.)
>
> More than a century and a half *have* elapsed since the first publication of "Gondibert."—D'ISRAELI, *Quarrels of Authors.* (Wrong.)
>
> Concerning some of them little more than the names *are* to be learnt from literary history.—HALLAM'S *Literature of Europe.* (Wrong.)
>
> At present the trade is thought to be in a depressed state, if less than a million of tons *are* produced in a year.—MACAULAY, *Hist. Eng.* (Wrong.)

20. "Many a."—This should be followed by a Singular verb :—

> Many a man *comes* and *goes.*
>
> And many a holy text around she strews,
> That *teach* the rustic moralist to die.—GRAY. (More correctly, *teaches.*)

Note.—Sometimes, however, a Plural is demanded by the context:—

> There *sleep* many a Homer and Virgil, legitimate *heirs* of their genius.—D'ISRAELI, *The Literary Character.* (Repeat *many a* before "Virgil.")

Note to § 11, Pendent Nominative.

Than whom.—Under the heading of Pendent Nominative it will be convenient to allude in this place to the combination *than whom.* The late Professor Nichol says that *whom* is in the wrong case after *than* and should be *who* (see *English Composition*, p. 23). To the same effect Dr. Gow, in his *Method of English*, p. 78, pt. i. says :—"A relative pronoun after *than* is always put in the Objective, even when it ought to be in the Nominative." Similarly, Mr. West, in *Elements of English Grammar*, p. 257, "condemns the expression as ungrammatical," and says that "the case of *whom* is indefensible from the standpoint of grammatical principles." According to these authorities, then, *whom* is wrong, though custom is in its favour, and if "grammatical principles" are not to be violated, *whom* should be changed to *who.* In the present instance, however, custom is more correct than the grammarians ; for if we change *whom* to *who*, we are confronted with the monstrosity of a Pendent Nominative,—a Nominative without a Finite verb to go with it. This is against all "grammatical principles." But it is well in keeping with the spirit of the English language to have *than*, like *before, after, since,* and many other words in very common use, used at one time as an adverb or conjunction, and at another as a preposition. That *than* is used as a preposition in the phrase "than whom" is the explanation, given by Dr. Abbott in *How to Parse*, p. 278, § 496, where the author shows that *than* in the phrase referred to "has assumed the force of a preposition." Sweet, the highest living authority, in § 380 of his *New English Grammar* says :—"In fact, *than* governs an objective case like a preposition in such a construction as—

Beelzebub, than whom

Satan except, none higher sat.—MILTON.

A critic in Southern India fancies that he gets over the difficulty by saying that *than whom* is "an idiom which cannot be parsed," "a triumph of anomaly over grammar." Such a statement contains two blunders : (*a*) It is against all grammar to say *who*, unless you can point to the verb of which it is the subject ; (*b*) *whom* can always be parsed in gender, number, and person with reference to its antecedent.

There is a third blunder involved in calling *than* a conjunction in the phrase *than whom*. This phrase is found only in that clause in which the comparative adjective occurs. But whenever *than* is a conjunction, the comparative adjective occurs in some previous clause,—some clause quite distinct from that containing *than* ; as "He is taller than I am." Here the conjunction or conjunctive word is *than*. But in the sentence—"A man, than whom I never saw a taller, has come,"—the only conjunctive word is *whom, than* having no conjunctive force whatever.

Lastly, it may be as well to point out in this place that Mr. Mason's assertion that "in A.S. *than* (þonne or þanne) was a relative or conjunctive adverb, equivalent to our *when*," is entirely erroneous. "In this sense," he says, "it was used after comparatives to introduce the standard of comparison. 'John is taller than Charles' meant originally—'When Charles is tall (*i.e.* when the tallness of Charles is regarded) John is taller.'" The truth is, *than* was a Demonstrative, not a Relative, adverb in A.S., and it signified, as its modified form *then* does in modern English, "after that." Probably, therefore, the original meaning of "John is taller than Charles" was "John is taller, after that (*i.e.* in a lower degree) Charles is tall."

Correct, improve, or justify the following sentences :—

1. The rightful position and influence of laymen in our Church is the vital question on which hangs the issues of its pending disputes.— *Church Gazette*, p. 43, April 29, 1899.

2. The intelligent and generally peaceable character of the tribes visited by Livingstone in Central Africa are a guarantee that with the introduction of agricultural implements, etc., such a desirable state of matters may speedily follow the opening up of the country.—*Life and Explorations of David Livingstone*, p. 113, chap. vi.

3. Not till then does the old woman seek again the shelter of the workhouse, there to wait for the oblivion and rest that has come to her daughter.—*Review of Reviews*, p. 260, March 1900.

4. To write, to speak, or to act seem uncommonly easy to a number of over-confident persons.—*Fortnightly Review*, p. 749, May 1900.

5. The colonel was very proud of me for offering to go and spike the enemy's cannon, but said he could not afford to lose such men as me.—Letter quoted in *Morning Leader*, p. 6, March 21, 1900.

6. In what manner the Powers could succeed in adjusting their relations upon a peaceful basis, passes the wit of man to predict.— *Daily Telegraph*, p. 9, July 2, 1900.

7. This book would be regarded by our modern wits as one of the most shining tracts of morality that is extant.—ADDISON, *Spectator*, No. 68, para. 2.

8. But each and all of these satisfying, if hopeless, theories is successively crushed by the evidence to hand within the covers of this one blue book.—*Pioneer Mail*, p. 6, May 11, 1900.

9. He submitted that upon all the facts of the case the Crown were entitled to judgment.—*Daily Telegraph*, p. 4, May 9, 1900.

10. Keen disappointment and chagrin is felt that we have lost the services of Admiral Seymour on the sea.—*Daily Express*, p. 1, June 19, 1900.

11. Before the mines can begin work again, much pumping and repairing of machinery is required.—*Daily Telegraph*, p. 9, July 9, 1900.

12. A cabman applied to Mr. Plowman for a summons against a fare, whom he alleged had not paid the proper amount.—*Ibid.* p. 9, April 27, 1899.

13. The Little England sect is separated from the Liberal Imperialists by a deeper gulf than divides the latter from the Ministerialists.—*Ibid.* p. 4, Aug. 7, 1900.

14. Neither of the sisters were very much displeased.—THACKERAY.

15. The rapidity of Lord Roberts's movements are deserving of the highest praise.—*Daily Express*, p. 1, May 14, 1900.

16. There are a score of large hotels in the centre of London, the public rooms of which are perhaps too accessible.—*Daily Telegraph*, p. 8, July 13, 1900.

17. The habit of looking for and noticing the smallest signs of objects teach a man to note and carry in his mind those little marks by which he can often obtain important information.—*Ibid.* p. 10, May 18, 1900.

18. England and the world is to be congratulated on the result.— *Ibid.* p. 7, June 1, 1900.

19. The number of Jews in the Russian army are equal to nearly half the whole of the British regular army.—*Pearson's Weekly*, p. 10, Nov. 18, 1899.

20. From one inch to one and a half inches of rain have fallen, extending over the colony generally eastward of the Darling river.— *St. James's Gazette*, p. 9, March 8, 1900.

21. An influential meeting of his constituents at Herschel were solidly adopting resolutions demanding their member's resignation.— *Daily Telegraph*, p. 7, Aug. 2, 1900.

22. Though the strenuous efforts to produce a brilliant effect in all externals has achieved astonishing success, the bright edifices are still far from being completed within.—*Ibid.* p. 9, April 30, 1900.

23. In these phrases of Carlyle lie the secret of the solidarity of the race.—*Literature*, p. 33, April 28, 1900.

24. In colonies, where the ancient quarrels have been after long

years appeased and done with, as in Canada, the goodwill, the sincerity, and the honesty of the English Government is heartily recognised and thoroughly repaid by their affection.—Quoted in *Daily Telegraph*, p. 10, May 30, 1900.

25. The truth is that neither Lord Carnarvon nor Mr. Froude seem to have realised the true character of South African feeling with regard to confederation.—*Fortnightly Review*, p. 672, April 1900.

26. " Who's got a bit of smoked glass ?" demanded a passenger in the front seat.   "Not me," said another, "but I'll soon make one." —*Daily Express*, p. 5, May 29, 1900.

27. A number of cattle was captured.—*Ibid.* p. 1, May 17, 1900.

28. Where a British merchant could do much in opening up new markets lies in learning the language of the country.—Quoted in *Daily Telegraph*, p. 3, Aug. 22, 1900.

29. The news, which the magistrate had almost hesitated to communicate to them, were at length announced.—SCOTT, *Heart of Midlothian*, chap. iii. para. 6.

30. Whomever the would-be assassin might have been, he was not found.—Quoted in *Literature*, p. 556, May 27, 1899.

31. In the case of bad weather a great variety of places of entertainment are open to visitors.—*Pearson's Weekly*, p. 710, April 28, 1900.

32. To every paragraph of praise there is added two of blame and depreciation.—*Review of Reviews*, p. 391, April 1900.

33. To aim at public and private good are so far from being inconsistent, that they mutually promote each other. — BISHOP BUTLER, *Sermon* 1, p. 5.

34. There is characteristic rancour and arrogance in this disdainful attitude.—*Daily Telegraph*, p. 9, April 13, 1900.

35. The strong force under D. W. are completely surrounded at Reitzburg.—*Ibid.* p. 5, Aug. 6, 1900.

36. Its contents, so far as the disaster is concerned, is confirmed by a despatch received at the Berlin Foreign Office.—*Ibid.* p. 9, April 13, 1899.

37. I don't think that ever any series of services were arranged for with more good feeling between all denominations.—*Review of Reviews*, p. 121, Feb. 1900.

38. Our General is considering the question of another campaign against the foe whom we were led to believe had fallen never to rise again.—*Ibid.* p. 412, Oct. 1899.

39. A tribe of Jews form the dominant race among the fierce fighting people of the Atlas Mountains.—*Pearson's Weekly*, p. 10, Nov. 18, 1899.

40. That is the form in which athleticism and sport as a legacy of war realises themselves in time and circumstances.—Quoted in *Literature*, p. 556, May 27, 1899.

41. There are likewise a comparatively numerous body of Jews in the navy, though it is a small one.—*Pearson's Weekly*, p. 10, Nov. 18, 1899.

42. Amongst you, amongst all active races, there is constantly and for ever these two controlling and opposing forces, the active and the passive, the conservatives and the changers.—Quoted in *Educational Review* (Madras), p. 79, Feb. 1900.

43. The event of these things do sufficiently witness.—NORTH's *Plutarch*, 1st ed. p. 553.

44. Yet were their number far above Pompey's.—*Ibid.* p. 309.

45. Oxford were seen to great advantage in the inter-university match at Lord's.—*Daily Telegraph*, p. 6, July 6, 1900.

46. In all their rejoicings the ancients used fires ; but they were intended merely to burn their sacrifices, and which, as the generality of them were performed at night, the illuminations served to give light to the ceremonies.—D'ISRAELI, *Curiosities of Literature*.

47. As far as the Council and Sanitary Inspector is concerned, it is "Theirs not to reason why, Theirs but to do," even though the official may be wrong, but in this case they have their remedy.—*Ealing Guardian*, p. 2, March, 10, 1900.

48. I protest against Mr. T.'s caricature of an individual, whom, I presume, he would have us believe represents some body of people.—Quoted in *Daily Telegraph*, p. 3, Feb. 2, 1900.

49. Plaintiff's horse and cab was overturned, the horse being severely injured and the cab smashed.—*Morning Post*, p. 4, Feb. 28, 1899.

50. Mr. D.'s controversial methods, judging by his letter in the last *Fortnightly Review*, is to evade his opponent's cardinal points and obscure the real issues by incoherent digressions.—CANON MACCOLL in *Fortnightly Review*, p. 717, April 1900.

51. The entire indifference and disbelief of the French public in Central African projects is shown by the following recent case.—*Fortnightly Review*, p. 856, Dec. 1898.

52. Half a million pounds' worth of realisable securities have been found by the military authorities.—*Daily Telegraph*, p. 6, March 30, 1900.

53. The presence of numerous small French posts on Egyptian territory raise questions of the gravest political importance.—*Fortnightly Review*, p. 850, Dec. 1898.

54. Dar Fertit and its ivory was profitable and therefore concealed itself.—*Ibid.* p. 851.

55. A population of 1,500,000, half of which have never been ruled or organised at all.—*Ibid.* p. 855.

56. The narrative of the three Synoptic Gospels are fairly consistent.—LAING, *Problems of the Future*, p. 264, ed. 1893.

57. At this time of day the Absolution of a priest pronounced over a poor dying soul and followed by extreme unction have got to be regarded more charitably than in the days when Protestantism was iron.—*Church Gazette*, p. 424, Feb. 4, 1899.

58. It must be humiliating to those members of the church, who think that the odour of sanctity and intrigue are inconsistent.—*Daily News*, p. 8, May 3, 1899.

59. The riches he has made from the discovery of the yellow metal in South Africa has greatly increased his fortune and his reputation.—*Pearson's Weekly*, p. 841, May 20, 1899.

60. Should he possess any personal sympathy with those under his charge, he rarely dare allow it to find expression in his actions.—*Fortnightly Review*, p. 823, May 1900.

61. By the term "Christian" I mean that quality of conscience and

sympathy, which suffer not a man to rest short of some altar, however rude, on which he offers his life for the common service, the social good.—Dr. HERRON, *Between Cæsar and Jesus,* p. 19.

62. Here then lies the head and front of their offending.—*Church Gazette,* p. 197, June 10, 1899.

63. Nothing is more striking in this controversy than the care with which the really fundamental question, what the spirit and method of Christ's teaching, what His whole religious attitude were, is always shirked.—*Ibid.* p. 151, May 27, 1899.

64. I am pleased to intimate that the expenses of a civil suit against the Company's late local agent has been avoided.—*Upper India Paper Mills Report,* Lucknow, Feb. 25, 1899.

65. It is superfluous to call attention to Dr. Moeller's merits as an historian,—his immense industry and invariably sound judgment,— which does not fail him even in dealing with the thorny period here covered.—*Literature,* p. 187, March 3, 1900.

66. The clerical costume and countenance does not attract confidence from the average man. —*Church Gazette,* p. 189, June 3, 1899.

67. The conscious pioneers of all the wealth and commerce and beauty and science, which has in later centuries made that lovely isle the richest gem of all the tropic seas.—KINGSLEY, *Westward Ho!* ch. xvii. p. 281.

68. That the books will be High Church in tone, the names of the gentlemen who will be responsible for the different volumes leaves no doubt, while at the same time they afford a promise of fairness of treatment.—*Church Gazette,* p. 203, June 10, 1899.

69. The evidence of Picquart and Bertulus contains the pith and marrow of this entangled question.—*Daily Telegraph,* p. 10, Aug. 19, 1900.

70. Hence this autobiography, in which is recorded the opinions of Augustine the Man on Augustine the King.—*Review of Reviews,* p. 418, Oct. 1899.

71. The very quality of the effort, its admirable consistency, its success won in the face of self-created difficulties, makes this point but the more evident.—*Daily Telegraph,* p. 10, Feb. 13, 1900.

72. They did not enter into these questions of sects, and neither Hanan nor Habakkuk appear to have been disturbed.—RENAN, *Hist. of Israel,* ch. xxi. pp. 153-54.

73. The entry of the allies into Pekin and the relief of the Europeans has been officially confirmed here as elsewhere. —*Daily Telegraph,* p. 3, Aug. 20, 1900.

74. They received travelling expenses varying from 15 to 30 guineas, two-thirds of which is paid before they start.—*Review of Reviews,* p. 119, Aug. 1900.

75. Splendour and grace was lent to the work of my father by my august and venerated mother.—Quoted in *Spectator,* p. 199, Aug. 18, 1900.

76. Thou who art a man of influence among thine own people lie here wounded.—BINION, *Quo Vadis?* p. 191, ch. i.

77. The elaboration, the completeness, and the exactitude with which this task is executed, distinguishes the *Century Dictionary*

from every other published.—Advertisement published in all the news-papers in May 1899.

78. To the interstices cling many a bush and even trees, while from the gate-towers frown tier upon tier of painted representations of cannon.—COLQUHOUN's *China*, quoted in *Review of Reviews*, p. 89, July 1900.

79. The possession of mathematical genius and the study of mathematical principles is no adequate guarantee for the solidity or comprehensiveness of the moral and speculative judgment.—HUTTON, quoted in *Church Gazette*, p. 50, April 29, 1899.

80. The remembrance of these things were still fresh.—NORTH's *Plutarch*, p. 1003, 1st ed.

81. There was mingled now and then pastime and pleasure.—*Ibid.* p. 66.

82. The spiritual and the temporal ruler ever thus appear in the theocracy.—M'ILWAINE, *A Religious Establishment*, p. 32 (H).

83. Sacred and profane wisdom agree in declaring that "pride goeth before a fall."—*Church Times*, p. 227, June 11, 1869 (H).

84. The wanton destructiveness and vindictiveness of the enemy is simply unsurpassable, and there is no limit to his audacity.—Quoted in *Daily Telegraph*, p. 9, Sept. 19, 1900.

85. That this set of plants have a square stem, while that is always round in sections,—that one had pale and another vivid blossoms,—such things have long been known and used for purposes of classification.—*Literature*, p. 489, April 29, 1899.

86. At that period when maternal vigilance and supervision were more strict than at present, there were a greater number of runaway matches than are now recorded.—*Daily Telegraph*, p. 7, Sept. 27, 1900.

87. Among the causes, then, that co-operated in fixing this period —December 25—as the birthday of Christ, was, as we have already seen, that almost every nation of the earth held a festival on this day in commemoration of the birth of the new-born sun.—DOANE, *Bible Parallels*, p. 366, ch. xxxiv.

88. In a chapel belonging to the monastery of Pootala, which was found in Manchow-Tartary, was to be seen representations of Fo in the form of three persons.—*Ibid.* p. 372, ch. xxxv.

89. His knowledge of the Chinese language, customs, and character have given him an immense influence over the people of China.—Quoted in *Spectator*, p. 411, Sept. 29, 1900.

90. The material and mental world have their points of union, blending them together.—FOX, *Works*, vol. iii. p. 280 (H).

91. He defends the admission of heathen ceremonies into the service of the church by the authority of the wisest prelates and governors, whom, he says, found it necessary for the conversion of the heathen to wink at many things and yield to the times.—DOANE, *Bible Parallels*, p. 409.

92. Thanks to the help of willing workers, by far the greater proportion of its valuable contents were rescued.—*Daily Telegraph*, p. 9. Oct. 6, 1900.

93. The flower of the auxiliary forces have gone to the help—how sorely needed!—of our troops in South Africa.—*Fortnightly Review*, p. 535, Oct. 1900.

94. There was a dulness and stiffness in every relation in life, between husband and wife, parents and children.—*Ibid*. p. 629, Oct. 1900.

95. The same affection, devotion, and happiness exists, but the wife is now a citizen with rights and means of her own.—*Ibid*. p. 631, Oct. 1900.

96. Thirty years is not a long period to look back on ; therefore we can easily measure the changes we are discussing by comparison.— *Ibid*. p. 631, Oct. 1900.

97. There is at present in Regent's Park a museum, lecture theatre, and small library and herbarium.—*Daily Telegraph*, p. 10, Oct. 20, 1900.

98. Of the eight States named, a part were carried by only slight pluralities.—*Review of Reviews*, p. 356, Oct. 1900.

99. He stated that such as himself, who were behind the scenes, knew that progress, though slow, was markedly steady.— *Daily Telegraph*, p. 7, Oct. 25, 1900.

100. By the strict law of the Church in England, the right of hearing confession and the power of giving absolution is vested in every baptized layman.—Quoted in *Church Gazette*, p. 68, May 6, 1899.

101. The North-Eastern Railway are among the heaviest losers. Their train service was much disorganised.—*Daily Telegraph*, p. 8, Oct. 29, 1900.

102.   Their strength or speed or vigilance were given
            In aid of our defects.—COWPER.

103. There will be sure to be a special race-meeting at Flemington, where the Duke and Duchess will see as complete a race-course as can be found in the world.—*Daily Telegraph*, p. 7, Nov. 1, 1900.

104. Those who take an interest in motor vehicles will find in this book more definite information, description, and explanation than has yet been placed before him on these subjects.—*Spectator*, p. 624, Nov. 3, 1900.

105. Yet when all is said, Oxford are not the great side which their runaway victories over Richmond and Blackheath and their defeat of the Scottish would imply.—*Daily Express*, p. 7, Nov. 12, 1900.

106. No authentic news has been received from China, but there are a quantity of rumours, all of one kind, which point to a serious evil prevailing there.—*Spectator*, p. 646, Nov. 10, 1900.

107. Persia filled a great place in the world. Jewish and Christian progress owe it immense gratitude.—RENAN, *History of Israel*, vol. iii. pp. 380, 381.

108. Jewish goods are now made here, and £150,000 (according to Messrs. Hitchcock and Williams) is distributed annually among the manufacturers and wage-earners.—*Daily Telegraph*, p. 4, Nov. 16, 1900.

109. If the weather or a breakdown do not account for his non-arrival, the mystery of the missing ex-President has begun.—*Daily Express*, p. 1, Nov. 22, 1900.

110. There is something in the breed and character of the Briton and the better-class Boer which secure mutual respect.—BUTTERY, *Why Kruger Made War*, 1900.

111. The edict also, in which she instructed the provincial viceroys to show a determined opposition to foreigners, and in which she conferred on them the extraordinary power of declaring war on their own account, with the State papers in which she directed the same authorities to show every leniency to the Boxers, who were at all times engaged in an anti-foreign crusade, furnish quite sufficient evidence to satisfy any Old Bailey jury of her complicity in the plot of assassination.—*Blackwood's Magazine*, p. 288, Aug. 1900.

112. The idea that there are a class of people who live in slums because they like them, owing to natural depravity, has been long since abandoned, except apparently at Spring Gardens.—*Fortnightly Review*, p. 970, Dec. 1900.

113. It may be at once admitted that the resource, determination, and energy with which they blamed others for their own shortcomings is unsurpassed.—*Ibid.* p. 973, Dec. 1900.

114. Happily it is a world where all manner of things are amusing in all manner of ways.—*Ibid.* p. 1032, Dec. 1900.

115. *Mr. Justice Ridley* : I think you require protection, not me. I never heard of Mr. B., and I have nothing to do with the Stock Exchange.—*Daily Telegraph*, p. 9, Dec. 20, 1900.

116. That the poor is always with us is shown by the accounts of charitable works that fill the papers.—*Ibid.* p. 5, Dec. 25, 1900.

117. From these savings landed property consisting of 175 villages have been bought at a cost of 31 lakhs of rupees.—*Pioneer Mail*, p. 12, Dec. 7, 1900.

118. The work of a District Superintendent of Police is of a quantity and quality that demands proportionate inducements for an ordinary individual to attempt.—*Ibid.* p. 24, Dec. 7, 1900.

119. The General also paid a tribute to the Boers, whom he observed were a brave nation, who fought gallantly and well.—*Daily Telegraph*, p. 8, Dec. 31, 1900.

120. Fourteen degrees below zero has been the lowest reading on one or two nights at Davos, and some place it even lower.—*Ibid.* p. 10, Jan. 8, 1901.

121. Of the many hundred pages of advice and comment, good and bad, which has been lavished on the Liberal Party and Lord Rosebery during the last few months, we have not come across anything quite so remarkable as the paper in December's *Fortnightly*.—*Ibid.* p. 36, Jan. 1901.

122. Their oppressive conduct reached such a point that, while England was at war with Russia for the defence of Turkey, they attempted to aid the Russians, whom they believed had taken up arms for the deliverance of the Holy Land.—*Ibid.* p. 158, Jan. 1901.

123. Owing to the previous heavy recruiting, under a thousand men have joined the Colonial Defence corps for service in the field.—*Ibid.* p. 8, Jan. 14, 1901.

124. Neither the history nor the style nor the tone strike us as admirable ; but apparently the publishers and the non-educational press seem to think that Dr. Stables' works are "splendid books for boys."—*School World*, p. 75, Feb. 1901.

125. It is not the less hostile to order, property, and law, as the incendiary speeches of the men who direct it and the conduct of its

subordinate agencies in many instances proves.—*Fortnightly Review*, p. 268, Feb. 1901.

126. Let us hope that the policy, which insists on placing economy before efficiency, has at last reached the limit of that endurance which pleasing illusion and misplaced patience has accorded to it.—*Ibid.* p. 313, Feb. 1901.

127. There was frequently £200 or £300 with which to pay European and native soldiers, to all of which the prisoner might have helped himself, had he chosen.—*Daily Telegraph*, p. 10, Feb. 23, 1901.

128. The moral and inference, so far as England's naval supremacy is concerned, to be drawn from the last remarks is that if England is determined to adhere to the voluntary system, her naval supremacy is being relatively undermined by the sum of the individual efforts of her rivals.—*Ibid.* p. 9, March 11, 1901.

129. The finding of the Commission has been challenged ; its composition has been assailed ; its *bona fides* have been questioned.—*Daily Telegraph*, p. 396, March 1901.

130. The vigorous reality of Her Majesty's influence in State affairs and its beneficent results is shown by her action on this important occasion.—*Fortnightly Review*, p. 437, March 1901.

131. Outside Buckingham Palace has been selected as a fitting site for a memorial to the late Queen Victoria.—*Daily Telegraph*, p. 8, March 20, 1901.

132. Henry George referred several times to Mr. Parnell, whom he considered made the mistake of his life in entering into the Kilmainham treaty with Mr. Chamberlain. — *Review of Reviews*, p. 297, March 1901.

133. For this person to accuse us of want of knowledge can only create amusement in the minds of those who have studied the views and know the facts as I have and do.—Quoted in *Middlesex County Times*, April 30, 1898.

134. Why should the Lieutenant-Governor (of the Panjab), or his chief secretary, who have to administer not frontier affairs alone, but the complicated interests of a vast and civilised province, be required to undergo so limited and inadequate a training ?—*Empire Review*, p. 278, April 1901.

135. The crowing in early morning and note of alarm is identical, or so nearly so as to be indistinguishable by the ordinary ear.—*Ibid.* p. 308, April 1901.

136. He admitted that the legal twelve miles (for motor-cars) was a mere formality, and that many drivers went beyond it.—Quoted in *Daily Express*, p. 5, April 16, 1901.

137. Dear Sir—It is a matter of much regret to me that, notwithstanding all the interest I have taken in the U.S.F.P. Fund, and the letters that I have from time to time addressed to the Board of Direction on subjects connected with the welfare and the future possible better arrangements for the management of its working, remain unanswered, or if a reply is vouchsafed, it is the usual stereotyped one, "The subject of your communication will be considered by the Directors," and there it invariably ends ; for I hear no more about it.—*Circular from a Subscriber*, Calcutta, April 1901.

138. Great was the disappointment and anger of the Iron Chan-

cellor when the British Government required both France and Prussia to sign a treaty with England and respect the neutrality of Belgium.— *Fortnightly Review*, p. 666, April 1901.

139. As to the charge of jury-packing, with which every administration was charged, it was right and just that they should be able to set aside men whom they believed would not give a fair verdict.— Quoted in *Daily Telegraph*, p. 7, May 4, 1901.

140. With a little further push the word "ended" may be truthfully written of this war.   It is time ; for the degeneracy of the enemy's operations are becoming outrageous. —*Ibid.* p. 9, May 8, 1901.

141. We are apt to wonder at the obstinacy and the foolishness of our ancestors in maintaining and enduring for so long a policy of Restriction and a system of Finance which seems so obviously mistaken.—*Fortnightly Review*, p. 785, May 1901.

142. What they are, or why they are what they are, seem likely to remain mysteries.—*Spectator*, p. 759, May 25, 1901.

143. In the last thirty years no less than four hundred thousand square miles of virgin soil has laughed into one illimitable expanse of corn.—*Daily Telegraph*, p. 9, June 3, 1901.

144. There is a Christian and a criminal in Dick's skin, and the reader seldom fails, when the swift "go" of the story leaves him time to reflect, to pronounce the diversity "bad art."—*Spectator*, p. 869, June 15, 1901.

145. Within the past few years such an extraordinary number of books of this character have been published, that they form a distinct body of literature, to which have been given the name of the Higher Criticism.—Dr. WALLACE, *Fortnightly Review*, p. 1063, June 1901.

146. The shareholder owns the world *de jure* (by right), by the common recognition of the rights of property ; and this incumbency of knowledge, management, and toil fall entirely to others.—H. G. WELLS, *Fortnightly Review*, p. 1108, June 1901.

147. When the Transvaal and the Orange River Colony were proclaimed British territory, it was naturally supposed that organised war was at an end.—C. DE THIERRY, *Imperial Review*, p. 501, June 1901.

148. The alarm and indignation of the clerical party is therefore very great, and it becomes a matter of high interest to understand why that fear and anger have proved in the actual conflict of parties so nearly impotent.—*Spectator*, p. 7, July 6, 1901.

149. Consideration of the schemes for widening Piccadilly and providing a refreshment tent on the Victoria embankment were postponed.—*Daily Telegraph*, p. 7, July 17, 1901.

150. Before such terrifying facts the attitude of both unions and employers become intelligible.—*Fortnightly Review*, p. 84, July 1901.

151. What had characterised the epoch of the Judges, and had led to the defeats of Israel, were the want of precautions and the inferiority of arms.—RENAN, *History of Israel*, ed. Chapman and Hall, vol. ii. p. 11.

152. The whole of what Elizabeth had already heard, his claims on Mr. Davey, and all that he had suffered from him, was now openly

acknowledged and publicly canvassed.—JANE ÁUSTEN, *Pride and Prejudice*, ch. xxiv.

153. Indeed, in the whole Empire, under 2 per cent of the population hold land on the strength of any personal title.—Quoted in *Review of Reviews*, p. 265, Sept. 1900.

154. There will always be medical unpreparedness for war, until each regimental unit, each brigade, and each division have their medical staff and equipment complete.—*Empire Review*, p. 431, May 1901.

155. The conciliatory course Mr. A. H. contends should have been pursued after the withdrawal of the proposal, was actually pursued.—*Fortnightly Review*, p. 496, March 1900.

156. Fortunately or unfortunately neither heaven nor hell retains their efficacy even for the purpose above described.—*Ibid.* p. 637, Sept. 1901.

157. The history of South African diplomacy from 1895 to the Boer ultimatum of October 1899, and of warfare from the latter date to the present, constitute a proof such as few payers of a shilling and twopenny income tax would care to dispute.—*Ibid.* p. 582, Oct. 1901.

158. The disestablishment and disendowment of the Irish Church was carried, not against the wishes, but in accordance with the demand of the overwhelming mass of the Irish people.—MACNEILL, *Ibid.* p. 666, Oct. 1901.

159. There is a little mere in the very centre of the Norfolk town of D. 17 feet deep, but the major part are shallow, tree-fringed, and greatly beloved of fish and fowl.—*Spectator*, p. 656, Nov. 2, 1901.

160. Neither the Russian literature, nor the Russian language, nor the Russian civilisation as a whole have the qualities to make them irresistible to the energetic and intelligent millions of the Far East.—H. G. WELLS, *Fortnightly Review*, p. 914, Nov. 1901.

161. The expression of these ideas are anathema to those who belong to the official clique.—*Ibid.* p. 37, Jan. 1901.

162. The delay makes fewer demands upon our patience ; for now all the news of our armies is good.—*Morning Leader*, p. 4, March 21, 1900.

163. The form of his (Richardson's) future masterpieces were determined by his bent towards letter-writing.—H. B. FORMAN, *Fortnightly Review*, p. 949, Dec. 1901.

164. If this is so, surely the days of shock tactics may be considered over. Granted this, then the *raison d'être* of the heavy man and horse have gone too.—*Parliamentary Paper*, quoted in *Daily Telegraph*, p. 10, March 4, 1902.

165. The logical absurdity of such a jump never appeared to strike the lecturer ; the possibility of any other alternatives were left entirely out of account.—*Middlesex County Times*, p. 7, March 29, 1902.

166. Including the hauls of prisoners separately reported, a total of 325 men were captured in South Africa last week.—*Daily Telegraph*, p. 8, April 22, 1902.

167. The difficulty we—not us, but those among us who contemplate a preferential arrangement with the Colonies—have had is this, that when we are asked to arrange our tariff in their favour, we have to reply that we have no tariff that we can arrange.—Sir CAMPBELL-BANNERMAN, quoted in *Daily Telegraph*, p. 11, May 26, 1902.

168. After all, no substitute for it has been found. Latin or Greek do train in boys the faculty of problem-solving or investigation more completely than any other subject taught by any method yet invented.—*School World*, p. 141, April 1902.

169. The obstinate maintenance, in the interest of a class, of an alien church and an alien land-law in Ireland are faults, not misfortunes, now.—GOLDWIN SMITH, *Three English Statesmen*, p. 99.

170. Valentia is one of the most delightful cities which is to be found in Europe.—ALISON, *History of Europe*.

171. I offer a prize of six pairs of gloves to whomsoever will tell me what idea in this second part is mine.—CHARLES DICKENS, *Letters*, p. 426, vol. ii.

172. The true doctrine and function of the Subjunctive mood is a part of grammar that is much misunderstood.—*Educational Review* (Madras), p. 68, Feb. 1900.

173. The Council have acquired the freehold residence of the late Mr. S. G. B.—*Daily Telegraph*, p. 6, July 12, 1890.

174. It is a speculation upon which neither his works nor his life throws any light.—*Review of Reviews*, p. 440, May 1901.

175. But the jury, having given their verdict, surely it must be respected, and we cannot see how the English people can feel affronted by the acquittal of Sipido on the grounds of his lack of discernment.—Quoted in *Daily Telegraph*, p. 5, Aug. 4, 1900.

176. These are processes not of growth, but decay,—they distort, they render obsolete, and they destroy. The obsolescence and destruction of words and phrases cuts us off from the nobility of our past, etc.—H. G. WELLS, *Fortnightly Review*, p. 172, Jan. 1903.

177. There are a force of police numbering some 150,000, and these, for the most part, are armed only with truncheons.—*Weekly Times and Echo*, p. 8, Feb. 15, 1903.

178. At the outset I wish emphatically to say that neither Colonel K. (my brother-in-law) nor I has ever attempted, or will ever attempt, to condone or excuse the abuses complained of.—*Daily Express*, p. 1, Feb. 12, 1903.

179. It follows, therefore—and I have authority for saying so—that it is not true that the German Government, in contrast with that of England, are opposed to the acceptance of the principle of arbitration.—*Daily Telegraph*, p. 7, Dec. 20, 1902.

180. Neither on the one side nor on the other was there the strength and unity of action which result from single and individual aims.—TRENCH.

181. Neither Kent nor Sussex were among the greatest of the kingdoms which our forefathers founded in Britain.—FREEMAN.

182.   I am no orator, as Brutus is ;
     But, as you know me all, a plain blunt man,
     That love my friend.—*Julius Cæsar*, iii. 2.

183. It is in such moments that the immortal superiority of genius and virtue most strongly appear.—ALISON, *Essay on Chateaubriand*.

184. Either a pestilence or a famine, a victory or a defeat, an oracle of the gods or the eloquence of a daring leader, were sufficient to impel the Gothic arms.—GIBBON, *Decline and Fall*.

185. Mr. Dodsley this year brought out his *Preceptor*, one of

the most valuable books for the improvement of young minds that has appeared in any language.—BOSWELL's *Life of Johnson.*

186. Alexander, Emperor of Russia, is one of the sovereigns of modern times who has left the greatest name in history.—ALISON, *History of Europe.*

187. The use of fraud and perfidy, of cruelty and injustice, were often subservient to the propagation of the faith.—GIBBON, *Decline and Fall.*

188. Neither (of these) bear any sign of care at all.—LATHAM, *English Language.*

189. Each of these chimerical personages come from different provinces in the gesticulating land of pantomime.—D'ISRAELI, *Curiosities of Literature.*

190. The duchy of Pomerania with the island of Rugen were added by Sweden to the Danish crown.—ALISON, *History of Europe.*

191. This Thyre, surnamed Bolöxe, with her twelve children were notorious robbers.—THORPE, *Northern Mythology.*

192. The masterly boldness and precision of his outline, which astonish those who have trodden parts of the same field, is apt to escape an uninformed reader.—HALLAM, *Literature of Europe.*

193. We suppose in England that the abstract and the practical knowledge are at variance.—BULWER LYTTON, *England and the English.*

194. The blessings which political and intellectual freedom have brought in their train.—MACAULAY, *History of England.*

195. The logical and historical analysis of a language generally in some degree coincides.—LATHAM, *The English Language.*

196. The literature of France, Germany, and England are at least as necessary for a man born in the nineteenth century as that of Rome and Athens.—BULWER LYTTON, *England and the English.*

197. The praise of the statesman, the warrior, or the orator furnish more splendid topics for ambitious eloquence.—VERPLANCK, *The Schoolmaster.*

198. We have already made such progress that some four or five millions of reduction in our expenditure has taken place.—*Cobden's Speech at Manchester,* 1851.

199. A few hours of mutual intercourse dispels the alienation which years of separation may have produced.—ALISON, *Essay on the Royal Progress.*

200. The Germans of the present day, although greatly superior to their ancestors, there are who opine that they are still distant from that acme of taste which characterises the finished compositions of the French and English authors.—D'ISRAELI, *Curiosities of Literature.*

201. The logic, though the religious zeal of its pious, sincere, and benevolent author has led him into the very great error of taking his examples of self-evident propositions from amongst those, many of which great numbers of men think to be not self-evident, it is a work wherein profound learning is conveyed in a style the most simple and in a manner the most pleasing.—COBBETT, *Letter* xxi.

(b) *Miscellaneous.*

Under this heading have been placed sentences involving any point of Accidence, Concord, or Government not already exemplified in Section (*a*). A few notes are appended.

1. Verb and Object.—The points in which mistakes are most frequently made are the following :—

(*a*) The Relative "who," when it is the object of a verb, must take the Objective form *whom*,—a rule which is frequently neglected through inadvertence :—

> A fortnight or less later, *who* was Sir W. entertaining at his beloved Malwood, but this same terrible fox of his ?—*Daily Express,* p. 1, June 14, 1900. (Wrong. Say *whom.*)

(*b*) When the Relative is in different cases, one Objective and the other Nominative, it must be mentioned twice (once for each verb), and with the necessary difference of form, if any such difference exists :—

> Considerable anxiety prevails, *which* (Objective) nothing but an authoritative announcement can dispel, and *which* (Nominative) is bound to deepen, as the hours roll by.—*Daily Telegraph,* p. 6, Feb. 5, 1900. (Correct.)
>
> In 1896 he made a statement to her about a woman named Clara, *who* he said he met in Birmingham, and *who* was a nurse in the County Asylum. *Ibid.* p. 6, July 12, 1900. (Wrong. The first *who* should be *whom*, object of the verb "met.")

(*c*) The proximity of the Relative to a Transitive verb is apt to lead the writer to put the Relative in the Objective case, when in fact it is the Subject of some verb that stands farther off. ·This is the snare of attraction. (See Section (*a*), 5.)

> An anonymous Belgian general, *whom* I should like to think was not General Brialmont, denounced England a few months back, etc.—*Fortnightly Review,* p. 759, Nov. 1900. (Wrong. *Whom* should be *who*, subject of the verb "was." The words "I should like to think" are parenthetical.)
>
> The Goorkha subaltern's eyes glisten, as he tells of the dark little devils *whom* he believes would follow, wherever he would dare to go.—Quoted in *Daily Telegraph,* p. 4, Nov. 8, 1899. (*Who* is needed as the subject of "would follow.")
>
> Why should not Mr. A. be regarded as the Liberal Premier of the future,—the man *whom* all the other leaders would inform the King was their choice ?—*Spectator,* p. 360, March 7, 1903. (*Who* is needed as the subject of "was." Say, "the man who, as all the other leaders would inform the King, was their choice.")

2. Verb and Complement.—When the verb is Transitive

(Factitive), the Complement, if it is expressed by a Pronoun, must be in the Objective form ; if the verb is Intransitive (Copulative), in the Nominative form :—

> "Is it *thee*, Actæa?" said she at last, seeing in the darkness the face of the Grecian.—BINION, *Quo Vadis?* ch. ix. p. 87. (Change *thee* to *thou*.)

3. Adjective and Noun.—As English adjectives have discarded their inflections, no question of concord arises, except that *this* and *that* with a Plural noun must assume the Plural form, *these* and *those* :—

> I always delight in overthrowing *those* kind of schemes.—JANE AUSTEN, *Pride and Prejudice*, ch. x. (Say, "schemes of that kind.")

4. Noun used as Adjective.—If a noun is used as an adjective or (what comes to the same thing) is compounded with another noun, the second noun must be mentioned immediately after it. (See further examples given below in Chapter II. Section (*b*), 10.)

> He paid as much attention to *home* as to foreign politics. (Say, "to home politics as to foreign" ; or say, "to domestic as to foreign politics.")

5. Absolute Construction.—If the absolute construction is used, take care that the noun or pronoun connected with the participle is not repeated in the same sentence in the Nominative case :—

> One of them being asked what he thought of the Master, he replied : "He is without self-conceit, without prejudice, and without egotism."—*Church Gazette*, p. 507, Feb. 25, 1899. (Cancel *he*, and cancel the comma after *Master*.)

6. Pendent Adjective or Participle.—An adjective or participle must not be left pendent or "swinging," *i.e.* having no noun or pronoun (either expressed or understood) with which it can be construed :—

> *Referring* to the paragraph in your issue of the 2nd, *re* the London United Tramway Company and my supposed attitude thereto, you owe me an apology for a mistake on your part.—*Middlesex County Times*, p. 9, June 9, 1900. (Change "referring" to "with reference to.")
>
> Having perceived the weakness of his poems upon the Franco-German war, they now reappear to us under new titles, and largely pruned or otherwise remodelled.—STEDMAN, *Victorian Poets*, p. 354. (Insert *he* before "having," absolute construction.)

Note 1.—We have, however, a class of pendent participles (sometimes called Impersonal Absolutes) in the Active or Passive voice; such as *owing to, considering, concerning, judging, regarding, provided, granted*, etc. These have become well established by custom.

Note 2.—When participles are used after *though, when, unless, till, if, whether . . . or*, and *while* (*i.e.* when the copulative verb and its Subject are not expressed), care must be taken that there is some noun or pronoun to which the participle can be referred. Otherwise, the construction is faulty and must be put right by supplying this omitted Copulative verb and its Subject.

> Though much disappointed, there is still ground for hope. (Say, "Though he or some one else is much disappointed, there is still ground for hope.")
> Though much disappointed, we can still find ground for hope. (Correct, since *disappointed* is not pendent, but refers to *we*.)

7. Pronoun and Antecedent.—Relative and Demonstrative pronouns must be of the same number, person, and gender as their antecedents. In the examples given below the corrections are shown in brackets :—

> Every man held *their* (his) peace.—NORTH's *Plutarch*, p. 184.
> As to national humiliation and national discomfiture,—*it* does not exist. (Change *and* to *or :* the Singular "it" can then remain.)
> I am one of those who cannot describe what *I* do not see.—RUSSELL, *Diary during the Last Great War*, ch. xvi. p. 514. (Say, "what they do not see.")
> There are few demonstrations of affection; one is made to feel that *he* must trust *himself*, that man is a soldier, and life is a fight. —*The British Weekly*, Jan. 16, 1902. (If *one* is changed to "a man," the *he* can remain : otherwise it must be changed to "one," and *himself* to "oneself.")

8. Pendent Pronoun.—A pronoun (except when it is an Indefinite Demonstrative) must not be left pendent, *i.e.* having no noun or other pronoun to which it can be referred :—

> Those who are given to hero-worship do not really respect *him* more than other men do." (Say, "do not really respect the hero.")
> The result was a feeling of constant anxiety, a dread of the future. *It* was haunted by fears, and as the years went on, *their* difficulties increased. — *The British Weekly*, Jan. 16, 1902. (What is *it?* and what is *their?* Change *it* to "the mind," and *their* to "the.")

9. Apposition.—Apposition requires the same case :—

> In this state Frank Churchill had found her, *she* trembling, they loud and insolent.—JANE AUSTEN. ("She" cannot be used absolutely immediately after *her;* yet if *she* is cancelled or changed to *her*, the sentence is pointless. Say : "This was the state in which Frank Churchill found her ; she was trembling, while they were loud and insolent.")

Of one of them—*he* of the *Morning Post*—you hear little **save**
that he is a good fellow and a man of parts, etc.—CROSLAND,
The Unspeakable Scot, p. 63. (Change *he* to *him*.)

10. Preposition and Object. — When the Object of a
Preposition is the Relative "who," writers sometimes forget to
give it the form of the Objective *whom :*—

I received no reply to a letter asking *who* (whom) he was with and
what he was doing.—*Middlesex County Times*, March 7, 1899.
The cherished plan of publication between Sir J. Leicester and *I*
was thus announced.—JERDAN, *Autobiography*.

Note.—Custom has sanctioned the ungrammatical phrases *but he,
but she, but they.* But no one need be afraid to say *but him, but her,
but them*, which would be far better grammar.

11. Adverb and Adjective.—Their functions are quite distinct.   But writers sometimes make an adjective qualify another
adjective, and an adverb qualify a noun :—

The people there loved him and were *marvellous* sorry for him.[1]—
NORTH's *Plutarch*, p. 121, Skeat's edition. (Say, "marvel-
lously.")
The assertions of this author are *easier* detected.—SWIFT, on the
Whigs. (Say, "more easily.")
Quite a crowd (a large number) of people afterwards secured bunches
of blossom from the fallen limb.—*Daily Telegraph*, p. 10, May
10, 1900.
A suppressed and *seldom* (unusual or seldom seen) anger.—JEREMY
TAYLOR.

Note.—The use of an Adverb qualifying a noun is not entirely
condemned by Sweet, *New English Grammar*, Part II. § 1836. He
says—"An adverb before a group-noun,—even if the group consists
only of article + noun,—still remains an adverb, although of course
it approaches in meaning to an adjective, as in *quite the gentleman,
not at all the lady, fully master* of the subject." Such examples,
however, are exceptional, not sufficient to invalidate the general rule.

12. Co-ordinative Conjunctions. —Co-ordinative conjunctions connect similar parts of speech, similar cases in nouns and
pronouns, and similar numbers, persons, tenses, and moods in
verbs :—

My Lord Duke's entertainments were both *seldom* and *shabby*.—
THACKERAY, *Esmond*, bk. ii. ch. xiv. (Substitute the adjective
infrequent for the adverb *seldom*.)
We are in an age of weak beliefs, *and in which* such belief as men
have is much more determined by their wish, etc.—J. S.

---

[1] In the Tudor period "marvellous" could be used adverbially. Yet
even North in the preceding paragraph (p. 120) wrote "they *marvellously*
reviled him."

MILL, *Essays on Religion*, p. 70. (Say, "We are in an age of weak beliefs,—an age in which," etc.)

The diverting character of the State Secretary's *woeful* and *otherwise* ballads deserves a wider fame than it has secured for them as yet.—*Daily Telegraph*, p. 9, May 27, 1901. (Insert some adjective such as "remarkable" after "otherwise.")

The London County Council was the *drainage* and *sanitary* authority for five millions of people.—*Ibid.* p. 6, March 27, 1901. (Say, "the authority for drainage and sanitation affecting five millions," etc.)

13. Subordinative Conjunctions, "as," "than."—The verb in the Subordinate clause should not be omitted, if the form of it is different, or if the verb itself is different, or relates to a different Subject from that of the verb in the Principal clause :—

The India Office had other experts to consult quite as good as he. —*Review of Reviews*, p. 497, Nov. 1900. (Say, "as he was.")

This has been pointed out by a much more considerable philosopher than he.—*Fortnightly Review*, p. 762, April 1901. (Say, "than he *is* or he *was*.")

We welcomed his popularity and the security of his seat as proof that there is still room for such as he in the House of Commons.—*Spectator*, p. 818, Nov. 29, 1902. (Say, "such as he *is*." Here the verb "is" is the same as that going before, but it relates to a different Subject.")

Note.—The omission of the verb in the Subordinate clause has led Mr. Hodgson into the error of saying that "as" and "than" connect nouns and pronouns in the same case.[1] According to this rule (which applies only to Co-ordinative conjunctions, never to Subordinate ones), the *he* in each of the above examples should be *him*, because in each of these the noun going before is in the Objective case. Certainly the pendent Nominatives *as he, than he*, sound very awkward. But the true remedy lies in supplying the omitted Finite verb.

14. Case after the verb "to be."—The rule in grammar is that the verb *to be* must have the same case after it that it has before it :—

> It is *I*. It is *he*. It is *they*. (Right.)
> I knew that man to be *him*. (Right.)

---

[1] See *Errors in the Use of English*, p. 158 and p. 100. The following may be selected from the examples that he gives :—

God will send no more such fools as *I* upon His errands.—KINGSLEY, *Westward Ho!* ch. xxxii. p. 513.

He was a mystery to wiser and honester men *than he*.—DICKENS, *Tale of Two Cities*, ch. viii.

Mr. Hodgson corrects *I* to *me* and *he* to *him*, because *I* is preceded by the Objective "fools," and *he* by the Objective "men." Such reasoning, however, is inadmissible altogether. The Finite verb should be supplied after each of the Subordinative conjunctions.

Art thou *he* that should come or do we look for another?—*New Testament.* (Right.)

Whom do men say that I the Son of Man am?—*Matt.* xvi. 13. (Wrong. Change *whom* to *who*, which is here the complement of the verb "am.")

Note.—Some authorities make an exception of the phrase *It's me*, which has evidently been borrowed from the French *C'est moi.* Others, admitting both phrases, make a distinction, and say that there is more emphasis and more dignity in *It is I* than in *It's me.*[1]

He said unto them, It is *I;* be not afraid.—*New Testament.*

Correct, improve, or justify the following sentences :—

1. Harken to me, O Christian! Yesterday I was with ye in Ostranium. I listened to your teachings.—BINION, *Quo Vadis?* ch. i. p. 192.

2. Accused of murdering all who opposed her will, and of gratifying her pride by assuming semi-divine titles, the example of her reign has been held as striking evidence of the evil of allowing women to meddle in politics.—*Fortnightly Review,* p. 962, June 1900.

3. The projector having thus settled matters to the satisfaction of all that heard him, he left his seat at the table and planted himself before the fire.—ADDISON, *Spectator,* No. 31, para. 4.

4. Then putting out his light he approached and said: "Is it thee, Ursus?" The giant turned his head, and said, "Who art thou?" —BINION, *Quo Vadis?* ch. xvii. p. 447.

5. There is no class of society, whom so many persons regard with affection as actors.—*Fortnightly Review,* p. 752, May 1900.

6. Immediately on his death popular estimation exalted him to the rank of a saint or martyr, though his public and private actions very far from entitled him to such a character.—*Short History of England,* p. 118.

7. About 5 o'clock the wounded were placed on stretchers, preparatory to removal.—*Ibid.* p. 10, June 2, 1900.

8. Every one with a sense of beauty, however small their knowledge of Japanese, can find joy in these harmonious representations of simple, primitive passions.—*Literature,* p. 450, June 16, 1900.

9. Now he had lost her, he wanted her back ; and perhaps every one present except he guessed why.—KINGSLEY, *Westward Ho!* ch. xxv. p. 398.

10. I don't forget the danger and woe of one weak woman, and she the daughter of a man who once stood in this room.—*Ibid.* p. 469.

11. Sometimes he would say, pointing to his favourite dog: "He alone loves me ; he alone can I trust. Every one else is always trying to use me for his own purposes."—*Review of Reviews,* p. 131, Aug. 1899.

12. But, unlike North, it was not necessary for him to surrender his own judgment to that of George III.—*Short History of England,* p. 378.

---

[1] The point is discussed with much ability in Alford's *Queen's English,* p. 114, ed. 1895.

13. I agreed to match the spectacles, agreeable to her commission. —SCOTT, *Ivanhoe*, Ded. Epist. p. 22.

14. The charge against Dr. H. was of a very serious nature, having regard to the high position he held in the noble profession to which he belonged.—Quoted in *Daily Telegraph*, p. 11, March 8, 1900.

15. No man actuated only by commercial principles will sell his manufactory or works, unless he hopes to gain more by selling it than by keeping it in his own hands.—*Fortnightly Review*, p. 819, May 1900.

16. The agenda in itself is a complete review of matters theatrical. —*Daily Telegraph*, p. 11, April 24, 1900.

17. I may mention that, when ironing, it is necessary to have a damped piece of flannel by you. —*Weldon's Bazaar of Children's Fashions*, p. 14, May 1895.

18. "I notice," said she, "that when it's me, you say I am cross; but when it's you, you say you are nervous."—*Pearson's Weekly*, p. 702, April 28, 1900.

19. When camping out in uncivilised parts, the pot has to be supplied by the gun.—*Fortnightly Review*, p. 385, March 1900.

20. Russia, instead of maintaining a due balance between imports and exports, which should increase proportionately where trade takes a healthy course, aims at decreasing the former as she increases the latter, and thus gradually absorb the wealth of other nations.—*Ibid.* p. 213, Aug. 1899.

21. By trying to see the art and position of the actor as it really is, it may be possible to explain, if not to allay, these periodical bursts of indignation, etc.—*Ibid.* p. 743, May 1900.

22. This party have stopped at no language, however strong, against those who they consider the authors of the war and are at all events the representatives of the nation.—Quoted in *Daily Telegraph*, p. 7, May 12, 1900.

23. Who should I meet at the door the other night but my old friend, Mr. President.—STEELE, *Spectator*, No. 32, para. 2.

24. I observed a fish feeding as is their wont.—STUART, *Lochs and Loch-fishing*, p. 89.

25. It is a well-known trait of we Britishers to found a club, whenever the least possible excuse presents itself. —*Pearson's Weekly*, p. 833, May 28, 1899.

26. Let me awake the King of Morven, he that smiles in danger— he that is like the sun of heaven rising in a storm.—MACPHERSON, *Ossian*.

27. I expected some difficulty in coming out, but the enemy being completely frightened on the 15th July seems to have frightened them —*Yorkshire Post*, July 24, p. 5, 1900.

28. Care must also be taken, when drying in the open, to protect as far as possible against smuts.—*Weldon's Bazaar of Children's Fashions*, p. 12, May 1895.

29. The "cattle king of Australia" is the only one supreme millionaire which Australia has produced.—*Australasian Review of Reviews*, quoted in *Review of Reviews*, p. 156, Feb. 1899.

30. In reply to a question as to the duration of the campaign, Mr. S. expressed his firm conviction that weighing up the present situa-

tion, the war was but half over.—*Daily Telegraph*, p. 6, April 13 1900.

31. Will the Under-Secretary for Foreign Affairs state who is in command of the allied forces at present, and who it is proposed to put in command when the advance on Pekin commences.—*Ibid.* p. 11, July 14, 1900.

32. I notice by the way that the newspapers, who have so long and so firmly supported the cause of Dreyfus, are protesting loudly, etc.—*Ibid.* p. 9, Sept. 16, 1899.

33. If I were ordered to choose who should sit at my side,—thee or Venus,—thee would I choose, my divine maiden.—BINION, *Quo Vadis?* p. 65, chap. vii.

34. An order came out that any one of eighteen years' service could get their discharge on a modified pension.—Quoted in *Spectator*, p. 141, August 4, 1900.

35. This imaginative element contains some details which we have allowed a warm place in our regard, and it would pain us to miss from the history of Israel.—*Encycl. Biblica*, "David," p. 1019.

36. Herr von Brandt, than whom perhaps there is no abler living critic of international affairs, recently put the argument with unanswerable force.—*Daily Telegraph*, p. 6, April 20, 1900.

37. Reflecting on the laws of gravity, it will be readily perceived that a comet's approach to the earth might cause the most woeful events.—*Fortnightly Review*, p. 779, 1899.

38. There could be no doubt what the result of an armed conflict between us and the republics would be, because, using Swift's language, ten men armed to the teeth were in a general way a match for one man in his shirt.—MORLEY, quoted in *Daily Telegraph*, p. 8, Jan. 25, 1900.

39. The local papers have been full of utterances which, under less benign or easy-going auspices than that of England, would have been denounced as rank and virulent treason.—*Fortnightly Review*, p. 178, Feb. 1900.

40. The nations not so blest as thee
  Must in their turn to tyrants fall.
  Rule Britannia.

41. Assuming the invention, it gives to the world an almost perfect insulator of gigantic value.—*Daily Telegraph*, p. 7, Aug. 18, 1900.

42. Acting as he did, the pyjamas got to the patients at once.—*Ibid.* p. 9, Aug. 2 1900.

43. Remember Bruce's certain corn cure—who it's for, what it does, what it is.—*Advertisement.*

44. It is I who guides you ; it is I who protects you, and who saves you.—DOANE, *Bible Parallels in other Religions*, p. 193.

45. Simultaneous with the concentration of the Federals, he moved the ever trusty Colonial division to a point midway.—*Daily Telegraph*, p. 8, Sept. 3, 1900.

46. What is called morality is an artificial product evolved by the slave-mind to further his own interests.—*Spectator*, p. 266, Sept. 1, 1900.

47. The railway will be long before it approaches paying.—*Church Gazette*, p. 45, April 29, 1899.

48. Mr. H. writes as a High Churchman, but he is less partisan than Mr. W.—*Literature*, p. 187, March 3, 1900.

49. The least optimist held with Dr. J. that it might be necessary to put 30,000 men on the water, before the resistance of the enemy would collapse.—*Review of Reviews*, p. 463, Nov. 1899.

50. The almost impossibility of frontal attacks, which Mr. Bloch predicted, is another blow to those foreigners who believed in the possibility of an invasion of France.—*Ibid.* p. 347, April 1900.

51. In answering Mill he (Comte) declares in the same grandiloquent way, that his English friends seem to him to be after all sufficiently his admirers to justify the continuation of their subsidy.—*Literature*, p. 438, April 29, 1899.

52. Between the far ago dates of these deposits, the layers of conglomerate rock had to be rolled and spread, and vast intervals of time were wanted for it all.—Sir EDWIN ARNOLD, in *Daily Telegraph*, p. 5, June 2, 1900.

53. He went to four or five of the hospitals, and, considering, they were very good.—Quoted in *Daily Telegraph*, p. 9, Aug. 2, 1900.

54. Instead, every obstacle to prevent the elucidation of the truth was raised.—Quoted in *Review of Reviews*, p. 579, June 1900.

55. Let us make a covenant, I and thou.—*Genesis* xxxi. 44.

56. The indwelling of the Father in the humanity of Christ made whatever he did and was divine.—Quoted in *Spectator*, p. 346, Sept. 15, 1900.

57. General Pole-Carew avoided this six or seven miles of difficult pass.—*Daily Telegraph*, p. 7, Sept. 20, 1900.

58. In him we have given that country one of our best men, than whom no better could have been sent to deal with the tangle to be unravelled.—Quoted in *Daily Telegraph*, p. 8, May 19, 1899.

59. Failing the ordinary courts, it is essential to have some tribunal that has legal validity.—*Times Weekly*, p. iii. April 13, 1900.

60. If she has sinned, she has sorrowed and suffered, and you know better than me that we must forgive others, as we pray to be forgiven. —SCOTT, *Heart of Midlothian*, chap. xxvii. para. 6.

61. Mr. B., the Radical candidate, declares in his address that he approves Disestablishment, because "it would give to the Church of England the power of correcting their own abuses."—*Daily Telegraph*, p. 7, Sept. 21, 1900.

62. This is essentially a business, a practical age.—Quoted in *Review of Reviews*, p. 227, Sept. 1900.

63. Sylvie of course marries Aubrey Leigh, though to do so she breaks with the Romish Church, to the intense chagrin of the holy Monsignori, she having great possessions.—*Ibid.* p. 2955, Sept. 1900.

64. The stocks (of cotton) in the world, relative to the consumptive requirements, have been reduced to a lower point than at any time since the American War.—*Spectator*, p. 406, Sept. 29, 1900.

65. This very inconsistency rendered him more congenial to a man such as myself, who has always had a keen sympathy with Pontius Pilate's inability to discover what is truth.—*Fortnightly Review*, p. 582, Oct. 1900.

66. Public opinion has less influence now than formerly ; for every one is a gospel to themselves.—*Ibid.* p. 630, Oct. 1900.

67. Youth in this age of reason requires to be convinced that the verdict rests on a basis which recommends itself to the immature and inexperienced mind, which has complete faith in the wisdom of every opinion they hold.—*Ibid.* p. 632, Oct. 1900.

68. O tree, that knoweth the history of this woman, and canst best determine the claims of these suitors, give judgment.—*Tales of a Parrot (The Four Travellers).*

69. No party ever came before the country demanding a mandate for five years, who had such an account given of its situation by its best friends.—*Daily Telegraph,* p. 5, Oct. 12, 1900.

70. The amusements of girls have come to acquire a practical and financial turn.   If a good tennis player, it is possible to take a couple of pounds of prizes in a season.—*Ibid.* p. 10, Oct. 16, 1900.

71. He read the warrant, and when he mentioned the prosecutor's name, prisoner said, "Oh, is it him? I don't care for him. I have got bills for it, and have a complete answer to it."—*Ibid.* p. 5, Oct. 18, 1900.

72. Instead of the chariot and horses of fire that transported Elijah, we have (for the ascension of Christ) the enveloping cloud and the removal while holding a farewell conversation.—STRAUSS, *Life of Jesus,* vol. iii. p. 394.

73. Not alone spiritually will the Spirit of Christ animate those in whom he dwells, but corporeally also ; for at the end of their earthly course God through Christ will resuscitate their bodies, as he did the body of Christ.—*Ibid.* vol. iii. p. 401.

74. It is to the credit of our Generals as men, but to their detriment as soldiers, that they seem throughout the campaign to have shown extraordinary little powers of dissimulation.—CONAN DOYLE, *The Great Boer War,* quoted in *Spectator,* p. 562, Oct. 27, 1900.

75. To make living and real personages of past ages, hampered, as the writer must be, with the necessity of creating a remote atmosphere and a strange medium, is the task of a master.—HEINEMANN in *Literature,* June 23, 1900.

76. You recently spoke of the demolition of house property caused by the railway companies whose termini is in the borough.—Quoted in *Daily Telegraph,* p. 7, Nov. 5, 1900.

77. My readers too have the satisfaction to find that there is no rank or degree among them who have not their representation in this club.—ADDISON, *Spectator,* No. 34.

78. By that time he will have come in contact with some of the most gifted genius of the earth.—*Cassell's Family Magazine,* p. 158, Jan. 1898.

79. The ancestors of the Chinese established the coinage of the square-holed copper cash, which are still practically the only currency in the United Kingdom.—*Spectator,* p. 604, Nov. 3, 1900.

80. The truth, simply, literally, and in all fulness, is (as he would argue) the one thing the historian is concerned about.—GRAHAM, *Victorian Literature,* p. 212.

81. I flatter myself that few biographers have entered upon such a work as this with more advantages ; independent of literary abilities, in which I am not vain enough to compare myself with some great

names who have gone before me in this kind of literature.—BOSWELL's *Life of Johnson.*

82. We may be quite certain that there exist no surer means of contradicting Wahabee bigotry than that of unconditional and friendly intercourse between the French and Arab inhabitants of Africa.—Miss EDWARDS, *A Winter with the Swallows,* chap. xiv. p. 213 (H).

83. The quality (of British officers) needs direction and control, certainly ; but having been reproached for two centuries, the question is apt—Where has it placed Great Britain among the nations of the earth ?—Quoted in *Daily Express,* p. 4, Nov. 15, 1900.

84. This is admitted even by Mr. Rider Haggard, who has done for the Zulus at least as much as Fenimore Cooper has done for the Red Indians of North America, which latter, be it remembered, delighted in nothing so much as the torture of their captives.—*Spectator,* p. 705, Nov. 17, 1900.

85. These trivial raids, passing events now unforeseen and scarcely to be anticipated, cannot change the issue, which has become simply a question of endurance between combatants immeasurably unequal in resources.—Captain A. T. MAHAN, *Story of the War in South Africa,* 1899-1900.

86. An extremely clever boy in every sort of way, his accomplishments were numerous.—*Daily Telegraph,* p. 11, May 19, 1900.

87. We all know that it is not in the interests of purity, but an attack on one man,—who has made his power felt throughout the country, and who honourable gentlemen opposite regard with very especial aversion.—Quoted in *Daily Telegraph,* p. 7, Dec. 11, 1900.

88. In the days of long ago the duty of an officer in war was merely a "question of dash," but both officers and men needed to be better educated to meet the demands of modern warfare.—*Ibid.* p. 9, Dec. 22, 1900.

89. He does not seem to see that although the German vote has a great influence on a Presidential election, the very fact of their surroundings compels the German-American to learn English.—*Review of Reviews,* p. 583, Dec. 1900.

90. The revolt of Arabi was rendered exceptionally serious by the relative weakness of Turkey, who had just emerged from a disastrous war, and who was in the midst of a financial crisis.—*Fortnightly Review,* p. 168, Jan. 1901.

91. Leaving Miss Cusack and Miss Ransom, we then went into the old man's bedroom, where the three claimants undressed and were carefully weighed. Having resumed their attire, Miss Cusack and Miss Ransom were summoned, and the lawyer went across the room to a large iron safe which had been built into the wall.—*Harmsworth's Magazine,* p. 262, April 1899.

92. Such being the case, the relief force was right to strain every nerve,—right to strike terror along the route, while pressing forward to Pekin ; nor is it unnatural to expect that fitting punishment would be meted out, once arrived, alike to officials, who more or less took active part in the lawless proceeding, and to a population who moved not a finger to prevent it.—Sir ROBERT HART, *Fortnightly Review,* p. 194, Jan. 1901.

93. Now there's no use me describing the filthy, stinking, slippery

job of flenching a whale,—or flensing as the books call it.—*Pearson's Magazine*, p. 28, Jan. 1901.

94. In the hope of an inevitable justice, in terror of which his father and mother have lived for ten years and have at last incurred, the fashionable physician becomes one of some poor Brethren devoted to the service of the sick.—*Daily Telegraph*, p. 5, Feb. 6, 1901.

95. Coal measures reappeared at Lisle, in France, where there were large collieries from which the same strata of coal was extracted at great profit.—*Ibid.* p. 5, Feb. 14, 1901.

96. His remedy for this state of things is equally root-and-branch. —*Daily Express*, p. 4, Feb. 15, 1901.

97. The Government, nevertheless, making every allowance, showed much remissness in this matter,—nay, readiness to traffic with Nationalist faction.—*Ibid.* p. 267, Feb. 1901.

98. Miss W. receives a limited number of girls to educate under her own personal supervision. The life and surroundings are made as home-like as possible, consistent with school-work.—*School Prospectus.*

99. To make up an apple-pie bed, to roll a guest in the snow, or to stuff up his dress-coat pockets with sticky sweets, are among some of the pranks which he played on those whom he knew could be used as butts for this roystering humour.—*Review of Reviews*, p. 137, Feb. 1901.

100. Speaking as a South African, it can hardly be said that our experience of Crown Colony Government has been altogether a happy one.—*Empire Review*, p. 35, Feb. 1901.

101. His chief argument is that habitual criminals should be punished having regard to their past offences, and not merely in the light of the present offence. — *Review of Reviews*, p. 178, Feb. 1901.

102. The enemy's scouts were soon afterwards seen to be approaching, they apparently being unaware of their proximity to the British camp.—*Daily Telegraph*, p. 9, March 11, 1901.

103. Like Mr. S., however, the eloquence of Mr. J. R. I. suffers from the continual rapidity of his delivery.—*Fortnightly Review*, p. 519, March 1901.

104. Conversation is not allowed, but when working in association, opportunities do occur when remarks are exchanged, and these they are not slow to avail themselves of.—*Ibid.* p. 564, March 1901.

105. Dr. Dillon greatly admires M. de Witte, the Russian Chancellor of the Exchequer, who is trying, like a new Colbert, to control and foster Russian trade, and who he believes to possess the complete confidence of the Czar.—*Spectator*, p. 503, April 6, 1901.

106. In the larger cities of Germany still more science and commercial schools have been opened.—*Daily Telegraph*, p. 9, April 17, 1901.

107. The late Lady M. E. was the only one in whom unpunctuality was tolerated ; but she was a licensed libertine and in the dread circle of lateness none durst tread but she.—*Quarterly Review*, p. 100, April 1901.

108. "I asked," continued the man, "who I should tell you wanted to see the ship, and they said *the owners.*" — *Fortnightly Review*, p. 710, April 1901.

109. For these kind of people this is the best of all possible worlds. —*Ibid.* p. 836, April 1901.

110. There was a toothache in everything. The wine was so bitter cold, that it forced a little scream from Miss Fox, which she had great difficulty in turning into a "Hem!"—DICKENS, *Dombey and Son*, ch. v.

111. The general tone of the document is universally praised even, it is said, by that section of Cape politicians which do not always agree with our policy across the Vaal.—*Empire Review*, p. 659, July 1901.

112. If he were to return to his party, were loyally to abide by the party-system, and let the country know whom were the men he was acting with, then he might expect a call, etc.—*Spectator*, p. 112, July 27, 1901.

113. I cannot pretend to be sorry that he or that any man should not be estimated beyond their deserts.—JANE AUSTEN, *Pride and Prejudice*, ch. xvi.

114. Everybody was pleased to think how much they had always disliked Mr. Darcy, before they had known anything of the matter.— *Ibid.* ch. xxiv.

115. Elizabeth was shocked to think that, however incapable of such coarseness of expression herself, the coarseness of sentiment was little other than her own breast had formerly harboured and fancied liberal.—*Ibid.* ch. xxxix.

116. Nobody wants him to come, though I shall always say that he used my daughter extremely ill ; and if I was her, I would not have put up with it.—*Ibid.* ch. xl.

117.   Now either spoke, as hope or fear impressed
        Each their alternate triumph in his breast.—POPE.

118. Though the storm was considerably abated, yet the sea went dreadful high upon the shore, and might well be called *Den Wild Zee*, as the Dutch call the sea in a storm.—DE FOE, *Robinson Crusoe*, p. 36 (Chandos Classics).

119. Would Irish discontent be diminished, if their country was brought into closer connection with Great Britain ?—*Daily Telegraph*, p. 8, Sept. 26, 1901.

120. A widower inscribed on his late wife's tomb, "The light of mine eyes is gone from me." Taking unto himself another wife with remarkable promptitude, a Dorset yokel scrawled upon the tablet, as his comment on the text, "But he soon struck another match."— Quoted in *Review of Reviews*, p. 173, Aug. 1900.

121. The only thing approaching cruelty in their eyes is that we insist upon cleanliness and proper attention to sanitary regulations, which the average individual, being a stranger to, utterly dislikes.— *Daily Telegraph*, p. 10, July 1901.

122. It was impossible, walking along Piccadilly Circus last night, where the enthusiasm was at its highest, to forget the homely assurance made at a time when the siege of Kimberley had not been raised.— *Daily Telegraph*, p. 9, May 19, 1900.

123. Feeling thus, it was surely a work of supererogation on his part to have produced the book in question.—*Daily Express*, p. 2, May 14, 1900.

124. He (Alfred the Great) actually invented ships longer and heavier manned than the Danes.—*Daily Telegraph*, p. 8, Sept. 19, 1901.

125. Sixteen persons were injured in this accident, but only four of them sufficiently serious to necessitate their removal to hospital.—*Ibid.* p. 8, Nov. 18, 1901.

126. Such notions would be avowed at this time by none but Rosicrucians and fanatics as mad as them.—BOLINGBROKE, *Ph. Fr.* 24.

127. Each of the sexes should keep within its particular bounds, and content themselves to exult within their respective districts.—ADDISON, *Freeholder*, No. 38.

128. Priests are constantly being arrested for appearing in the streets dressed in their ecclesiastical habit, regardless of the fact that according to law they are liable to imprisonment for going abroad in any other costume.—*Fortnightly Review*, p. 1005, Dec. 1901.

129. Charles II. dared not commit illegal acts as Charles I. had done, nor dared he rule without the advice of ministers whom he knew were answerable to Parliament for all they did.—*School History of England*, Clarendon Press, p. 220.

130. He was anxious to maintain the British connection, not out of any love for Great Britain, but because the independence of South Africa was at the mercy of whomsoever had command of the sea.—*Daily Telegraph*, p. 9, March 27, 1902.

131. Quite a small crowd of enthusiasts, who are persistent admirers of the excitable count, gathered to welcome both prisoners back to the glorious light of freedom.—*Ibid.* p. 10, June 21, 1899.

132. I always delight in overthrowing these kind of schemes.—JANE AUSTEN, *Pride and Prejudice*, ch. x.

133. As to national humiliation and national discomfiture—it does not exist.—*Daily Telegraph*, p. 8, May 10, 1899.

134. The ceremonies of betrothal and marriage, which is based on purchase, are for the most part of a civilised nature, though here and there a few survivals crop up.—*Folklore*, vol. xi. No. 3, p. 306.

135. "Speak, dear, speak," she said, "I am Sornia who love thee."—*Fortnightly Review*, p. 1058, Dec. 1900.

136. I wish that little Mavey would find them closeted together, he softened by her tears, and she receiving his devotions with effusion.—Mrs. LYNN LINTON, *Sowing the Wind*, vol. iii. p. 215.

137. The inscrutability of Carton,—who was a mystery to wiser and honester men than he.—DICKENS, *Tale of Two Cities*, ch. viii.

138. It was marvellous necessary to suppress the insolence of noblemen, who being far from the king made almost an ordinary war among themselves.—Quoted in GOLDWIN SMITH's *United Kingdom*, vol. i. p. 286.

139. The main fact, however, is that the whole of what was L. B.'s army have placed themselves out of action, though a small number have made off to the north-west.—*Daily Telegraph*, p. 9, Sept. 25, 1900.

140. The Sultan is an indefatigable worker. Rising early, a day of labour begins that is not equalled by the poorest scribbler or accountant in London.—Captain GAMBIER, *Fortnightly Review*, p. 755, Nov. 1902.

141. Those of us who are wanting in literary genius may appro-

priately confine ourselves to those more modest tasks, which expose our powers of expression to a less exacting trial.—*Fortnightly Review*, p. 822, Nov. 1902.

142. A catena of documents, the dissection of dubious evidence, or the naked severity of an analytical monograph require little more of their exponents than, etc.—*Ibid.* p. 823, Nov. 1902.

143. Personally I should prefer Greek ; but that is out of the question. But to learn a little Latin in a year for the purpose of matriculating is useless and folly.—*Ibid.* p. 867, Nov. 1902.

144. They edged their way out among the quietly moving crowd, and happening to push past General Bernhoff, that personage gave an almost imperceptible salute, etc.—MARIE CORELLI, *Temporal Power*, ch. xix.

145. The English dramatists are truer to the substance of things, to universal human nature, while the French seem to be in great part an imitation, having root neither in the soil of France nor Attica.— C. D. WARNER, *The People for whom Shakespeare wrote*, p. 173.

146. Following out the same idea, the execution was left to the Romans.—RENAN's *Life of Jesus* (tr. W. M. Thomson), p. 240.

147. How does he set about it ? To begin with, he gives us a man in whom Othello's friends and intimates believe, a man whom they are ready to swear is honest.—Col. W. HUGHES HALLETT, *Fortnightly Review*, p. 277, Feb. 1903.

148. Into the bottom all kinds of rough stones and clinkers may be buried, taking care, as the filling in advances upwards, that smaller and closer-fitting material is used.—*Daily Telegraph*, p. 11, Jan. 15, 1903.

149. Such are some of the main features of the new regulations, which will, I have no doubt, be welcomed by all those schools who hitherto have suffered from the London matriculation.—*School World*, p. 65, Feb. 1903.

150. This I filled with the feathers of several birds I had taken with springs made of yahoos' hairs and were excellent food.—SWIFT, *Gulliver*, ch. x.

151. I shall endeavour to live hereafter suitable to a man in my station.—ADDISON, *Spectator*, No. 530.

152. The firm will take proceedings against any persons or firms importing or using these cars if acquired other than through the medium of the above firm.—*Daily Telegraph*, *Advertisement*, p. 5, March 18, 1903.

153. De —— had a painful complaint, which sometimes keeping him awake made him sleep, perhaps, when it did come, the deeper.— DE QUINCEY, *English Opium-Eater* (U.S. ed. 1852), p. 25 (H).

154. No man securely commands save he who hath learned well to obey.—Quoted in *Free Lance of To-day*, by HUGH CLIFFORD.

155. No one can have lost their character by this sort of exercise.— D'ISRAELI, *Curiosities of Literature.*

156. Seated in their high saddles, with stirrups so short that their knees are up to their elbows, and the reins of a powerful bit in their hands, the Turkish horseman pushes on with fearless hardihood at the gallop, confident in his sure-footed steed.—ALISON, *History of Europe from the Fall of Napoleon.*

157. The wealth of the great Audley may be considered as the cloudy medium through which a bright genius shone, and which, had it been thrown into a nobler sphere of action, the greatness would have been less ambiguous.—D'ISRAELI, *Curiosities of Literature.*

158. How fortunate then was James Naylor, who, desirous of entering Bristol on an ass, Hume informs us that all Bristol could not afford him one.—*Ibid.*

159. I strike the harp in praise of Bragela, she that I left in the isle of mist.—MACPHERSON'S *Ossian.*

160. Between Alaric Watts and I no such event ever occurred to be lamented now.—JERDAN, *Autobiography.*

161. What shall we gain by it but that we should speedily become as poor as them?—ALISON, *Essay on Macaulay.*

162. Robert is there, the very outcome of him and indeed of many generations of such as him.—CARLYLE, *Heroes and Hero-Worship.*

163. The very scullion who cleans the brasses in the kitchen becomes of more consideration and importance than him.—FRANKLIN, *Essays.*

164. It is to prevent all this disorder and to enjoy all the usefulness and the pleasure of this various knowledge, which has produced the invention of notes in literary history.—D'ISRAELI, Preface to *Quarrels of Authors.*

165. The reindeer, that useful animal, from whom the savage of the north derives the best comforts of his dreary life.—GIBBON, *Decline and Fall.*

166. There is a certain tune in every language, to which the ear of a native is set, and which often decides on the preferable pronunciation, though entirely ignorant of the reasons for it.—WALKER, Preface to *Dictionary.*

167. The soil and climate of Scotland, even where it is susceptible of cultivation, is incomparably less favoured by nature than that of the southern parts of the island.—ALISON, *History of Europe.*

168. The feeble parapet of the wall was soon levelled by the French cannon ; and the heroic Spanish gunners had no defence but bags of earth, which the citizens replaced as fast as they were shattered by the enemy's shot, joined to their own unconquerable courage.—*Ibid.*

169. Weighing the grounds of comparison, was a viler treason ever perpetrated?—DE QUINCEY (Masson's Edition), vol. vii. p. 146.

170. Sensible that not having hanged Josephus at first it was now become their duty to reward him, they did not do the thing by halves. —*Ibid.* p. 133.

CHAPTER II.—ERRORS OF CONSTRUCTION.

We sometimes meet with forms of expression, which, though not amounting to errors of Grammar, may be called Errors of Construction. Between these two classes of errors it is not necessary, nor would it be possible, to draw a sharp line of distinction. Roughly speaking, errors of Grammar (as explained in Chapter I.) have reference to Accidence, Concord, and Government ; while errors of Construction refer chiefly to some incongruity between the surroundings of a word and the way in which the word is used in the given sentence. The sentences involving questions of this class have been arranged under certain headings—(a), (b), (c), etc., as shown below, and under a final heading (j) Miscellaneous. As before, the answers or solutions will be found in Part II. The student is advised, as before, not to consult any answer until he has first examined the sentence himself and come to his own conclusion as to whether it needs correction or not, and in what form the correction, if any, should be made.

(a) Nouns.

1. Separate or joint Possession.—When two nouns in the Possessive case are connected by *and*, the apostrophe *s* is added to both nouns to denote separate possession, and to the last only to denote joint possession :—

> *Clement's and Paget's* forces entered Bethlehem on the 7th inst. The former on nearing the town demanded its surrender. The latter made a wide turning movement, etc.—*Daily Telegraph,* p. 9, July 11, 1900. (Separate possession, as the context shows.)

> The second edition of *Johnson and Steeven's* version appeared in the volumes in 1778.—Sidney Lee, *Life of Shakespeare,* p. 321. (Joint possession, since Steeven's version was practically the same as Johnson's.)

2. Restricted use of the flexional Possessive.—According

41

to the rule usually laid down the Possessive inflection is restricted to nouns denoting (a) living things, as "a man's foot," "a cat's tail"; (b) things personified as living, as "Fortune's favourite"; (c) space, time, or weight, as "a day's journey," "a boat's length," "a pound's weight"; (d) certain dignified objects, as "the court's decree"; (e) a few familiar objects occurring in familiar phrases, as "out of harm's way," "at his fingers' ends."

In the daily press, however (not in literature, nor, as a rule, in the higher class of journalism), a practice has lately sprung up of adding the apostrophe s to almost any kind of noun, and sometimes even to adjectives:—

The *dead's* last appeal.—*Daily Express,* p. 5, June 20, 1900.
The *public's* attitude.—*Fortnightly Review,* p. 912, May 1901.
Richmond Hill's appeal.—*Daily Express,* p. 5, June 17, 1901.
Windermere's size.—*School World,* p. 314, August 1901.
The *steamer's* damage.—*Central News,* Hong-Kong, May 6, 1901.
The *Siberian railway's* construction.—*Review of Reviews,* p. 388, October 1900.
The *community's* well-being.—*Fortnightly Review,* p. 369, February 1901.
The *station's* approaches.—*Daily Telegragh,* p. 9, May 8, 1900.
Mafeking's relief.—*Ibid.* p. 10, May 21, 1900.

Examples could be multiplied almost without end. The Possessive in the above examples is used in a great variety of senses. Thus "Richmond Hill's appeal" = the appeal made by the citizens of Richmond respecting Richmond Hill; "the steamer's damage" = the damage done to the steamer; "the station's approaches" = the approaches leading to the railway station; in "Mafeking's relief" Mafeking is the name of the place that received relief, not the name of the place which gave it. Time will show whether this innovation will ever find its way into literature or into journalism of the best class. Meanwhile the student will do well to avoid it. The prediction made by Archbishop Trench in 1877—"The flexional genitive formed in s or es will finally disappear, or will survive only in the diction of poetry,"—is at present very far from being fulfilled.[1]

3. The same Noun with two Adjectives. — When two

---

[1] Sweet, in his *New English Grammar,* Part II. §§ 1996-2000, gives no countenance to the unrestricted use of the Possessive, admitting only those uses which I have shown in the text. He points out that "the objective relation is expressed by the prepositional Possessive, as in "*the love of God,*" *i.e.* the love of which God is the object. Yet we now see the objective relation expressed by the flexional Possessive in such examples as "the steamer's damage," "Mafeking's relief."

adjectives connected by *and*, and having one noun between them, are intended to describe two distinct things, the noun must be pluralised, or if not pluralised it must be repeated after each adjective, or if the noun is neither pluralised nor repeated, the two adjectives must be distinguished by each having an article placed before it :—

> Ornate and grotesque music have common faults.—BUCHANAN, *Life of David Gray*, p. 47 (H). (Repeat *music* after "ornate." No other method is here possible, since we cannot pluralise *music*, neither can we place an article before it.)

> The assimilation of the Finnish and Russian system was not required.—*Review of Reviews*, p. 33, July 1900. (Either place the article *the* before "Russian"; or put *system* into the plural number; or insert *system* after "Finnish." The third method is the least commendable on account of its cumbrousness. Even when the noun is pluralised, there is no harm whatever in repeating the article before the second adjective.)

4. The same Noun as double Object.—The same noun should not be used in the same sentence first as the object of a Transitive verb and then as the object of a preposition following an Intransitive verb :—

> The more he weighed the less was he disposed to subscribe to the Thirty-Nine Articles of the Church of England.—GIBBON, *Autobiography*.

Here "articles" is the object first of the Trans. verb "weigh" and then of the preposition "to" following the Intrans. verb "subscribe." It would be better to repeat the object in the form of a Demonstrative pronoun :—"The more he weighed the Thirty-Nine Articles, the less was he disposed to subscribe to them."

5. Apostrophe "s."—Much uncertainty appears to exist as to whether the apostrophe *s* should or should not be used after words ending in *s* or in the sound of *s*. All possible cases, however, are covered by one simple rule :—WRITE, AS YOU SPEAK.

After plurals ending in *s* we never articulate, and therefore we should never write, apostrophe *s*. In all such words the Possessive case is indicated merely by the apostrophe :—

> *Horses'* tails. The *ladies'* boots. The *monkeys'* chatter.

After Singular nouns ending in *s* or in the sound of *s*, we always articulate, and therefore we should always write, apostrophe *s*.

> A *horse's* tail. *Epps's* cocoa. *James's* hat. *Guinness's* stout.

When the noun following the Possessive is "sake," we add

apostrophe *s*, if the last syllable is accented, but only the
apostrophe, if the last syllable is unaccented.

> For *Ross's* sake.   For *James's* sake.   (*Accented.*)
> For *Jenkins'* sake.   For *conscience'* sake.   (*Unaccented.*)

Correct, improve, or justify the following sentences ;—

1. The theatrical audience's power of sustained attention is by no
means what it was.—*Literature*, p. 329, April 28, 1900.

2. Now we distinctly object to have our instructor write us down
an ass after this summary fashion.—*Blackwood's Magazine*, p. 217,
August 1855.

3. All the three races were great warriors, and much fighting went
on.—RANSOME, *Short History of England*, ch. i. p. 8.

4. Germany's Kaiser learnt of our reverses with deep regret and
sympathy for the brave men who fell.—*Daily Telegraph*, p. 10, June 6,
1900.

5. The pair bore each other and bicker together.—*Literature*, p. 257,
March 31, 1900.

6. This consideration may not be untimely at this hour of the great
island-continent's federation into a vast united commonwealth.—*Ibid.*
p. 255, March 31, 1900.

7. They found two armed Federals in a Kaffir kraal, and took them
prisoner.—*Daily Telegraph*, p. 9, July 12, 1900.

8. I say nothing about the Duke of Orleans' letter, because the
behaviour of that exalted personage is entirely unimportant.—*Fortnightly Review*, p. 723, May 1900.

9. Mr. B. C. has been the means, apart from his original intention,
of rendering an immense service to the reputation of Lord Roberts and
Lord Kitchener.—*Daily Telegraph*, p. 9, June 30, 1900.

10. At the other extreme you have another party who believe, I
have no doubt honestly, that the Federals are injured innocents,—
that they are the lamb of the fable who have been worried by the
greedy British wolf.—*Ibid.* p. 7, May 12, 1900.

11. The first settlers were low types. They were drawn from the
criminal classes of Europe, and were, many of them, kidnapped by the
agents of the company.—*Pioneer Mail*, p. 13, May 11, 1900.

12. The telegram shows that the fighting which French and Ian
Hamilton's Brigades had near Johannesburg began on Sunday. The
result of the operations of the two Generals was entirely successful.—
Daily Telegraph, p. 7, June 1, 1900.

13. Now when the last of London season's theatrical successes has
given up the ghost, you will see a sorrowful procession of players who
are resting.—*Ibid.* p. 3, August 24, 1900.

14. In the Queen's Bench Division yesterday Mr. Justice W.
granted a declaration that the property belonging to St. Bartholomew's, St. Thomas's, and the Bridewell Hospitals is exempt from income tax.—*Ibid.* p. 8, November 27, 1900.

15. These speeds are justified by Sir William White's rule that the
cost of these swift ships is justified by their power and efficiency.—
Ibid. p. 8, Dec. 26, 1899.

16. If he does not distinguish between the province of reason and emotion,—the most difficult of philosophical problems,—he keeps clear of the cruder mysticism.—LESLIE STEPHEN, *Hours in a Library*, p. 199.

17. The Cabinet in Paris was delighted that the ground should be thus further smoothed by this proclamation of the policies of England and Germany, which declared for the open door and against any tampering with Chinese territory.—*Daily Telegraph*, p. 9, Oct. 23, 1900.

18. The popular misconception of the tune's having been derived from a hornpipe melody leads the popular mind to see what it expects to see.—Quoted in *Review of Reviews*, p. 376, Oct. 1900.

19. The nine other disciples were all moderate men, and the church at the time few in number and easily managed.—G. REBER, *Christ of Paul*, p. 85.

20. Music's firm hold on the community was made manifest at the annual presentation of prizes and certificates to the successful students in the local examinations.—*Daily Telegraph*, p. 10, Nov. 6, 1900.

21. The position of the Cabinet is exceedingly difficult between the danger of foreign and civil war, either of which may be precipitated by a single error.—*Ibid.*, *Telegram from Madrid*, April 14, 1898.

22. Both charges have been made through a conspicuous set of articles in a St. Petersburg newspaper, in which American and German criticism was directed with equal severity against the same faults.—*Daily Telegraph*, p. 9, Dec. 15, 1900.

23. She got away, but was rearrested. The couple were each fined ten shillings and costs.—*Ibid.* p. 9, Dec. 20, 1900.

24. The result is that although space has not been abolished, every one is nearer neighbours to every one else. The world has become perceptibly smaller.—*Review of Reviews*, p. 536, Dec. 1900.

25. As administrators they had not made their reputations, and one may say, most of them were a failure.—*Fortnightly Review*, p. 72, Jan. 1901.

26. Among the legislation to be introduced at a near date was a conciliation and arbitration bill in labour disputes, and a bill for a transcontinental railway.—*Daily Telegraph*, p. 8, Jan. 18, 1901.

27. The existence of malarial germs and mosquitos is alike essential to the perpetuation of malaria.—*Spectator*, p. 206, Feb. 9, 1901.

28. Mr. Baghot draws a clear distinction between the principles which govern the Maffia and the Camorra (secret societies in Italy) and throws fresh light on the former.—*Ibid.* p. 211, Feb. 9, 1901.

29. Excessive heats are reported from France, Switzerland, and Russia. There have been many deaths.—*Daily Express*, p. 1, June 24, 1901.

30. A member of our old nobility may not be indifferently spoken of as *Lord Everard Appleyard* and as *Lord Appleyard.* The two styles indicate widely different status.—*Punch*, p. 234, Sept. 25, 1901.

31. Among peoples not actually subject to British or American rule, and who are neither waiters nor commercial travellers, the inducements to learn English rather than French or German do not increase. —*Fortnightly Review*, p. 733, Oct. 1901.

32. These are the book's faults ; on the other hand, its earnestness

is so indisputable that we are willing to pardon them.—*Spectator*, p. 599, April 27, 1901.

33. Like Joshua in earlier days, my heart burns within me, and my mind is unpiloted and unanchored.—*True History of Joshua Davidson*, E. LINN LINTON, last paragraph.

34. Richelieu's portrait was encircled by a crown of forty rays, in each of which was written the name of the celebrated forty academicians.—D'ISRAELI, *Curiosities of Literature*.

35. One of the many contrasts which strike a stranger most in that extraordinary country is the strange contrasts which exist between the nobility and the great body of the people.—ALISON, *History of Europe from Fall of Napoleon*.

(b) Adjectives (including Articles).

1. "Few," "a few," "little," "a little."—When *few* and *little* are preceded by the indefinite article, they have an affirmative force; when they are not so preceded, they have a negative one. "Few" = not many. "Little" = not much.

> Few men escaped, and these were rewarded. (Insert *a* before "few," which is evidently required by the sense : "some few men escaped, and these were rewarded.")
> The line through Siberia is a Russian railway, and little foreign aid has been sought or accepted.—*Review of Reviews*, p. 88, July 1900. (Here *little*, having a negative force (= not much), is correctly followed by "or." If *a little* had been written instead of *little*, the clause would have been—"*though a* little foreign aid has been sought *and* accepted.")

2. "Whole," "all." — The former denotes a Collective Singular, and should therefore be followed by a Singular noun or pronoun. The latter, though sometimes used collectively before a Singular noun, has always a distributive force before a Plural one.

> A motion was passed declaring *the whole* resolutions and acts passed by the majority on Tuesday to be unconstitutional.— Quoted in *Daily Telegraph*, p. 11, Nov. 1, 1900. (Change *the whole* to "all the.")

3. "Any," "either."—The latter is used for two things ; the former for more than two :—

> There have been three famous talkers in Great Britain, *either* of whom would illustrate what I say about dogmatists well enough for my purpose.—HOLMES, *Poet at the Breakfast Table*, p. 278. (Change *either* to "any one.")

4. "Each," "every."—There are three differences in the use of these two words. (*a*) "Every" can be used only of any number exceeding two ; whereas "each" can be used both of two and of more than two. (*b*) "Each" is merely dis-

tributive; while "every" has the further sense that no
individual is left out; thus "each and every" means "each
individually and all without exception."   (c) "Every" may
denote the periodic recurrence of a thing, as "every other or
second day."

> These men, if they are not satisfied, must make good *each and every*
> deficiency.—*Spectator*, p. 164, Aug. 11, 1900.   (Correct.)

But "every," though it signifies all without exception,
never loses the sense of "one at a time," and must not be
used as equivalent to "all" (Plural), or followed by a Plural
pronoun :—

> When perspective was first discovered, everybody amused *themselves*
> with it.—RUSKIN, *Elements of Drawing*, Preface, p. xviii.
> (Say "amused himself." Here "himself" may stand for both
> genders, as "horse" may stand for either horse or mare. Or say,
> "drawers of every kind amused themselves," etc.)
> Every man in the jury was agreed that the prisoner was guilty.
> (Say, "all men were agreed.")

5. "Each other," "one another."—A distinction (of no
great importance) is generally observed by careful writers
between these two phrases, "each other" having reference to
two, "one another" to more than two :—

> The leaders and the men often agree with one another what should
> be done.—*Daily Telegraph*, p. 11, May 14, 1900.   (Correct.)
> His knees smote one against another.—*Dan.* v. 6.   (Say, "against
> each other," or "the one against the other.")

6. "A," "an."—Much uncertainty appears to exist as to
when "a" should be used and when "an." The cardinal rule
covering all possible cases may be expressed in four words :
WRITE, AS YOU SPEAK.

In accordance with this rule, we write "an" before an
open vowel *when it is sounded as open*, and before *h, when the
"h" is not sounded.* In all other cases we write "a."

> *An* heroic romantic comedy by Mr. E. V. was produced at Drury
> Lane Theatre on Saturday night.—*Daily Telegraph*, p. 8, April
> 23, 1900. (Correct. The *h* in "heroic" is not sounded, because
> the accent is on the second syllable. We say *an 'eroic*, not *a
> heroic*.)
> This was not *an* heroic figure.—FIRTH, *Augustus Cæsar*. (Correct.)
> The poet before us has not only found out *an* hero in his own
> country, but raises the reputation of it by several beautiful
> incidents.—ADDISON, *Spectator*, No. 70, May 21, 1711.   (Wrong.
> Here *an* should be *a*, because the accent on the first syllable
> of "hero" causes the *h* to be sounded.)

His father kept *an* hotel in the little hamlet of Obersalybrun.—
Fortnightly Review, p. 459, Sept. 1901. (Correct. The *h* in
"hotel" is not sounded, because the accent is on the second
syllable. In talking we always say *an 'otel*, not *a hotel*.)

On the whole the Stuart family takes *a* unique position in the pages
of fiction.—*Pearson's Weekly*, p. 700, April 28, 1900. (Correct.
The *u* of "unique," though written as an open vowel, is not
sounded as one. The *u* is sounded as *yoo*.)

The German magazine for October contains *a* eulogistic sketch of
Moltke.—*Review of Reviews*, p. 485, Nov. 1900. (Correct, for
the same reason as that just stated.)

7. Repetition of Article or of Preposition.—To separate

the sense of one noun or adjective from that of another, so as
to show that two different things are intended, or that one thing
is to be seen in two different lights or aspects, the article should
be repeated. On the other hand, when one noun or adjective
is intended merely to supplement the sense of another, or when
one noun is closely connected with the other in sense, the
article should not be repeated. (See Chap. I. (*a*), 2.)

A fatalist or *a* fanatic is a hard man to beat in battle, but perhaps
the man of unconquerable high spirits is harder still.—*Daily
Telegraph*, p. 11, April 25, 1900. (Correct.)

They possessed both the civil and criminal jurisdiction.—HUME.
(Wrong. Say, "both the civil and the criminal," etc.)

What is the use and object of building pinnacles?—HELPS.
(Correct. "Use" and "object" mean the same thing.)

It is at once a picturesque and *a* political pamphlet, and we know
not which aspect to prefer.—*Spectator*, p. 771, May 17, 1902.
(Correct. Here the same thing "pamphlet" is exhibited in
two different lights.)

Accordingly the editor and manager were ordered to appear at the
bar on Friday.—*Ibid*. p. 206, Aug. 17, 1901. (By sheer
accident the form of the verb, *were*, shows that two different
persons are intended. *The* should, none the less, have been
repeated before "manager.")

In dealing with the historical portions of the Old Testament, it is
important to keep clearly in view the distinction between *the*
historical and *the* religious and moral elements.—LAING, *Human
Origins*, ch. vii. p. 209. (Correct. Observe that "moral"
merely supplements the meaning of "religious," and therefore
there is no article before it.)

It is the supreme importance of the dynastic and personal factors in
German monarchy, that lends a unique interest to the coming
of age of the prince in Berlin.—*Daily Telegraph*, p. 9, May 5,
1900. (Here the absence of an article before "personal" is
correct, because "personal" supplements the meaning of
"dynastic.")

When no article can be used, but the two adjectives placed
before the noun are intended to denote two distinct persons or

things, some preposition must be employed if possible, or the noun must be repeated, or some other device adopted, in order to mark the distinction :—

> To compare the republics of ancient and *of* modern times is a means of throwing light upon the republican system in general.— BAIN's *Rhetoric*, vol. i. p. 157. (Correct. The repetition of "*of*" serves to separate the sense of "ancient" from that of "modern." The writer might have said, "to compare the republics of ancient with those of modern times.")

8. "The" before a Comparative.

—When *the* is placed before an adjective in the Comparative degree, it gives the Comparative a selective sense :—

> Both were men of the highest talents, courage, and enterprise. Hodgson himself was *the* lesser figure, but *the* more mysterious. —*Spectator*, p. 631, Nov. 2, 1901. (Correct.)
> On the whole, then, though the President is often cruelly hampered, while an English Prime Minister remains free and untrammelled, *the* greater power and responsibility must be admitted to remain with the President.—*Ibid.* p. 655, Nov. 1, 1902. (Correct.)
> English readers will certainly find the first of Sir Henry's two volumes *the* more interesting.—*Daily Telegraph*, p. 4, Feb. 22, 1901. (Correct.)

9. "Other" with nouns of kindred reference.

—When one thing is spoken of in connection with another *of the same class*, the word "other" should not be omitted :—

> Believe it, my good friend, to love truth for truth's sake is the principal part of human perfection in this world and the seed-plot of all *other* virtues.—LOCKE, quoted in p. 220 of Quick's *Essays on Educational Reformers*. (Correct. Here the love of truth is spoken of as one amongst other virtues).
> The only fault we have to find is one which this author shares with many American writers. —*School World*, p. 277, July 1899. (Insert *other* before "American," since the author referred to is Mr. S. T. Dalton of Massachusetts.)
> Let us not howl against the Government for omitting to do what every Cabinet would have equally omitted.—*Review of Reviews*, p. 137, Feb. 1900. (Insert *other* before "Cabinet.")
> The Jingo element is strong in London, stronger than it is in the other provincial towns.—Quoted in *Daily Telegraph*, p. 6, Aug. 24, 1900. (Cancel *other*, since London is not a "provincial town." If *other* is to be retained, then *provincial* must be cancelled.)

10. Noun coupled with Adjective.

—When a noun is used as an adjective to qualify some other noun,[1] it should not be

---

[1] Professor Bain, in his *Companion to Higher English Grammar*, devotes several pages to showing that "these short expressions (a noun qualified

E

coupled by *and* with a real adjective. Such a construction offends the ear and may cause ambiguity. The ear would be better satisfied and ambiguity would be removed, if the adjective were placed first and the qualifying noun last :—

> He had to give expression to political and social emotions, to set forth *class and national* grievances.—*Spectator*, p. 667, Nov. 1, 1902. (Say "national and class grievances.")
>
> The United Irish League has replaced *the Land and the National* Leagues of another time. —*Fortnightly Review*, p. 649, Oct. 1902. (This is defensible, because the writer has been careful enough to make "Leagues" plural and to separate "National" from "Land" by saying "*the* National." It would be better, however, to say—"the National and the Land Leagues.")
>
> Questioned as to the respective positions of the Board and Voluntary school teacher under the Education Bill, Mr. B. said that the measure on the whole would be enormously to the advantage of the latter.—*Daily Telegraph*, p. 8, Dec. 9, 1902. (It would sound better to say "the Voluntary and the Board school teacher." The article should be repeated.)

11. "Only," "alone."—"Only" is more properly an adverb than an adjective, though it is occasionally used as an adjective in certain contexts. As a general rule "alone" should be so used in preference :—

> No book has been published since your departure of which much notice is taken. Faction *only* fills the town with pamphlets, and greater subjects are forgotten.—JOHNSON, *Letter to Rev. Mr. White.* (Change *only* to *alone.*)
>
> It is a hereditary aristocracy which alone can be depended on in such a contest, because it *only* possesses lasting interests which are liable to be affected by the efforts of tyranny.—ALISON, *History of Europe.* (Change *only* to *alone.* Also change *a* to *an* before the unaccented and practically silent *h* of "hereditary." It would sound better to say "this alone" than "it alone.")

Similar care must be taken not to use *alone* (adjective) in contexts where *only* (adverb) is required :—

> It (the seizure of Kiaochau) was undertaken not alone without the knowledge of the Chancellor, but directly against his will.— WOLF VON SCHIEBRAND, *Germany as a World-Power.*—Quoted in *Daily Telegraph*, p. 11, April 16, 1903. (Change *alone* to *only.*)

---

by another noun) are the remnants of explanatory clauses" (p. 92). One cannot, however, believe that this remark contains the true account of their origin. The two nouns simply make a compound ; but the omission of the hyphen,—the neglect to write the two nouns together as compounds, has led grammarians to speak of the qualifying noun as if it were " a noun used as an adjective." For the sake of convenience I have used this phrase in the text.

Correct, improve, or justify the following sentences :—

1. Both sides confidently expected victory for their candidate, and up to the time when the last vote was recorded, it was difficult to decide whether victory lay with Conservatives or Liberals.—*Daily Telegraph,* Jan. 13, 1898.

2. The men are the pictures of health and energy, are splendidly mounted and armed, and present thorough types of our Colonial material.—*Ibid.* p. 7, Dec. 29, 1899.

3. The only alternative to amendment is postponement. We unhesitatingly say that the latter is more objectionable.—*Ibid.* p. 9, April 23, 1900.

4. This was the cost for removing snow from the whole of the thoroughfares of the metropolis.—*Ibid.* p. 8, Feb. 15, 1900.

5. Another detail in connection with the Hague conference is the utter breakdown of the French as the universal language.—*Ibid.* p. 9, June 6, 1899.

6. The kingdoms were weak, because the shires had little sympathy with each other.—RANSOME'S *Short History of England,* chap. iii. last para.

7. The whole fleet of their ships were taken.—NORTH'S *Plutarch,* p. 1096.

8. A waiting policy, or a policy of indifference, is shown by the Metropolitan and Metropolitan District Railways.—*Daily Telegraph,* p. 11, July 31, 1900.

9. In no other country in the world is so little attention paid either by the military or civilian shots as to what other countries are doing. —Quoted in *Review of Reviews,* p. 137, Feb. 1900.

10. What a historic week this is, even if its events be yet completed.—*Daily Mail,* p. 4, March 3, 1900.

11. How could I hear such words from any other man but he ?— Mrs. CRAIK, *Ogilvies,* chap. x.

12. I should think myself happy, if I could be admitted into your protection and service as house-steward, clerk, butler, or bailiff, for either of which I think myself tolerably well qualified.—SMOLLETT, *Humphrey Clinker,* p. 176 (H).

13. Although I rarely find something in your journal with which I do not fundamentally disagree, I always read it with interest and profit.—Quoted in *Spectator,* p. 407, Sept. 29, 1900.

14. Between the Radical and Unionist democracy comes the decisive intervention of the odd man, the cross-bench elector, who is usually not a democrat at all.—Quoted in *Review of Reviews,* p. 162, Aug. 1899.

15. This state numbers less inhabitants all told than Sheffield.— *Ibid.* p. 8, July 29, 1899.

16. With the ambition of William conspired an ambition not less grasping, not less ruthless, not less sanctimonious than his own.— GOLDWIN SMITH, *United Kingdom,* vol. i. pp. 17, 18.

17. It is contrary to the habits of the Tsar to profit by the difficulties of any other friendly state.—*Daily Telegraph,* p. 9, Feb. 1900.

18. We should be creating a difficulty in the way of consolidating South Africa into an united and homogeneous confederation.—*Fortnightly Review,* p. 862, May 1900.

19. We have in the Pacific three complete naval stations—the China, Pacific, and Australian.—*Ibid.* p. 264, Aug. 1900.

20. Every nation was blended under the name and standard of the great company.—GIBBON, *Decline and Fall*, chap. lii.

21. In the expansions of the heart the Eternal City (Rome) always takes precedence of all Italian towns.—Quoted in *Daily Telegraph*, p. 8, Aug. 2, 1900.

22. The declaration of Lord S. that England sought neither gold nor territory has been transformed into a cunning resolve to seize both one and the other.—*Review of Reviews*, p. 487, May 1900.

23. The leaders of the cotton trade will take effectual steps to secure that in future the true character of the cotton crop in the United States shall be known to them and to all concerned both early and accurately.—*Spectator*, p. 364, Sept. 22, 1900.

24. Every morning our scouts and patrols got in touch with the enemy, saluting each other with a shot or two.—*Daily Telegraph*, p. 10, May 14, 1900.

25. It denies the existence of a science of politics ; for it denies the existence of any first principles on which that science, like every science, must be based.—*Fortnightly Review*, p. 923, June 2, 1900.

26. The whole of the coal-carts had been furbished up for the occasion, and were eloquent of labour's toiling hands. — *Ealing Guardian*, p. 5, May 6, 1899.

27. France has under her hand the share assigned to her, but she prefers, with all the Powers, the principle of the integrity of the Chinese empire.—*Daily Telegraph*, p. 7, Sept. 27, 1900.

28. No stronger and stranger a figure than his is described in the modern history of England.—M'CARTHY's *Our Own Times*, I. chap. ii. p. 31.

29. Henry had intended to balance the two parties—the Conservative and Progressive—or, as he called them, the dull and rash, against each other.—GOLDWIN SMITH, *United Kingdom*, vol. i. p. 342.

30. The secret societies of West Africa could be divided under five heads : tribal, mystical, the medical, the slave, and the temporary, which only existed for carrying out certain purposes, and then fell apart.—*Daily Telegraph*, p. 7, Feb. 14, 1900.

31. It behoves the interpreter of life to exercise greatest care in the manner of handling and admitting mystery. — *Fortnightly Review*, p. 919, June 2, 1900.

32. The whole of our party-system is based upon a manifest lie and crying wrong.—*Ibid.* p. 930, June 2, 1900.

33. The belief is still prevalent in France that the sale of a wife in the market-place is a habitual and an accepted fact in English life.— *Daily Telegraph*, p. 11, June 6, 1900.

34. This practically creates an independent state extending from Hoangho to the British and French frontier.—*Ibid.* p. 9, July 3, 1900.

35. The partition wall which separated the Jews and Gentiles is broken down.—STRAUSS, *Life of Jesus*, vol. iii. p. 401.

36. Errors have been many, but no more, we may be sure, than would have overtaken any troops in like situations.—*Fortnightly Review*, p. 618, Oct. 1900.

37. The various Powers cast upon us looks of tiger-like voracity,

hustling each other in their endeavours to seize upon our innermost territories.—*Ibid.* p. 514, Sept. 1900.

38. The worst of the casualties were Russian and Japanese.—*Review of Reviews*, p. 242, Sept. 1900.

39. It is understood here that the whole of the other Governments have heretofore given assurances on these lines.—*Daily Telegraph*, p. 10, Oct. 22, 1900.

40. We already possess four times as great a trade with China as every other nation put together.—*Report of G. Balfour's Speech*, Feb. 4, 1898.

41. It (the work of Abbé Dubois) records the impressions of an acute and a patient observer of the actual life of the Hindus.—*Times Weekly*, p. 92, Feb. 11, 1898.

42. He gathered that the Government were not altogether satisfied with each other.—*Daily Telegraph*, June 23, 1898.

43. A Woman's Era Exhibition has lately made up for lack of popularity by an ubiquitous presence upon street hoardings.—*Fortnightly Review*, p. 850, Nov. 1900.

44. The Court find the prisoner is not guilty of all the charges, and honourably acquit him of the same.—Quoted in *Daily Telegraph*, p. 11, Nov. 23, 1900.

45. Rear-Admiral Fitzgerald contributes an eulogy on the Japanese navy, ships and men.—*Review of Reviews*, p. 473, Nov. 1900.

46. More than one qualified student of ethnology believes that there is now little or no racial difference between the higher and lower Hindu castes.—*Pioneer Mail*, p. 5, Nov. 16, 1900.

47. It is hardly possible that the lion, tiger, or bear will ever become domestic animals, in spite of the fact that their strength and endurance would prove valuable qualities, if they could be used.—JENKS, *History of Politics*, Temple Primers, p. 21.

48. The Commander-in-chief must order a Court-martial in South Africa to go into the whole of the disasters—they have not been defeats—and to forward the evidence to a specially constituted Board. —*The Sun*, p. 2, Jan. 3, 1901.

49. To him, as he states in his Exordium, Richard showed "two natures, sport of two fates ; the hymned and the reviled, the loved and loathed, spendthrift and a miser, king and a beggar, the bond and the free, god and man."—*Fortnightly Review*, p. 64, Jan. 1901.

50. There are probably one hundred thousand women and one hundred thousand men in London at this moment, who are separated from each other by an invisible barrier. They may be in very much the same, or in the identical social circle, but there is no one to introduce them to one another.—*Review of Reviews*, p. 97, Jan. 1901.

51. Greek dramatists based their plays either on the blind or logical evolutions of Fate.—*Daily Telegraph*, p. 10, Feb. 16, 1901.

52. A pacificator of the bold and intuitive temper like the Earl of Durham, who dealt with Canada, would much sooner pin his faith to the second formula.—*Fortnightly Review*, p. 343, Feb. 1901.

53. By direct implication the United States Government has recognised the Transvaal and Orange River Colony to be British Territory.—*Daily Telegraph*, p. 8, March 18, 1901.

54. It was a heroic attempt, and the labour involved must have been prodigious.—*Spectator,* p. 600, April 27, 1901.

55. The Professor was pursued by hostile students ; free fights ensued between the clerical and liberal students, blood being freely shed.—*Daily Express,* p. 4, April 30, 1901.

56. An informal engagement with the *Times* as an occasional contributor from Montenegro led to his regular attachment to the staff of that paper for upwards of twenty years as war and resident correspondent.—*Spectator,* p. 624, April 27, 1901.

57. The dogma (of infallibility) separates the Pope finally from all other of mankind.—*Ibid.* p. 689, May 11, 1901.

58. It is now confidently hoped that both the British and Native army will be fully armed with the new weapon before the close of the year.—Quoted in *Pioneer Mail,* p. 5, May 10, 1901.

59. He (Mr. Chamberlain) commands at the present moment beyond all question the popularity and admiration of the Empire to an extent as great as any British statesman has enjoyed.—*Daily Telegraph,* p. 9, Aug. 17, 1901.

60. Happily there was no danger of such an issue in the case of the editor and publisher of the *Globe.* They had no option but to obey the unanimous vote of the House.—*Ibid.* p. 9, Aug. 17, 1901.

61. She could not determine whether the silent contempt of the gentleman or the insolent smiles of the ladies were more intolerable.— Jane Austen, *Pride and Prejudice,* ch. xviii.

62. Wisdom and folly, the virtuous and the vile, the learned and ignorant, the temperate and debauched, all give and return the jest.— Brown, *Characteristics,* Ep. i. Lect. 5.

63. Not for an instant must we allow the cheerful and the helpful note, which has become inseparable in the mind of the country from the thought of Mafeking, to minimise the stern and splendid reality of the sheer heroism and born military genius, etc.—*Daily Telegraph,* p. 8, May 19, 1900.

64. The only difference in appearance between the tame and wild buffalo is that the horns of the former do not grow to the size attained in the wild specimens.—*Spectator,* p. 279, Aug. 31, 1901.

65. Radicalism must reshape its creed, if it wishes to be entrusted with the control of imperial interests or to attain power for any purpose.—*Daily Telegraph,* p. 8, Oct. 18, 1900.

66. As time goes on, English is as much the language of the German American, and he is as good a citizen of the United States as any one.—*Review of Reviews,* p. 583, Dec. 1900.

67. The Queen's portrait I print as a frontispiece ; for her reign has covered more of the century than that of any living sovereign.— *Ibid.* p. 587, Dec. 1900.

68. The treaty between Russia and Persia concluded at the end of December 1899 presupposes the neutrality of Persia in the event of hostilities arising between Russia and any power in Asia.—*Daily Telegraph,* p. 7, Jan. 7, 1901.

69. The one thing which is universally allowed to have done more than anything in the bringing about of the Progressive triumph is the public working of a part of the tramways of London.—*Fortnightly Review,* p. 639, April 1901.

70. Archangel is like most Russian towns in having fine churches, with much riches in their treasuries, and the poorest and vilest of roads.—*Pearson's Magazine*, p. 356, April 1901.

71. Newton was piling up—he and hundreds of great men—a cairn, ever mounting higher, from the top of which the horizon is ever widening and widening.—*Daily Telegraph*, p. 8, Sept. 25, 1901.

72. You have added more ideas to contemporary politics than any one since Lord Beaconsfield.—*Fortnightly Review*, p. 380, Sept. 1901.

73. The vice of covetousness is what enters deepest into the soul of any other.—*Guardian*, No. 19.

74. The coal strike and famine added fuel to the flames, contradictory as the term may seem.—*Daily Telegraph*, p. 7, Oct. 27, 1902.

75. He has been responsible for an increase in the revenue (of Russia) unparalleled in any other European or American State.— *Fortnightly Review*, p. 112, Jan. 1903.

76. Both resolutions referred specially to the relations between Germany and Argentina, and Germany and the United States of America.—*Daily Telegraph*, p. 10, Jan. 15, 1903.

77. The most of them are concerned with things more serious than pageants and ceremonies. Two of the tracts describe expeditions into some foreign country.—*Spectator*, p. 259, Feb. 14, 1903.

78. Cranmer held that his own spiritual functions, like the secular functions of the Chancellor and Treasurer, were at once determined by a demise of the crown.—MACAULAY, *History of England*, i. 56.

79. There were considerations which told with still more effect upon the able statesmen who at that time directed the foreign affairs of France and England.—ALISON, *History of Europe*.

80. The light must not be suffered to conceal from us the real standard by which only his greatness can be determined.—D'ISRAELI, *Quarrels of Authors*.

81. Of various natural and acquired excellence it is hard to say whether the British or French soldiers were the most admirable.— ALISON, *History of Europe*.

82. But half his heart was in his profession, which of all others would require the whole.—GILFILLAN, *Literary Portraits*.

(c) Comparison of Adjectives.

1. Comparatives.—When two things are referred to, use the Comparative in preference to the Superlative :—

> Hope, brother of Fear, more gaily clad,
> The *merrier* fool of the two, yet quite as mad.—COWLEY.

Cowper was indisputably the *most* virtuous man, as Rousseau was the *greatest* intellectual power.—LESLIE STEPHEN, *Hours in a Library*, vol. iii. p. 98. (Change *most* to *more*, and *greatest* to *greater*.)

Note.—In some traditional phrases the Comparative is used where we should expect the Superlative; as, "the *latter* end," "*utter* contempt." Sometimes, on the other hand, we use a Superlative where we should expect a Comparative; as, "He came in *first* of the two"; "Of two evils choose the *least*"; "They are both good, but A. is the *best* of the two."

2. Comparatives in " or."—Avoid using "than" after Latin comparatives ending in "or" :—

His work is superior, and deserves to be better paid than yours. (Say, " is superior to yours, and deserves to be better paid.")

3. " Other " after a Comparative.—When two objects or two kinds of objects are compared with each other, the word " other " must not be omitted after an adjective in the Comparative degree :—

"An object can be compared only with an object or a class of objects other than itself ; or, if with itself, then with itself at some different stage of its existence. Thus we may compare the population of England of to-day with that of France or of Elizabethan England, but to compare the census of 1871 with the census of 1871 were like asking the price of a penny bun " (Hodgson). It is by means of the word "other" that the thing compared is excluded from the class of things with which it is compared.

The moulting season is a *more* delicate and interesting period for birds than for the bipeds of any country. (This is as good as saying that birds are not bipeds. Insert "other" before "bipeds.")

Sir Michael has had a *more* difficult task than any *other* British Chancellor of the Exchequer within living memory.—*Daily Telegraph*, p. 9, Nov. 5, 1901. (Correct.)

4. " Other " after a Superlative.—When one thing is said to surpass all other things of the same kind, take care *not* to use the word " other " after the adjective in the Superlative degree. Here the exclusive force of " other " is entirely out of place, since the thing to which the Superlative refers must be *included* amongst things of its own class ; otherwise no such comparison can be made.

The place to which she was going was the very spot which of all *others* in this wide world she had wished most to see.—SOUTHEY, *The Doctor*. (Cancel *others* and insert "spots" in its place.)

The study of nature in her animal and vegetable kingdoms, although of all *others* the most obvious and simple, seems to be one of the last which attracted the attention of mankind.—ROSCOE, *Life of Leo X.* (Cancel *others* and substitute *studies*.)

5. " Any " after a Superlative.—The noun that follows a Superlative should not be in the Singular number, and should not be qualified by " any," but by " all " :—

This student has the best memory of any boy in the same class. (Wrong.)

This sentence can be corrected in two different ways :—

This student has the best memory of all boys in the same class.
This student has a better memory than any other boy in the same class.

6. Adjectives not susceptible of Comparison.—Adjectives denoting qualities which do not admit of degrees, should be used only as Positives, not as Comparatives or Superlatives :—

President K. is the *chiefest* offender in this respect.—*Review of Reviews*, p. 89, Jan. 1899.   (Say *chief.*)
The feeling of the country has been *most unanimous* on this point.—Speech quoted in *Daily Telegraph*.   (Say *quite*. Or perhaps the writer meant "more generally agreed on this point than on any other.")

To this class belong such adjectives as *unique, square, round, golden, universal, impossible, preferable, perpetual*, etc.   When we say "a more perfect method," this is a short, though scarcely correct, way of saying "a method that makes a nearer approach to perfection."

Correct, improve, or justify the following sentences :—

1. Sir Charles Dilke suggested that it might be of great advantage to us, if we had a larger reserve of guns than any of the Powers had at the present time.—*Daily Telegraph*, p. 6, March 9, 1890.

2. Coleridge on a solemn occasion described Frere as deserving of all men he had ever known to be characterised as a gentleman.—*Literature*, p. 111, July 29, 1899.

3. These great qualities (on the part of the Queen) have added to that popularity, which was already greater than that of any monarch in history.—Quoted in *Daily Telegraph*, p. 10, May 17, 1900.

4. Mr. Stanley was the only one of his predecessors who slaughtered the natives of the region he passed through.—*Examiner*, p. 204, Feb. 16, 1878.

5. They were of a country which of all others in Europe has been most familiar with war.—Scott, *Life of Napoleon.*

6. The Liberal party, which formerly drew its chiefest strength from the large centres of population, has now come to look for its account in the minor boroughs.—*Ibid.* p. 8, Oct. 3, 1900.

7. The writer contends that happiness in married life would be more universal, if every wife had a separate income, to be at her independent disposal.—Quoted in *Review of Reviews*, p. 249, Sept. 1900.

8. Sir H. C.-B. said the Ministry was thankful for small mercies, but then Sir H. had the shortest memory of any distinguished politician.—Speech quoted in *Daily Telegraph*, p. 7, Oct. 10, 1900.

9. Would not a man of far inferior abilities than Bismarck have become cognisant from that moment of France's exact power of resistance ?—*Fortnightly Review*, p. 407, Sept. 1898.

10. The nations which can make the best use of such external elements will probably prove to be the stronger competitors in all that makes for modern progress.—*Spectator*, p. 616, Nov. 3, 1900.

11. The caravan, which founded the new order of things, was that of Jerubbabel, the grandson of Jehoiachin, aided by Joshua, the grandson of the priest Seraiah. Joshua was far the most capable of the two.—RENAN, *History of Israel*, vol. iii. p. 425.

12. This is a weekly journal which has of late years risen to one of the most widespread circulations of any paper in Great Britain.—*Pioneer Mail*, p. 7, Nov. 2, 1900.

13. Mr. Bock's humour is of course more impossible to transfer than Mr. Wiggins's.—*Spectator*, p. 779, Dec. 1, 1900.

14. How different from my beloved Letitia, who finds her chiefest joys in the gaieties of the town.—*Ibid*. p. 1020, 1900.

15. There are still three well-known beverages left, namely, cocoa, milk, and coffee. Too much of the latter has been condemned long ago ; cocoa induces rotundity ; and milk disagrees with the majority of adults.—*Daily Telegraph*, p. 8, Dec. 31, 1900.

16. The second principle, which is in reality much the most important, is that every citizen who is not himself in want is expected to be willing to undertake for a term of three years the duty of being helper to the poor.—*Review of Reviews*, p. 293, March 1901.

17. Should time permit, progress will be made with the War Loan Bill, the Public Works Loan Bill, the Pacific Cable Bill, and the Light Railways Bill. Remarkable eagerness is evinced by some members on the Opposition side to prevent the latter measure from adorning the statute book this session.—*Daily Telegraph*, p. 6, Aug. 5, 1901.

18. Jane Austen has been described as the most obscure of her sisters.—MATHEW, *History of English Literature*, 1901.

19. It celebrates the Church of England as the most perfect of all others.—SWIFT, *Apology for the Tale of a Tub*.

20. Under these conditions the forces of the Triple and Dual Alliances might well be balanced, and it would be difficult to say at the present moment which of the two Alliances has the strongest force.—Quoted in *Daily Telegraph*, p. 10, Jan. 28, 1902.

21. Three schemes were submitted to him on the point of remuneration—(1) payment by salary, (2) payment by bonus, (3) payment by salary and bonus. He selected the latter system.—*Ibid*. p. 11, April 19, 1902.

22. Being without a guide, we took a wrong path used only by the shepherds, and certainly the steepest I ever climbed before.—R. FERGUSON, *Swiss Men and Swiss Mountains*, ch. xx. p. 137 (H).

23. I had previously travelled on the English, French, and German packets running to Zanzibar, and I must confess that I found the latter so superior to their rivals that I decided to use again this route. —Quoted in *Daily Telegraph*, p. 8, Sept. 29, 1899.

24. The position of Buller and French and Pole-Carew, the former of whom is said to have gone north-westward, makes further resistance impossible.—*Ibid*. p. 7, Sept. 3, 1900.

25. Dr. Johnson, and Oliver Goldsmith, and last, but not least, the ill-fated Eugene Aram, were schoolmasters. Not many may reach the latter's elevation in death.—*Ibid*. p. 10, May 30, 1900.

26. Subsequently the party visited St. John's, Corpus, Oriel, and Merton Colleges, the latter causing especial interest by the beauty of its buildings and its associations.—*Ibid*. p. 9, June 21, 1899.

27. Mr. Rhodes has been received by the Kaiser with a heartier welcome than he accords to few who are not his subjects.—*Ibid.* p. 9, May 3, 1899.

28. Mr. Sch. and Mr. S. are opposing the Bond Congress, the former the most strongly. It will therefore probably be abandoned.—*Daily Express*, p. 1, May 25, 1900.

29. Northumberland was the most extensive of any Anglo-Saxon state.—HALLAM.

30. This noble nation hath of all others admitted fewer corruptions.—SWIFT, *Mechanical Operations.*

31. The vice of covetousness is what enters deepest into the soul of any other.—*Guardian*, No. 19.

32. The principles of the Reformation were deeper in the prince's mind than to be easily eradicated.—HUME, *History of England.*

33. Sachet's administration was incomparably the least offensive of that of any of the French generals in the Peninsula.—ALISON, *History of Europe.*

34. We have a profession set apart for the purposes of persuasion, wherein a talent of this kind would prove the likeliest perhaps of any other.—FITZ-OSBORN'S *Letters*, B. i. Letter 24.

35. Money, in a word, is the most universal incitement of human misery.—GIBBON, *Decline and Fall.*

36. Astronomy, that "star-eyed science," which of all others most denotes the grandeur of our destiny.—GILFILLAN, *Literary Portraits.*

37. The event of all others, which the Orleans party most ardently desired to avoid.—ALISON, *History of Europe.*

(d). *Pronouns.*

1. Redundant pronouns.—A pronoun must not be used if the noun for which it stands occurs in the same syntactical relation :—

> The Federals not having forfeited the right to be an independent state, *they* are bound to observe the supreme law of state life,—the maintenance of independence and state-preservation.—*Review of Reviews*, p. 375, Oct. 1899. (Cancel *they*, and place a comma after "Federals.")

> Then Cæsar, because he would be more assured of Pompey's power and friendship, *he* gave him his daughter Julia in marriage.—NORTH'S *Plutarch, Julius Cæsar*, 12. (Cancel *he.*)

Note.—In poetry, however (as formerly in Tudor prose), the pronoun is sometimes given as well as the noun :—

> The skipper he blew a whiff from his pipe.—LONGFELLOW.

2. Reflexive pronoun as Subject.—A Reflexive (or Emphatic) pronoun cannot, alone, be the Subject of a verb ; it must be preceded by some noun or by some other pronoun :—

> For they, and not *he himself*, pay the penalty of his errors.—*Daily Mail*, p. 5, April 20, 1900. (Correct.)

Indeed both *himself* and Wolf had so much in common with Jonas,
that they became very amicable.—DICKENS, *Martin Chuzzlewit,*
ch. xxviii. (Insert *he* before "himself.")

Note.—The reason of this rule is that the Reflexive, though apparently in apposition with a Nom. Personal pronoun, is really in the
Objective case, some preposition such as *for* being understood.

3. "One" as Antecedent.

—When this word is used as an
Indefinite Demonstrative pronoun, it ought not to have a Definite
Demonstrative pronoun for its consequent :—

One must not be confident of *his* own success. (Wrong. Say, "*one's*
own success.")

4. Possessive pronouns as Antecedents.

—The Possessive
forms have more of the character of adjectives qualifying nouns
than of independent pronouns. Hence they are seldom used as
antecedents to a Relative ; and their use as such is not to be
commended.

Hungry and thirsty, *their* soul fainted in them.—*Psalm* cvii. 5.
The more accurately we search into the human mind, the stronger
traces we find everywhere of His wisdom who made it.—BURKE,
Inquiry into Origin of the Sublime. (Say, "the wisdom of Him,
who," etc.)
But that verbal questions, if treated as verbal questions, and not
mistaken for what they are not, may lead to the most useful results, I need not express *my* conviction, who have compiled the
following observations for the sake of explaining the significa-
tion of political words.—G. C. LEWIS. (Say, "the conviction
held by myself, who have," etc.)

5. Demonstratives before a Preposition.

—To save the
repetition of a noun, a Demonstrative pronoun can be used before
a preposition :—

One root-difference between *English methods* in technical education
and *those* in vogue on the Continent lies in the fact, etc.—
School World, p. 23, Jan. 1901. (Correct. It would have been
better, however, to say "English and Continental methods,"
since *those* might refer to *English methods,* whereas it is intended to refer only to *methods.*)

But care must be taken (*a*) not to leave the Demonstrative
out, in places where it is wanted ; (*b*) to use it correctly, if it is
to be used at all ; and (*c*) not to put it in if it is not wanted :—

There is no period in ancient or modern history so interesting as
the French Revolution.—*Daily Telegraph,* p. 6, March 8, 1899.
(Say, "as *that of* the French Revolution.")
Those who have explored with strictest scrutiny the secret of their
own bosoms will be least apt to rush with intolerable violence

into that of other men's.—CARLYLE, *Miscellanies.* (Either
cancel *that of*, or change *men's* to *men.*)

My personal views are quite in accordance with the Loyal Churchman's Union.—Quoted in *Church Gazette*, p. 149, May 27, 1899.
(Say "*those of* the Loyal Churchman's Union.")

There is a great difference between an ox of Indian and English
breed. (Say, "and *one of* English breed.")

Another mode of spending the leisure time is *that* of books.—
COBBETT, *Advice*, p. 79. (It makes no sense to say "the mode
of books." But the phrase can easily be put right by saying
"that afforded by books"; and no doubt this is what the
writer meant.)

6. Relative as Subject.—When a Relative is the object of
a verb it may be omitted sometimes, but when it is the subject,
never :—

Mr. Prince has a genius would prompt him to better things.—
STEELE, *Spectator*, No. 466. (Insert *which* before "would.")

Note.—The omission sometimes occurs in poetry, but must not be
imitated in prose.

I have a brother is condemn'd to die.—*Measure for Measure.*
'Tis distance lends enchantment to the view.—CAMPBELL.

7. Relative as Object.—The omission of the Relative as
object of a verb is an idiom peculiar to English. The omission
can hardly be considered as anything else than a defect. The
omission, when it occurs in the middle of a long sentence, often
gives rise to obscurity :—

Here is a specimen from *Hamlet* which illustrates the unmethodical
character conversation will assume when a principal interlocutor
is pursuing a private train of thought with intense eagerness.—
ABBOTT AND SEELEY, *English Lessons for English Readers*, p.
231. (Insert *that* between the two nouns "character" and
"conversation.")

8. "In which."—This relative phrase must not be omitted
after such nouns as "manner," "way," and others. But the
habit is becoming rather common.

It is really amusing to see *the way in which* some of our local fathers
attack the great problems that have grown to be part of our
complex social system.—*Daily Telegraph*, p. 2, Sept. 10, 1900.
(Correct.)

Some alarmist news about the alleged way the lads of the Public
Schools battalions suffered from sunstroke during the field-day
last Friday, caused a flutter in many fond maternal breasts.—
Ibid. p. 7, Aug. 8, 1900. (Insert *in which* after "way.")

9. Restrictive, Continuative.—The Relative *that* is used
only in a Restrictive sense, and then only in the Nominative or
the Objective case, since it has no Possessive form :—

(1) Several questions were put to Mr. Chamberlain, *who* was received with loud and prolonged cheers from the Government benches on entering the House. — *Daily Telegraph*, p. 8, March 17, 1903.

Here *who* does not express any qualification or restriction regarding the person denoted by its Antecedent; but it mentions an additional and independent fact in continuation of what has been said about him already. It is therefore "Continuative." *That* could not have been used in its place. *That* is called by Bain (*Higher English Grammar*, p. 36) "the restrictive, explicative, limiting, or defining relative." For such a purpose it is more suitable than *who* or *which*, though it labours under the disadvantages that it cannot have a preposition placed before it, and cannot be used in the Possessive case.

(2) Troubles fell thick and fast on the unfortunate priest, *who* in a series of years came into difficult relations with a number of human beings, in each of *whom* he saw and recognised the glint of the demon's eye.—*Review of Reviews*, p. 70, Jan. 1901.

Here *who* is Continuative, while *whom* is Restrictive or explicative. Such confusion of use in the same sentence should be avoided. Say: —"Troubles fell thick and fast on the unfortunate priest. In a series of years he came into difficult relations," etc.

(3) President Roosevelt has asked the Admiral for an explanation, which he considers satisfactory, Admiral Dewey disclaiming hostility to Germany, and there will therefore be no diplomatic consequences of the incident, which has only one importance.—*Spectator*, p. 518, April 4, 1903.

Here in both cases the *which* is simply Continuative. The sentence can hardly be commended for imitation. It might be rewritten :— "President Roosevelt has asked the Admiral for an explanation, and he considers the explanation that he has received satisfactory, etc. There will therefore be no diplomatic," etc.

The non-observance of the distinction here asserted between *that* on the one hand and *who* or *which* on the other may produce ambiguity—one of the greatest faults in composition :—

There were very few men on the battlefield, who escaped without being seriously wounded.

This will bear two meanings :—

(1) There were very few men, etc., *and these* escaped, etc. (**Continuative.**)

(2) There were very few men, etc., *that* escaped, etc. (**Restrictive.**)

Sometimes *who* or *which* (Continuative) is used to imply or suggest the reason, or purpose, for which something is said to be done or thought of :—

My second boy, Moses, *whom* I designed for business, received a sort of miscellaneous education at home.—GOLDSMITH, *Vicar of Wakefield*, ch. i.

This means that the boy was given a miscellaneous education at home, *because* he was designed for business, and not for one of the learned professions, that require a training in some public school, to be followed by a training in some university.

Sometimes, again, *who* or *which* (Continuative relative) does the work of a Continuative conjunction :—

> Advices from Somaliland state that Colonel Swann has dispatched 750 camels to General Manning, *who*, if his transport allowed it, was to have left Galkayu yesterday.—*Daily Telegraph*, p. 8, March 23, 1903.

This might be rewritten—"that Colonel Swann has dispatched 750 camels to General Manning, and that General Manning, if his transport allowed it, was to have left," etc.

10. "Who," "who"; "which," "which."—It does not sound well to use the same Relative twice in the same sentence for the same Antecedent, unless the Relatives so used are in different cases or have some conjunction such as *and* or *but* to connect their respective clauses :—

> There are some men *who* witnessed what happened, *who* can give better evidence than I can. (Say, "some men, who, having witnessed what happened, can give," etc.)
> There is considerable doubt who these invaders were, who were known as Hyksos or Shepherd Kings.—S. LAING, *Human Origins*, ch. i. p. 29. (Substitute *that* for the second *who*. The first who is interrogative, the second restrictive.)
> As Mr. Balfour says, it was not the gift, but the words *that* accompanied the gift, *which* did the true service.—*Spectator*, p. 662, Nov. 2, 1901. (Here all awkwardness is avoided by using *that* in one clause and *which* in the other.)
> Where is there one *who* has died so young, *whose* fame has survived so long?—J. DIX, *Life of Chatterton*, p. 297. (Say, "Where is there one, whose fame has survived so long after a life so short?")
> There are many words *which* are adjectives *which* have nothing to do with the qualities of the nouns to which they are put.— COBBETT. (Three *whiches* in two lines. Say, "many words *that* are adjectives having nothing to do," etc.)

11. Demonstrative mixed with Relative.—A Demonstrative should not be used in a clause co-ordinate with a Relative clause :—

> The actions of princes are like those great rivers, *whose* course every one beholds, but *their* springs have been seen by few.—HELPS. (Change *their* to *whose*.)
> I ought to have thought it too strong for the presence of a lady ; *whom*, or any of *her* sex, in a matter of politics I would allow to chase me like a football all round the tropics, etc.—DE QUINCEY (Masson's Edition), vol. vii. p. 179. (Change *her* to *whose*.)

12. "And which"; "but which," etc.—A Relative clause preceded by a co-ordinative conjunction such as "and" or "but," should not be used, unless another Relative clause has been used already. Even then a second Relative after the conjunction is not required, unless it is in a different case from the first Relative or is made to introduce a statement entirely distinct.

> Our Lord's teachings were probably simpler than we find them in the Gospels and Epistles written years after from memory, *and which* are tinged by the individuality of the minds wherein they lay for years.—*Church Gazette*, p. 712, April 15, 1899. (Say, "which were written years after from memory and are tinged," etc.)
>
> The result of his explorations on this site has been to show that a still larger and more wealthy city existed here for a longer period than Troy, *and which* affected a more extensive area.— LAING, *Human Origins*, ch. iii. p. 98. (Say, "that there stood here a city, which was larger and wealthier than Troy, existed for a longer period, and affected a more extensive area.")
>
> We refer to two telegrams *which* the widow sent to the Mayor of Rome *and which* are published.—*Daily Telegraph*, p. 8, Aug. 2, 1900. (Correct. *Which* must be repeated because the cases are different.)
>
> I saw her again laid up with a fever she had caught in her vocation as sick-nurse, *and which* proved fatal.—AMY DALTON, *The Streets and Lanes of a City*, ch. iii. p. 74. (Insert *which* after "fever." This insertion will make the sequence of *and which* correct.)
>
> His action came to the ears of Mr. Rowe, another director of the corporation, who thought that it was "immoral traffic" for one of his colleagues to dispose of stock below par when much of it had not yet been issued, and who took upon himself to say so at a board meeting.—*Daily Telegraph*, p. 8, Nov. 5, 1901. (Here the repetition of *who* is correct for two reasons—(*a*) the two statements are quite distinct ; (*b*) the first *who* is at a great distance from the verb "took.")

13. "Same," "such," as Antecedents.—"Same" may be followed by *as* or *that*. "Such" can be followed only by *as.* At one time, and this not very distant, "such" was frequently followed by *who* or *that ;* but this practice is entirely forbidden by modern idiom.

Such an act

That blurs the grace and blush of modesty.—SHAKESPEARE.
Let *such* teach others *who* themselves excel.—POPE.

"As" must not be made to take the place of *who* or *which* with a preposition : —

He put his theories into practice with the same levity *as* he had maintained them in the sparkling conversaziones of the capital. —WHITE, *History of France.* (Say, "as that with which he had," etc.)

14. "They," "them," "those," as Antecedents.—Pronouns of the Third person, when they are in the Plural number, are not suitable antecedents for "who" or "that." The same objection does not lie against the same pronouns in the Singular number.

> *They that* are whole have no need of a physician, but *they that* are sick.—*Mark* ii. 17.

Such language was common in the Tudor period. But modern idiom requires us to use "those" in preference to "they" or "them":—

> *Those that* are whole have no need of a physician, but *those that* are sick.

Similarly, if "those" is used as a qualifying adjective with some noun, and not as a Demonstrative pronoun standing alone, the noun which it qualifies acquires precision as an antecedent through having "those" placed before it :—

> Mr. Ch. made a strong declaration in favour of compensation being paid to publicans whose licenses were withdrawn for no fault of their own. —*Daily Express*, p. 1, March 25, 1903. (Insert *those* before "publicans." Without it the antecedent is weak, and the sentence is not entirely free from ambiguity.)

15. Uncertain reference of Pronouns.—Since pronouns (all except those which are used indefinitely) are substitute words, there should be no uncertainty as to the noun to which a pronoun refers or for which it has been made a substitute :—

> Generally at war with each other, the Rajahs repeated the scene presented by the robber Barons of Europe in the Middle Ages, with this aggravation, that they had no Christian ideal to which their victims could appeal, even though it might be in vain.—*Spectator*, p. 978, Dec. 20, 1902. (There is no noun to which "it" in the last clause can refer. For "it" say "the appeal.")

16. Want of Common Gender in Pronouns of Third person Singular.—"Each," "every," "any," "some" will include both males and females, and are therefore applicable to either gender. When one of these words is the subject of a sentence, or at least a part of the subject, a difficulty arises as to the gender of the Third personal Singular, if it should be

F

necessary to use such a pronoun anywhere in the remainder of the sentence. Four ways of meeting this difficulty have been suggested :—

(*a*) By mentioning both genders, as in the following :—

> If *any one* comes, let *him* or *her* wait till I am ready.
> Everybody called for *his* or *her* carriage.

This is grammatically correct, but too clumsy for general use. Consequently it has never, in point of fact, come into use.

(*b*) By using the Plural number, the gender of which is common,—including males and females alike. Many examples can be quoted from literature :—

> Let *each* esteem other better than *themselves.—Phil.* ii. 3.
> *Every person's* happiness depends in part upon the respect *they* meet with in the world.—PALEY.
> *Every one* must judge of *their own* feelings.—BYRON.
> *Everybody* was pleased to think how much *they* had always disliked Mr. Darcy.—JANE AUSTEN, *Pride and Prejudice.*

Such language is open to the fatal objection that the pronouns are made to disagree in number with the antecedents, the pronouns being Plural and their antecedents Singular. The grammar is as faulty as the sound is awkward.[1]

(*c*) By changing "each," "every" to "all" or "both," whichever of these words will suit the sense. This will always suit the grammar and almost always the sense : [2]—

> Each of them was busy in arranging their particular concerns, and endeavouring, by placing around them their books and other possessions, to form for themselves a home.—Miss AUSTEN, *Sense and Sensibility,* i. p. 67. (It would have suited the sense as well as the grammar to say, "Both of them were busy," etc.)
> One fine afternoon everybody was on deck, amusing themselves as they could.—CHARLES READE, *Hard Cash,* i. p. 308. (Say, "all the passengers were on deck," etc.)

(*d*) By using *him* and leaving the reader to infer from the context that the pronoun is used in a general sense and

---

[1] This construction, however, is declared to be "allowable" by the late Professor Bain, in p. 310, *Higher English Grammar,* ed. 1896,—a rather strange assertion from an author who, four pages before, had told us that "the strong individualising force of 'every' affects the number of the predicate verb." The example there given is—"*every* smile and *every* feature *appears* with *its* appropriate grace."

[2] This is the method adopted by Hodgson, pp. 153-154, from which the above examples are taken.

applicable to both genders.[1] This use of *him* is common both
in the spoken language and in literature :—

> Let *him* that thinketh *he* standeth take heed lest he fall.—*1 Cor.*
>   x. 12.
> *Every one* that is perfect shall be made as *his* master.—*Luke* vi. 40.
> *Every one* that exalteth *himself* shall be abased ; and *he* that
> humbleth *himself* shall be exalted.—*Luke* xviii. 14.

In all these examples (and many more might be quoted),
women are referred to quite as much as men. A similar idiom is
at work, when we use *colt, dog, horse* (all of which properly
denote males), or when we use *duck, bee, goose* (all names for
females), to denote either sex. But such confusions as the
following cannot be allowed :—

> The heart is a secret, even to *him* (or *her*) who has it in *his own*
> breast.—THACKERAY.
> The institution of property, reduced to its essential elements,
> consists in the recognition, in *each* person, of a right to the
> exclusive disposal of what *he* or *she* has produced by *their* own
> exertions.—J. S. MILL.

17. Pronominal use of "same."—To avoid the repetition
of a noun, "the same" is sometimes used as a pronoun. Its
use, however, is apt to lead to obscurity ; and even when it
causes no obscurity, its use is rarely met with in the best
authors. It is better to repeat the noun or to use some other
kind of pronoun.

> After much angry dispute relative to the enormous and illegal
> exaction of fees, a tariff of *the same* was fixed.—MARTIN,
> *History of the Colonies.* (Say, a fee-tariff was fixed.)
> The jealousy of the Spanish monarch led to a renewed discussion of
> the territorial rights of our settlers, which the imbecile ministers
> of Charles II. so far admitted, as to direct the Governor of
> Jamaica to inquire into *the same.*—*Ibid.*

What is the antecedent of *the same?* This ill-worded sentence
might be rewritten as follows :—"A renewed discussion of the territorial rights of our settlers arose out of the jealousy of the Spanish
monarch, the grounds of which the imbecile ministers of Charles II.
so far admitted as to direct the Governor of Jamaica to inquire into
them."

---

[1] This, I find, is the solution adopted by Mr. Sweet, in p. 72, Part II.
of *New English Grammar,* where he says : "One way (of evading the
difficulty) is by using *he* only, leaving the application of the statement to
women as well as to men to be taken for granted." It is worth noticing
that this is the plan adopted in the wording of Acts of Parliament, where
it is often stated that nouns or pronouns denoting males must be understood to include females, except where the sense shows that only males
can be intended.

Correct, improve, or justify the following sentences :—

1. He was armed with a long sword slung in a belt, and which bumped ceaselessly against the calves of his legs.—*The Conspirators,* DUMAS, Eng. Trans., ch. i. p. 1.

2. Her Majesty's self-devotion and self-sacrifice on behalf of the country, which she rules so wisely and which loves and reveres her so well, are beyond all praise.—*Daily Telegraph,* p. 8, March 8, 1900.

3. Her passion will die like a lamp for want of that the flame should feed upon.—SCOTT, *Bride of Lammermoor,* ch. xviii., last paragraph but one.

4. At the bar the temperance drinks were sold by the same attendants who sold the intoxicating liquors.—Quoted in *Daily Telegraph,* p. 2, April 12, 1900.

5. Some exceedingly charming letters of George Sand, and which are full of human as well as of literary interest, are published in the second number of the *Revue.*—*Review of Reviews,* p. 619, Dec. 1899.

6. Such of the enemy who escaped the first onslaught fled without offering much resistance.—*Daily Graphic,* p. 10, Feb. 19, 1900.

7. The Princess showed precisely the same composure, courage, and absolute presence of mind manifested by the Prince of Wales himself. —*Daily Telegraph,* p. 9, May 2, 1900.

8. He feared there was no man among us who had borne that responsibility who could truthfully say he had been free from mistakes. —Quoted in *Daily Telegraph,* p. 10, Nov. 14, 1899.

9. Of all our fellow-craftsmen I never knew one but gave you the name of honesty and kindness.—Quoted in *Literature,* p. 401, Oct. 21, 1899.

10. It may be that for once they may have misjudged the pace our men can move with their new mounts.—*Daily Telegraph,* p. 10, April 26, 1900.

11. The clerk suddenly returning, he was knocked down, and both the culprits escaped.—*Daily Express,* p. 2, May 3, 1900.

12. "Is he hooked, do you think?" whispered Crimple, as himself and partner stood in a distant part of the room observing him as he lay.—DICKENS, *Martin Chuzzlewit,* ch. xxviii.

13. To elect Directors in the stead of A. and B. retiring by rotation, but who are eligible for re-election.—*Upper India Paper Mills,* Feb. 25, 1899.

14. There are others in England who must have foreseen and felt the need for reform, who can take up the question.—*Daily Telegraph,* p. 11, May 14, 1900.

15. War, new victories, fresh glories were, as himself avowed, indispensable to his hold on France.—GOLDWIN SMITH, *United Kingdom,* vol. ii. p. 300.

16. Mr. M. unlocked the stables in which were twenty-three horses. They stampeded at once. Four of them kicked themselves, one very severely.—*Middlesex County Times,* p. 3, Jan. 20, 1900.

17. I was able to rest for the night with all the comforts of a roof to one's head.—Quoted in *Daily Telegraph,* p. 4, April 19, 1900.

18. On this subject there is nothing which is raised by the right

honourable gentleman, which has not been touched, and indeed elaborated, by one speaker after another.—*Ibid.* p. 7, Feb. 7, 1900.

19. My personal views are quite in accord with the Loyal Laymen's Union.—Letter quoted in *Church Gazette,* p. 149, May 27, 1899.

20. The charge is inconsistent with the facts as evinced by the wages sheet now forwarded, clearly defining how the men were employed, and which did not escape the attention of your auditor.— *Ealing Guardian,* p. 2, May 6, 1899.

21. A form, which had given much dissatisfaction to the leading American statesmen, and which was treated with contempt by the individual states.—*Educational Review* (Madras), p. 41, Jan. 1900.

22. To see the Master, late so haughty and reserved, and whom she had always supposed the injured person, supplicating her father for forgiveness, was a change at once surprising, flattering, and affecting. —SCOTT, *Bride of Lammermoor,* ch. xvi. para. 13.

23. In England the external restriction has been removed (from the Jews), as it has from every sect who conceives it to be their duty to spread their faith.—*Fortnightly Review,* p. 674, April 1899.

24. Salvation, when employed in the phraseology of a Jewish theologian, refers to the conditions of this life, and not to the life hereafter.—*Ibid.* p. 668, April 1899.

25. Who can measure their responsibilities, whose incredible traditions and discredited arguments estrange men of intellect from Christianity?—*Ibid.* p. 352, Feb. 1900.

26. I shall speak first of a hope that is dear to me, and next of a matter perhaps irrelevant, but which I dwell upon with a continual pleasure.—*Ibid.* p. 508, March 1900.

27. There is no little skill in the way Orestes is taught Hermione's real nature by the influence of Andromache.—*Literature,* p. 368, May 12, 1900.

28. It is the people above all, whom faint-hearted Liberals assumed to be wedded to the cramping notions of the Manchester school, who have discovered that Great Britain is a name and symbol for an Oceanic power.—*Daily Telegraph,* p. 9, May 17, 1900.

29. Under the shelter of these Acts, abuses and evils have been allowed to grow, which go far to counterbalance the advantages the Acts of 1862 and 1867 have conferred upon the community.—*Fortnightly Review,* p. 815, May 1900.

30. It is therefore most desirable that British public opinion should understand the general character of the problem our Government will in all likelihood be called upon to solve at no distant date.—*Ibid.* p. 860, May 1900.

31. One feature of *Pearson's Weekly* is the insurance coupon which is with each number, the signing of which by the purchaser entitles his or her next-of-kin to claim £200, if they should happen to be killed on the railway with the coupon in their pocket.—*Review of Reviews,* p. 424, May 1900.

32. If any attempt were made to govern either Canada or Australia the way Sir A. M. has governed Cape Colony in the last twelve months, Canada and Australia would be in open revolt.—*Ibid.* p. 446, May 1900.

33. He made so great a show of mistrusting his own judgment and

esteeming his with whom he conferred for the present, that he seemed to have no opinions and resolutions but such as he contracted from the discourses of others. —*Ibid.* p. 451, May 1900 (quoted from CLARENDON).

34. There is no one who has studied the question who would see without reluctance the new province governed as a Crown colony.—*Daily Telegraph*, p. 6, Sept. 6, 1899.

35. There used to be lots of things as Bright Trollop carved in gentlefolks' houses at one time.—Quoted in *Nineteenth Century*, p. 790, May 1900.

36. Almost equally fine is the petulant outburst of temper, when at last Jane opposes his wishes, and which Emma humanely cures by pointing out to him the door of the dining-room in Doverell Abbey.—*Ibid.* p. 814, May 1900.

37. "Well, if you call this an eclipse," said a policeman at the street corner, "all as I can say is, I don't see why anybody should go to Spain to see it."—*Daily Express*, p. 5, May 29, 1900.

38. Would they (the Colonies) be with us, if they were sordid considerations which guided us in the path in which we had embarked ?—Speech quoted in *Daily Telegraph*, p. 10, May 9, 1900.

39. The characters of Bothwell, Moray, and Darnley are well conceived, but the Queen is inadequate.—*Literature*, p. 368, May 12, 1900.

40. Then, thirdly and lastly, there is another party which leans to both sides at once,—a party which endeavours to ride two horses at the same time, who tells you in one breath that this war is unnecessary and demands in the next that it shall be vigorously prosecuted.—Speech quoted in *Daily Telegraph*, p. 7, May 12, 1900.

41. It would be unfair to postpone its adoption pending the submission of the remedial measures still unready, and which may not prove satisfactory.—*Daily Telegraph*, p. 7, May 11, 1900.

42. When the English Government took over the Cape, it found a race which had a passionate sense of personal independence, and which at the same time were bigoted, stern, and unbending.—*Pioneer Mail*, p. 14, May 11, 1900.

43. By losing the Caliphate the Sultan would lose the nominal hold over the Moslems he has had hitherto, but which is always growing weaker.—*Daily Telegraph*, p. 5, June 2, 1900.

44. It behoves the interpreter of life, no less than those who are living that life, to exercise the greatest care in their manner of handling and admitting mystery.—*Fortnightly Review*, p. 919, June 2, 1900.

45. "I did not dare !" Such was Mr. A.'s reply to the query flung at him in the House of Commons as to why, when himself in office, he had not transformed our procedure with regard to dangerous trades.—*Ibid.* p. 972, June 1900.

46. He was not altogether lenient to such ambassadors, who had purposely contributed to hiding their light under a bushel.—*Daily Telegraph*, p. 10, June 22, 1900.

47. He was not in a position to state the speed the ship travelled. —*Ibid.* p. 4, June 29, 1900.

48. My attention has been called to a letter which has appeared in

the *Guardian* newspaper, which imputes to the reporters that they are in the habit of taking money.—*Ibid.* p. 10, July 11, 1900.

49. Remembering that we have absolutely no ships of our own to catch these German ships, remembering also the pronounced hostility of German opinion, is this safe ?—Quoted in *Review of Reviews*, p. 361, April 1900.

50. She relates an ingenious way the Mexican Government has of dealing with its desperadoes.—*Review of Reviews*, p. 178, Aug. 1900.

51. Look at the present Emperor ! Every coolie grins at the way his step-mother locks him up and bullies him.—Quoted in *Literature*, p. 64, July 28, 1900.

52. There is not one single case which has been pending against the Chinese Government, in which Her Majesty's Government has not sooner or later obtained a satisfactory settlement.—Quoted in *Daily Telegraph*, p. 5, Aug. 9, 1900.

53. He volunteered to assist in storming Majuba, he being then a burgher of the Free State, with which England was not at war.—*Ibid.* p. 5, Aug. 11, 1900.

54. The French lieutenant complains of the way the English treated him when he was a prisoner.—*Ibid.* p. 5, Aug. 24, 1900.

55. This honour comes to me from a body of public men, among whom, and among their predecessors, I have lived and moved through thirty years of their political life.—*Ibid.* p. 5, Feb. 7, 1899.

56. It was the popular interest which their sacrifices excited in Russia itself which led Alexander II., sorely against his will, to pledge his Imperial word, that if no other power would intervene, the Slav should not look to Russia in vain.—Quoted in *Review of Reviews*, p. 135, Aug. 1899.

57. It was those gentlemen who were loudest in denunciation of the Government who were least willing to take the opinion of their constituents on their actions.—Quoted in *Daily Telegraph*, p. 11, Nov. 25, 1899.

58. There is not a single one of those 670 gentlemen who walked last Monday and who could boast himself M.P., who has this Thursday evening the slightest right to those honourable and responsible initials. —*Ibid.* p. 8, Sept. 28, 1900.

59. The Buddhist ascetic not aspiring to elevate himself only, he practised virtue and applied himself to perfection to make other men share in its belief.—*China, Tartary, and Thibet*, vol. i. p. 329.

60. I have a shyness of disposition, which looks like pride, but it is not, which makes me awkward in speaking to my household domestics.—Quoted in *Spectator*, p. 413, Sept. 29, 1900.

61. Captain L. is one of those who have broken with Mr. Gladstone's Irish policy, and who has not concealed his genuine opinions in order to turn a dishonest penny out of the Irish vote.—*Daily Telegraph*, p. 7, Oct. 3, 1900.

62. That sentence was right and tactful, as is everything which the new Commander-in-Chief says, and which will please the professional soldier throughout the British empire.—*Ibid.* p. 8, Oct. 5, 1900.

63. I have no doubt that to people he did not like, and who rubbed him up the wrong way, he could and did make himself uncommonly unpleasant.—*Fortnightly Review*, p. 580, Oct. 1900.

64. It is just the class whose labour is most exhausting and unremitting, whose pay and food are of the scantiest, who never tire and never complain.—*Daily Telegraph*, p. 6, Oct. 9, 1900.

65. The manners of the girl of the present day are infinitely preferable to those of the shy, shrinking girl of the past, with no ideas, no conception of life, and no opinions of her own, and who was generally a faded reproduction of the narrow society in which she lived.—*Fortnightly Review*, p. 635, Oct. 1900.

66. It was Imperial officers, whose peacock feathers denoted exceptionally high rank, who mounted the guns on the city wall to pound the representatives of the Powers in their Legations.—*Daily Telegraph*, p. 7, Oct. 16, 1900.

67. Armed with his whisky, gin, and cotton cloths, the white man brings about a sickness which exterminates the people whom he came to benefit, to bless, to rescue from their savagery, and to make them wise and just.—Quoted in *Review of Reviews*, p. 400, Oct. 1900.

68. I was less able to praise what the Canadians had done in fiction, especially the sort we other Americans imagine ourselves to have surpassed the rest of the Anglo-Saxon world in.—*Literature*, p. 473, May 6, 1899.

69. A few months ago we gave publicity to the strong measures a clergyman announced he intended to take against sleepers in church.—*Church Gazette*, p. 169, June 3, 1899.

70. His attack hardly went beyond that playful badinage which we expect in a Parliamentary debate which is not intended to be taken very seriously.—*Daily Telegraph*, p. 8, Feb. 7, 1900.

71. We can best illustrate the claim that the three Gospels were written in the order they appeared by taking some subject that is mentioned by all.—G. REBER, *Christ of Paul*, p. 72.

72. Through covetousness shall they with feigned words make merchandise of you : whose judgment now of a long time lingereth not, and their damnation slumbereth not.—2 *Peter* ii. 3.

73. There are now extant writings which learned men refer to the apostolic age, which have no value except as they may throw some light on the age in which they were written.—REBER, *Christ of Paul*, p. 321.

74. The whole question is accordingly remitted to a committee, the composition of which has already been announced in our columns, who will consider and report with all convenient speed upon the proposals of the Government of India.—*Times*, May 3, 1898.

75. Chung Chih Tung, Viceroy of Nankin, a thorough Chinaman, a Progressive, though disliking foreigners, but who has the unique distinction of being absolutely honest and incorruptible, has engaged German instructors for his army.—*Daily Telegraph*, April 19, 1898.

76. No one is more fully alive than himself to the heavy burden of his responsibilities.—*Standard*, p. 4, Aug. 11, 1898.

77. Apparently there was an appreciable section of those who paraded the streets in the evening who were more or less intoxicated with the spectacular excitement of the day.—*Spectator*, p. 614, Nov. 3, 1900.

-*Ibi.*The proper test-question would be to take a city-bred and city-
48.

reared youth of eighteen, and compare his vision with a Boer or Zulu of the same age.—Quoted in *Spectator*, p. 746, Nov. 24, 1900.

79. The only ally which Mr. Spender found who rendered the least service to him was Mr. Chamberlain, who with characteristic adroitness and assiduity proceeded to demonstrate the indivisibility of the Liberal party.—*Review of Reviews*, p. 453, Nov. 1900.

80. He invented an English prose-style of his own, limpid, dignified, perhaps somewhat nerveless, which is only a little behind Addison.—*Spectator*, p. 775, Dec. 1, 1900.

81. We are able to distinguish easily between the Boer of French and Dutch origin.—*The Free Lance*, p. 218, Dec. 8, 1900.

82. The way he is encouraging authors of patriotic plays is more hurtful than beneficial, both to the authors and to that sort of poetry. —*Fortnightly Review*, p. 949, Dec. 1900.

83. I am as far apart as the poles from Mr. Addison's idea of women, whose toilet is their great scene of business, and the right adjusting of their hair the principal employment of their lives.—*Ibid.* p. 1020, Dec. 1900.

84. I have sat with hundreds of them standing around and wandering about my camp, no one of whom carried fewer than three spears, and most of them also with a gun.—*Government Report*, quoted in *Man*, p. 18, Jan. 1901.

85. They have contrived to obtain a large share of the education of the rising generation, which they train in hatred of the Republic.— *Daily Telegraph*, p. 5, Jan. 11, 1901.

86. Dissatisfaction was felt in regard to the way business was being conducted.—*Middlesex County Times*, p. 7, Jan. 19, 1901.

87. A small pony, which had become a pet in the family, and of which the children, who often rode on him, were especially fond, was grazing near by.—*Our Boys and Girls*, p. 58.

88. All that one may do with propriety is to indicate what he regards as the most plausible opinion.—*Encyclopædia Biblica*, vol. ii. p. 2435.

89. A serious attack upon the R. and M. mines has been made by the same commando which wrecked the Kleinfontein and Brackpan works.—*Daily Telegraph*, p. 9, Feb. 1, 1901.

90. Australia had in the past fifty years been developed by such men, Scotchmen, Irishmen, and Englishmen, who, going into the land, had found how to exercise their intelligence, not for their own benefit, but for the benefit of mankind in general.—Quoted in *Commerce*, p. 1006, Dec. 19, 1901.

91. Doubtless the great captain would soon have brought our present war to an end by means our much-maligned humanity will not permit us to use, but which perhaps no other nation would scruple to employ.—Quoted in *Spectator*, p. 201, Feb. 9, 1901.

92. The basin having its northern portion in the tropics, it acts like an oven under the daily sun.—RANKEN, *Dominion of Australia*, quoted in *Encyclopædia Britannica*.

93. Is the agency referred to the same agency which the right honourable gentleman repudiated the other day?—Quoted in *Daily Telegraph*, p. 9, Feb. 22, 1901.

94. I may not agree with Mr. N. in many things, but I admire the

firm way he sticks to his principles.—Quoted in *Middlesex County Times*, p. 6, March 2, 1901.

95. It is a matter of order, but if there is any case in which any honourable member has been reported to me, and who has been named and suspended, who in point of fact has been named under a mistake, the proper course would be for that honourable member to communicate with me and inform me what the facts are.—SPEAKER IN HOUSE OF COMMONS, quoted in *Daily Telegraph*, p. 6, March 7, 1901.

96. But there were circumstances, over which he has no control, which are bound to make for a modification of his practice of those traditions.—*Fortnightly Review*, p. 418, March 1901.

97. In the former country there are numerous large private works, some with a monthly capacity far greater than either of the private British works.—*Ibid.* p. 529, March 1901.

98. The prophets were importunate, proud in their humility, masters of power, and without pleasing whom it was hopeless to expect success.—RENAN's *Israel*, vol. ii. chap. viii. p. 101.

99. Expecting to be seized, and wrought up to a state of desperation, they resolved at least not to die without having revenged themselves on Hipparchus ; whom they found within the city gates near the chapel called the Leôkorion, and immediately slew him.—GROTE, *History of Greece*, part ii. chap. xxx.

100. When one arrives at the end of such a puzzled sentence, he is surprised to find himself gone to so great a distance from the object with which he at first set out.—BLAIR's *Rhetoric*, vol. i. p. 169.

101. The colonial settler, too, with work as hard as a navvy's, and continual dangers and risks, no wonder he eats largely of meat, and where he cannot get it he has an admirable substitute in oatmeal and dairy produce.—*Spectator*, p. 429, March 23, 1901.

102. But there was a second party which with the same aim in view as Samuel and his followers—the union of the tribes—saw no hope of reaching it but by having a king who could lead them to battle.—CLODD, *Jesus of Nazareth*, p. 66.

103. Mr. Grohman does not accept the argument . . . but replies that there are thousands of men who would join the rifle clubs but who would not become volunteers.—*Review of Reviews*, p. 279, Mar. 1901.

104. It was to the effect, "That this meeting, representing the whole of the mining districts of the nation, hereby enters its protest against the imposition of an export duty on coals, as in our opinion it is economically unsound and highly dangerous to our position as wage-earners."—Quoted in *Daily Telegraph*, p. 8, April 26, 1901.

105. One knows scores of cases of men who never had military education of any sort, who in the present war have greatly distinguished themselves.—Quoted in *Spectator*, p. 565, April 20, 1901.

106. They were prepared to hear the evidence of the five gentlemen from Holland. These are the only witnesses which the Dutch Government propose to bring forward.—*Daily Telegraph*, p. 9, May 1, 1901.

107. A malarial district in Virginia, which was drained and all the ponds, marshes, and wells saturated with petroleum, is now quite free from the scourge (of malaria).—*Review of Reviews*, p. 388, April 1901.

108. He counselled Mr. Childers, if bent upon making any declara-

tion at all, to confine himself to an expression of willingness to consider the Irish claim to have a legislature of their own on non-imperial questions.—*Ibid.* p. 396, April 1901.

109. The German people as a whole has never shown its characteristic defect of political instinct more clearly than in its present absolute alienation from the Kaiser upon the issue of their relations towards this country.—*Fortnightly Review*, p. 577, April 1901.

110. And this is without taking into account any new taxes, or imposts upon mines, other than formerly existing.—*Daily Telegraph*, p. 10, May 14, 1901.

111. The cold composure of their features made it impossible for any outsider to say whether it was dismay the anti-reform fiat of the court had occasioned or triumph.—Sir ROBERT HART, *Fortnightly Review*, p. 764, May 1901.

112. The reform edict as above epitomised is forcible and promising. With the Emperor at the helm and the Empress-Dowager supplying the motive power prestige conserves, the ship of the state will take a new departure, and the order of the day will be Full Steam Ahead!—*Ibid.* p. 784, May 1901.

113. Of course you are mortified and disappointed, but your disappointment is nothing to mine, who had a horse with whom I hoped to win the Derby, and he went amiss at the last moment.—Quoted in *Fortnightly Review*, p. 790, May 1901.

114. Bankruptcy and revolution, the ruin of her French bond-holders, the necessity of trying to repair all at the expense of the peasants, taxed to the point of torture, and whom further pressure would make mad,—these might not be the worst evils.—*Fortnightly Review*, p. 1037, June 1901.

115. They show a devotion to duty, a capacity for sacrifice, a connection of life with high aims and objects, that may well rebuke them who know Christ and live with God in this world.—Dr. MARSHALL LANG, *Ibid.* p. 1066, June 1901.

116. The full measure of public enthusiasm is roused by what may be called political chivalry, sometimes described as magnanimity, sometimes as conciliation, and sometimes as humanity, but which always spells weakness.—C. DE THIERRY, *Empire Review*, p. 499, June 1901.

117. Let it be no detraction from the merits of Miss Tox to hint that in Mr. Dombey's eyes, as in some others that occasionally see the light, they only achieved that mighty piece of knowledge, the understanding of their own position, who showed a fitting reverence for his.—DICKENS, *Dombey and Son*, chap. v.

118. He doubts the wastefulness of our military system, and certainly shows that much of our expenditure, as compared with Russia and France, is due to the larger pay we are obliged to offer.—*Spectator*, p. 23, July 6, 1901.

119. How shall I look to have any part of my desire herein satisfied, unless myself be careful to satisfy the like desire which is in other men?—HOOKER.

120. The highest reading of the thermometer yesterday in the shade was eighty-three degrees, which is six degrees lower than Thursday last.—*Daily Express*, p. 1, July 17, 1901.

121. We have to think of the suffering population in South Africa, not only of those Boer women and children in the camps whose hardships we deplore, and many among us are doing our best to alleviate them ; but we have to deal with the suffering population in South Africa—the loyalists, the refugees—those who, in spite of almost indescribable temptations and of almost irresistible pressure, have remained faithful to their allegiance.—Mr. Asquith's *Speech*, quoted from *Daily Telegraph*, p. 10, July 20, 1901.

122. A railway from the Bosphorus to the Persian Gulf would be an enterprise impossible to separate from politics, and which would never have been backed by the Kaiser with personal enthusiasm except for the purpose of some ultimate political design.—*Fortnightly Review*, p. 128, July 1901.

123. This is a type of woman there are excellent reasons for anticipating will become more frequent.—*Ibid.* p. 182, July 1901.

124. One of the points still unsettled is—whether the Whang-Po Commission shall represent only the largest commercial interests, including England, Germany, and Japan, or shall also include those of the smaller ones, as the United States and France.—*Daily Telegraph*, p. 8, August 27, 1901.

125. But Bucklaw had so far derived wisdom from adversity, that he would listen to no proposal which Craigengelt could invent, which had the slightest tendency to risk his newly-acquired independence.—*Bride of Lammermoor*, chap. xx.

126. Under the present conditions declared by the management it is pretty evident that the above fund now exists merely for their sole and special benefit.—*Pioneer Mail*, p. 22, May 4, 1900.

127. It states : "Myself and the Emperor have during the past year slept on wormood and eaten gall." This is a Chinese metaphor for nourishing vengeance.—*Fortnightly Review*, p. 10, Oct. 14, 1901.

128. From the scientific superintending engineer to the humble road-sergeant there is hardly a man who ever served under General Cotton who does not speak of that service as one of the happiest periods of his life.—*Daily Telegraph*, p. 10, Oct. 16, 1901.

129. The situation opened the door for fraud, and many there were who attempted to enter in whose "patriotism" had been, in very truth, the last resource of the scoundrel.—*Ibid.* p. 9, Oct. 19, 1901.

130. When they throw the blame on the shoulders of British statesmanship, leaving themselves out of account, they forget that they are a self-governing community, who has the right and the duty of regulating its destinies.—*Fortnightly Review*, p. 635, Oct. 1901.

131. But the sway of these islands was greater and more glorious than ancient Rome. Their sway rested, not on the pride of the sword, although the sword could not be laid aside, but it rested upon industry and the arts of peace.—John Morley, *Daily Telegraph*, p. 10, Nov. 5, 1901.

132. Nicholson and Hodson have each left a reputation different in kind from any other of their contemporaries.—*Spectator*, p. 631, Nov. 2, 1901.

133. Another mode of spending the leisure time is that of books.—Cobbett, *Advice*, p. 79.

134. The murder of a king, or a queen, or a bishop, or a father

are only common homicides; and if the people are by any chance or in any way gainers by it, a sort of homicide much the most pardonable, and into which we ought not to make too severe a scrutiny.—BURKE, *Reflections on the French Revolution*, p. 115.

135. In the strain and on the plan Mr. Burke was writing, he might have written on to as many thousands (of pages).—THOMAS PAINE, *The Rights of Man.*

136. No diplomacy can be termed intelligent which excites universal distrust,—which cynically ignores solemn agreements and allows its ambassadors to make statements like Shouvaloff, on the honour of the sovereign, which are immediately found to be false. —Sir LEPEL GRIFFIN, *Fortnightly Review*, p. 758, Nov. 1901.

137. I see no reason whatever to anticipate that the campaign may not be brought to a successful termination well within the period to which I and the estimates have referred.—Quoted in *Daily Telegraph*, p. 7, Oct. 24, 1899.

138. These are the spring-tides of public affairs, which we see often happen, but seek in vain to discover any certain causes of them.—COWLEY.

139. In the earlier part of this period men who were mere traders in politics,—whose motives were obviously base and their lives contemptible,—became for a time powers in the state.—*Encyclopædia Britannica*, vol. xvii. p. 416.

140. A few months after the war began we amassed against them an army much larger than Marlborough or Wellington had at any time under their command.—*Fortnightly Review*, p. 26, Jan. 1902.

141. It has been too often forgotten that the special word "guerilla" is applied to an enemy which cannot dispute a field.—*Daily Telegraph*, p. 8, Feb. 15, 1901.

142. The results of these lengthy investigations have not yet been published, but from the manner he has pursued them and the time expended on them, it is confidently expected that the monograph will be of immense interest.—Sir H. M. STANLEY, *Fortnightly Review*, p. 745, Nov. 1902.

143. There seems to be a kind of madness seizes on nations at certain times.—*Ibid.* p. 749, Nov. 1902.

144. But there are certain features connected with the educational conference which I disapprove, and would fain see them modified.—Quoted in *Pioneer Mail*, p. 28, Nov. 7, 1902.

145. It requireth few talents to which most men are not born, or at least may not acquire.—SWIFT on *Conversation.*

146. I shall do all I can to persuade others to take the same measures for their care which I have (taken).—*Guardian*, No. 1.

147. For we are his workmanship, created unto good works, which God hath before ordained that we should walk in them.—*Ephesians* ii. 10.

148. In the temper of mind he was then, he called them (pieces of good fortune) mercies, favours of providence, and blessings upon an honest industry.—ADDISON, *Spectator*, No. 549.

149. Everybody is to judge for themselves.—JANE AUSTEN, *Pride and Prejudice.*

150. Originality in politics, as in every field of art, consists in the

use and application of the ideas which we get or are given to us.—
JUSTIN M'CARTHY, *History of our own Times*, chap. ii. p. 44.

151. The House was aware that the system of education in Ireland
was different from either England or Scotland.—"House of Commons,"
Daily Telegraph, p. 11, April 3, 1903.

152. An officer on European and on Indian service are in very
different situations.—SYDNEY SMITH, *Essays*.

153. Precision imports pruning the expression, so as to exhibit
neither more nor less than an exact copy of his idea who uses it.—
BLAIR'S *Lectures on Rhetoric*.

154. Observe the tortures of a mind, even of so great a mind as
that of Warburton's.—DISRAELI, *Quarrels of Authors*.

155. Dr. Wittman might have brought us back anile conjecture,
but sound evidence of events which must determine his character
who must determine our fate.—SYDNEY SMITH, *Essays*.

156. For the history of the Empire no works exist of equal ability or
authority as those regarding the Revolution.—ALISON, *Hist. of Europe*.

157. Skinner, it is well known, held the same political opinions
with his illustrious friend.—MACAULAY, *Essay on Milton*.

158. She looked at her own neat white stockings, and thought
how glad she would be to cover their poor feet with the same.—
LAMB, *Essays of Elia*.

159. There is no doubt upon his mind, first as to every part of his
creed, and next to his individual capacity for expounding the same.—
GILFILLAN, *Literary Portraits*.

160. He will have no difficulty in appreciating both the magnitude
of the embarrassment which this resistance imposed on the sovereign,
and of the guilt of those who occasioned it.—ALISON, *History of Europe*.

161. As Mr. R. pointed out lately, the sources of the national
income before the Crimean War and to-day contrast thus :—etc.—
Daily Telegraph, p. 9, April 16, 1903.

(e) *Finite Moods and Tenses.*

1. Present in a Future sense.—The Present tense can be
used in a Future sense, provided that futurity is implied by some
adverb or other word in the sentence ; but not otherwise :—

> When *do* you start (=will you start) for Edinburgh ? (Here
> futurity is implied by the context.)
> He promised to come here to-day ; I hope he *does*. (Wrong.
> Change *does* to "will." The verb "hope" does not always
> imply futurity. We may hope for what is past or present, as
> well as for what is future.)

2. Present Perfect.—This tense connects a *completed* event
in some sense or other with *present* time. It is therefore
called the "Present Perfect." [1]   If the reference is to something

---

[1] Mr. Sweet in his *New English Grammar*, p. 104, Part II., points out
that the Present Perfect is used instead of the Future Perfect in clauses
dependent on a sentence which has a verb in the future :—

By the time you *have washed* and *dressed*, breakfast will be ready.

past, the past is still present in thought and has something to do with present time.

> The British Empire in India *has succeeded* to the Mogul. (Correct, because the British Empire still exists. If the *has* were cancelled, the sentence would mean that the British Empire succeeded to the Mogul in some past time, but has since been itself superseded by some other empire.)

> Yet if he never could make a fortune, he *has exercised* to the full the rarer and more enviable gift of making friends. Nor could anything exceed the warmth and affection with which he acknowledges his indebtedness to those who befriended him in his need.—*Spectator*, p. 624, April 27, 1901. (Here *has exercised* is correct, because it is clear from the verb "acknowledges" that the person referred to is still living.)

> Turn wheresoe'er I may,
> By night or day,
> The things which I *have seen* I now can see no more.
> WORDSWORTH.

(Correct. The last line means "The things which I once saw and which *are* still in my thoughts I now can see no more." Here past time "once saw" is connected with present time "are still in my thoughts.")

> Britain *has been infested* with wolves from that remote period conventionally called "the earliest times."—*Spect.* p. 134, Jan. 26, 1901. (Here *has been* is obviously wrong, since we know that in the British Isles wolves have long been extinct. The tense "has been" implies that Britain is still infested with wolves.)

> I have written to him twice these ten years. (Correct, because *these* connects the completed action with present time.)

> I have written to him several times since I received his reply. (Correct, because *since* denotes present time dating back to some past event.)

Note.—It follows from what has been said that the Present Perfect tense can never be qualified by an adverb or adverbial phrase denoting past time and excluding present.

> I have walked ten miles last Saturday. (Cancel *have*.)
> I have returned ten days ago. (Cancel *have*.)
> Our club *has* recommenced last Friday, but I was not there.—JOHNSON, *Letter to Boswell*, 1777. (Cancel *has*.)
> I *have* formerly talked with you about a military dictionary.—*Ibid. Letter to Mr. Cane.* (Cancel *have*. Or retain *have* and say, "I have talked with you before now," etc.)
> During the last century no Prime Minister, however powerful, *has* become rich in office.—MACAULAY, *History of England*. (Change *has become* to *became*.)

3. Past Perfect.—This tense (sometimes called the Pluperfect) is used whenever we wish to say that some action had been completed before another was commenced. It should never be used at all in any other sense.

He *had been* ill for two days, when the doctor came. (This is better than saying " he *was* ill for two days," etc.)

4. One Auxiliary with two Principal verbs.—Repeat the Auxiliary, if the voice or number of one Principal verb is not the same as the voice or number of the other. The construction of the Auxiliary must be made complete.

> The growth of tobacco has been established in India for the last 300 years and overspread the country. (Wrong. Say "*has* overspread." The tense of this verb is the same as that of "has been established," viz. Present Perfect, but the voice is different.)
>
> Since his last summary was sent off, twenty-five of the enemy *have been* killed, eighteen wounded, one hundred and ninety captured, and fifty more *have* tendered their submission. — *Daily Telegraph*, p. 8, Oct. 22, 1901. (Correct. "Have tendered" is in the Active voice, while the two preceding verbs are in the Passive.)
>
> The country was divided into counties, and the counties placed under magistrates.—FREEMAN, *History of England*. (Insert *were* before "placed," since its Subject is plural, whereas the Subject of the previous verb is singular.)

5. Two Auxiliaries with one Principal verb.—When two Auxiliaries are used with one Principal verb, the Principal verb need not be repeated, if the same form will do for both. If, however, one form will not suffice for both, two forms must be given, one for each Auxiliary.

> This England never did, nor never shall,
> Lie at the proud foot of a conqueror.—SHAKESPEARE.

(Here *did lie* and *shall lie* are both correct forms, and therefore the Principal verb "lie" need not be repeated.)

> I never have, and I never will, accuse a man falsely. (Wrong. Say, I never *have accused* and I never *will accuse* a man falsely.)
>
> Guerilla tactics alone have never expelled and never will expel a resolute invader.—J. B. FIRTH, *Fortnightly Review*, p. 810, Nov. 1901. (Correct. *Have expelled* and *will expel* are both complete forms.)
>
> It is not worthy of the powers of its author, who can and has at other times risen into much loftier ground. — GILFILLAN, *Literary Portraits*. (Wrong. Insert *rise* after *can*.)

6. Subjunctive mood.—The Subjunctive mood, though it has fallen somewhat into disuse in the literary style and is still more rarely used in the colloquial, can still be rightly used in any kinds of clauses, in which doubt, uncertainty, or denial is intended to be implied, but never to express a fact, or what is regarded as one. In the latter case the only mood that can be correctly used is the Indicative. "If it *be* so" implies a doubt, while "if it *is* so" conveys no such meaning. Hence the Subjunctive mood has been well called "the thought-mood" (Sweet).[1]

In the Past tense no difficulty arises; for the Subjunctive has in modern English become identical in form with the Indicative, excepting only in the verb *to be*, which has retained the form *were*, in marked contrast with the Indicative form *was*. But in the Present tense, Third person, there is no final *s* in the Subjunctive as in the Indicative; and hence the writer must be guided by his own intention as to which mood he should use in any given context. If he desires to suggest a doubt or a denial, he will use the Subjunctive. If he desires to express a fact, or what for the purposes of the argument is regarded as one, he will use the Indicative. If he is indifferent as to whether his words imply a certainty or an uncertainty, he can use the Indicative. Mistakes are much more frequently made in using the Subjunctive for the Indicative than in using the Indicative for the Subjunctive.

(1) If thou *meet* thine enemy's ox or his ass going astray, thou shalt surely bring it back to him again.—*Exodus* xxiii. 4.

Here the use of the Subjunctive though not necessary, is not unsuitable, since it alludes to a contingency which may or may not arise.

(2)   The noble Brutus
Hath told you Cæsar was ambitious :
If it *were* so, it *was* a grievous fault,
And grievously hath Cæsar answer'd it.
                    Julius Cæsar, iii. 2.

Here the suggestion of doubt or disbelief is admirably expressed by *were*. Mark Antony in this oration over the corpse of Cæsar does not at all desire to admit as a fact that Cæsar was ambitious and therefore deserved to be assassinated.

(3) Blank verse, if it sometimes *fail* to convey the movement and swing of the original, has the merit of passing into the reader's inner sense without jar or resistance.—*Literature*, p. 299, April 14, 1900.

Here *fails* would be as suitable as *fail*, since the writer seems to be conceding a point rather than suggesting an uncertainty. "However true it may be that blank verse lacks sometimes the swing and movement of a rhymed original, it has the merit," etc.

---

[1] *New English Grammar*, § 2259. The following definitions are worth quoting in this connection :—"In the Subjunctive mood the action is not stated as a fact, though it may be one, but as a conception of the mind" (Peile). "In the Conjunctive a thing is asserted simply as an idea conceived in the mind ; so that the speaker does not at the same time declare it as actually existing" (Mudrig).

(4) If John *were* satisfied, why should she be discontented.—*Too Much Alone*, ch. xv.

Here *were* is obviously wrong ; it spoils the sense.   Change it to *was*.

The Subjunctive mood may also be used to express a wish or a purpose.   (It is more usual, however, to employ auxiliaries.)

> Hallowed *be* thy name ; thy kingdom *come*.   (Wish.)
> Judge not, that ye *be* not judged.   (Purpose.)

Correct, improve, or justify the following sentences :—

1. There has been gradually growing up a feeling that, although Dr. C. is one of the most broad-minded and tolerant of men, yet there be limits to his patience.—*Church Gazette*, p. 44, April 29, 1899.

2. The recovery of Germany from that cruel period was less rapid, than is the recovery now going on in those provinces of China, which have been for a time almost depopulated by the rebellions of 1848-1873.—*Fortnightly Review*, p. 953, June 1899.

3. William and Mary had no children.   The Princess Anne, married to Prince George of Denmark, had several, but they were all dead.—*Short History of England*, p. 318.

4. It is clear to any outsider that he has and is acting without any relic of the obedience due from a priest to his lawful superiors.—*Middlesex County Times*, p. 9, Sept. 16, 1899.

5. The breach in the defence of the Legations at Pekin has been made, and after a gallant defence, during which the ammunition gave out, all the foreigners were killed.—*Daily Telegraph*, p. 8, July 16, 1900.

6. Messrs. Skeffington and Son publish immediately six hymns for the commemoration of the Queen's eightieth birthday.—*Church Gazette*, p. 129, May 20, 1899.

7. He (Ruskin) has made thousands of persons care for art as they never cared for it before, and never but for him.—Quoted in *Literature*, p. 197, March 10, 1900.

8. Maritime operations always have and always must involve the prompt application of military force as their necessary complement.—*Fortnightly Review*, p. 263, Aug. 1900.

9. Here we simply stand by and look on in amazement, and inquire : "How long is this sort of thing going on ?"—*Daily Telegraph*, p. 11, March 1, 1900.

10. Candles vary in price according to size, are exposed for sale near the shrine with their prices marked, and a money-box fixed near for the reception of the candle-money.—*Church Gazette*, p. 128, May 20, 1899.

11. In the opinion of Vinitius, the Christians not only could, but they ought to have killed Chilo. — Dr. BINION, *Quo Vadis?* p. 204, ch. iii.

12. No educated man can or ought to be indifferent to Mr. Chamberlain's scheme for the establishment of a school of tropical medicine.—*Educational Review*, Madras, p. 304, July 1899.

13. The men-at-arms then boarded, and in this way line after line was defeated, and the ships either sunk or taken prisoners.—RANSOME, *Short History of England*, p. 114.

14. London, the place of meeting, is Puritan and hostile to the court. In this as in the French Revolution the patriotism of the Assembly has the street on its side, and sometimes brings mob intimidation to bear. The London apprentices especially were always ready.—GOLDWIN SMITH, *United Kingdom*, vol. i. p. 512.

15. Living too in the Balearic Islands is dear, and cookery, or things be greatly changed, is an unknown art.—Quoted in *Church Gazette*, p. 50, April 29, 1900.

16. If it does not take Republicans to make a republic, they must be there to give it a soul : in 1848 Republicans there were none, or at least but a mere sprinkling of them.—*Fortnightly Review*, p. 1026, June 1899.

17. "It will get him through now most likely, though, of course —of course, Miss Carson, I hope it does."—*Morning Leader*, p. 2, Aug. 17, 1899.

18. There are thousands yet living who, if they delay not, may begin to read in Trollope of a world, the counterpart of which memory may yet recall, or which experience discover.—*Literature*, p. 254, March 31, 1900.

19. The book is a mere record of a summer spent chiefly without visitors, although towards its close there be too many.—*Church Gazette*, p. 218, June 10, 1899.

20. The passenger was killed and several injured by an accident to the Irish mail.—*Daily Telegraph*, p. 8, Dec. 9, 1899.

21. An immediate survey of all British dependencies is required, so that leaders in case of war do not have to operate on unknown ground, as at present in South Africa.—Quoted in *Review of Reviews*, p. 460, May 1900.

22. For some years past he has lived in the presence of the lakes and mountains that he loved.—*Literature*, p. 91, June 27, 1900. (Said of Ruskin about a week after his death.)

23. The German Government has refused to enter into peace negotiations with Li Hung Chang, until it be distinctly known with what government the Powers have to deal.—*Daily Telegraph*, p. 5, Aug. 24, 1900.

24. The absolution of a priest pronounced over a poor dying soul has got to be regarded more charitably than in the days when Protestantism was iron instead of putty.—*Church Gazette*, p. 424, Feb. 4, 1899.

25. I am anxious for the time when he will talk as much nonsense to me as I have to him.—*Biography of W. S. Landor*, by FORSTER, vol. i. p. 452.

26. Lord Fairfax of Cameron, who has lived the life of a gentleman farmer in America, has died, and the title descends to Albert Kirby Fairfax.—*Daily Telegraph*, p. 8, Oct. 1, 1900.

27. Cotton seed is used for making artificial butter, and its other products for fattening cattle in the South.—*Review of Reviews*, p. 383, Oct. 1900.

28. I received my training in my country, and I have experienced

disappointments in the early years, when I would gladly have changed my profession.—*Engineering*, p. 543, Oct. 26, 1900.

29. I saw her again, laid up with a fever she had caught in her vocation as sick-nurse, and which had proved fatal.—AMY DALTON, *The Streets and Lanes of a City*, ch. iii. p. 74 (H).

30. An attempt has been lately made to minimise and disparage the part played by England in 1830 in the creation and preservation of Belgium. An anonymous Belgian general denounced England for having acted as she has done on behalf of Belgium only from egotism and personal interest.—*Fortnightly Review*, p. 759, Nov. 1900.

31. To the investigation of this work Mr. G. W. has wisely given his immediate personal attention on his appointment to succeed Mr. G. B. as Chief Secretary.—*Spectator*, p. 738, Nov. 24, 1900.

32. It is no doubt India, and not Great Britain, which is primarily aimed at ; for Great Britain does not and never has imposed compensation taxes on imported sugar.—*Pioneer Mail*, p. 8, Nov. 2, 1900.

33. There is abundant evidence to show that they acted in unison, well aware that serious danger to life and property was the probable result of their actions.—*Ibid.* p. 17, Nov. 2, 1900.

34. No nation ever fell but by its own vices. If Venice were blotted out from the sovereignties of Europe, it was because Venice with her own hands had taken off the crown that in purer days sat upon her bold, bright brow.—MACLAREN, *A Spring Holiday in Italy*, p. 127.

35. Though nations were of more importance than we can conceive, and therefore the need of intercommunication a primary necessity, they had no international language.—*Review of Reviews*, p. 536, Dec. 1900.

36. Eight Turkish soldiers have been killed at Ishtib, a town forty miles south-east of Uskub, while attempting to arrest some Bulgarians, who are believed to be agents of the Macedonian committee.—*Daily Telegraph*, p. 6, Jan. 5, 1901.

37. I scarcely saw a gun or a spear the whole journey through these States, and I have formerly sat with hundreds of them standing around, not one of whom carried fewer than three spears, and most of them also with a gun.—*Government Report*, quoted in *Man*, p. 15, Jan. 1901.

38. The poet understands very well that no one will or ought to think the better of his righteousness for his being a seer.—COVENTRY PATMORE, quoted in *Fortnightly Review*, p. 310, Feb. 1901.

39. England and Greece, each after its own guise, have founded the most splendid empires over-sea ; and Greece succeeded in one direction where England has failed.—*Spectator*, p. 276, Feb. 23, 1901.

40. These are the book's faults : on the other hand its correctness is so indisputable and its observations often so true, that we are willing to pardon them.—*Ibid.* p. 599, April 27, 1901.

41. Through the same excellent source I heard that the family life of the late King (of Italy), far from going each his own way, has been a model of conjugal relations.—*Review of Reviews*, p. 377, April 1901.

42. At that time the *Pall Mall Gazette* was almost alone in maintaining that there was no cause for war, and to make war about the Pandjeh collision was a monstrous crime.—*Ibid.* p. 397, April 1901.

43. The peasantry have been told by their fathers that under the Second Empire prices were higher than they have ever been either since or before.—*Daily Express*, p. 4, June 18, 1901.

44. Nations do not act in pursuance of abstract principle, whether ethical or other, but upon motives of urgent expediency, and their proceedings never have or can be limited by scruples, but only by obstacles.—*Fortnightly Review*, p. 1033, June 1901.

45. So stagnant has the pool of domestic politics been since the prorogation, that the little ripple caused by a contested election in East Lanarkshire, which is brought to a conclusion this week, is giving entertainment, if not instruction.—*Daily Telegraph*, p. 6, Monday, Sept. 23, 1901.

46. That the rule of Spain has lasted so long in spite of its abuses —and it has lasted between three and four centuries over vast countries —is due to the splendid organisation of the Roman Church.—*Spectator*, p. 426, Sept. 28, 1901. (What little remained of the Spanish empire came to an end in 1899. The bulk of it had gone many years before.)

47. The desolation will be so great that when the child will be weaned, he will be fed, as among nomadic tribes, with curdled milk and wild honey.—J. M'SWENEY, *Translation of the Psalms and Canticles*.

48. Dr. Stein has employed his vacations for several years in obtaining in Kashmir the local information that is absolutely essential to the proper elucidation of Kalhana's text. The result was not only an accurate edition of the Sanskrit text, in 1892, but the present translation, which is accompanied by an ample commentary on the Chronicle in the form of footnotes.—*Spectator*, p. 504, Oct. 19, 1901.

49. What Senator Lodge thinks improbable, a highly imaginative, but also highly able, writer like Mr. Brooks Adams seems to think extremely probable, unless America shall look well and quickly to her armour.—*Fortnightly Review*, p. 559, Oct. 1901.

50. It was very hard for Abel Fletcher to have for his only child such a sickly creature as I, now at sixteen as helpless and useless to him as a baby.—Mrs. CRAIK, *John Halifax Gentleman*, ch. i.

51. I shall do all I can to persuade others to take the same measures for their care which I have.—*Guardian*, No. 1.

52. Cordite has been condemned by the committee appointed by the Admiralty and the War Office eighteen months ago in favour of another and, as it is believed, a more effective and serviceable explosive. —*Daily Telegraph*, p. 9, Jan. 9, 1902.

53. Surely no soldier of his century—save only the great Duke— has done more for his country, or has met with so little gratitude from his countrymen.—*Spectator*, p. 661, Nov. 1, 1902. (Said of Lord Raglan, who died before Sevastopol in the Crimean war.)

54. If ever there were a woman unfit by her own character, by her training, and by her beliefs for such a life as that which George Eliot chose, it was George Eliot.—*T. P.'s Weekly*, p. 2, Nov. 14, 1902.

55. France has obtained a firm footing at Tonking ; England is settled at Hong-Kong for some time past ; Russia is at the Amoor.— *Daily Telegraph*, Feb. 8, 1898.

56. The highest honours of the State are given to the successful

generals, but to the inventors of the guns and scientific weapons that made their victories even possible nothing more than is within the easy reach of successful tradesmen.—*Fortnightly Review*, p. 83, Jan. 1903.

57. This dedication may serve for almost any book that has, is, or shall be published.—CAMPBELL'S *Philosophy of Rhetoric*, p. 186.

58. Though he avoid commonplace, he does not straightway fall into paradox ; and he has given us a clear, unbiassed account of the true founder of the Roman Empire.—*Spectator*, p. 336, Feb. 28, 1903.

59. When the Emperor Alexander elevated the standard of the cross, he invoked the only power that ever has or ever will arrest the march of temporal revolution.—ALISON, *History of Europe*.

60. South, as great a wit as a preacher, has separated the superior and the domestic.—D'ISRAELI, *Miscellanies*.

61. The following facts may or have been adduced as reasons on the other side.—LATHAM, *The English Language*.

62. This union shared the fate of nearly all (unions) in every rank, which are formed by parental authority, before the disposition has declared itself, the constitution strengthened, or the tastes formed.— ALISON, *History of Europe from the Fall of Napoleon*.

63. If it has been shown that the foundations of our system of logic are falsely laid, an essential service has been rendered to the future logician, and smoothed his way to what Locke calls "a very different sort of logic and critic" from any with which he has hitherto been made acquainted.—RICHARDSON, *The Study of Language*.

64. Sir Thomas More in general so writes it, although not many others so late as him.—TRENCH, *English Past and Present*.

65. It is now about four hundred years since the art of multiplying books has been discovered.—D'ISRAELI, *Curiosities of Literature*.

66. Many years before this article was written, has appeared the *History of Dramatic Poetry*, by Mr. Collier.—*Ibid*.

67. Of this admirable work a subsequent edition has been published in 1822.—ALISON, *Essay on Humbolt*.

68. Out of the walls of Cadiz, in 1810 and 1811, has issued the cloud that now overspreads the world.—ALISON, *History of Europe*.

(*f*) "*Shall*," "*should*" ; "*will*," "*would*."

1. **"Shall," "should," in the First person.**—(*a*) *Shall*. When the verb is in the First person, future time in its simplest sense is expressed by "shall" :—

I (or we) *shall* write to you soon.

(*b*) *Should*.   Similarly future time in the First person is expressed by "should" (1) in a Principal clause, when the future is meant to be understood in a contingent or uncertain sense, (2) in a Subordinate clause, provided that the verb of the Principal clause is in a Past tense :—

I *should* be very glad to help you.   (*Contingent future*.)
I told him that I *should* be at home.   (*Indirect speech*.)
I was in hopes that I *should* meet him.   (*Dependent clause*.)

2. "Will," "would," in the Second and Third persons.

—(a) *Will.* When the verb is in the Second or Third person, future time in its simplest sense is expressed by "will."

> You *will* go. He, she, or they *will* go.

(b) *Would.* Similarly future time in the Second or Third person is expressed by "would" (1) in a Principal clause, when the future is meant to be understood in a contingent or uncertain sense ; (2) in a Subordinate clause, provided that the verb of the Principal clause is in a Past tense :—

> He *would* be very glad to help you. (*Contingent future.*)
> He told me that he *would* be at home. (*Indirect speech.*)
> He was in hopes that he *would* meet me. (*Dependent clause.*)
> It is understood that continued contumacy on the part of the Ottoman Government would have been met by the blockade of a port.—*Daily Telegraph*, p. 8, May 21, 1901. (*Contingent future.*)
> In both directions *we should* appear to the Afghans in the light of invaders and enemies, and *they would* welcome any assistance in expelling us from their country.—*Fortnightly Review*, p. 990, June 1900. (*Contingent future* in both clauses.)

3. "Shall," "should," in the Second and Third persons.

—When "shall" or "should" is used with a verb in the Second or Third person, the verb so formed does not express merely future time, but future time combined with some notion of command, demand, promise, previous arrangement, threat, determination, recommendation, assurance, or confident prediction :—

> These are things which never can be, never ought to be, and never *shall* be, forgotten.—*Daily Telegraph*, p. 9, April 28, 1900. (Assurance.)
> It has now been decided that Lord Kitchener *shall* leave Alexandria by despatch boat on Friday for Malta.—*Ibid.* Dec. 21, 1899. (Command or arrangement.)
> The country in its turn will demand of them that not an instant *shall* be lost.—*Ibid.* p. 6, Dec. 18, 1899. (Demand.)
> Colonel Baden-Powell has prophesied that the relief of the town *shall* be a birthday gratification for Her Majesty the Queen.—*Ibid.* p. 10, April 27, 1900. (Confident prediction.)
> The only address they put on their goods is intentionally such that even the acutest of their rivals *shall* be unable to tell whom they are for or where they are going.—*Spectator*, p. 932, Dec. 22, 1900. (Intention.)
> It is a federation in which Cape Colony and Natal, the Orange Free State, the Transvaal and Rhodesia *shall* be united under the federal constitution, under the British flag, and under the sovereignty of England.—*Daily Telegraph*, p. 10, March 14, 1901. (Determination.)

It has been definitely arranged that Mr. K. *shall* visit Amsterdam on the 10th inst., and leave the next day for Rotterdam.—*Ibid.* p. 9, Dec. 13, 1900. (Arrangement.)

The Spinners' Society of Oldham has decided that grants from the funds *shall* be made, etc. —*Ibid.* p. 10, Sept. 11, 1900. (Decision.)

What I have in mind is that the demands to be made in China, though simple in form, *shall* be conceived in the spirit of a large policy of reconstruction.—*Fortnightly Review*, p. 513, Sept. 1900. (Recommendation.)

Job, sitting aloof from men in his bodily degradation, yet lifts his eyes to heaven and knows that he *shall* be vindicated.—*Spectator*, p. 343, March 9, 1901. (He knows this on the strength of the divine promise.)

Little has been done of late by the Commander-in-Chief to redeem the promise which he made that the faithful hamlet *should* be relieved.—*Daily Telegraph*, p. 10, April 27, 1900. (Promise.)

He knew who *should* betray him.—*New Testament.* (Here *should* implies that the subject (Judas) referred to by *who* is under the control of destiny. "He knew who was destined to betray Him.")

It was the popular interest excited by their sacrifices which led Alexander II. to pledge his imperial word that if no other power *would* intervene, the Slav *should* not look to Russia in vain.—*Review of Reviews*, p. 135, Aug. 1899. (Here *would* expresses simple futurity, and *should* expresses a promise. Both are in the past form, because "led" is past.)

4. "Will," "would," in the First person.—When *will* or *would* is used in the First person, it does not express merely future time, but future time combined with the sense of intention or the exercise of will-power on the part of the doer :—

I *will* never do such a thing again. (Intention, promise.)

I *would* never do such a thing again, even if I were tempted. (Contingent promise ; a promise less strongly expressed.)

If we *will* adhere resolutely to that policy, we *shall* carry it through. — *Spectator*, p. 840, March 9, 1901. (Here *will* expresses intention, and *shall* simple futurity.)

I *will* leave my mark somewhere, and it *shall* be clear and distinct and free from the abominable blur of cant, humbug, and self-seeking which surrounds everything in this present world.—HUXLEY's *Letter to his Sister*. (Here *will* in the First person, and *shall* in the Third, both express intention.)

We know to what causes our past reverses have been owing, and we *will* have ourselves to blame if they are again incurred.—ALISON, *History of Europe*. (Wrong. Change *will* to *shall*.)

Note.—In interrogative sentences *will* is not used in the First person, for the obvious reason that it would be absurd for a man to question himself about his own intentions.

Mr. Ch. The Rhodesian papers will come later.

Mr. L. Will we have the papers before the budget?—House of Commons, *Daily Telegraph*, p. 11, April 3, 1903. (Change *will* to *shall*.)

5. Misuse of "shall" for "may" or "can."—Under no circumstances whatever ought *shall* to be used as an equivalent to *may* or *can*. It is this careless use of *shall* which leads to misapprehension as to its right uses.

What shall compensate Dreyfus for the mental agony and physical sufferings of these five long years?—*Church Gazette*, p. 198, June 10, 1899. (Change *shall* into *can*.)

I am taking a pony as far as the Portuguese frontier, and a donkey who will go as far as he *shall* live.—*Daily Telegraph*, p. 8, Dec. 26, 1899. (Change *shall* to *may*.)

6. "Should" in Conditional clauses.—In a Conditional clause, *i.e.* a clause preceded by "if" or any other conjunction that implies a condition, *should* is used in all three persons, and not merely in the First person. The same rule holds good when no conditional conjunction is expressed :—

Conditional.	*Consequent.*
If I *should* see him,	I *should* know him.
If you *should* see him,	you *would* know him.
If he *should* see him,	he *would* know him.

Observe that *should* is used in all three persons on the conditional side, while on the consequent-side contingent futurity is expressed by *should* (according to rule) in the First person, and by *would* (according to rule) in the Second and Third persons.

Note.—If the writer or speaker desires in the conditional clause to combine the sense of will or intention with that of mere supposition, he can substitute *would* for *should*. The construction in such a case is equally correct, but the sense is not the same. "If you *would* lower your terms, he would be very glad": *i.e.* "if you were willing to lower you terms, he would be very glad."

7. Remaining uses of "should."—There are two more uses of "should" still to be mentioned :—

(*a*) It is used in all three persons after the conjunction "lest"; and is the only auxiliary used after this conjunction, whatever may be the tense of the verb going before :—

He *works* or *worked* hard, lest he *should* fail = that he *may not* or *might not* fail.

(*b*) It is used in the sense of duty in all three persons. Here *should* is equivalent to "ought."

Present tense.—I (or he) *should do* (=ought to do) this.

Past tense.—I (or he) *should have done* this.   (I (or he) ought to have done this, but neglected to do it.)

The feeling on the subject in the City is that change should not (=ought not to, is not likely to) materially alter the situation. —*Daily Telegraph*, p. 4, Nov. 1, 1900.

A simple child—
What should it know of death ?—WORDSWORTH.

(What ought it to know ?   What can it be expected to know ?)

He states that the water-supply of the Mudug district *should* be (=is likely to be) closed to the Mullah by the end of the month. —*Daily Telegraph*, p. 8, March 20, 1903.

Note.—Under the heading (*b*) may be included those examples in which *should* expresses duty or propriety in a contingent sense :—

It is recommended that he *should* have a month's rest.

What we advise is that he *should* be promoted.

It is expedient for us that one man *should* die for the people, and that the whole nation perish not. —*John* xi. 50.

8. Remaining use of "will," "would."—*Will* and *would* can be used in the sense of habit in all Three persons, Present time being denoted by "will," and Past by "would" :—

> The methods of the pirates are characteristically practical and efficacious.   A band of pirates *will* buy a regular passage on a river steamer, and when they come to a convenient place over-awe the officials of the ship, etc.—REINSCH, *World Politics*, p. 187.

> A number of stories have been told of the manner in which the Princess in these early days *would* recognise ladies of the neigh-bourhood who happened to meet the royal party in Kensington Gardens.—*Daily Telegraph*, p. 10, Jan. 30, 1901.

> At length such friendship sprang up between the hound and the hare that they *would* daily play together and caress each other. —COWPER'S *Tame Hares*.

Correct, improve, or justify the following sentences :—

1. It may be hoped that this provincial note shall disappear both from the poetry and the polity of the United Commonwealth.— *Literature*, p. 255, March 31, 1900.

2. A little farther down in the century we will find men engaged in laying the foundations of a church whose claims are based on apostolic succession.—G. REBER, *Christ of Paul*, p. 60.

3. Inspector Summers finally announced that he should not eject the man who had made the allegation above named.—*Daily Telegraph*, p. 10, May 7, 1900.

4. It shall go hard with our generals, if they do not intercept some of that heavy artillery.—*Ibid.* p. 5, Dec. 26, 1899.

5. The nation confidently expected that the Government should do whatever was necessary to give our arms an irresistible superiority of strength.—*Ibid.* p. 6, Dec. 18, 1899.

6. If good old President Brand had been living, we and our country should not have been in this mess to-day.—*Ibid.* p. 6, Feb. 13, 1900.

7. I feel that it is my duty to indicate what I have said elsewhere, namely, how the Jewish Theistic Church shall speak of the great Jew of Tarsus.—*Fortnightly Review*, p. 672, April 1899.

8. A countryman, telling us what he had seen, remarked that if the conflagration went on as it was doing, we would have as our next season of employment the Old Town of Edinburgh to rebuild.—H. MILLER, quoted in *Webster's Dictionary.*

9. We can see an allusion to the debates which already divided the Church, and which shall fill up the history of Christian theology some centuries later.—RENAN'S *Antichrist*, ch. ii. p. 26.

10. I could hardly have dreamed that an old pupil of mine should have accused me of advocating a policy, the foundation of which is a lie.—*Review of Reviews*, p. 372, Oct. 1899.

11. We shall not be surprised if the interesting episode of the Queen's visit to Ireland shall mark the re-establishment of a union of hearts between Great Britain and Ireland.—*Daily Mail*, p. 4, March 30, 1900.

12. We have much pleasure in announcing that we are about to publish a military history of the present campaign in South Africa, which shall supply the public with an impartial and connected account of these stirring events.—Advert. *Literature*, p. iv. March 10, 1900.

13. But all these imperfections will count as little in the judgment of those, who shall turn to this book for solace and instruction.—*Ibid.* p. 149, Feb. 17, 1900. (Continuation of the same advertisement.)

14. Brandis finds the inimitable touch of the master in just these scenes, which Mr. Lee decides that it is impossible Shakespeare should have written.—*Ibid.* p. 346, May 5, 1900.

15. Nor would we be surprised to hear that satisfactory explanations have already been exchanged at Berlin.—*Daily Telegraph*, p. 8, April 13, 1899.

16. In the face of the resignation of those two thousand preachers, who shall say that Puritanism was mercenary or hollow?—GOLDWIN SMITH, *United Kingdom.*

17. When he left, the brushes disappeared, and the master of the house waited some days thinking he should receive them back.—Quoted in *Review of Reviews*, p. 391, April 1900.

18. We would be at Russia's mercy; for treaties would count for nothing then.—*Daily Mail*, p. 3, April 17, 1900.

19. Not until that has taken place will we have any security that we may not have again to fight for the unity of the empire.—Quoted in *Daily Telegraph*, p. 10, Nov. 1, 1899.

20. Great dangers and evils are before us, unless it shall be found possible to restore the discipline which has been so seriously impaired. —Quoted in *Daily Telegraph*, p. 9, May 9, 1899.

21. I would hold very different views, if this were the question of the presentation of an address to the Lord-Lieutenant.—Quoted in *Daily Telegraph*, p. 7, March 15, 1900.

22. Dig, search, read in museums local and national, and perchance you shall light on a bare record of these architects' births and deaths. —*Fortnightly Review*, p. 440, Sept. 1898.

23. We will see the **same** thing occur in the war between the Federals and Great Britain.—*Daily Telegraph*, p. 11, March 5, 1900.

24. If other dangers are to be successfully met, it must be done by public opinion insisting that steps shall be taken now to give a permanent character to its decisions, so that they shall remain effective when the interest excited by present events shall have died away, and the present outburst of patriotism shall be a thing of the past.— *Nineteenth Century*, p. 737, May 1900.

25. So long as our army is under the control of Parliament, we never will be prepared when the time comes.—Quoted in *Spectator*, p. 231, Aug. 25, 1900.

26. Tell that to your journal, and through it to the world, that this Republic shall fight to the bitter end. What do you take us for? —*Daily Telegraph*, p. 9, July 9, 1900.

27. I feel pleasure in my own home, among works of art. I know that in life I will never find anything above what I have already found.—Dr. Bixion, *Quo Vadis?* p. 248, ch. viii.

28. Vinitius believed that Nero's hour had struck, that the falling ruins of the city should overwhelm the mountebank and all his crimes. —*Ibid.* p. 321, ch. xxi.

29. The more I know of Buddha, the more I admire him ; and the sooner all mankind shall have been made acquainted with his doctrines, the better will it be.—Fausböll, quoted in *Bible Parallels*, p. 289.

30. I believe we will have a better man for the President of the United States for the next four years.—Quoted in *Daily Express*, p. 1, Sept. 7, 1900.

31. When that General shall have heard the opinions of the allied Generals, and shall have thoroughly considered the military situation, he will report.—*Daily Telegraph*, p. 9, Sept. 11, 1900.

32. Complaint has been made that Mr. Chamberlain should have published Mr. E.'s "stream of facts" letter.—*Ibid.* p. 10, Oct. 10, 1900.

33. Our language not being an inflected one to any extent, we would cut our parsing down to very small compass, if we confined ourselves to the distinctions expressed by the inflections of verbs.—Quoted in *Australasian Schoolmaster*, p. 37, Aug. 1900.

34. A coxcomb, flushed with many of these infamous victories (over young women), shall say he is sorry for the poor fools, protest and vow he never thought of matrimony.—Steele, *Spectator*, No. 288.

35. You shall seldom find a dull fellow of good education but, if he have any leisure on his hands, will turn his head to one of these two amusements for all fools of eminence—politics or poetry.—Steele, *Ibid.* No. 43.

36. The worst of it is, we have paid the men ourselves and I don't know how we will get our money back.—Quoted in *Daily Telegraph*, p. 9, Nov. 24, 1900.

37. He drew down upon him one anti-imperialist who believed that the annexation of the Philippines should be prevented by the Senate's refusal to ratify the Treaty of Peace.—*Review of Reviews*, p. 437, Nov. 1900.

38. In painting the British seaman in his true colours Mr. Bullen looks forward to that day when our sailors will be appreciated at their

true worth, and when the British seaman shall no longer feel that he is completely isolated from the thoughts and sympathies of his countrymen.—*Ibid.* p. 500, Nov. 1900.

39. I am not able to devote as much time and attention to other subjects as I will be under the necessity of doing next winter.— CHALMERS, quoted in *Webster's Dictionary.*

40. We are prepared to expend from £1,000,000 to £4,000,000 in this work. Of course we will have to secure franchises, and they will in many cases be difficult to obtain.—*Daily Express*, p. 1, Dec. 5, 1900.

41. I do not think the honourable member can appreciate what would be the result of such a statement, because we would be giving to the strangers in arms against us a great deal more than we have been giving to our own subjects.—Quoted in *Daily Telegraph*, p. 7, Dec. 8, 1900.

42. If so, we would be voting money to set up those injured by the war, although the injury is due to their own actions or to those who represented them.—*Ibid.* p. 7, Dec. 8, 1900.

43. If they were to have Wall Street methods thrust upon them, they should be paying very dearly for the very small sum which would be saved in the matter of commission.—*Ibid.* p. 9, Dec. 14, 1900.

44. There need be no war, but there must be a clear knowledge of our interests ; otherwise we will negotiate vaguely till we find too late that we have been elbowed out of what we really wanted.—*Spectator*, p. 60, Jan. 12, 1901.

45. From the moment war is declared, all foreign markets would of course be closed to us, and we would have to fall back upon our reserve stock and upon our home resources.—*Fortnightly Review*, p. 527, March 1901.

46. Nor would I feel called upon to utter one syllable on the subject but for the fact that some of my honourable friend's arguments have been so unfair, so unjust to the British Government.—Quoted in *Daily Telegraph*, p. 10, March 14, 1901.

47. It is important that members, irrespective of party, should realise the existing dissatisfaction with their recent performances and the expectations that they shall set themselves to bring about a change.—*Ibid.* p. 8, April 15, 1901.

48. My first appointment under the Colonial Office was that of Colonial Secretary in British Honduras, and I principally rejoiced in the fact that to get there I would have to travel to New York, which I had never seen.—*Empire Review*, p. 380, May 1901.

49. Some of us from time to time have expressed doubts and fears lest the next great war would show that the medical organisation was not suited to meet the sanitary and other conditions of modern warfare. —*Ibid.* p. 430, May 1901.

50. It being our duty to watch over the interests of British commerce in that part of the world, we feel that we would not be justified in allowing British trade to be made, as it were, a milch cow for the purpose of facilitating payment of these large indemnities.— Quoted in *Daily Telegraph*, p. 6, May 22, 1901.

51. You shall not find much or any mention of the beautiful blossom (of the lilac) till you come to the "Survey of the Nonsuch Palace," 1650, where it is written " a fountaine is sette round with six

trees called lelack trees."—Sir EDWIN ARNOLD, *Daily Telegraph*, p. 5, May 25, 1901.

52. He is well aware that it may be only a question of days before some emissary from the Empress, more fanatic or more cunning than the others, shall succeed in the ever imminent attempt upon his life. —*Fortnightly Review*, p. 2, July 1901.

53. Not only would we attract numbers of steady and ambitious young men to the ranks, but by gradually improving—as we certainly should—the class and the prestige of our non-commissioned officers, we should find it was much easier to maintain a sound system of discipline. By taking this step, moreover, we would strike a heavy blow at another cause of waste—desertion.—*Ibid.* p. 17, July 1901.

54. But how shall they get the constant market for bridges, which has enabled American bridge companies to invest large sums in labour-saving machinery and other appliances ?—Quoted in *Fortnightly Review*, p. 83, July 1901.

55. Colonel K. S. hoped that in future campaigns they should not again see a staff of those in high command filled up by gentlemen, however personally eminent or charming, whose trade was not the army.—Quoted in *Daily Telegraph*, p. 5, July 26, 1901.

56. A few succeeding years laid him in the earth, and though the marble (statue) shall preserve for ages the exact resemblance of his form and features, his own strong pen shall outlive that.—*Fortnightly Review*, p. 252, Feb. 1900.

57. The experiment which we then made has proved, I believe, a great success, and I cannot doubt that it will be widely extended to all other classes of the industrial community. When that is done, we will hear very little of the litigation of which you hear now a great deal too much.—Quoted in *Daily Telegraph*, p. 10, Oct. 28, 1901.

58. The attempt to make the Unionist party solely, or even chiefly, responsible for him and his doings is a monstrous perversion of the truth, and shall never be passed over by us without protest.—*Spectator*, p. 787, Nov. 23, 1901.

59. I will speak, and the word that I shall speak shall be performed.—*Ezekiel* xii. 25.

60. There is need for the most careful consideration of the naval needs of the empire, lest, when the time comes for action, a requisite fleet is not ready.—*Daily Telegraph*, p. 9, March 9, 1903.

61. If we look within the rough and awkward outside, we will be richly rewarded by its perusal.—GILFILLAN, *Literary Portraits*.

(g) Sequence of Tense and Mood.

1. Past tense in Principal clause.—If there is a Past tense in the Principal clause, this must be followed by a Past tense in the Dependent clause. There must be no conflict or incongruity. This has been well called "tense-attraction" (Dr. Earle). In each of the examples given below, the verb in the Dependent clause would be in the Present tense but for the attractive power of the Past tense of the verb in the Principal clause.

Victor Emmanuel III.'s first words *inspired* the confidence that he *could* and *would* take as monarch the place he must occupy, if Italian monarchy is to be saved from the breakers of civil war.—Quoted in *Review of Reviews*, p. 279, March 1901.

Mr. S. V. *was* pleased that the Admiralty *did* not propose to set up as armour-plated manufacturers, since the Sheffield firms *could* do all that *was* required.—*Daily Telegraph*, p. 6, Feb. 28, 1900.

To the policy of "standing by" with the fleet and relying upon the ultimate strength of sea-power to obtain respect for our rights we *would* have invited any other Powers to adhere that *desired* to do so.—*Spectator*, p. 366, Feb. 23, 1901.

I *was*, however, assured to-day by a Chinese official that the Emperor *had* no intention of leaving Haian-fu while the present situation *lasted*. The same official also *stated* that if the Powers *persisted* in their present intention with regard to the Legation quarters, it *was* extremely probable that the Court *would* never return to Pekin at all.—*Daily Telegraph*, p. 10, March 7, 1901.

The same principle holds good in the Oblique Narration. In such narration all that is said by the speaker must be in the Past tense, if the verb which introduces his speech is in the Past tense.

It *was* certain, said Lord R., that when the leading representatives of the colonies *came* together, something further *would* be accomplished in the direction of welding and uniting the empire.—May 3, 1887. (In the Direct Narration the words used by the speaker are : It *is* certain that when the representatives, etc., *come* together, something further *will* be accomplished, etc.)

In all these examples the sequence of tense is correct, a Past tense in the Principal clause being accompanied by a Past tense in the Dependent clause or clauses. In the following example the sequence is wrong :—

Sir W. Foster, M.P., *pointed* out to the Secretary of State for War that in all probability there *will* be a great loss of life from fever and other maladies.—*Fortnightly Review*, p. 494, Sept. 1890. (Change *will* to *would*.)

One exception, however, must be noted. To express some universal, habitual, or generally recognised fact, the Present tense (which is the proper tense for expressing facts of this kind) may be retained in the Dependent clause in spite of there being a Past tense in the Principal clause.

Principal clause.	*Dependent clause.*
The students *were* taught,	that the earth *moves* round the sun.
His illness convinced him,	that all men *are* mortal.

2. Present or Future tense in Principal clause.—If there is a Present (including the Present Perfect) or a Future tense in

the Principal clause, this can be followed by any tense whatever in the Dependent clause. The tense given to the verb in
the Dependent clause will depend upon the time (past, present,
or future), that the writer wishes to express.

	what he does	*Present Indefinite.*
	what he is doing . . .	*Present Continuous.*
a.	what he has done . . .	*Present Perfect.*
	what he has been doing .	*Present Perf. Cont.*
I know or	what he will do . . .	*Future Indefinite.*
shall know	*b.* what he will be doing . .	*Future Continuous.*
	what he will have done . .	*Future Perfect.*
	what he will have been doing .	*Future Perf. Cont.*
	what he did	*Past Indefinite.*
	what he was doing . . .	*Past Continuous.*
c.	what he had done . . .	*Past Perfect.*
	what he had been doing . .	*Past Perf. Cont.*

If for *know* or *shall know* we write *knew*, so as to give the
verb of the Principal clause a Past tense, then (*a*) must be
cancelled altogether, (*b*) must have the *will* changed to *would*,
and (*c*) will remain as it is.

One exception, however, must be noted. To express a
purpose in the Dependent clause by means of the conjunction
" that," the verb in this clause must be formed with the
Auxiliary " may," if the verb in the Principal clause is Present
or Future, and with the Auxiliary " might," if the verb in the
Principal clause is Past.

> He *works* or *will work* that he *may* succeed.
> He *worked* that he *might* succeed.

Note.—If " lest " is the conjunction used for expressing a purpose,
it is followed by the Auxiliary " should," whatever may be the tense
of the verb in the Principal clause. See above 7 (*a*), p. 89.

3. Conjunctions of comparison.— When two facts are
compared with each other by means of a Principal and a Dependent
clause, equality is expressed by " as well as," and inequality
by " than." Here the question of time is altogether absent.
Any tense can be followed by any tense according to the
intention of the writer.

> He *liked* you { better than he *likes* me.
> as well as he *likes* me.
> better than he *will like* me.
> as well as he *will like* me.

If no verb is expressed after these conjunctions, the verb of the Dependent clause is *understood* to be of the same tense as that *expressed* in the Principal clause.

4. Co-ordinate clauses.—Verbs connected by *and, nor, but,* and referring to simultaneous acts, should agree in tense and mood. The proper agreement of tenses has been carefully preserved by the writer of the following sentence :—

> The able statesmen and thinkers who *directed* and *direct* German affairs *realised* and *realise* that the making and maintenance of the nation in the first rank *depended* and *depends* absolutely on the technical and industrial efficiency of the people.—*Spectator*, p. 155, Aug. 2, 1902.

If, as sometimes happens, one Dependent clause is co-ordinate with another, the verbs of the co-ordinate clauses should agree in tense and mood. In the following example this principle has been violated :—

> If Keble *was* a scholar, a divine, a remarkably gifted poet, if he *were* exemplary as a friend, a brother, son and husband, so he was admirable in the discharge of his duties as a parish priest. —Sir J. T. COLERIDGE, *Memoir of John Keble*, vol. ii. p. 575.

Here *were* should be changed to *was* (not *was* to *were*), since *were* would imply a doubt, which is the opposite to the author's meaning. The sentence is faulty on other grounds. Say, "as a friend, a brother, *a* son, and *a* husband."

5. Condition and consequent.—To express a condition and its consequent, the Indicative mood should be followed by the Indicative and the Subjunctive by the Subjunctive. The sequences given below all express the same meaning, and all have reference to Present or Future time, whatever the form of the tense may be.

Indicative.	If I *meet* him . .	I *shall* know him.
Subjunctive.	If I *met* him . . If I *should meet* him If I *were to meet* him	I *should* know him.

Observe the agreement of moods in the following sentences :—

I *will* never do such a thing again, even if I *am* paid to do it. (Both Indicative.)

I *would* never do such a thing again, even if I *were* paid to do it. (Both Subjunctive.)

Note.—In such sentences as the following, the sequence is irregular, and appears to have arisen from a confusion between two constructions :—

> It *is* a pity that he *should* behave thus.

This might be split up into two sentences, in each of which the sequence is correct and regular :—

H

It *would* be a pity that (if) he *should* behave thus.
It *is* a pity that he *does* behave thus.

Apparently from a confusion between these two has arisen the irregular sequence above noted.

Correct, improve, or justify the following sentences :—

1. It was then that the Tsar made use of the memorable words in question, that it is contrary to his habits to profit by the difficulties of any other friendly State, even though its rulers were wholly unrelated to his house.—Quoted in *Daily Telegraph*, p. 9, Feb. 24, 1900.

2. He trusted that peace will soon be made, and a satisfactory agreement arrived at.—*Ibid.* p. 10, March 3, 1900.

3. There have been unmistakable signs that this campaign would be a fiasco.—*Daily Mail*, p. 4, March 7, 1900.

4. His party connections matter little or nothing, provided he were not in principle opposed to national action.—Quoted in *Review of Reviews*, p. 251, March 1900.

5. Admiral Tirpitz on his part declared that colonial possessions and a world-trade without a proper fleet remind one of a cavalry-man who can ride well, but has no horse.—*Fortnightly Review*, p. 612, April 1900.

6. He explained that the priests read the lessons so fast that no one can possibly follow them, but the people understand their purport, which is considered sufficient.—*Church Gazette*, p. 8, May 6, 1899.

7. Mr. Wallace in his book on Russia says that the bishops select wives for the priests, but a Russian lady whom I asked the question denied that this is so.—*Ibid.* p. 138, May 20, 1899.

8. As a result of this message Secretary Alger said this afternoon that he felt confident that the trouble will be satisfactorily adjusted.—Quoted in *Daily Telegraph*, p. 10, May 17, 1899.

9. His Honour does not believe that England would resort to extreme measures.—*Ibid.* p. 9, May 6, 1899.

10. The Works Committee recommended that if Mr. S. will cover the shed with corrugated iron, he be granted a licence for five years.—*Middlesex County Times*, p. 7, Nov. 25, 1899.

11. He performed many feats of valour, and was fabled to have performed many more ; but the crusade was, so far as its main object is concerned, a failure.—*Short History of England*, p. 84.

12. In brief, the delegates revealed unwittingly their belief that the struggle of their compatriots is quite hopeless.—*Daily Express*, p. 4, May 17, 1900.

13. He considers that the Tsar should issue an edict, that no Russian subject could be molested for his religious opinions.—*Church Gazette*, p. 138, May 20, 1899.

14. Some of our Unionist friends urge upon us that it would be a disgrace to the strongest government of modern times, if we allow this parliament to close without doing something to redress this glaring anomaly.—*Daily Telegraph*, p. 10, May 17, 1900.

15. But he could not have fought yesterday or on Monday, unless

indeed an opportunity had presented itself, which he dare not throw away.—*Ibid.* p. 9, Jan. 11, 1900.

16. It was unfortunately the case that the Japanese who have settled in Korea belong to a very low class.—*Ibid.* p. 10, March 31, 1900.

17. It points out that the British were at their door, and that if they continued fighting, their farms and towns would be destroyed.—*Daily Express*, p. 1, May 25, 1900.

18. He expressed the fear that the ambitious desire of France will be an accomplished fact before England's voice is raised.—*Ibid.* p. 1, May 25, 1900.

19. It is doubtful whether any man living has ridden to hounds oftener than the late Mr. Bevan.—*Daily Telegraph*, p. 8, Feb. 16, 1900.

20. The result of the operations of the two Generals was that British troops occupy secure positions between Johannesburg and Pretoria.—*Ibid.* p. 8, June 1, 1900.

21. General Buller telegraphed last night that he has occupied positions at Laing's Nek, which will enable him to render the position of the Federals untenable.—*Ibid.* p. 8, June 9, 1900.

22. The Premier adds, however, that should the Imperial Parliament resolve to amend the measure as proposed, it is unlikely that any difficulty would be caused.—*Ibid.* p. 9, June 22, 1900.

23. I for my part claim a restitution of every penny paid by me into the fund, inveigled thereto under what is obviously false pretences.—Quoted in *Pioneer Mail*, p. 22, May 4, 1900.

24. The interests of those who have to live in South Africa, our enemies as well as those on our side, will demand that there should not be two antagonistic political systems in what nature and history have decided must be one country.—Quoted in *Daily Telegraph*, p. 5, April 13, 1900.

25. Contrary to expectation, Mr. Brodrick stated yesterday that the Government has received no further news of any sort from the City of Mystery and perhaps of Death.—*Daily Telegraph*, p. 6, July 13, 1900.

26. Two merchants from Pretoria, who are at present staying at Machadodorp, have offered a reward of £100 to the first burgher who succeeded in rehoisting the Transvaal flag over the Government buildings in Pretoria.—Quoted in *Daily Telegraph*, p. 7, July 30, 1900.

27. I understand, however, on good authority that the supply of food for the prisoners is insufficient, that they had no meat or salt for eleven days, and that the ordinary allowance of meat was one pound a week.—*Ibid.* p. 5, Aug. 1, 1900.

28. It will be well, if one or more of those responsible were summarily hanged.—*Review of Reviews*, p. 13, July 1900.

29. The Russian engineers have declared that in 1902 the last section of the railway, that connecting Port Arthur with Siberia, would be completed.—*Ibid.* p. 88, July 1900.

30. They have always encouraged the back-country rustic in his ignorance and isolation; they have patted him on the back and told him what a fine and clever fellow he was.—*Fortnightly Review*, p. 258, Aug. 1900.

31. The filching of Kiau-Chou stirred up the whole Far-Eastern

question at a moment when the rivalries of the Powers in that region bid fair to sleep a long sleep.—*Ibid.* p. 328, Aug. 1900.

32. It is highly desirable that an enemy should see another wall of defence behind the first and a third behind that, so that the whole prospect might be too much for a future possible successor of Napoleon. —*Nineteenth Century,* p. 735, May 1900.

33. At the recent general meeting of the Agricultural Committee the hope was expressed that the Board of Education will introduce some modifications into the curricula of the Training Colleges.— *School World,* p. 303, Aug. 1900.

34. What we want is this, that the work we do may be consecrated to God, and that He might accept and bless it.—*Sunday Magazine,* quoted in *Review of Reviews,* p. 247, March 1900.

35. They might hope that generous democratic expansiveness will also obtain the willing co-operation of those distant kinsfolk of ours in South Africa.—*Daily Express,* p. 5, Sept. 7, 1900.

36. It was not deemed likely in official circles that the German reply will be published, but it has been communicated to all the other Governments.—*Daily Telegraph,* p. 7, Sept. 8, 1900.

37. Clause 74 provides that questions arising out of the Federation scheme itself should only be referred to the proposed Supreme Court of Appeal established under the Federation scheme in Australia.— *Review of Reviews,* p. 445, May 1900.

38. Sir William found the great starting-point of modern biological science in Schwann's enunciation of the principle that the elementary tissues consisted of cells.—*Spectator,* p. 291, Sept. 10, 1900.

39. Although much of our forethought may be of an unproductive nature under the dire pressure of war, still the satisfaction would remain of having done all that prescience suggests.—*Fortnightly Review,* p. 494, Sept. 1900.

40. The great scene when Pilate was overruled, having challenged the Jews to prove that public opinion is on their side and against Jesus of Nazareth, was simply the General Election anticipated.— *Review of Reviews,* p. 355, Oct. 1900.

41. He stated that men like himself, who were behind the scenes, knew that the progress, though slow, is markedly steady. —*Daily Telegraph,* p. 7, Oct. 25, 1900.

42. He will stay at the Hôtel de Noailles during his brief sojourn in the Southern port, and when he came on to Paris, he would alight at the Hôtel S—e, already the headquarters of the delegates.—*Ibid.* p. 10, Nov. 1, 1900.

43. Sir Roger was saying last night that he was of opinion that none but men of fine parts deserve to be hung.—STEELE, *Spectator,* No. 6.

44. They say that the moment the tax is imposed, publicity is inevitable, and that publicity would expose every well-to-do man to an amount of envy which would ultimately prove unendurable.— *Spectator,* p. 613, Nov 3, 1900.

45. A heavy succession-duty on Sir William Harcourt's plan would not be exposed to this drawback, and has the advantage, very great in France, that few of those who vote for it in the Chambers will be called upon to pay it.—*Ibid.* p. 613, Nov. 3, 1900.

46. From time immemorial there have been midnight street-prowlers, brutes of strength, but lacking the courage even of the common thief, who skulked in lonely places, ready to pounce out or attack any drunken person who rashly exhibits a watch-chain, or any old or enfeebled individual easily felled with one blow of a fist.—*Daily Telegraph*, p. 4, Dec. 14, 1900.

47. It is matter for exceeding regret that they allowed the Colonials to go away empty, and refused to receive a deputation on the subject of trade because they dare not say what they would, and would not say what they knew.—*Fortnightly Review*, p. 1015, Dec. 1900.

48. It has always been said by experts that there was in the Colonies the finest military material in the world.—*Ibid.* p. 1017, Dec. 1900.

49. Many old residents, who are by no means alarmists, regard the rising of the Dutch as quite likely, and are of opinion that to meet this strong reinforcements would be necessary.—*Daily Telegraph*, p. 7, Jan. 4, 1901.

50. It is a not unnatural instinct; but Lettice Trent, who fancied she has an experience of the ways of the world, had very little knowledge of the strings that govern the relations of men and women.—*Ibid.* p. 4, Jan. 4, 1900.

51. If only this money were drawn from the rates and the Board was elected *ad hoc*, the irate citizen would long ere this have arisen to protest against such misplaced use of wealth earmarked for a definite purpose.—*Fortnightly Review*, p. 177, Jan. 1901.

52. Nor is it unnatural to expect that fitting punishment would be meted out alike to officials, who took a more or less active part in the lawless proceeding, and to a population who moved not a finger to prevent it.—Sir ROBERT HART, *Fortnightly Review*, p. 194, Jan. 1901.

53. It is said that employers in the Philippines have rather preferred men who drank, gambled, and played the *gallera*, because such men, having more wants to satisfy, would work with greater energy and persistence.—REINSCH, *World Politics*, 1900, p. 322.

54. Last night there was a terrible thunderstorm, accompanied by torrents of rain. It appeared to travel north and to extend over a wide area, so that the river will undoubtedly again be swollen.—*Daily Telegraph*, p. 9, March 1, 1901.

55. If no general conditions, political or otherwise, shall arise, such as the appearance of bands of robbers, or if the behaviour of the regular troops should not necessitate it, the Court is inclined to agree to Li Hung Chang's request that no more expeditions should be dispatched.—*Ibid.* p. 10, March 7, 1901.

56. The burghers may be assured that, even if we have to fight them for another twenty years, the British people would see the thing through.—*Spectator*, p. 414, March 23, 1901.

57. In quoting these rates it is understood that a siding would be constructed whereby the traffic would be brought to the railway, and that no terminal services would be performed at either end.—JENKINS, *First Guide to Commercial Correspondence*, p. 52.

58. The sons of dukes may now be found in the offices of wine

merchants and stockbrokers, which would be deemed an impossibility fifty years ago.—*Daily Express*, p. 4, April 11, 1901.

59. His advice, even when it had to do with matters which directly affected his own sphere of action, has been several times set aside.—*Contemporary Review*, April 1901.

60. Sooner or later it is inevitable that the battery of the comparative method should breach these venerable walls mantled over with the ivy and mosses and wild flowers of a thousand tender and sacred associations.—FRAZER, *Golden Bough*, I. xxii.

61. The association by twenty-nine votes to nine declared that his conduct was inconsistent with Unionist principles, and that by voting with the Nationalists he has broken his pledges to the electorate.—*Daily Express*, p. 5, May 28, 1901.

62. Fifteen cases, it is said, are already down for hearing, and the probability is that some twopenny-halfpenny question will arise, which would interest no person in the world excepting the two litigants.—*Review of Reviews*, p. 419, May 1901.

63. To call it an estimate is a misuse of terms. It was merely a guess based on information supplied by men who are not in a position to give it.—*Fortnightly Review*, p. 1093, June 1901.

64. The statements of Mr. D. drew an indignant protest from Mr. L., who declared that the honourable member dare not repeat outside the House the charges that he had made against British troops.—*Daily Telegraph*, p. 8, July 5, 1901.

65. If the British element were to yield to the contagion of a bad example (in its treatment of the blacks), South Africa is doomed.—*Ibid.* p. 240, Aug. 24, 1901.

66. Russia's sphere of influence in this region had been so clearly defined, and her interests were so vital and generally acknowledged, that England can have no objection to the occupation.—Quoted in *Homeward Mail*, p. 1145, Sept. 2, 1901.

67. The notion that the regulation (for fixing the rate of wages) was impartial, and a proof that the economical and social policy of these days was in a higher spirit than ours, is manifestly absurd, when the avowed object of the statute is to prevent the demand for excessive wages.—GOLDWIN SMITH, *United Kingdom*, vol. i. p. 226.

68. In the course of a long discussion it was made clear that in the opinion of the reformers, the evil has a diversity of causes, and can be remedied only by the application of as many cures.—*Daily Telegraph*, p. 8, Feb. 23, 1901.

69. Accidents arising from shows of performing lions and other wild beasts are so many and so frequent that to enumerate those even of the last two or three years would occupy space that can be better used.—*Fortnightly Review*, p. 388, March 1900.

70. Ye will not come unto me, that ye might have life.—*John* v. 40.

71. If thou bring thy gift to the altar, and there rememberest that thy brother hath ought against thee ; leave there thy gift before the altar, and go thy way, etc.—*Matthew* v. 23, 24.

72. What Wordsworth's poetic life lacked was energy, and he refused to recognise that no amount of energy will suffice for continual production.—*Fortnightly Review*, p. 40, Jan. 1902.

73. In his official report General B. states that were it not for the action of Colonel Long and the subsequent disaster to the artillery, he thought that the battle might have been a successful one.—CONAN DOYLE, *The Great Beer War*, pp. 102, 103, ed. 1900.

74.   Fate hath decreed Ulysses should abide
        More toils and fiercer than all men beside :
        Heavily homeward must he win his way
        Through lure, through darkness, anguish, and delay.
                        STEPHEN PHILLIPS, *Ulysses*.

75. It took the jury only five minutes to find him guilty. Sentence was deferred till the case against Kelly and Stiles has been gone into.—*Daily Telegraph*, p. 8, Feb. 20, 1902.

76. At a Cabinet Council held at the Elysée yesterday it was decided that President Loubet shall set out on his journey to Russia in the second week of May.—*Ibid.* p. 8, March 13, 1902.

77. Many are neither archaic nor modern, but seem to think that the further their style were from any known model, the closer it might convey foreign ideas. — *Nineteenth Century*, p. 1012, Dec. 1902.

78. President Castro has forwarded through Mr. Bowen a proposal that the British and German claims shall be submitted to arbitration. —*Daily Telegraph*, p. 8, Dec. 13, 1902.

79. There was a discussion as to whether the ballet should be dropped, and it was announced that the general manager, Mr. C. Dundas Slater, will shortly retire.—*Daily Express*, p. 2, Feb. 10, 1903.

80. But though we hold that arbitration would be much the best way out of our present difficulties, we fear that it is not very likely that Germany will agree to such a course even if Venezuela were to prove reasonable.—*Spectator*, p. 977, Dec. 20, 1902.

81. It is confidently reported that two young gentlemen of real hopes, bright wit, and profound judgment have made a discovery that there was no God.—SWIFT, *Argument against abolishing Christianity*.

82. If there be but one body of legislators, it is no better than a tyranny ; if there are only two, there will want a casting vote.—ADDISON, *Spectator*, No. 287.

83. In order, therefore, to try our good nature, whether it arises from the body or the mind, whether it be founded in the animal or rational part of our nature, we must examine it by the following rules.—ADDISON, *Spectator*, No. 177.

84. If that system were vigorously carried into execution,—if a first imprisonment was in every instance made so long as to teach the young novice in crime an honest trade, the continual stream of depravity which now pollutes the British islands would be lessened.—ALISON, *History of Europe*.

(h) *Infinitive, Verbal Noun, Gerund, Participle.*

1. The Noun-Infinitive.—The Noun-infinitive (as distinct from the Gerundial or Qualifying Infinitive to be explained below) is so called because it does the work of a noun, and may therefore be the subject, the object, or the complement of a verb ; and sometimes even the object of a preposition.

> *A walk* is good for one's health. (*Common Noun.*)
> *Walking* is good for one's health. (*Verbal Noun.*)
> *To walk* is good for one's health. (*Noun-Infinitive.*)

The Noun-Infinitive has been also called the Simple Infinitive, because in certain connections it is used without *to.* Such connections are the following :—

(*a*) After *hear, see, need not, dare not, feel, make, let, bid, watch, behold, know :*—

> He dare not *come.* He need not *go.* I heard him *speak.* I made him *laugh.* I have known him *laugh* for nothing.

Note.—In the Passive voice the *to* is used after *hear, see, feel, make, bid, know* : as, "He was heard *to say*"; "The stick is seen or felt *to be* crooked"; "He was bidden or made *to go*"; "He is known *to be* clever."

(*b*) After Auxiliary and Defective verbs :—

> I shall *go.* I will *go.* I can *go.* I may *go.* I did *go.* I must *go* (But "I ought *to go*" is an exception.)

(*c*) After the prepositions "but" and "than" :—

> He did nothing but *laugh.* He did nothing else than *laugh.*

(*d*) After the phrases "had better," "had rather" :—

> You had better not *remain* here.
> I had rather *take* this than that.

With the above exceptions, the Noun-Infinitive is invariably preceded by *to.* But writers are very apt to leave the *to* pendent, *i.e.* to put no verb after it, leaving the verb to be understood. This is not good English, and is not sanctioned by literature.

> If a hill is steep enough to coast on,[1] I do not want to back-pedal unless I have *to.*—*Fortnightly Review,* p. 119, Jan. 1899. (Say "unless I have or am forced *to do so.*")

2. Noun-Infinitive, Present and Perfect forms.—I. The **Present** form of the Infinitive is used for expressing any action that is simultaneous with or subsequent to the time indicated by the Principal verb, whether that time be Past, Present, or Future.

> I hope, or hoped, or shall hope *to see* you.
> I *am* able, or *was* able, or *shall be* able to do this.

---

[1] To "coast" means to allow the bicycle to run down the incline of itself, without using the pedal to move it forward.

II. The **Perfect** form of the Infinitive is used for three different purposes :—

(*a*) To describe some action as *completed*. Here the sense of the Perfect Infinitive tallies precisely with that of the Present Perfect, Indicative.

> *To have accomplished* this task is the crown of my ambition. (This is equal to saying "That *I have accomplished* (Present Perfect) this task is, etc.)

(*b*) To show that some supposition, expectation, opportunity, duty, or desire was *not realised.*[1]

> Neglected grievances grow into active discontent, and what might *have ended* in a formidable rising had to be quelled by the dispatch of troops from Cape Town.—*Empire Review*, p. 35, Feb. 1901. (Here observe the difference between *have ended* (Perf. Infin.) and *to be quelled* (Pres. Infin.). The former refers to an event that could have happened, but did not happen ; the latter to an event that happened simultaneously with the time indicated by the Principal verb "had.")
>
> The annual banquet of the Birmingham Chamber of Commerce, at which Mr. Gerald Balfour, Mr. Jesse Collins, and Mr. Austen Chamberlain were *to have been* present, has been abandoned.—*Evening News*, p. 3, Jan. 2, 1901. (Correct.)
>
> It was the Lord Advocate's intention *to have introduced* an amending bill ; but the state of public business prevented him.—*Scotsman*, June 30, 1875. (Correct. But here the Perfect Infinitive is unnecessary, since the final clause shows that the intention was frustrated.)

---

[1] Campbell, in *Philosophy of Rhetoric*, p. 212, ed. 1841, makes the extraordinary and very erroneous statement that "all verbs expressive of hope, desire, intention, or command, must be invariably followed by the Present, and not the Perfect, of the Infinitive." He sees no difference between "I expected to find him" and "I expected to have found him." The latter means "I expected to find him, but was disappointed." The former merely expresses the expectation, and makes no implication whatever as to the upshot.

Mr. Hodgson, in *Errors in the Use of English*, stigmatises as an "error" the use of "the Perfect form of the Infinitive after a Perfect verb," except when the action or state denoted by the Infinitive is prior in point of time to that denoted by the Finite verb. Thus he admits as correct, "He *was proved to have been born* in France" ; but condemns as wrong, "He paid me many compliments upon my sermon against bad husbands, so that it is clear he *intended to have made* a very good one." The last sentence, however, is not necessarily wrong. It might mean that he intended to make a good husband, but failed to do so. Nevertheless it is a common blunder to use a Perfect Infinitive after a Past Finite verb in sentences where the Present Infinitive should have been used in preference ; and Hodgson has done well in cautioning his readers against it.

They ought *to have saved* us from sensualism and metaphysics, but they ran us aground on both reefs.—Quoted in *Spectator*, p. 807, Dec. 1, 1900. (Correct.)

He speaks foolishly of "the common English prejudice against Paul Jones," whereas a little thought might *have convinced* him that the prejudice which he denounces is far too true.—*Spectator*, p. 875, Dec. 15, 1900. (Correct.)

They, supposing him *to have gone* in the company, went a day's journey.—*Luke* ii. 44. (History shows that he had not gone ; and therefore the Perfect Infinitive is correct.)

(*c*) To show that some action or state belongs to a time earlier than that referred to by the Finite verb. This use of the Perfect Infinitive occurs only after verbs (in the Passive voice) of saying, believing, showing, reporting, and after a few Neuter verbs, as "seem," "appear." The sense of the Perfect Infinitive as thus used tallies precisely with that of the Past Indefinite or Past Perfect, Indicative.

Herodotus is shown *to have erred*, not so much in his description, as in his dates.—*School World*, p. 57, Feb. 1902. (This is equivalent to saying, "It is shown that Herodotus *erred*," Past Indefinite.)

The coronation of George I. seems *to have created* very little excitement in London.—*Notes and Queries*, p. 313, Oct. 18, 1902. (This is equivalent to saying, "The coronation, it seems, *created*," Past Indefinite.)

He was believed *to have died* in the year before last. (This is equivalent to saying, "He *had died* (Past Perfect), as was believed, in the year before last.")

When none of the above three purposes is served, the Present Infinitive should be used, and not the Perfect. It is a common blunder, however, to put a Perfect Infinitive after a Finite verb in the Past tense on the mistaken notion that past time in the Finite verb requires to be followed by past time in the Infinitive. (This is another example of Attraction or the Error of Proximity : see above, p. 5.)

Gray might perhaps have been able *to have rendered* him more temperate in his political views.—SOUTHEY, *The Doctor*.

Swift, but a few months before, was willing *to have hazarded* all the horrors of a civil war.—JEFFREY, *Essays*.

3. Gerundial or Qualifying Infinitive.—This Infinitive, though it is now the same in form as the Noun-Infinitive, had once a separate form of its own, and is still entirely distinct from the Noun-Infinitive in its uses. Far from being a Noun or doing the work of a Noun, it does the work of an Adjective in qualifying nouns, or of an adverb in qualifying verbs and adjectives.   It might hence be fitly called the Qualifying Infinitive.[1]

> Quick *to hear* and slow *to speak*.   (*Adj. qualified.*)
> He came *to see* the sport.   (*Verb qualified.*)
> I have no pen *to write* with.   (*Noun qualified.*)

Note.—When this Infinitive is made to qualify a noun, as it is made to do in the last example, it must be accompanied by the same preposition that it would have if the verb were Finite.   " I write *with* a pen " ; " a pen to write *with*."

> For Russia any stick is good enough to beat the Ottoman dog.— Captain GAMBIER, *Fortnightly Review,* p. 749, Nov. 1902. (Say "to beat the Ottoman dog with"; or say "with which to beat the Ottoman dog.")

4. Future Sense of Qualifying Infinitive.—As there is no form of Future Participle in English, the Gerundial or Qualifying Infinitive takes the place of one.

> In 1789 the great French Revolution began ; and a democratic republic, soon *to pass* into a military despotism, was set up.— HUNTER's *Short History of England,* p. 383.
> By a statue of Lord Russell of Killowen, *to be placed* in the courts, the memory of the late Lord Chief Justice will be handed down from generation to generation of lawyers.—*Daily Telegraph,* p. 8, Oct. 27, 1900.
> The caul was put up in a raffle, the winner *to pay* five shillings.— DICKENS, *David Copperfield.* (Here the noun and the infinitive are used absolutely, just as a noun and a participle often are.)

5. Qualifying Infinitive, Active or Passive.—It is often a moot point whether the Qualifying Infinitive, when it is used to qualify a noun or an adjective, should be in the Active or the Passive voice.   On the whole the Active voice is the more common.   But no absolute rule can be laid down ; the writer must be guided by ear or by what he knows of custom.

> A house *to let*.   A house *to be let*.   (Both correct.)
> A vigour and watchfulness which leave nothing *to seek.*—*Daily Telegraph,* p. 9, June 15, 1900.   (Correct.)

---

[1] In A.S. the Noun-Infinitive ended in *-an* or *-ian*, which, after being changed to *-en* in Middle English, was eventually lost.   Thus we have "bind-*an*," "bind-*en*," "bind." In A.S. this Infinitive was never preceded by *to*.   What I have called the Gerundial or Qualifying Infinitive was in A.S. a phrase formed by the preposition *to* and by the inflexion *-anne* or *-enne*, which after being shortened to *-en* was, like the preceding, eventually dropped.   When the *to* came to be added to the Noun-Infinitive, as it always had been to the Gerundial, no difference in *form* between the two Infinitives remained.

In point of clearness his speech leaves something *to be desired.—*
Ibid. (Correct).

These societies were too powerful *to suppress* or *to ignore.—Ibid.*
p. 7, Feb. 14, 1900. (Here it would be better to say " to be
suppressed or ignored.")

6. Gerund and Verbal Noun.

—Although the Gerund has
sprung from the Verbal Noun (which in Anglo-Saxon ended in
-ung, and sometimes in *-ing*, as in Modern English), and though
both end in *-ing*, yet the two cannot now be considered as
identical. The differences are :—

(*a*) The Verbal Noun is followed by " of " and preceded by
the Definite article ; the Gerund has neither of these accompaniments :—

> *The* gathering *of* flowers delighted her. (*Verbal Noun.*)
> Gathering flowers delighted her. (*Gerund.*)

(*b*) The Verbal Noun is qualified by an Adjective, the
Gerund by an Abverb :—

> The *rapid* reading of a book is useless. (*Verbal Noun.*)
> Reading a book *rapidly* is useless. (*Gerund.*)

(*c*) The Verbal noun has only one form, viz. that which
tallies with the Present Participle in *-ing ;* the Gerund can take
the form not only of the Present Participle, but also that of the
Past Participle, and it can do this in both the Active and the
Passive voices :—

> I profited much by *having read* the book. (*Active.*)
> The soil was loosened by *being dug.* (*Passive.*)

(*d*) The Verbal noun is a pure noun,—a noun and nothing
more,—a noun formed from a verb, but retaining none of the
functions of a verb. A Gerund, on the other hand, is a noun
and verb mixed, *i.e.* partly a noun and partly a verb. In the
phrase " by having read the book," *having read* is a noun
because it is the Object of the preposition " of " ; and it is a
verb, because it has " the book " for its Object.

7. Confusion of Gerund with Verbal Noun.

—Since a
Gerund and a Verbal noun have acquired distinct positions in
English grammar, no confusion between the two ought to be
made in composition.

> The giving to the courts the power to review hard and unconscion-
> able bargains will control the rest.—*Review of Reviews,* p. 165,
> Aug. 1898. (Cancel *the* before " giving." It would not sound
> well to insert *of* before " the power.")

It is against euphony, though not against grammar, to mix up the two constructions in the same sentence, as is done in the following examples :—

> Poverty turns our thoughts too much upon *the* supplying *of* our wants, and riches upon enjoying our superfluities.—ADDISON, *Spectator*, No. 464. (Either cancel *the* and *of*, or convert "enjoying" from a Gerund to a Verbal noun by applying to it a similar construction.)
>
> I had the misfortune to displease him by unveiling of the future and revealing all the dangers, etc.—H. L. BULWER, *Historical Characters*, vol. i. p. 378. (Cancel *of* after "unveiling." If *of* is to be retained "unveiling" must be preceded by *the* and a similar construction must be used with "revealing.")

8. Confusion of Gerund with Infinitive.—"It" is often used to introduce a Noun-Infinitive, as "It is easy to do this = To do this is easy." A Gerund should not be substituted for an Infinitive in such a context.

> It is easy *distinguishing* the rude fragment of a rock from the splinter of a statue.—GILFILLAN, *Literary Portraits*. (Say, "to distinguish.")
>
> It was great in him *promoting* one to whom he had done some wrong.—*Ibid.* (Say, "to promote.")

9. Reference of Gerund to Subject.—A Gerund, when it is preceded by a preposition, has reference to the Subject of the sentence rather than to any other word ; and unless there is some subject to which the action expressed by the Gerund can be referred, the Gerund ought not to be used with a preposition.

> He gave us a bed after *having had* a good meal. (Change *after having had* to *after we had had*. Otherwise "after having had" will relate to the Subject "he.")
>
> Before *leaving* the old country I had wondered why it was that so little information was forthcoming in the Maritime Provinces.—*Empire Review*, p. 324, April 1901. (Correct, because the Gerund is intended to refer to the Subject "I.")
>
> We came upon a number of Boers, who were cleaning their rifles after *being engaged* with us.—HALDANE, *Blackwood's Magazine*, p. 157, Aug. 1900. (Correct, because "being engaged" is intended to refer to the Subject "who.")
>
> Dr. —— well remembered that he had a salary to receive, and only forgot that he had duties to perform. Instead of *guiding* the studies and *watching* over the behaviour of his disciple, I was never summoned to attend even the formality of a lecture.—GIBBON, *Autobiography*. (Wrong. The gerunds in the text have reference to *I;* but this is against the sense. Say, "Instead of guiding, etc., and watching, etc., he never summoned me," etc.)

10. Possessive before Gerunds.—If a noun is used before a Gerund, it should be in the Possessive case provided that the noun is one that can take the Possessive form. Pronouns too should be in the Possessive.

> Bingley urged *Mr. Jones's* being sent for immediately.—JANE AUSTEN, *Pride and Prejudice*, close of ch. viii. (Correct.)
>
> It is, however, almost impossible to believe that such transactions would have been carried on without *Lord Kitchener* being informed.—*Daily Telegraph*, p. 6, Sept. 20, 1901. (Say, *Lord Kitchener's.*)
>
> Don't fear *me* being any hindrance to you ; I have no more to say. —DICKENS, *David Copperfield*, ch. ii. 290. (Say, *my.*)
>
> We shall in any case be the only large users of the line, the patrons whose custom is essential to it paying a dividend.—*Spectator*, p. 521, April 4, 1903. (Say, *its paying.*)

11. Gerundive use of Participles.—Owing to the fact that there are many nouns which do not take the Possessive form, a mixed construction has arisen which has been called "the Gerundive use of Participles."[1]

> A bishop may be untiring in every one of his duties without his *name being known* beyond the limits of his diocese.—*Spectator*, p. 79, Jan. 19, 1901. (Since we cannot say *name's*, "being known" must be considered a participle used gerundively. The sense is equivalent to "without the being known of his name" ; but such a phrase is against idiom.)
>
> The nearness of the Basuto frontier prevented *the enemy going* into the valley of the greater river.—*Daily Telegraph*, p. 6, Aug. 3, 1900. (Say, "the enemy's going"; or say, "the enemy from going." The construction in the original, though we often meet with it, is a confusion.)

Sometimes, when the noun happens to be separated by several intervening words from the Gerund to which it belongs, it is more convenient not to use the Possessive case with a Gerund, but to use a Participle gerundively instead.

> I remember a true *representative* of Brabant, who had positively declared that a German occupation of Belgium would be intolerable, *being pulled up* by a Flemish gentlemen with the remark, etc.—*Fortnightly Review*, p. 762, Nov. 1900.
>
> The Cantabs were handicapped by *one* of their best players *being* absent through illness.—*Daily Telegraph*, p. 8, Dec. 20, 1900.

These sentences are bad enough already ; but they would be made worse than they are by saying "representative's" for "representative," and "one's" for "one."

---

[1] Mr. Sweet in *New English Grammar*, § 2330, calls the participle in such constructions a "half-gerund." Dr. Abbot calls such use of participles "gerundive."

It would be better to rewrite them as follows :—

I remember the incident in which a true representative, etc., was pulled up, etc.

The Cantabs were handicapped by the absence of one of their best players on account of illness.

12. Participles used absolutely.—A participle is said to be used "absolutely" with a noun or pronoun in the Nominative case, when the said noun or pronoun has no syntactical connection with any other word in the sentence. Though grammatically disconnected from any one word in the sentence, the absolute phrase modifies the sense of the sentence as a whole.

For hours he kept us waiting in the boat, until presents had been exchanged, *we* giving them a coloured pocket-handkerchief, and *they* pushing out to us on a canoe a few cocoanuts.—*Empire Review*, p. 572, June 1901.

But the absolute construction should not be used, if the noun or pronoun has been employed already in some connection other than that of the participle :—

The pains which his father had taken to train *him* for business and war, *he* being apt for neither, may have increased his distaste for both.—GOLDWIN SMITH, *United Kingdom*, vol. i. p. 203. (Change "he being apt for neither" to "apt though he was for neither.")

Man being what he is, man was certain to pin his faith on practically useful ghosts, ghost-gods, and fetishes which he could keep in his wallet or medicine bag.—ANDREW LANG, *Making of Religion*, p. 282. (Put a comma after the first *man*, and cancel the second one.)

There must be no confusion between the absolute and the adjectival uses of a participle in the same sentence :—

Accident *having opened* a new and most congenial career to him, and *having become* a great favourite of and of much use to Mr. Nash, he ultimately accompanied his patron to London.—*Hodgson*, p. 103. (Here *having opened* is absolute, while *having become* is adjectival. Say, "Accident having opened, etc., he became a great favourite, etc., and ultimately accompanied," etc.)

13. Impersonal Absolute.—The Present participle of certain verbs can be used absolutely without any noun or pronoun being attached to it. This is called the Impersonal Absolute (see above, ch. i. (*b*), 6). To this class belong such words as "regarding," "concerning," "considering," "touching," "owing to," which have practically become prepositions. There are a few other participles similarly used ; but no one is justified in resorting to such a construction whenever it pleases him, without the authority of custom or literature.

As the Federals, *judging* from their previous tactics, are not likely to take the initiative in any attack, he will have time to gather his forces for a stronger effort.—*Daily Telegraph*, p. 9, Dec. 16, 1900. (Admissible.)

Generally *speaking*, these peculiar orgies obtained their admission and their influence at periods of distress, disease, public calamity or danger.—GROTE, *History of Greece*, ch. i. p. 25, ed. 1888. (Admissible.)

The route on Saturday will be lined by 23,000 troops, *including* colonials, volunteers, and militia.—*Daily Express*, p. 1, Jan. 30, 1901. (Admissible.)

There was in these regiments, *taking* one with another, a considerable number of officers who were pre-eminently leaders of men, etc.—*National Review*, Jan. 1901. (Admissible.)

On the contrary, there was probably never a time when Ireland was more prosperous (*calculating* per head of population), or when there was less destitution and the standard of living was higher.—*Spectator*, p. 902, June 22, 1901. (Admissible.)

It is to be regretted that the thieves escaped, but, *having escaped*, the search must none the less be continued. (Inadmissible. Say, "the escape having been made.")

14. Participle qualifying Possessive pronoun.—Such a construction, though not common, is defensible perhaps, because a Possessive like *his* is equivalent to *of him*. The construction, however, is not one that can be recommended.

Engaging in mining in Brazil, *his* great business ability had brought him wealth, and having paid all his obligations he will return to his country.—*Daily Express*, p. 1, Dec. 29, 1900.

In poetry a similar construction is sometimes met with :—

Thus repulsed, our final hope
Is flat despair.—*Paradise Lost*, ii.

15. Past Participle of Intransitive verbs.—There are very few Intransitive verbs in English, which form a Past participle, though all such verbs form a Perfect participle with "having." Thus we can say, "The messenger, *having come* from Thebes," etc. But we cannot say, "The messenger *come* from Thebes." The latter can only be expressed by saying, "The messenger, *who had come* or *who came* from Thebes." The following examples are exceptional :—

A *faded* rose. A *retired* tradesman. The *returned* soldier. The *fallen* city. The *risen* sun. A *withered* flower. A *departed* guest. *Past* history. In times *past*. A man *sprung* or *descended* from a noble ancestry.

But we cannot say :—

A *come* messenger. A *laughed* man. A *smiled* girl. A *remained* guest. A *knelt* suppliant. A *fled* fox. A *flown* bird.

Note.—A Past participle is sometimes used to express some permanent habit, state, or character.

A well-*read* man (one who has read well and read much). A *reserved* man (one who makes a habit of reserving or keeping back his opinions). A *mistaken* man (one who has formed erroneous notions). A well-*behaved* man. The *ravined* salt-sea shark.—SHAKES. (the shark whose character it is to ravin or be ravenous). A plain-*spoken* man (one who is in the habit of speaking plain). A *travelled* man (one who has been a great traveller).

Correct, improve, or justify the following sentences :—

1. In the event of it being found impossible to come to an agreement, the United States desires that the Russian and American commanders should arrange for a simultaneous withdrawal.—Quoted in *Daily Telegraph*, p. 7, Sept. 3, 1900.

2. After all, why should not the frequenters of the Free Library take out 70 per cent of fiction, if they want to ?—*Literature*, p. 492, June 30, 1900.

3. The sentiment of the French in favour of the South African republics is fed by the knowledge of a sprinkling of descendants from French Huguenots being contained in the Boer population.—*Fortnightly Review*, p. 33, July 1900.

4. "I don't object to you explaining," said Mr. Chamberlain, "but I cannot allow you to introduce a new argument."—*Yorkshire Post*, p. 4, July 26, 1900.

5. Herod would not have dared to have taken upon himself the odium and responsibility of such a sacrifice.—DOANE, *Bible Parallels in other Religions*, p. 174, ch. xviii.

6. People live longer now than they used to.—*Nineteenth Century*, p. 727, May 1900.

7. Mr. H. S., porter, was brought up for sentence, he having last sessions been found guilty of stealing a pair of earrings from a trunk.—*Middlesex County Times*, p. 5, Aug. 11, 1900.

8. It is unfortunate that this somewhat delicate situation should have arisen ; but, having developed, it is of the first importance that the main reasons should be understood by the public.—*Daily Telegraph*, p. 7, May 11, 1900.

9. The man Bean fired at Her Majesty,—that is, he attempted to ; but two brothers, named Dasset, fell upon the rascal at the right moment.—*Pearson's Weekly*, p. 704, April 28, 1900.

10. We were greeted in the dark by our Scotch friend, who put us up for the night, after enjoying a refreshing cup of tea, with kindly, hospitable care.—*Daily Telegraph*, p. 5, April 14, 1900.

11. Another death has occurred at Glasgow, accompanied by symptoms which pointed to it being due to plague.—*Ibid.* p. 6, Sept. 3, 1900.

12. Had he done so, he might have been able to have made peace

with the allies on advantageous terms.—*Review of Reviews*, p. 491, May 1900.

13. History is much easier to be taught than geography.—*Educational Review*, Madras, p. 64, Feb. 1900.

14. Chatham had done more than any other statesman to build up the empire in America, and was aghast at the idea of it being so soon ruined.—RANSOME, *Short History of England*, p. 362.

15. "I will insure five hundred pounds," said the unhappy man, grasping Wildfire's hand,—"five hundred pounds for to save my life."—SCOTT, *Heart of Midlothian*, ch. vi. para. 18.

16. The Castilian having made his addresses to her and married her, they lived together in perfect happiness for some time.—*Spectator*, No. 198, Oct. 17, 1711.

17. The English farmer is so crippled by the obstacles that prevent him rising in his business of agriculture, that his lack of intelligent enterprise is proverbial.—*Church Gazette*, p. 202, June 10, 1899.

18. Just as they used to of old, the water-hens steal up from the moat after dark and pilfer what food the peacocks and guinea fowls have left.—*Outlook*, p. 379, Oct. 21, 1899.

19. On 11th April 1743, Edward Thurlow, afterwards Lord High Chancellor of England, was entered at the schools, he being then eleven years of age.—*Nineteenth Century*, p. 777, May 1900.

20. The error which our reformers make, when there is some evil affecting the community, is to seek some one whom they shall hang : but the people who are to hang and all their friends make the utmost resistance to the process.—Speech quoted in *Daily Telegraph*, p. 10, May 30, 1900.

21. If Colonel Bertin did not say that, Dreyfus having been imposed upon the General Staff, he and his Christian colleagues would know how to get rid of him, he certainly might have said it with prophetic truth.—*Daily Telegraph*, p. 8, Aug. 23, 1900.

22. After a church surely the most disgraceful place to pick pockets is a cricket ground during the game.—*Ibid.* p. 9, July 5, 1899.

23. Rev. S. D. is a ritualist, and Mr. K. felt bound to protest against him being allowed to rise any higher in the priestly hierarchy. —*Ibid.* p. 10, March 12, 1900.

24. One account speaks of them having been found in force there by General H.—*Ibid.* p. 9, May 10, 1900.

25. These societies were too powerful to suppress or ignore, but if dealt with in the right way, were capable of rendering great assistance to the new rulers of the country.—*Ibid.* p. 7, Feb. 14, 1900.

26. You had children whenever you wanted to. You bought and paid for them, just as you might have obtained two puppies.—Quoted in *Daily Express*, p. 5, May 31, 1900.

27. Nationalist papers say that the resignation of General de G. is the direct result of M. Waldeck-Rousseau insulting the army.—*Ibid.* p. 1, May 31, 1900.

28. The real danger of it spreading lay in the fact that a country like China always had within it large numbers of inflammable people. —*Ibid.* p. 1, May 31, 1900.

29. What happened after Germinston, occupied, as we have said,

last Tuesday, is still by no means clear.—*Daily Telegraph*, p. 9, June 1, 1900.

30. On pretence that the waistcoat needed a button sewn on, it was handed to Bennett.—*Ibid.* p. 11, Feb. 8, 1900.

31. He turned towards the retainers knelt in the room.—Quoted in *Literature*, p. 190, March 3, 1900.

32. On the other hand it has emboldened some to proceed to further extravagances, they considering that, if not complained of, these will have obtained a sort of ecclesiastical sanction.—*Church Gazette*, p. 661, April 1, 1899.

33. The sincerity of the demand for intervention now, I trust, established, I suppose I ought next to recapitulate the wearisome story of our grievances.—*Fortnightly Review*, p. 1040, June 1899.

34. It would be a grave omission if the present session were to pass away without insisting on the institution of a committee of inquiry on this subject.—*Nineteenth Century*, p. 775, May 1900.

35. The erratic Charles XII. of Sweden was propitiated by assuring him that Marlborough would gladly serve in a campaign under so great a captain to perfect himself in the art of war.—GOLDWIN SMITH, *United Kingdom*, vol. ii. p. 132.

36. Hunger satisfied, I was able to rest for the night with all the comforts of a roof to one's head.—*Daily Telegraph*, p. 4, April 19, 1900.

37. The traditional friendship of the United States with Russia may lead to them mediating with success between Russia and Great Britain.—*Review of Reviews*, p. 539, June 1899.

38. Those born in the colony would all be on the side of the republic in the event of it refusing to observe its treaty obligations.—*Fortnightly Review*, p. 847, May 1900.

39. The whole prospect might be too much for a future possible successor of Napoleon risen in response to an overwhelming, if unreasoning, cry for action.—*Nineteenth Century*, p. 735, May 1900.

40. The position held by the Federals was carried without our forces suffering any great loss.—*Daily Telegraph*, p. 9, Sept. 11, 1900.

41. Accident having opened a new and most congenial career to him, and having become a great favourite and of much use to Mr. Nash, he ultimately accompanied his patron to London.—MATHEWS, *Autobiography*, vol. ii. p. 39 (H).

42. Vico observes that the wife bringing a dowry is evidence of her freedom.—BUCKLE, *Works*, vol. i. p. 369.

43. I should like to find in all the world a stick that would not be good enough to beat the Colonial Secretary.—Quoted in *Daily Telegraph*, p. 6, Sept. 24, 1900.

44. The future of Sikhism as an independent creed depends on its votaries rebelling against the authority of Hinduism.—*Pioneer Mail*, p. 22, May 13, 1900.

45. But we had six months to do it, and all the mercantile marine of the British empire to draw upon for transport.—*Review of Reviews*, p. 304, April 1900.

46. Sir Walter Forster, M.P., volunteered to form one of a small commission to go out in a sanitary capacity, his offer being declined.—*Fortnightly Review*, p. 494, Sept. 1900.

47. Two lives have been lost owing to a bog in North-West Clare, extending over a number of acres, sweeping with terrific force over some low-lying land, burying a house.—*Daily Telegraph*, p. 89, Oct. 11, 1900.

48. So much accomplished, it will be asked what are the legitimate consequences to which the nation may frame its expectations?—*Ibid.* p. 8, Oct. 15, 1900.

49. Nothing but compulsory military service will suffice to create an adequate working capital to carry on the business on the present lines. —*Review of Reviews*, p. 318, Oct. 1900.

50. They will point to two thousand years of suffering for their Mosaic faith and ask you with a look of scorn, if the ancestors of such a people could ever be apostles.—REBER, *Christ of Paul*, p. 362.

51. When the Cape was reoccupied in 1806, it having been restored to Holland in the peace of 1802, Sir Hume Topham was able to trust very largely to the colonists for the defence of the place.—*With the Flag to Pretoria*, ch. i. p. 7.

52. As the Mosaic law is no longer binding on the believer, he being dead to it with Christ, the partition wall which separated Jew and Gentile is broken down.—STRAUSS, *Life of Jesus*, vol. iii. p. 401.

53. The Church rejected the idea of a subordinate God become man in Jesus, because on this theory the image of the Godhead would not have been manifested in Christ.—*Ibid.* vol. iii. p. 404.

54. After this they arise possessed of the strength and agility of maniacs, and wield swords and spears in a way they are unable to at other times.—*Fortnightly Review*, p, 716, Nov. 1900.

55. Mr. H. A., in allusion to the Foreign Office code, parried a question as to the possibility of it being of use to a foreign government by saying that the accused believed it to possess that value.—*Daily Telegraph*, p. 8, Nov. 13, 1900.

56. There was no lack of visitors come to take a last long lingering look at the now defunct exhibition.—*Ibid.* p. 9, Nov. 13, 1900.

57. Letters passed between the husband and wife, she reproaching him for not returning to her, and alleging a change of his feelings towards her.—*Ibid.* p. 11, Nov. 20, 1900.

58. Under these circumstances Major B. could not conceive him making a false charge against an officer.—*Daily Express*, p. 5, Nov. 22, 1900.

59. Upon it being pointed out to him that willows need a marshy ground, while the spot in question was dry and sandy, he replied, etc.—*Ibid.* p. 4, Nov. 2, 1900.

60. He was convinced that, his cause being just, God would not abandon it, and that it would triumph.—*Daily Telegraph*, p. 9, Nov. 24, 1900.

61. In several bills power was asked for to construct and manage refreshment-rooms in parks.—Quoted in *Review of Reviews*, p. 466, Nov. 1900.

62. The Overseers of the Poor demand payment of the Poor Rate made the 5th day of November 1900.—*Demand Note : Brentford Union, Parish of Ealing.*

63. The morning of my capture,—which took place at 8.50 P.M. after defending the armoured train for an hour and a half,—was

raw and damp.—HALDANE, in *Blackwood's Magazine*, p. 156, August 1900.

64. What violence did the accused show to necessitate you using the truncheon ?—Quoted in *Daily Telegraph*, p. 5, Dec. 6, 1900.

65. Guerilla warfare obstructed our railway communication so frequently and so seriously that we had scarcely enough food to feed the troops.—*Ibid.* p. 9, Dec. 7, 1900.

66. England cannot bring her case before any just tribunal in the world without it being knocked to pieces.—*Ibid.* p. 9, Dec. 8, 1900.

67. W. H. W. pleaded guilty of bigamy, he having married Miss H. C. R., a hospital nurse, while his wife was alive.—*Ibid.* p. 4, Dec. 11, 1900.

68. Could not some arrangement be made for men being continuously employed ? In Ludgate Hill yesterday only two men were employed, although there were excavations from end to end.—*Ibid.* p. 7, Dec. 15, 1900.

69. It is said that the regular clergy, the bishops excepted, are by no means hostile to the Bill, they finding that the stream of benefactions is carried under the present system into channels over which they have no control.—*Spectator*, p. 918, Dec. 22, 1900.

70. His death was very tragic. On February 15, 1766, he being at the time eighty-eight years of age, he was severely burnt.—*Review of Reviews*, p. 581, Dec. 1900.

71. The Amir of Afghanistan has employed thousands of men for twelve years in fortifying the province of Bokh. Having thus fortified Bokh, Russia turned her attention towards Bavakshun, in answer to which challenge the Amir prepared himself to meet the Russians in that quarter also.—*Ibid.* p. 589, Dec. 1900.

72. He turned, the order for the murder given, into the arms of his unsuspecting queen, who had never loved him so much as she did at this moment.—*Fortnightly Review*, p. 181, Jan. 1901.

73. When the girl went in search of health for her brother, almost the first person she met was her father, long since turned over a new leaf, and for some weeks having been on the look-out for his two children.—*Our Boys and Girls*, p. 67.

74. The truth is that the out-of-the-way chances,—the risk of a man committing suicide, or of being hanged, or of suddenly going to Timbuctoo,—are so small that a good Insurance Company ignores them altogether.—*Review of Reviews*, p. 58, Jan. 1901.

75. He was an Irishman, a Gaelic speaker, and a Catholic, come of an old Irish family ; in a word as near the pure Irish Celtic type as any man could be.—*Spectator*, p. 114, Jan. 26, 1901.

76. Do not worry about me being miserable ; you do not know how sad it makes me feel to think that I add to your worry.—Quoted in *Daily Telegraph*, p. 4, Feb. 1, 1901.

77. Do you remember him asking you for your permission to tell the plaintiff ? Yes : I gave it him.—*Ibid.* p. 6, Feb. 9, 1901.

78. Mrs. Botha has left Pretoria on a visit to her husband, Commandant-General Louis Botha, she having been passed through the British lines.—*Daily Express*, p. 1, Feb. 18, 1901.

79. Without dwelling upon a most unlucky appointment, believed to be the result of a crooked intrigue for which he must be held in

part responsible, he has deeply offended thousands of the best men in Ireland.—*Fortnightly Review*, p. 266, Feb. 1901.

80. When he first came into our society, he was told that he must pay his court to the Comtesse de Bragade. He said that he did not want to : she frightened him.—*Ibid.* p. 379, Feb. 1901.

81. In cross-examination she said she did not at the time tell Mr. Woolley about the matter, because she did not like to.—*Daily Telegraph*, p. 4, Feb. 22, 1901.

82. Pupils are prepared for the University Local Examinations, if desired.—*School Prospectus.*

83. The second great weapon of attack just proven successful at Sandy Hook is a shell charged with maximite, the new explosive.—*Daily Express*, p. 1, March 20, 1901.

84. Mr. K.'s state of health for the time being would prevent him undertaking such a journey.—Quoted in *Daily Telegraph*, p. 9, March 11, 1901.

85. On Mr. Sauer reaching King William's Town, where Gordon was in residence, he at once asked him to accompany him to Basutoland.—*Life of Gordon*, p. 82.

86. Since elected by you three years ago it has been my endeavour to fulfil the pledges I then made to you, and I venture to hope I have done so with success.—*Extract from Electioneering Address.*

87. Next to the Marylebone tribunal, the Metropolitan County Courts are delightful places to spend a merry afternoon.—*Daily Telegraph*, p. 10, March 20, 1901.

88. Have you seen the correspondence that passed between Mr. J. and Mr. C. prior to you getting the order for the 600 tons? No.—Quoted in *Daily Telegraph*, p. 7, March 22, 1901.

89. He considered it his duty to repeat the Emperor's words. The Emperor, moreover, had bidden him and the Vice-President to repeat them.—*Ibid.* p. 10, March 25, 1901.

90. Let the Government do what they wanted to openly, and not make the Prime Minister a sort of a Pooh-Bah, etc.—*Ibid*, p. 6, March 27, 1901.

91. Consequent upon so many soldiers returned from South Africa being placed on furlough pending discharge, a difficulty has been experienced of men obtaining employment, resulting from having no document to testify to the characters they bore whilst serving.—*Ibid.* p. 7, April 4, 1901.

92. Then as to servant maids' chances of marriage. The English tradesman might look for a wife from among them, but even he quickly takes up with the traditions of the place ; and the Colonial tradesman, whose sisters have been brought up to despise service, is not likely to. —Quoted in *Spectator*, p. 457, March 30, 1901.

93. The Company being now, as I have said, under British financial control, it does not attach the same importance as the original founders of the line may be assumed to have done to the facts, etc.—*Empire Review*, p. 304, April 1901.

94. Having decided upon a spot which the deer seem to most frequent, it is usual to return to camp for the night, if not too far. —*Ibid.* p. 307, April 1901.

95. Persecuted, forcibly converted, and finally expelled, the tie

between French Protestants and French Catholics was never a strong one.—*Ibid.* p. 320, April 1901.

96. One of the objects in view, when founding the *Empire Review*, was to give accurate and practical information concerning various phases of colonial life.—*Ibid.* p. 323, April 1901.

97. When praising a thing, everything is either "nice" or "not nice," and an action or deed is simply "good" or "bad," with some people, whose store of adjectives is meagre.—WOOD's *Word-building*, etc., part vi. p. 52.

98. The work of the great mass of the candidates showed that in their preparation too much reliance had been placed on memory, and that insufficient attention had been given to exciting interest and bringing out intelligence.—*Annual Report of Syndicate, Cambridge Locals*, p. 24, 1901.

99. In talking over this matter in Paris last month with Dr. Leyds, he told me that it was quite preposterous to expect his countrymen to give in.—*Review of Reviews*, p. 322, April 1901.

100. Through the same excellent source I also heard that the family life of the late King (of Italy), far from going each their own way, has been a model of conjugal relations.—*Ibid.* p. 377, April 1901.

101. However strongly such a place may be fortified, the Chinese will be able to capture it if they wish to.—*Daily Express*, p. 4, May 24, 1901.

102. We wish to draw the attention of capitalists to the inexhaustible quantities of high-grade iron ore throughout the Mysore Province, and especially to our water power. Besides supplying the gold mines at Kolar with electric power, electrical furnaces could be set up at Ullagoor, nine miles from the head works of the Cauveri River scheme.—Quoted in *Pioneer Mail*, p. 19, May 10, 1901.

103. The coal-tax was sure to affect the miners' wages, and he objected to them being made to pay in this way a double tax.— Quoted in *Daily Telegraph*, p. 10, May 31, 1901.

104. Pekin herself has been plundered to the bare walls, the Forbidden City suffering especially at the hands of the Russians, who have sent home all the Empress-Regent's accumulated treasures.— *Spectator*, p. 754, May 25, 1901.

105. They had been disappointed also in the climate of Canada, finding it difficult to grow fruit, as they were accustomed to do in their former homes.—*Review of Reviews*, p. 437, May 1901.

106. Taking all circumstances into consideration, it is fairly evident that the Empress (of China) did not anticipate all that has happened. —*Daily Telegraph*, p. 7, July 11, 1900.

107. Still at least he appreciated the Sabbath for it having kept the schoolboys at home.—*Pioneer Mail*, p. 18, May 17, 1901.

108. J. M. S. was charged on a warrant at Southwark with travelling on the L.B. and S.C. Railway without having paid his proper fare, and with intent to avoid payment, he having been previously convicted of a like offence.—*Daily Telegraph*, p. 5, June 24, 1901.

109. When it became necessary to remove him, he being too like a mean kind of Eli, the Chamber discovered that, although removal

was not contemplated by the Constitution, that document gave them one irresistible weapon.—*Spectator*, p. 962, June 29, 1901.

110. Sir, Assuming the expediency (which may be questioned), as well as the justice (which I do not doubt), of correcting the over-representation of Ireland, it might be done without all the complication of a general Redistribution Bill.—*Ibid.* p. 972, June 29, 1901.

111. For those slaves whose qualifications do not warrant the dealer taking much trouble in their disposition, there is the market. —*Empire Review*, p. 652, July 1901.

112. But this scrupulous use of cover while shooting if pushed home leads to another modification or development of shooting.—*Spectator*, p. 114, July 27, 1901.

113. It is stated that his name (O'Malley) procured him the votes of the Irish Catholics of that State who knew nothing of him, they assuming that he was one of themselves.—*Standard*, p. 5, Aug. 30, 1901.

114. Formerly people generally wrote novels because they were impelled to by an inner prompting, by the desire to deliver their minds, by the fact that they had something to say.—*Spectator*, p. 278, Aug. 31, 1901.

115. Expressing himself strongly in favour of reciprocity, I ventured to point out that in the whole world there was only one country whose ports and markets were open to all products of the United States, and to suggest that reciprocity should begin there.—*Daily Telegraph*, p. 5, Sept. 16, 1901.

116. "I might be at this time," continued the gentleman, "about five or six years old ; and from that time till I was thirteen, I worked in the mine where we were yesterday."—MARION EDGEWORTH, *Lame Jervas*, p. 5.

117. The Commonwealth depends for general revenue upon its Customs duties, which will be ample even after paying to the separate States their stipulated shares.—*Spectator*, p. 503, Oct. 12, 1901.

118. We cannot produce the same thing that we see in others ; we have no need to ; but we can and must produce its equivalent.—*Ibid.* p. 509, Oct. 12, 1901.

119. The sides of high roads are the natural positions for a population to settle, and it is there, if anywhere, that the new building will take place.—*Ibid.* p. 552, Oct. 19, 1901.

120. *Mr. Rawlinson:* Is there a hill where the bicycle was?— Yes ; and I was surprised at him trying to ride there a second time. —Report of trial in *Daily Telegraph*, p. 6, Oct. 22, 1901.

121. In the recent naval manœuvres, for example, any ship that had a mind to seems to have intercepted the messages of any other ship ; and it is said that in one case one of our cruisers read all the orders from a French man-of-war within whose "sphere of influence" she had come by accident in a fog.—Quoted in *Spectator*, p. 600, Oct. 26, 1901.

122. The scheme was put into practice, with the result that the enemy were severely cut up, and those that were able to, quickly retreated.—*Middlesex County Times*, p. 2, Nov. 9, 1901.

123. I pointed out to him that the Turkish empire, which by its geographical position was so closely bound to the interests of civilisation and humanity, could continue to exist under the sceptre of the

Ottoman Sultans on the sole condition of introducing reforms.—
Fortnightly Review, p. 148, Jan. 1901.

124. The story about Rawlinson having thus introduced the kilt
is certainly open to suspicion ; but, on the other hand, and while
admitting that Lord Archibald has made the most of his case, it can
scarcely be said that the arguments for the high antiquity of the kilt
in the Highlands are altogether convincing.—*Literature*, p. 127, Aug.
5, 1899.

125. The matter being thus reduced within clearly defined limits
and prepared for business-like discussion, it was submitted to the
deliberations of a committee of Imperial and Colonial delegates.—
Times Weekly, p. 34, Jan. 21, 1898.

126. Oct. 7, 1819. Heard a cock pheasant, which nowadays is like
a wild beast on my property, and in half an hour came home with
two fine old cock pheasants, I having found another with the one
reported, and bagged them both.—*Hawker's Diary*, quoted in *Fortnightly Review*, p. 833, Nov. 1901.

127. On inquiry at the offices of the London County Council it was
pointed out that, so far from having approved, or even encouraged,
this scheme, it has as yet had no official recognition.—*Daily Telegraph*,
p. 10, Nov. 21, 1901.

128. A conspiracy against her having been discovered, and she,
suspecting that Frederick the Great of Prussia was at the bottom of
it, embraced the alliance of Austria, which was at war with him.—
Blackwood's Magazine, p. 191, Aug. 1855.

129. Overlooking "Theodric" and "The Pilgrim of Glencoe,"
which are considered as failures, his lyrical pieces may be described
as perhaps the most successful efforts of the genius of Campbell.—
CHAMBERS, *History of English Literature*, Seventh Period, p. 203.

130. The originators of the theory claimed to discover in the Earl
of Pembroke the only young man of rank and wealth to whom the
initials "W. H." applied at the needful dates.—SIDNEY LEE, *Life
of Shakespeare*, p. 407.

131. His (Darius's) Scythian Expedition, instead of a meaningless
raid, appears to be aimed at substituting an "ethnic frontier" for an
artificial one, and thus anticipates the most modern lessons of political
science.—*School World*, pp. 56, 57, Feb. 1902.

132. Speaking as one who has closely studied the question, there
is an extraordinary concurrence of naval opinion in favour of the course
which His Majesty's Government have adopted.—*House of Commons*,
p. 6, Feb. 11, 1902.

133. This declaration on their part is one which certainly cannot
cause any surprise, having regard to all past and present circumstances.—*Spectator*, p. 204, Feb. 8, 1902.

134. The Company replaced the men, but the strike will cause
Lord Kitchener to be delayed, as he was to embark on board the
Cleopatra at Brindisi.—*Daily Telegraph*, p. 7, Oct. 27, 1902.

135. Owing to the rain, falling heavily for five days without a
break, inundating the fields the hay crop was ruined.—*Daily Express*,
Sept. 1900.

136. They are, be it noted, friendly critics from among his own
household, whose interests are identical with his, whose object is the

same,—that of improving the dividends earned by the company.—
Ibid. p. 8, Dec. 13, 1902.

137. Had this been a conclave and Lothair the future Pope, it would
have been impossible to have treated him with more consideration
than he experienced.—Lord BEACONSFIELD, *Lothair*, iii. 61.

138. I think it may assist the reader by placing these before him
in their chronological order.—AYTOUN, *Bothwell*, note 1, p. 223 (H).

139. The battle of Eylau should have been the signal for the
contracting the closest alliance with the Russian Government.—
ALISON, *History of Europe*.

140. In reading of poetry above all, what forces through this
ignorance are lost!—TRENCH, *English Past and Present*.

141. That he was willing to have made his peace with Walpole
is admitted by Mr. Scott.—JEFFREY, *Essays*.

142. It was universally expected that his first act upon being
elevated to the office of Prince Regent would have been to have sent
for Lords Grey and Grenville.—ALISON, *History of Europe*.

143. They would gladly have seen the Anglo-Saxon to have
predominated over the Latin element of our language.—TRENCH,
English Past and Present.

144. It were indeed worth while inquiring how much of this
coolness resulted from Crabbe's early practice as a surgeon.—
GILFILLAN, *Literary Portraits*.

145. How fine sometimes it is accompanying the prattle of a
beautiful child!—*Ibid.*

146. He was like the adventurous climber of the Alps, to whom
the surmounting the most tremendous precipices and ascending to
the most towering peaks only shows yet dizzier heights and higher
points of elevation.—SCOTT, *Life of Napoleon*.

(i) *Miscellaneous Examples.*

Correct, improve, or justify the following sentences :—

1. The Canadians and Queenslanders, who are dismounted, stood
the test of marching long distances through heavy sand with very
little rest.—*Daily Telegraph*, p. 9, May 22, 1900.

2. You shall find piles of corn at one port, and a starving crowd at
another. But the Sultan will not allow the corn to be taken to the
famine-stricken, because when they get food, they are apt to rebel
with success.—*Fortnightly Review*, p. 273, Aug. 1899.

3. He is reported to have told the burghers that the deputation
which went to Europe were sure to be welcomed.—*Daily Telegraph*,
p. 9, May 10, 1900.

4. The movable platform, imitated from the Chicago model, and
which is one of the features of the exhibition, does not please everybody.—*Ibid.* p. 9, April 19, 1900.

5. Most great London drapers lose some thousands of pounds every
year through thefts of people, that from dress and bearing are almost
impossible to detect.—*Daily Express*, p. 3, May 16, 1900.

6. In furnishing the new hotel comfort has not been sacrificed to
splendour.—*Daily Telegraph*, p. 7, June 7, 1890.

7. The Government have reserved their action, until the whole people of Australia has committed themselves to the provisions of this bill.—Quoted in *Daily Telegraph*, p. 7, May 15, 1900.

8. We have no right to consult any other circumstance but that we consider to be right for the public service.—*Ibid.* p. 6, May 5, 1900.

9. At last he (Becket) left the hall amidst a volley of insults, which, the soldier rising within him, he returned in kind.—GOLDWIN SMITH, *United Kingdom*, vol. i. p. 93.

10. I feel very deeply the kind words which have been uttered by the mover and the seconder of this resolution, and who have expressed their sense and your sense of the loss which my wife has lately sustained.—Report of Speech in *Daily Telegraph*, p. 7, May 12, 1900.

11. Various politicians maintained that, although there was a great gulf between France and Germany in Europe, they being separated by Alsace-Lorraine, they could at least bury the hatchet in other quarters of the globe.—*Daily Telegraph*, p. 8, Dec. 12, 1898.

12. Of a sickly constitution when a child, Louis XV., a king at five years old, was suffered unchecked to develop the inherited hard-heartedness of the Bourbons. He would sit at the council-board without uttering a word, playing now and then with a kitten.—*Literature*, p. 209, March 10, 1900.

13. The strange feature of the affair is that the thief, named Meonitz, being unknown to the tailor, and the tailor to him, he must have derived his information as to the tailor's property at second hand.—*Daily Telegraph*, p. 8, Aug. 25, 1900.

14. Artillery, both siege and field, was weak, till it was improved by Cromwell.—GOLDWIN SMITH, *United Kingdom*, vol. i. p. 538.

15. Some alarmist news about the alleged way the lads of the Public Schools battalions suffered from fatigue and sunstroke caused a flutter in many fond maternal breasts.—*Daily Telegraph*, p. 7, Aug. 8, 1899.

16. The troops which have borne the strain of a long imprisonment, and which General Buller tells us need a little nursing, are sure to be withdrawn.—*Ibid.* p. 9, March 2, 1900.

17. Myself and a few comrades were within an ace of twisting the brave General's sword into a sceptre.—*Ibid.* p. 7, July 11, 1899.

18. There are men who are impossible to work with with any degree of satisfaction.—*Church Gazette*, p. 690, April 8, 1899.

19. To-day we bask in almost tropical weather, behind the very ground so many lives were lost to gain.—*Daily Telegraph*, p. 11, May 2, 1900.

20. A bill for the acquisition of property for building a new land-registry and other public offices in London was read for a first time.—*Ibid.* p. 6, March 28, 1900.

21. Of sign that he realises the responsibilities of the position, from which he can no more extricate himself than he can get out of his skin, there is as yet none.—*Review of Reviews*, p. 416, May 1899.

22. We have had no occasion for them sort of books for many a long year.—Quoted in *Review of Reviews*, p. 391, April 1900.

23. The tsetse fly prevails along the first two to three hundred miles, rendering animal transport almost impossible with the exception of a few places.—*Daily Telegraph*, p. 8, Aug. 3, 1899.

24. There is, however, a section of the party which is indifferent

to all the considerations that actuate average intelligent Englishmen.
—*Ibid.* p. 8, Oct. 17, 1898.

25. It was all wrong, though absolutely in accordance with human nature, and especially of Conservative parties and oligarchies all the world over.—*Review of Reviews*, p. 370, Oct. 1899.

26. That curious league of so-called Dutch nationality, and which was always inconsistent with the supremacy of the British crown.—*Fortnightly Review*, p. 179, Feb. 1900.

27. It is just as well that Borrow's unfair attack on Scott has never got to be really familiar with the reading public.—*Literature*, p. 401, Oct. 21, 1899.

28. Relative pronouns are those which, in addition to being substitutes for the names of persons or things, also join by showing the relation between one sentence and another.—*New Morell Gram.* p. 21.

29. Mr. Churchill is not only the son of his great father, but a man come back with all the glamour of the war and its perils attaching to him.—*Daily Express*, p. 4, Oct. 2, 1900.

30. With these reports he seeks to make the flesh of the foreign investor to creep.—*Daily Telegraph*, p. 9, March 16, 1900.

31. Whether we like it or not, we have got to retain the direction of the war in the hands of the Ministry who still enjoy the confidence of Parliament.—*Ibid.* p. 10, Feb. 8, 1900.

32. The true interpreter of the past will not claim all for statistical history. But I think we will turn more and more to that which reveals the individual character than to that which narrates general events.—*Fortnightly Review*, p. 508, March 1900.

33. He wrote poetry of considerable merit at ten years old, and had greatly improved in the art at twelve.—CHAMBERS, *History of English Language and Literature*, p. 73.

34. Once more one of English blood sat on the royal throne, and kings of English extraction should hereafter rule in England.—*Short History of England*, p. 63.

35. Whenever I hear people saying, "Something has got to be done," I know beforehand that what they want to do is something foolish.—*Daily Telegraph*, p. 10, Feb. 8, 1900.

36. I should not be surprised to find this prove a third unsuccessful attempt.—*Middlesex County Times*, p. 3, Feb. 17, 1900.

37. China in its present stage is intensely interesting, full of "questions," but not enjoyable in enjoyment's literal sense.—*China, the Long-lived Empire*, quoted in *Daily Telegraph*, p. 9, Aug. 1, 1900.

38. The gentleman-usher shall linger with pride on the household he once marshalled ; the fallen statesman shall tell us of the rapid journey and skilful boldness which brought him fame and wealth at a bound in his youth ; and we read with respectful interest. The Lady of Crèqui shall greet her English guest with an English embrace, and a whole letter of Erasmus rushes to our memory. We shall ride beside the author to a boar-hunt more exciting than that Dumas has painted for us.—*Literature*, p. 569, Dec. 9, 1899.

39. There has been another mutiny in Uganda, which was promptly quelled and the ringleaders punished.—*Daily Telegraph*, Jan. 13, 1899.

40. The speech was after all only the culmination of a series of attacks not consistent with each other,—not based on knowledge, but

showing most extraordinary ingenuity in discovering the basest, the meanest, and (I will add) most far - fetched motives.—*Ibid.* p. 7, May 5, 1900.

41. English and Dutch have got to live together at the Cape.—*Ibid.* p. 7, Feb. 7, 1900.

42. Besides this I believe good fiction one of the most beneficial reliefs to the monotonous lives of the poor.—*Daily Express.* p. 3, May 3, 1900.

43. Remembering that we have absolutely nothing to catch these ships, remembering their immense radius of action,—is this safe ?—*Review of Reviews,* p. 361, April 1900.

44. I enclose Mr. M.'s account, and am sorry for his unbusiness-like delay, and which has been the cause of all this trouble and bother.—*Letter from a House Agent,* Jan. 10, 1900.

45. He lorded it over his debtors, built him a stately dwelling, and loved to display his wealth.—GOLDWIN SMITH, *United Kingdom,* vol. i. p. 109.

46. That issue had got to be tried ; that battle had got to be fought ; one or other party had to give way, if peace was to be preserved.—Report of Speech in *Daily Telegraph,* p. 7, Feb. 6, 1900.

47. When the actors were in possession of that forwarder space to act upon, the voice was then more in the centre of the house.—*Literature,* p. 329, April 28, 1900.

48. It had had the effect of bringing together our Colonies in a way they never could have been brought together.—Report of Speech in *Daily Telegraph,* p. 6, April 30, 1900.

49. It is plain now that we have to fight an enemy who has apparently still an abundant supply of all the munitions of war, and which, so long as it can choose its own ground, is as nearly invincible as any army we know of in history.—*Ibid.* p. 5, Dec. 18, 1899.

50. Why should the English alone have an accent or stress (on syllables) unknown to any other Teutonic or Latin people ?—*Literature,* p. 566, Dec. 9, 1899.

51. Sometimes I dream of the old prophecy that Christ shall come again upon Iona.—*Fortnightly Review,* p. 508, March 1900.

52. Ealing's celebration of the Queen's eighty-first birthday was marked by the enthusiasm which attended the news of the relief of Mafeking.—*Ealing Gazette,* p. 5, May 26, 1900.

53. Possibly part of the charm lies not only in the beautiful and delicate touch of the painter, but in the antique and long-ago feeling which pervades it.—*Fortnightly Review,* p. 1, 1027, June 1900.

54. The Chinese Government cannot even keep order at home, let alone protect itself from foreign aggression.—*Daily Express,* p. 1, June 12, 1900.

55. Their interpretation of the meaning of loyalty to the Crown could only be explained, much less justified, by the most practical casuist.—*Daily Telegraph,* p. 9, June 13, 1900.

56. Mr. S. urged a scheme recommended by Her Majesty's Government, and in which a special tribunal should be instituted to try rebels.—*Ibid.*

57. This is a check which not merely deprives the foreign residents in Pekin of the succour they had hoped to receive, but which is calcu-

lated to encourage the most dangerous instincts of the Chinese.—*Ibid.* p. 8, June 19, 1900.

58. He felt ashamed, when called upon to strike off the rolls a solicitor who had stolen less than a sovereign, while every one knew that there were leading solicitors who had stolen half a million sterling, who were not proceeded against.—*Ibid.* p. 9, June 22, 1900.

59. The hostility created by the Administration's friendly attitude towards England.—Quoted in *Review of Reviews*, p. 558, June 1900.

60. Where will the Netherlands Railway Company be anon, and its disseminators of hatred, jealousy, and racial follies? Shall they gnaw a file?—*Daily Telegraph*, p. 7, July 7, 1900.

61. There has been some malicious kind of method in the way the nations of Europe have been gradually enlightened about the fate of their fellow-countrymen in Pekin.—*Ibid.* p. 10, July 7, 1900.

62. Paul was instructing his countrymen in the mysteries of the new covenant, and was pointing out to them the relation which Christ bore to the same, as compared with Moses under the old.—REBER, *Christ of Paul*, p. 334.

63. The council do approve of action being taken for purchasing or leasing suitable houses already or hereafter to be built or provided for the purpose of supplying house accommodation.—Quoted in *Fortnightly Review*, p. 979, Dec. 1900.

64. People are saying that what is wanted is improvement in the regimental officers. If necessary, improve them by all means, though that does not touch the real point.—*Spectator*, p. 929, Dec. 22, 1900.

65. The most obvious gain from the Passion Play is that it strips the legendary Christ of a divinity whose ascription to His person has served no other purpose than to obscure the completeness of His humanity.—Quoted in *Review of Reviews*, p. 567, Dec. 1900.

66. Bombala, which is a seaport of its own, a twofold bay, is at present first favourite.—*Review of Reviews*, p. 569, Dec. 1900.

67. The so-called life-sketch of the Field-Marshal is little else save a rather long drawn out survey of the chief events of his life.—*Ibid.* p. 583, Dec. 1900.

68. So long as the Afghans can fight for themselves, they ought not, they would not, let one soldier of Russia or England put his foot in their country to expel the enemy, as it would be impossible to get rid of the army which they themselves had invited to help them, who would always have the excuse of remaining by saying that they were keeping the country peaceful.—*Life of Abdur Rahman*, quoted in *Review of Reviews*, p. 589, Dec. 1900.

69. It is computed that on Saturday the route will be lined by 23,000 troops, who will include Colonials, Volunteers, and Militia.— *Daily Express*, p. 1. Jan. 30, 1901.

70. How long did Satan consume in rising through Chaos and finding his way to the Sun and thence to Mount Niphates?—*School World*, p. 51, Feb. 1901.

71. It may be said of Mr. M. as Mommsen said of France, that she had shaken many empires and founded none ; Mr. M. has broken up ministries, but has never established one.—*Fort. Rev.* p. 234, Feb. 1901.

72. He found his chief enjoyment in the retired circle of select friends, in whose literary leisure, and in the amenities of female con-

verse, which for him had the highest charm, he sought the purest and most refined recreation.—*Ibid.* p. 365, Feb. 1901.

73. It is the allies who are spending between them something like a million a week on their armies and fleets, and whose forces are in constant need of replenishment, who are in a hurry (to see Pekin evacuated).—*Spectator*, p. 266, Feb. 23, 1901.

74. If there be opposition, and that persevered in, the question has to come before a House of Commons committee.—*Middlesex County Times*, p. 5, March 2, 1901.

75. To anybody else but Mr. H. the word implies that the statement was made not only without justification but without excuse.—Quoted in *Daily Telegraph*, p. 11, March 12, 1901.

76. Lord S. referred to the cry for the recall of Sir A. M., and said he did not know whether such a step would be the more unwise or dishonourable.—*Ibid.* p. 8, March 28, 1901.

77. The Dutch are as stubborn as Mr. R. is vindictive, and between the two they have brought South Africa very nearly to ruin.—*Review of Reviews*, p. 301, March 1901.

78. The kind of employés wanted for the Cape Colony and the new territories will of course be very different.—Quoted in *Spectator*, p. 495, April 12, 1901.

79. One of my friends informed me to-night that before leaving Kumási it was resolved that such a dinner as this should be held.—Quoted in *Daily Telegraph*, p. 10, April 18, 1901.

80. Shan-hai-kwan is to be garrisoned by contingents of 500 men, each furnished by France, Russia, Great Britain, and Germany, Italy supplying one company.—*Ibid.* p. 9, May 2, 1901.

81. These are matters which are not to be disposed of in a night, and the House of Commons will ill perform its functions if they endeavour for personal convenience to stifle this debate.—Sir W. HARCOURT, quoted from *Daily Telegraph*, p. 6, May 3, 1901.

82. Him he admires sincerely. "I do not think they will ever catch me," he said three months ago, "but if any one does, I hope the man is French."—*World's Work*, April 1901.

83. You cannot have a great public object-lesson like this without profoundly affecting men's thoughts about capital and capitalists, and such object-lessons are multiplying every day.—*Fortnightly Review*, p. 639, April 1901.

84. Well, every animal, from man downwards, uses those gifts and those weapons which Providence has put at their disposal.—Quoted in *Daily Telegraph*, p. 7, May 9, 1901.

85. In comparing British and American blast-furnace practice, ten years ago is ancient history.—*Engineering*, p. 641, May 17, 1901.

86. The Chinese are second to none in their respect for education, but they have their own views on the subject, together with their own books, their own schools, their own systems, and all these respond to demands that exist and supply wants the people are acquainted with and national life has developed.—Sir ROBERT HART, *Fortnightly Review*, p. 768, May 1901.

87. The Canadians will have some difficulty in demonstrating their claim owing to the fact that in 1878 the Government of the Dominion exhibited at the Exhibition in Paris a very elaborately drawn official

map, which for some time hung in the corridor of the Dominion Parliament at Ottawa, which defined the coast-line of Alaska exactly in accordance with the present American contention. — *Review of Reviews*, p. 421, May 1901.

88. At twelve years old his mother wisely thought that it was best for him to be with other boys and under the supervision of a man.— *Spectator*, p. 17, July 6, 1901.

89. The general official and unofficial feeling is in favour of the reform Lord Curzon has accomplished and previous viceroys contemplated.—*Empire Review*, p. 686, July 1901.

90. I believe that of late there have been very few cases in which even a skirmish has taken place in which the number of British soldiers engaged has been largely in excess, and in many cases less than the Boers.—Quoted in *Daily Telegraph*, p. 11, Aug. 3, 1901.

91. Sir H. C.-B.'s friends have given up the impossible task of trying to understand his distinction between the responsibility resting upon the Government and Field-Marshal respectively for the barbarous methods by which he alleges the war has been carried on.—*Daily Telegraph*, p. 8, Nov. 30, 1901.

92. It requireth few talents to which most men are not born or at least may not acquire.—SWIFT, on *Conversation*.

93. The Court of Chancery frequently mitigates and breaks the teeth of common law.—*Spectator*, No. 564.

94. The exercise of reason appears as little in them, as in the beasts they sometimes hunt and by whom they are sometimes hunted.— BOLINGBROKE, *Phil. Essays*, ii. sect. 2.

95. A professor of history, such as we understand Mr. M. is or has been, had better try to write a history of anything else in the world except the literature of England.—*School World*, p. 312, Aug. 1901.

96. Among the warders who took charge of Dreyfus immediately after his arrival here was one who has been transferred to another post some time ago.—*Daily Telegraph*, p. 11, May 29, 1899.

97. It seems to me that this year English cycle-makers are adopting all the bad American methods, while American makers are adopting all the good British ones. But what does it matter? Nobody hardly tours.—*Fortnightly Review*, p. 116, Jan. 1899.

98. Already, during my previous journey through the country, I visited Matabeleland.—*Daily Telegraph*, p. 8, Dec. 26, 1899.

99. The Imperial Embassy to France had never, neither directly nor indirectly, had any relation whatsoever with Captain Dreyfus.— *Ibid.* p. 9, Sept. 9, 1900.

100. It is hardly possible that a few Federals may manage to slip through our lines under cover of the night, but that is the most that the enemy can hope for.—*Ibid.* p. 9, Feb. 27, 1900.

101. This Government is disposed to hold the punishment of the responsible authors (of the outrage) essentially a condition to be embraced in the negotiations for a final settlement.—*Ibid.* p. 7, Sept. 25, 1900.

102. The problem is one which no research has hitherto solved, and probably never will.—HOLLAND, *Recollections of Past Life*, ch. xiii. p. 345.

103. Paris is trying its nerves preparatory to partaking of the

grand sensation which the visit of the ex-President promises. —*Daily Express*, p. 1, Nov. 22, 1900.

104. Musical composition, like everything else, is the outcome of hard work, and there is really nothing speculative nor spasmodic about it.—Sir A. SULLIVAN, *Autobiography*.

105. This principle once asserted in the statute-book, all that followed became not alone possible, but certain.—*Fortnightly Review*, p. 2, Jan. 1901.

106. "Nay then," said the grasshopper, "I was not idle neither; for I sang out the whole season." The situation is old as Æsop.—*Ibid.* p. 25, Jan. 1901.

107. As Mr. Balfour pointed out, it is very difficult to draw a line between personal interests as affected by private and public measures. —*Daily Telegraph*, p. 9, May 1, 1901.

108. Quite the sensation in political circles yesterday was the publication of a statement purporting to contain the truth about the Hawksley dossier.—*Ibid.* p. 9, Feb. 22, 1900.

109. Just such a roving life, sparkling with dangerous incident, would have suited our troops A1, and the end of the war would have been attained cheaper and more quickly.—*Spect.* p. 657, Nov. 2, 1901.

110. We sometimes wonder why there should be so much indignation now and so little before.—*Ibid.* p. 706, Nov. 8, 1902.

111. Meanwhile it is the cause of introducing ideas we shall have trouble in getting rid of when we realise that we have a past worth living up to.—*Fortnightly Review*, p. 672, Nov. 1902.

112. We are no longer storm-tossed : arrived at this stage we know pretty well what we are going to do,—those of us who thought they were going to do anything.—*Review of Reviews*, p. 264, March 1900.

113. The Laird would have done better to have transferred his glances to an object possessed of charms far superior to Jeanie's.— SCOTT, *Heart of Midlothian*, ch. ix. para. 2.

114. Such was Admiral Eden's version to me of an incident, which at ninety years old or thereabouts seemed to him as fresh as if it had happened only the day before.—*Spectator*, p. 138, Jan. 26, 1901.

115. General Stewart with difficulty made good his retreat, fighting all the way to Alexandria, where he arrived with a thousand fewer men than he had set out.—ALISON, *History of Europe*.

116. They are the wretched attempts towards an art of this kind, which have so often disgraced oratory.—BLAIR, *Lectures on Rhetoric*.

117. No people ever was more rudely assailed by the sword of conquest than those of this country ; none had its chains, to appearance, more firmly riveted round their necks.—ALISON, *History of Europe*.

118. He found himself at a loss to display his powers of criticism, only by lavishing his praise.—D'ISRAELI, *Curiosities of Literature*.

119. It were not difficult retorting upon many passages of his own writing.—GILFILLAN, *Literary Portraits*.

120. It is indeed ludicrous looking back through the vista of forty years.—*Ibid.*

121. If we would see what the aborigines of this country (England) were, what but for foreign intermixture they would still have been, we have only to look to the inhabitants of the south and west of Ireland, or of the highlands and islands of Scotland.—ALISON, *Hist. of Europe*.

K

CHAPTER III.—ERRORS OF ORDER.

IF words, phrases, and clauses are not put in their right places, the sense of a sentence is either rendered doubtful or is destroyed altogether. Observe how the sense of the following sentences is marred by the faultiness of the order :—

> *Paradise Lost* is the name of Milton's great epic poem on the loss of Paradise divided into twelve separate parts.
> You have already been informed of the sale of Ford's theatre where Mr. Lincoln was assassinated for religious purposes.
> Few people learn anything that is worth learning easily.
> He was shot by a secretary under notice to quit with whom he was finding fault very fortunately without effect.
> He repeated these lines after he had read them only once with perfect accuracy.
> Our correspondent saw several soldiers dead or wounded riding over the battlefield.

The cardinal rule is that *things which are to be thought of together must be mentioned as closely as possible together.* In no language is this more important than in modern English, which has lost almost all the inflections, which in Old English and in most other languages serve as a guide to the grammatical relations of words. In every one of the above examples this rule has been violated. By attending to this rule, we can correct these sentences as follows :—

> *Paradise Lost,* divided into twelve separate parts, is the name of Milton's great epic poem, etc.
> You have already been informed of the sale, for religious purposes, of Ford's theatre, where, etc.
> Few people learn easily anything that is worth learning.
> He was shot, fortunately without effect, by a secretary under notice to quit, with whom, etc.
> After he had read these lines only once, he repeated them with perfect accuracy.
> Our correspondent, riding over the battlefield, saw several soldiers dead or wounded.

Sometimes it is necessary to recast a sentence, a mere change of order being insufficient.

> Very tenderly does Arethusa appeal to her son not to deprive her of his protection, companionship, and help, who had devoted her life to him, by retiring into a monastery.—*Academy*, p. 196, May 15, 1872 (H).

The sentence can be recast as follows :—

> Very tenderly does Arethusa appeal to her son not to retire into a monastery, and thus deprive her, who had devoted her life to him, of his protection, companionship, and help.

(a) Subject, Object, Apposition.

1. Verb and Subject.—The Subject usually precedes its verb. The chief exceptions are—

(*a*) When the verb is used for asking a question :—

> Could *you* have made this, if you had tried ?

(*b*) When the verb is used for giving an order or entreaty (Here, however, the Subject is usually omitted) :—

Go *ye* into all the world, and preach the gospel to every creature.—*New Test.*

(*c*) When the verb is used for expressing a wish or prayer :—

> Long live *the king.* So be *it.*

(*d*) When the verb is used for expressing a condition, without the help of a conditional conjunction :—

> Should *he* meet me, he would know me.
> Were *I* in your place, I should start at once.

(*e*) When the verb is used to report a speech in the Direct Narration :—

> "Agreed," said *the prince,* "we will start to-night."

(*f*) When the verb is introduced by an adverb :—

The method is excellent, and excellently has *Mr. Tovey* carried it out.—*Spectator*, p. 173, Feb. 2, 1901.

Note.—The commonest form of this idiom is seen in the use of the introductory adverb *there:* "There comes a time when," etc. Here *there* is merely an introductory particle, and has no sense of "in that place."

(*g*) When the verb is introduced by *neither* or *nor,* signifying "and not" :—

> He did not say so ; neither did *I.*
> He promised to come, nor did *he* fail to do so.

(*h*) When the verb is introduced by a correlative conjunction :—

> As men sow, so will *they* also reap.
> No sooner did *he* begin to speak, than every one was silent.
> Scarcely had *we* reached home, when it began raining.

(*i*) When the complement is placed before the verb for the sake of emphasis :—

> Blessed are *the merciful.—New Test.*
> Great is *Diana* of the Ephesians. —*New Test.*

(*j*) When a dependent clause precedes a principal clause. This, however, is occasional only :—

> Not as the world gives, give *I* unto you.—*New Test.*

2. Subject after Intransitive verb.—When the Subject is accompanied by a good deal of description or comment, while the verb itself (Intransitive) is not so accompanied and is not emphatic, it is more convenient to place the Subject after its verb instead of before it. Observe, however, that when the verb is thus made to precede its Subject, it should not be the first word in the sentence, but should be introduced by some adverb such as *there* or by some adverbial or other qualifying phrase.

> Thus arises the *paradox*, that while we believe in the actuality of Miss Austen's pictures, we cannot realise them so vividly as we can the conventional figures of the historical romances.— *Literature*, p. 254, March 31, 1900.
> No sooner had *he* reached Thionville, than there commenced that incessant and apparently needless movement of troops, with which readers of this book have already been made familiar. —*Fortnightly Review*, p. 482, Sept. 1900.
>> There are *more things* in heaven and earth, Horatio,
>> Than are dreamt of in your philosophy.—*Hamlet*, i. 5.

(Here *there* is merely an introductory adverb ; it does not signify "in that place" ; in fact it has no meaning at all.)

> At the root of that life lay *an abiding sense* of God and duty,—of God as the sovereign not of nations only, but also of individual men and women,—of a duty and responsibility, all pervading, and descending from the greatest to the most trivial acts of a human life.—GRAHAM, *Victorian Literature*, p. 188.
> Permeating the report runs the *idea* that the successful development of the medical service in the future must be founded on professional, not on military lines.—*Empire Review*, p. 431, May 1901.

3. Verb and Object.—The main rule is that the Object, except where it is a Relative or Interrogative pronoun or where it is made the first word for the sake of emphasis, should be placed after its verb, and not before it.

> *Which* of these books do you prefer ?
> This is the book *that* you chose.

The *cost* of railway construction, which is so high in England, the writer attributes to the rapacity of landlords.—*Spectator*, p. 21, Jan. 3, 1903. (Here *cost* is placed at the beginning of the sentence for the sake of emphasising it.)

Another rule is that the Object should be placed immediately after its verb, so that nothing may be allowed to come between them. Sometimes, however, it is convenient to separate them by an adverb or even by a long adverbial phrase, when the said adverb or phrase is used to qualify the verb :—

Many officers who are deeply interested in this question intend to bring *before the British public* proposals somewhat in the nature of those I have mentioned.—*Daily Telegraph*, p. 7, April 19, 1900. (Observe, that if the italicised words had been placed after "mentioned," the sense would have been entirely different.)

Shall not the street preacher, if so minded, take *for the text of his sermon* the stones in the gutter ?—THACKERAY. (Correct.)

Jack meantime, who had just come below from his watch on deck, was attacking, *with a ferocity which made it appear as if he was contending with some bitter enemy instead of a plentiful dinner*, the boiled beef and biscuit that the boy had lately placed on the table.—KINGSTON, *Three Midshipmen*, ch. ii. (Correct. The italicised words could not stand at the end.)

4. Indirect Object.—If the preposition *to* is not used, the Indirect object should be placed between the verb and the Direct object, as—

> He gave *me* a book.

But if the preposition *to* is used, the Indirect object must be placed either after the Direct object, or (if it is emphatic) before the verb :—

> He gave a book *to me*.
> *To me* he gave a book.

5. Apposition.—When a noun or a noun-clause is in apposition with a noun, they should not be separated by any intervening word or words :—

For Herodias' sake, his brother Philip's wife.—*New Test.* (Say, "For the sake of Herodias, his brother Philip's wife.")

The Appositive noun or phrase more commonly stands after the Principal noun ; but it sometimes anticipates the Principal, and this adds to its impressiveness.

The realm would not, in the phrase of Comines, *the most judicious observer of that time,* suffice for them all.—MACAULAY, *History of England,* ch. i.

He had now, however, to experience *the most painful of all circumstances attending popular outcry,* the desertion or coldness of friends.—J. H. MONK, *Life of Bentley.*

6. Order of words in Parallel Constructions. — In parallel sentences or clauses, words or ideas of the same or kindred meaning should follow the same order.

> Be thou a spirit of health or goblin damn'd,
> Bring with thee airs from heaven or blasts from hell,
> Be thy intents wicked or charitable,
> Thou comest in such a questionable shape
> That I will speak to thee.—*Hamlet.*

(Here "airs from heaven" and "blasts from hell" in the second line follow the same order as "spirit of health" and "goblin damned." But in the third line "wicked" and "charitable" follow a different order from that of the first and second lines. Such discrepancy is not to be imitated in prose.)

Correct, improve, or justify the following sentences:—

1. The death took place at Rugby yesterday morning of Mr. David B., of Clare College, Cambridge, the well-known amateur cricketer, and slow round-hand bowler.—*Daily Telegraph,* p. 5, June 1, 1900.

2. Remains only the Great-Western Railway Company, and some five score of Ealing residents, who have yielded to the solicitations of an agent of the London General Omnibus Company. —*Middlesex County Times,* p. 5, April 28, 1900.

3. If I mistake not, Brandis finds in just those scenes which Mr. Lee decides that it is impossible Shakespeare could have written, the inimitable touch of the master.—*Literature,* p. 346, May 5, 1900.

4. Little by little the number rose of those who passed under the high arch of the gate, over which the beautiful four-horse chariot of Lysias was driven.—BINION, *Quo Vadis?* p. 62, ch. vii.

5. Rev. R. H. Quick was a schoolmaster whom the Harrow boys gave rather a bad time, but who theorised luminously on educational subjects.—*Literature,* p. 573, June 3, 1899.

6. During the engagement Major McKenzie nearly fell into a trap laid by a Kaffir, as well as Thorneycroft's Horse, who were similarly treacherously treated by another native guide.—*Daily Telegraph,* p. 7, April 14, 1900.

7. Many of the Free Staters, who gave in as proof of their submission their muskets, said very much the same thing.—*Ibid.* p. 10, May 4, 1900.

8. Three Russian, two Japanese, one British, and one American battalions have scoured the Imperial Park to the south of the city. —*Ibid.* p. 7, Aug. 30, 1900.

9. Africans most nearly reproduce of all surviving types the type of primitive man.—*Review of Reviews,* p. 582, June 1900.

10. Public opinion would be strong against this and the influence of governing bodies and headmasters.—*Literature*, p. 118, Feb. 10, 1900.

11. Henry had intended to balance in the composition of his administrative board the two parties, the Conservative and Progressive.—GOLDWIN SMITH, *United Kingdom*, vol. i. p. 342.

12. If such persons were indifferent to Cobbett's defection, they whose standard he joined hailed with enthusiasm his conversion.— BULWER, *Historical Characters*, vol. ii. p. 134.

13. Though we do not expect the abolition of foolish speculation from the labours of the Royal Commission, we do expect some good from its appointment.—*Spectator*, p. 365, March 24, 1877 (H).

14. Nobody could expect the Church to resign that spiritual independence which it holds essential to religion and which till now was never doubted without a struggle.—H. COCKBURN, *Memorials*, ch. viii. p. 290 (H).

15. The public blame the great officials, whose want of imagination and failure to make improvements admitted to be necessary in good time nearly landed us in irreparable disaster.—*Spectator*, p. 700, Nov. 17, 1900.

16. Upon our side there can be no anxiety as to the issue, and should be no impatience during the process.—*Daily Telegraph*, p. 9, Nov. 24, 1900.

17. He had never received, so far as I could gather, though he was a graduate of Trinity College, Dublin, what in England would be called a high classical education.—*Fortnightly Review*, p. 584, Oct. 1900.

18. Every profession needs to hearten it some grand prize, and probably as every sucking barrister dreams of the woolsack, so every priest dreams at his ordination of that far distant, but shining, tiara. —*Spectator*, p. 690, May 11, 1901.

19. There is a sort of suspicion among quiet Germans, especially in the non-industrial provinces, that he wishes to pose as a redresser of the world's wrongs.—*Ibid.* p. 737, Nov. 24, 1900.

20. In a recent number of *Literature* the discovery at Florence was announced of a series of documents bearing on the family of Dante.—*Literature*, p. 319, Sept. 30, 1899.

21. When this prevails in Madras schools, the centre of education, worse will be the case of the village schools.—*Educational Review* (Madras), p. 63, Feb. 1900.

22. As the leading and consistent champion of the oppressed, I trust you will permit me in your columns to advocate the cause of humanity towards helpless animals.—Quoted in *Daily Telegraph*, Jan. 6, 1898.

23. To him the spiritual and the physical world—the life of movement and the life of moral emotion—appeared as the double face of one mystery, Nature.—*Fortnightly Review*, Dec. 1902, p. 951.

24. We must suppose, therefore, that the public are quite wrong in attributing certain inconveniences under which they imagine themselves to be still suffering to injudicious competition.—*Spectator*, p. 979, Dec. 20, 1902.

(b) Adjective and Participle.

1. Adjective or Participle used attributively.—As a general rule an adjective or participle, or other qualifying word that does the work of an adjective, is placed immediately before the noun that it qualifies ; and it is very important to bear this rule in mind.[1] Thus there is a great difference between—

The author's best endeavours—The best author's endeavours.
A great gentleman's coat—A gentleman's greatcoat.
A little lady's dog—A lady's little dog.
An unquestioned man of genius—A man of unquestioned genius.
The half-yearly Directors' meeting—The Directors' half-yearly meeting.

(*a*) It is convenient to place the adjective or participle after the noun, if it is enlarged by some qualifying phrase or clause :—

A matter too *urgent to be put off any longer.*
A room not *large enough for a meeting that was likely to be attended by twenty persons.*
A man *convinced against his will* is of the same opinion still.

This order is better than that exemplified in such a sentence as the following :—

In the presence of Tennyson I felt the overshadowing of a so much loftier intellect than my own.—Edward FitzGerald. (Say, "an intellect so much loftier than my own.")

(*b*) If the participle is one formed with the help of an Auxiliary verb, it may stand either before or after the noun :—

The horse, *being tired out,* could go no further.
Being tired out, the horse could go no further.

(*c*) When several adjectives qualify the same noun, it often sounds better to place the noun first :—

God is the maker of all things *visible and invisible, animate and inanimate.*
The Lords *spiritual and temporal.*
Humanity will be more free to lead a life happy, moral, and intellectual.—*North American Review,* p. 585, June 1901.

---

[1] Professor Bain, in *Companion to Higher English Grammar,* p. 302, edit. 1877, says :—" By a fortunate convention of our language the simple adjective goes before the noun. This is the arrangement that is scientifically the most defensible. Before a thing is named, the mind should be prepared with all the qualifications and limitations, so as to conceive the thing at once as qualified and limited." Similarly when a noun is used to qualify another noun, the qualifying noun must invariably be placed first. Observe the difference in meaning between "horse-race" and "race-horse."

(*d*) There are a few well-established phrases, in which the adjective is placed last, apparently the result of French influence :—

> Notary *public*. Heir *apparent*. Governor-*general*. The sum *total*. Letters *patent*. Knight-*errant*. Court *martial*. Malice *pre- pense*. Bishop *elect*. Point *blank*. God *Almighty*.

(*e*) Sometimes the adjective is placed after its noun for the sake of emphasis :—

> The agenda paper in itself is a complete review of matters *theatrical*. —*Daily Telegraph*, p. 14, April 24, 1900.
>
> Yes, sir, puffing is of various sorts ; the principal are the puff *direct*, the puff *preliminary*, the puff *collateral*, the puff *collusive*, and the puff *oblique* or puff by implication.— SHERIDAN, *The Critic*, Act I.

(*f*) Adjectives, when given in the comparative or superla- tive degree, especially when either is expressed by *more* or *most*, can be freely placed after their nouns :—

> This programme affords room for the ventilation of views *the most diverse*.—*Standard*, March 17, 1891.
>
> Words *more sublime* or *more illuminative* never fell from the lips of man.—W. SANDAY, *Oracles*, iv.

(*g*) When two or more adjectives connected with a noun express entirely different meanings, it may be advantageous to separate them by placing the noun in the middle :—

> One of the most extraordinary things is *the utter past and present neglect* of British interests in Somaliland.—*Daily Telegraph*, p. 10, May 7, 1901. (The sense will be more obvious, and the sound will be more pleasing, if we say, "The utter neglect, past and present, of British interests," etc.)

(*h*) When a participle is used as an adjective, it is often put after the noun. "This order is of course the result of the participles being still felt to be half verbs" (Sweet).

> The day *following*. The time *being*. The money *required*. The reason *supposed*. The day *appointed*. The subject *referred to*. The fact *alleged*.

(*i*) When an adjective is used as an appellative, it is placed after the noun and has the definite article placed before it :—

> Alfred the *Great*. William the *Silent* (parallel to William the *Conqueror*). Edward the *First*. Henry *VIII*.

2. Adjective or Participle used predicatively.—When the sense of an adjective or participle is more closely connected with that of the verb of the sentence than with that of the Subject or Object, the adjective or participle must be placed both after the noun and after the verb. An adjective or participle so used is called Complementary, because it completes the sense of the verb.

(a) *Subject :—*

> He became *sad* and *dispirited.*
> He was found *carrying* his coat on his arm.

(Here the italicised adjectives and participles, though they qualify the Subject *he,* are more closely connected in sense with the verb than with the subject.)

(b) *Object :—*

> They painted the door *white.*
> They considered the man *courageous.*

(Here *white,* though it qualifies the Object *door,* is much more closely connected in sense with the verb *painted.* Similarly *courageous* is closely connected in sense with the verb *considered.* Both adjectives are therefore placed after the noun as well as after the verb.)

Observe how the sense of the following sentences depends on the position of the italicised adjectives :—

> My father left *poor* me. (My father deserted unlucky me.) *Attributive use.*
> My father left me *poor.* (When my father died, he did not leave much to support me.) *Predicative use.*
> He bought *cheap* material. (He bought cheap material, paying for it at the market rate.) *Attributive use.*
> He bought the material *cheap.* (He bought the material at a price below the market rate.) *Predicative use.*
> I *alone* can do it. (No one but me can do it.) *Attributive use.*
> I can do it *alone.* (I can do it without any assistance.) *Predicative use.*
> He made *public* confessions. *Attributive use.*
> He made his confessions *public.* *Predicative use.*

3. Participle used with a Conjunction.—Whenever a participle is used after such conjunctions as *though, when, if, while,* etc. (the Auxiliary verb and its Subject being omitted for the sake of brevity), the participle must be placed as close as possible to the noun or pronoun that it refers to, and if no such noun or pronoun is to be found in the sentence, the Auxiliary verb and its Subject must be supplied.

> While going home, a wolf met him. (Say, "A wolf met him, while going home"; or say, "While going home, he was met by a wolf.")
> While going home, a wolf appeared from behind a rock. (This is wrong. Say, "While he (or some one else) was going home, a wolf appeared," etc.)

4. Prepositional adjunct.—A prepositional adjunct, when it does the work of an adjective, is placed immediately after its noun :—

> Every turf *beneath their feet*
> Shall be a soldier's sepulchre.—CAMPBELL.

Note.—This subject is more fully dealt with under the heading (*e*) *Prepositions*, in this chapter.

Correct, improve, or justify the following sentences :—

1. As is often the case, being an inferior work, the author had a manifest partiality for it, and rated it among his best pieces.—*Fortnightly Review*, p. 250, Feb. 1900.

2. These excellent villas to be sold or let, freehold or leasehold.—*Builder's Notice.*

3. We are no longer storm-tossed : we know pretty well, arrived at this stage, what we are going to do,—those of us who thought they were going to do anything.—Quoted in *Review of Reviews*, p. 264, March 1900.

4. He was a saint indeed, not a hermit of asceticism, combining piety, meekness, humility, simplicity, with active benevolence and virtue.—GOLDWIN SMITH, *United Kingdom*, vol. i. p. 48.

5. The loyal British colony of Natal will look forward to the time when, not far distant, her northern frontier will reach to the Barberton goldfields and to the hinterland of Delagoa Bay.—*Fortnightly Review*, p. 733, Nov. 1899.

6. I feel that I am now in some way bound to place my services at the disposal of my fellow ratepayers, and not to shirk the work and responsibility involved in maturing these measures, having ample leisure for the purpose.—Quoted in *Middlesex County Times*, p. 4, Nov. 18, 1899.

7. Lady, spinster, orphan, twenty-one, medium height, considered nice-looking, is anxious to marry a gentleman, refined, of irreproachable character, and with thorough business capabilities, having recently inherited the property of a large and valuable tea-plantation in Ceylon, the affairs of which will require her to go out there.—*People*, July 9, 1900.—*Advertisement.*

8. Articles appear in our page for women dealing with "Early Autumn Fashions," "The Ladies' Golf Union," and "Russian Society."—*Daily Telegraph*, p. 8, Sept. 9, 1899.

9. The United States expressed the desire to have the questions of privateering and the neutrality of merchandise not contraband of war considered.—*Ibid.* p. 9, May 20, 1899.

10. Looked at from where one will, one could not but feel in comparison with this natural cathedral how poor was a temple made with hands.—*Cornhill*, p. 215, Feb. 1899.

11. The many duties and distractions of the king's office left him but little time to pursue letters for himself, though he did much to make them accessible to others ; much less, certainly, than he wished for.—*National Review*, quoted in *Literature*, p. 372, April 8, 1899.

12. A large number of volumes are announced or have already

appeared in Germany dealing with various aspects of the life and thought of the century.—*Literature*, p. 553, May 27, 1899.

13. On the 24th of July 1899, he alluded to "serious operations in which the use of anæsthetics is wholly or partly dispensed with" as taking place.—*Fortnightly Review*, p. 394, March 1900.

14. It was ordinary life which she alone depicted, but it was to her seeing that life not partially, as we see it, but in all its actual vastness, that she owed her great success.—*Review of Reviews*, p. 480, May 1900.

15. An extraordinary story is given currency by the editor of the *National Review*, first among the episodes of the month.—*Ibid*. p. 453, May 1899.

16. That the war will have the effect upon them predicted, I totally disbelieve.—*Fortnightly Review*, p. 740, May 1900.

17. Facts which are untrue about her (England's) foreign and home policy have been stated, and arguments and articles by the thousand have been written based on these false assertions.—*Weekly Times*, p. 231, April 13, 1900.

18. The oyster is a singularly interesting animal regarded from a naturalist's point of view.—*Middlesex County Times*, p. 7, March 24, 1900.

19. The clergy find a difficulty in deducing easy moral lessons from every-day occurrences suited to their hearers.—*Church Gazette*, p. 57, May 6, 1899.

20. Being the only child of a man well-to-do, nobody would have been surprised had Agnes Stanfield been sent to a boarding-school.— Mrs. OLIPHANT, *Agnes*, vol. i. p. 7 (H).

21. A glance deeper will show that each gains a solid advantage in the shape of security.—*Spectator*, p. 651, Nov. 10, 1900.

22. I shall not trouble you further, disliking controversy.—Quoted in *Spectator*, p. 745, Nov. 24, 1900.

23. We have hitherto, compared with several European countries, been singularly free from the machinations of anarchism.—*Daily Express*, p. 4, Nov. 29, 1900.

24. The anonymous author peremptorily dismisses the "attempt to merge Liberals in a new party reconstituted on Imperialist lines under Lord Rosebery as autocrat" as "hopeless."—*Spectator*, p. 848, Dec. 8, 1900.

25. Steps are being taken to form a corps for town-defence of men unable to proceed to the front. One drapery firm has promised one hundred men alone.—*Daily Telegraph*, p. 7, Jan. 4, 1900.

26. Eventually the motion was withdrawn on Lord Salisbury, who regretted that language of such indecent violence had been placed on the statute book, promising an inquiry.—*Ibid*. p. 8, March 20, 1901.

27. A few convictions (passed against furious drivers) would make fairly safe roads at present much more dangerous than the road to Comassie.—*Middlesex County Times*, p. 6, April 27, 1901.

28. What can be more glorious than to have played one's part, even though a modest one, in never-to-be-forgotten events?—Sir EDWARD MALET, *Shifting Scenes*, ed. 1901.

29. The ladder from the gutter to the university, by which we alone can hope to organise the selection of talent, and thereby organise and

recruit society, can never be really complete as long as there are rival authorities in the field.—*Fortnightly Review*, p. 829, May 1901.

30. A reduction of expenditure during the last half-year was effected amounting to £21,818.—*Daily Telegraph*, p. 4, May 25, 1901.

31. There is not a capital in Europe, especially if it is ultra-sceptical, where men and women of the world, who suppose themselves free from all superstitions, are not consulting wizards, trusting in diviners, believing that to some sort of priests of Isis knowledge has been communicated denied to the remainder of mankind.—*Spectator*, p. 761, May 25, 1901.

32. All experience shows that they cannot deal with the difficulties of housing alone.—G. HAW, *New Liberal Review*.

33. A great deal of attention has been attracted during the week to an article in the September *National Review*, by Sir Edward Grey, dealing with the causes of the war.—*Ibid.* p. 271, Aug. 31, 1901.

34. Sir, Dr. Elkind's letter in the *Spectator* of 24th August recalls to my mind an article I once read somewhere which illustrates the curious and out-of-the-way knowledge about the causes of baldness possessed by some barbers.—*Ibid.* p. 351, Sept. 14, 1901.

35. But relying upon your inability to make yourselves acquainted with the facts, you are deceived and played with by those party organs.—Quoted in *Daily Telegraph*, p. 10, Oct. 26, 1901.

36. The sitting closed definitely at five o'clock without the matter which had brought so many together having been practically entered upon.—*Ibid.*

37. There remains a very copious supply of creditable literature in the autumn lists to be dealt with.—*Fortnightly Review*, p. 1028, Dec. 1900.

38. With this small band they advanced against the city of Kiow, containing 80,000 inhabitants, where they would have found ample supplies of all sorts, closely followed by 4000 men.—ALISON'S *History of Europe*.

39. Claudian, in a fragment upon the wars of the giants, has contrived to render this idea of their throwing the mountains, which is in itself so grand, burlesque and ridiculous.—BLAIR'S *Lectures on Rhetoric*.

(c) *Pronouns.*

1. Relative and Antecedent.—A Relative pronoun or Relative adverb should be placed as close as possible to its antecedent :—

(1) I have read Plato's writings, who was a disciple of Socrates. (Say, "I have read the writings of Plato, who was a disciple of Socrates.")

(2) We find ourselves in sympathy with Miss Cynthia Lennox, the charming heroine's eccentric benefactress, who loved Ellen so passionately as a child.—*Spectator*, p. 907, Dec. 7, 1901. (Here the proper order has been well preserved. "Benefactress" is the antecedent of "who," and so the writer has done well in saying "heroine's benefactress" instead of saying "benefactress of heroine.")

(3) It is the system, not the individual, which I condemn. (Say, "It is the system which I condemn, not the individual"; or, "It is not the individual, but the system which I condemn.")

2. Demonstrative and Antecedent.—A Demonstrative
pronoun, being a word of reference, should not as a rule be mentioned until the word to which it refers has been mentioned. This rule is neglected in the following sentence :—

> Democracy loves spending, is devoted to dignity, and provided *they* are indirect or fall heaviest on the rich, will pay any amount of *taxes.—Quarterly Review*, No. 367, p. 84. (Say, "Provided *taxes* are indirect, etc., will pay any amount of *them.*")

Sometimes, however, it is not convenient to mention the Antecedent before giving the Demonstrative. In such a sentence as the following the inversion causes no offence to the ear :—

> This code was adopted as *their own* by the two other members of the triple alliance.—PRESCOTT, *History of Medicine*, i. 119.

3. Position of First person.—A pronoun in the First person
should be mentioned last :—

> I shall be obliged if Mr. Councillor J. will give me and your readers his authority for the statement.—Letter in *Daily Telegraph*, p. 6, July 14, 1900. (Say, "will give your readers and myself," etc.)
>
> Neither I nor my companion suffered from *ennui* during the months we spent together.—Quoted with disapproval by *Spectator*, p. 120, July 26, 1902, from a book under review.

4. Repetition of Antecedent.—Sometimes it is found to
be difficult, if not impossible, to place the antecedent as near as it should be to the relative. In such a case (if the sentence will not bear reconstruction), the best remedy lies in repeating the antecedent, as in the following examples :—

> During the last two years, since the outbreak of the war, there have been amongst us differences of opinion as to its origin, as to the causes which led to it,—*differences which* have been deep-seated, far-reaching, and acute.—From a Speech quoted in *Daily Telegraph*, p. 9, June 21, 1901. (Observe that when the antecedent is thus repeated, it should be preceded by a dash.)
>
> Among quiet Germans, especially in the non-industrial provinces, there is a sort of suspicion that he wishes to pose as a redresser of the world's wrongs,—a suspicion which we entirely believe to be unjust.—*Spectator*, p. 737, Nov. 24, 1900.

Correct, improve, or justify the following sentences :—

1. I have tried on more than one occasion to express the gratitude that I and my countrymen feel towards the people and government of

Natal for the assistance so loyally given during the past year.—Quoted in *Daily Telegraph*, p. 9, June 21, 1900.

2. For Herodias' sake, his brother Philip's wife.—*Matthew* xiv. 3.

3. We learn from Reuter that a relieving force of Haussas has been dispatched from Accra to Kumasi, which is considered insufficient.—*St. James's Gazette*, p. 4, April 11, 1900.

4. If he is still alive, it may be found possible to re-establish the Emperor on the throne.—*Daily Express*, p. 4, June 20, 1900.

5. Lord Salisbury made a statement in the House of Lords yesterday, which, though it only shot a canard on the wing, was of much importance.—*Daily Telegraph*, p. 9, Feb. 23, 1900.

6. The prison will be filled with soldiers and officials. Should they recognise thee, I and my family would perish.—BINION, *Quo Vadis?* p. 451, ch. xviii.

7. An exhibition has just been closed at Manchester which should be interesting to many more persons than those of the trade.—*Daily Graphic*, p. 7, May 26, 1900.

8. But the meaning was perfectly clear, which he intended to convey.—Quoted in *Daily Telegraph*, p. 4, Feb. 2, 1900.

9. Many people would have been of opinion that the Laird would have done better to have transferred his glances to an object possessed of far superior charms to Jeanie's, even when Jeanie's were in the bloom, who began now to be distinguished by all who visited the cottage at St. Leonard's Crags.—SCOTT, *Heart of Midlothian*, ch. ix. para. 2.

10. My study of Dar Fertit dates from the time when I and others planned Lupton Bey's escape from Khartoum.—*Fortnightly Review*, p. 863, Dec. 1898.

11. A wise foresight will see that he is the truest friend of the Republic who strives to rebuild the Home and recreate the Family.—Quoted in *Review of Reviews*, p. 512, Nov. 1899.

12. In the picturesque and well-wooded grounds of Wembley Park a white city of canvas will rise at midsummer next year, in which six thousand of our visitors from over-sea and from our own land will be accommodated.—*Ibid.* p. 352, Oct. 1899.

13. The principle of measuring other people by your own bushel is never so nauseous as when applied to cover his own ingenuity by an unscrupulous exploiter of public confidence.—*Daily Express*, p. 4, June 20, 1900.

14. The small prince is heir-presumptive to an enormous fortune. His mother is the only child of the King of Wurtemburg, to whom his large fortune will eventually go.—*Daily Telegraph*, p. 5, Sept. 30, 1899.

15. All men under twenty-one and over thirty, except sergeants, who were taken up to thirty-five years of age, who were considered unfit, were immediately rejected.—*Ibid.* p. 7, Sept. 6, 1899.

16. The German Emperor has decreed that the three new fortifications near Metz are to bear the names of the Crown Prince, the Empress, and Lothringen respectively, in order to show, in the words of the Emperor, "how closely I and my house are related to the Reichsland."—*Ibid.* p. 9, June 6, 1900.

17. They tell him that there shall be no reforms in the slovenly

methods common enough fifty years ago, some of which have survived to the present day, of which he does not approve.—*Church Gazette*, p. 710, April 15, 1899.

18. I am not minded to follow in Rufinus' tracks, whose story I was about to tell thee.—BINION, *Quo Vadis?* p. 28, ch. i.

19. There are one or two points raised by those who represent the art of acting as an inferior and unworthy art, that claim a passing consideration.—*Fortnightly Review*, p. 746, May 1900.

20. I never made the statement at the last meeting of the County Council or at any other time, which you have imputed to me.—*Middlesex County Times*, p. 9, June 9, 1900.

21. A long stretch of the Brent runs along the boundary line of the constituency that I represent, which requires constant watching on the part of the committee.—*Ibid.* p. 9, June 9, 1900.

22. The President gave a monopoly of the supply of dynamite to a German non-resident in the country, which taxed the miners for this article alone $2,600,000 a year beyond the highest price it could otherwise have been bought for.—*Nineteenth Century*, p. 746, May 1900.

23. No one can doubt how great and critical was the occasion who observed the keen and breathless interest of Parliament as Mr. Chamberlain began his speech.—*Daily Telegraph*, p. 9, May 22, 1900.

24. Mr. A. W. has an article entitled "Britannia and the Colonist," in which he protests against the current habit of looking at the Colonist as something outside and inferior, which is universal in Government circles.—*Review of Reviews*, p. 576, June 1900.

25. The book deals with the old story of horrid vengeance for centuries of wrong, wreaked usually on the innocent, which we have read so often before, and yet which is of eternal interest.—*Literature*, p. 47, July 21, 1900.

26. We cannot point to any novel since that which gave new life to the times of Erasmus, which leaves the same impression of power and breadth as *The Knights of the Cross.*—*Daily Telegraph*, p. 4, June 29, 1900.

27. More than one group of persons passed him, as he was whiling away the hours of darkness that yet remained, whom from the stifled tones of their discourse, the unwonted hour when they travelled, and the hasty pace at which they walked, he conjectured to have been engaged in the late fatal transactions.—SCOTT, *Heart of Midlothian*, ch. vi. para. 22.

28. Rumour says that after we left the niggers took the Federal camp and killed all but eleven of the enemy, who escaped.—*Daily Graphic*, p. 8, Feb. 14, 1900.

29. His object is to help on the work of the Association for securing greater efficiency in our whole administration, which has been set on foot in the *Nineteenth Century.*—*Spectator*, p. 294, Sept. 8, 1900.

30. Many a half-hour business men wasted with Mrs. Stern, trying to fish out the exact state of the chemist's concerns, which they thought afterwards might have been spent with about as much profit on the top of the Monument.—*Too Much Alone*, ch. xii. p. 112 (H).

31. I shall be obliged, if Mr. Councillor J. will give me and your readers his authority for the statement.—Quoted in *Daily Telegraph*, p. 6, July 14, 1900.

32. The following conversation may interest you, which I had with an intelligent young Yorkshire farmer about thirty years of age.—Quoted in *Spectator*, p. 408, Sept. 29, 1900.

33. When the war was carried into operation, the cause became the cause of my country, and I and my friends have given it the most loyal support in the House of Commons.—Quoted in *Daily Telegraph*, p. 10, Oct. 6, 1900.

34. Throughout it is the speech of a man who sees hostile forces which he defies, and who has plans to meet the difficulties of the hour which he intends to carry out.—*Spectator*, p. 613, Nov. 3, 1900.

35.   Had you enjoined them on me, given me soul,
        We might have risen to Rafael, I and you.
                    BROWNING, *The Ring and the Book.*

36. During the last five years I was a director not of several, but of one company, in which myself and family were largely interested.—Quoted in *Daily Telegraph*, p. 7, Dec. 8, 1900.

37. Our strange and heterogeneous succession of Poor Laws is one of the most remarkable and most pathetic illustrations of human intelligence and effort struggling towards the light, through error and shortsightedness, through failure and disaster, wnich the history of social organisation contains. —*Fortnightly Review*, p. 956, Dec. 1900.

38. Less than six months after the parting with Mr. Tweddell, Miss Gunning was married to General Alexander Ross, best known as the friend and aide-de-camp of Lord Cornwallis, who was then in his fifty-fourth year.—*Ibid.* p. 376, Feb. 1901.

39. To sweeten his discourse Dr. Creighton, with the rare courage which differentiated his intellect from that of most bishops, launched out into a defence of the pursuit of wealth as an end which would, we think, in its want of reserves and qualifications have made most of his brethren on the bench rub their eyes.—*Spectator*, p. 489, April 6, 1901.

40. In 1856 Sir Edward first introduced shorthand into his office work. "Otherwise," he writes, "I and others who have to do letters by the hundred and more a day would long ago have been mad or blind or both.—*Daily Telegraph*, p. 7, April 15, 1901.

41. They are some of the feather-bed soldiers who have never been away from home before that complain to their wives.—*Daily Mail*, p. 4, April 22, 1901.

42. I and many thousands more welcome with gratitude the agitation so vigorously taken up by the *Express* for the appointment of a Minister of Commerce.—*Daily Express*, p. 5, April 29, 1901.

43. Carlyle speaks somewhere of the matter-of-fact attitude towards all the daily wonders of the world, which ceases to regard the existence of the globe as anything more remarkable than the cooking of a dumpling.—*Daily Telegraph*, p. 9, April 30, 1901.

44. Reports were also current as to his determination to appropriate £5,000,000 to the creation of the greatest technical university at Pittsburg that the world has ever seen.—*Review of Reviews*, p. 343, April 1901.

L

45. In the difficult position of Indian Secretary he showed not only great force, but the power of seeing into the centre of a complicated mass of details, and of realising conditions among which he has not lived, which is unusual even among statesmen.—*Spectator*, p. 756, May 25, 1901.

46. Perhaps, unlearned as she was, she could have brought a dawning knowledge home to Mr. Dombey at that early day, which would not then have struck him in the end like lightning.—DICKENS, *Dombey and Son*, ch. ii.

47. I trust neither I nor Mr. Chamberlain are going to say anything which will be taken as a challenge to Lord Salisbury.—DUKE OF DEVONSHIRE, *Daily Telegraph*, p. 9, July 11, 1901.

48. The great distance from its original home in India at which we now find the buffalo established is evidence that the animal has a history of an exceedingly adventurous kind, were it possible to trace the story of its travels.—*Spectator*, p. 279, Aug. 31, 1901.

49. There in the valley six thousand feet below are the chapel and priests' house built by their own hands, with their own money, by the people of the wholly Christian village of Ta Tien Tze.—*Cornhill*, p. 215, Feb. 1899.

50. The university of Padua is a dying taper ; but Verona still boasts her amphitheatre, and his native Vicenza is adorned by the classic architecture of Palladio.—GIBBON, *Autobiography*, p. 79.

51. We are inclined to think that it was a real recognition that Wycliffism as left by its founder, and still more as expounded by his followers when deprived of his guidance, offered no basis for a Church in touch with the broad and many-sided character of the nation, which was largely accountable for the rapid failure of the Lollard movement.—*Spectator*, p. 463, Oct. 6, 1900.

52. He cannot be said to have died prematurely whose work was finished, nor does he deserve to be lamented who died so full of honours.—SOUTHEY.

53. There are not meanwhile critics wanting here, who assign this victory as regards moral and political supremacy in China to Russia.—Berlin Telegram, *Daily Telegraph*, Feb. 5, 1898.

54. No one is entitled to form or express an opinion on the relations between Nelson and Lady Hamilton, or on the parentage of Horatia, who has not carefully studied the letters to be found in this invaluable collection.—*Times Weekly*, March 4, 1898.

55. We may well ask what is the use of it, if energetic action in shipbuilding is not accompanied by parallel action in diplomacy.—*Homeward Mail*, July 25, 1898.

56. There is a huge cave among its cliffs, where the Mac Somethings had taken refuge from their foes, the Mac Something-elses, to the number of above two hundred men.—*Church Gazette*, p. 41, April 29, 1899.

57. It has long been acknowledged that the lessons of the war would not be rightly read, until we had their own view of the stubborn struggle and its possibilities from the pens of the Boer generals themselves.—*Spectator*, p. 894, Dec. 6, 1902.

58. At the appearance of Jesus to Mary Magdalene there is the eloquent interchange between the two, "Mary," "Master." On the solemn caution, "Touch me not," Mrs. Jameson explains it to mean that He had put on immortality ; that He had passed the gates of death, while she was still on our side of them.—HACKWOOD, *Christ-Lore*, pp. 169-171.

59. No book has been published since your departure of which much notice is taken.—JOHNSON, *Letter to Rev. Mr. White*.

60. How much more to them than to us, so long as we are ignorant of the same, would these words have conveyed !—TRENCH, *English Past and Present*.

61. Democracy loves spending, is devoted to dignity, and provided they are indirect and fall heaviest on the rich, will pay any amount of taxes.—*Quarterly Review*, No. 367, p. 84.

(d) Adverb, Adverbial Phrase, or Adverbial Clause.

The positions of an adverb or adverbial phrase are various, depending as they do on the character of the word or words which it is intended to qualify.

1. With Adjective, Preposition, Conjunction, or other Adverb.—The adverb or adverbial phrase must be placed immediately before any of the parts of speech here named :—

Surely it was *precisely because* Admiral Seymour may have been dominated by his early experience of the fighting mettle of the Chinese, that he imagined his experience would be a success.—*Daily Graphic*, p. 7, Aug. 16, 1900. (Here the adverb " precisely " qualifies a conjunction.)

Immortal Amarant, a flower which once
In Paradise, *fast by* the tree of life,
Began to bloom.—*Paradise Lost*, iii. 353-355. (Here the adverb " fast " qualifies a preposition.)

This was followed by a terrible headache *right across* the forehead.—Quoted in *Daily Telegraph*, p. 7, April 27, 1900. (Here the adverb " right " qualifies a preposition.)

A little while before business was concluded, these sales had lost their influence. — *Ibid.* p. 10, Feb. 17, 1900. (Here the adverbial phrase " a little while " qualifies a conjunction.)

It has become widely known, *largely on account of* the opposition of the medical profession.—*Ibid.* p. 9, May 31, 1901. (Here the adverb " largely " qualifies the prepositional phrase " on account of.")

2. With Intransitive verb.—When the verb is Intransitive, the adverb or adverbial phrase is usually placed after the verb, though sometimes for the sake of euphony it is placed before it :—

The children of Israel were fruitful, and increased *abundantly*.—*Exodus* i. 7.

If thou return at all *in peace*, the Lord hath not spoken by me.—1 *Kings* xxii. 28.

Innumerable trap-doors lay concealed in the bridge, which the passengers no sooner trod upon, but they fell through them into the tide and *immediately* disappeared.—ADDISON, *Spectator*, No. 159.

When the adverb or adverbial phrase denotes time, it is usually placed before the verb :—

He *always* laughed *heartily* at a good joke.
He *never* spoke *boastfully* about his own merits.
He *often* wept *bitterly* on passing that tomb.
He *seldom* slept *soundly* in any house.
The same day came to him the Sadducees.—*Matt.* xxii. 23.
Previously to the Bill last passed in favour of the Catholics, the opinions of the most celebrated of foreign universities were taken.—SIDNEY SMITH.
During the supremacy of Northumbria lived the venerable Bede, who wrote a history of the English Church.—RANSOME, *Short History of England*, ch. ii. p. 18.

So strong is the tendency in our language to place adverbs of time first, that we often find them placed before the wrong word :—

His last journey was to Cannes, whence he was *never* destined to return.—Mrs. GROTE, *Life of George Grote*, ch. xxix. p. 245. (Say, "destined never to return.")

3. With Transitive verb.—When the verb is Transitive, an adverb or adverbial phrase can be placed either before the verb, or after the Object, or (if the Object is accompanied by a phrase or clause or is expressed by several words) between the verb and the Object :—

He bore his losses *cheerfully*.
He *briefly* explained his meaning.
He *liberally* rewarded (or, he rewarded *liberally*) all those who had served him well.
Nobler and loftier emotions lit up *with a generous enthusiasm* the hearts of men who had still heavy sacrifices to make.
Your lordships will observe the propriety of opening *fully* to you this circumstance in the government of India.—BURKE, *Impeachment of Warren Hastings*.

It may be pointed out, however, that when the adverb is placed at the end, the emphatic character which it acquires from this position somewhat affects the sense :—

(1) I understand your feelings *perfectly*.
(2) I *perfectly* understand your feelings.

In (1) the adverb is very emphatic and must be taken in its most literal sense. In (2) it tends to become "a mere expletive," and a weaker word would have sufficed. (See Sweet, *New English Grammar*, § 1848.)

4. With Auxiliary verb.—An adverb or adverbial phrase is frequently placed between an Auxiliary verb and the Notional verb. This is to be expected, since it is the Notional verb, *i.e.* the notion or meaning expressed by the verb, that the adverb is intended to qualify.

But this position is by no means necessary : for the sake of emphasis or for any other reason the position may follow that shown in 2 or 3 :—

> What mean those great flights of birds that are *perpetually* hovering about the bridge.—ADDISON, *Spectator*, No. 159.
> This plan will *to a large extent* fit in with mine.

When the qualifying adverb is the negative "not," it is invariably placed between the Auxiliary verb and the Notional verb :—

> We have *not* seen him since Monday last.
> I do *not* think as you do on this point.

5. Several adjuncts to the same Verb.—When an action is beset with numerous adverbs or adverbial phrases, it sounds better to place some of these before and some after the verb :—

> A river flowing with equable current busily by great towns.—HELPS. (It would sound better to say, "with equable current flowing busily by great towns.")

6. The Split Infinitive.—There has been springing up of late the custom, common in journalism, but not (so far as I can find) sanctioned at present by literature, of placing an adverb or adverbial phrase between "to" and the Infinitive.[1] This usage is called "the Split Infinitive."

In the following examples the Infinitive is split :—

> The brigade, being met by the concentrated fire of the federal guns, was ordered to *temporarily* retire.—*Daily Telegraph*, p. 9, May 7, 1900.
> In the extra meeting the members failed to *entirely* clear the paper of business.—*Ibid.* p. 10, March 16, 1900.
> Meanwhile Mr. B. R. has given notice to *on Monday* ask Mr. B. whether, etc.—*Ibid.* p. 9, May 6, 1900.

---

[1] Dr. Earle, however, in his *Simple Grammar of English*, p. 96, quotes one example from literature,—the only one that I have seen :—

> Leafy huts made of the branches which the hill people know how to deftly interweave.—Sir W. HUNTER, *The Old Missionary.*

Dr. Earle terms it "an innovation," and does not recommend it for imitation. Nor is it endorsed by Hodgson, who speaks of it "as contrary to established precedent and otherwise assailable" (*Errors in the Use of English*, p. 178).

The delay is alleged to *seriously* hamper the **extension** of the undertaking.—*Ibid.* p. 10, Feb. 20, 1900.

In the following **examples** the Infinite has not been split, the adverb being placed according to rule either before the Infinitive or after it :—

The rights resolutely claimed by ourselves we are prepared *freely* to extend to others, when they are willing *loyally* to accept them.—*Daily Telegraph*, p. 5, April 13, 1900.

The Edinburgh club is doing an excellent work by encouraging the young people in the Scotch capital to read Scott's novels *intelligently.*—*Literature*, p. 325, April 28, 1900.

Excess in eating caused poorer people to spend *extravagantly* in order to imitate the wealthier classes.—*Pearson's Weekly*, p. 702, April 28, 1900.

The military engineer's mission in life is to build *firmly*, yet *temporarily*, but to destroy *effectually.*—*Ibid.* p. 703, April 28, 1900.

Their calculations were thrown out by their inability to measure *accurately* the strength of our reserve forces.—*Fortnightly Review*, p. 758, Nov. 1901.

Even in journalism the balance of authority or custom is decidedly against the Split Infinitive. The above sentences would all lose much of their force if the position of the adverb were changed. There is nothing to be gained, either in force or euphony or clearness, by putting the adverb between " to " and its verb ; and as literature is against the usage, it is best to make a habit of avoiding it altogether.

The splitting of the Infinitive sometimes mars the sense by impairing the energy of the sentence :—

A proposal *to specially convene* the members with a view to winding up their affairs was carried unanimously.—*Daily Telegraph*, p. 8, March 26, 1903. (Here "specially" should have been placed before "with a view." A proposal to convene the members specially with a view to (or with the special object of), etc.

7. Adverb qualifying a sentence.—An adverb or adverbial phrase should be placed at the beginning of a sentence, when it is intended to qualify, not any word in particular, but the sentence as a whole :—

Unfortunately great political problems do not wait on any one's convenience.—*Fortnightly Review*, p. 753, Nov. 1900.

Observe how the sense of the following sentences depends on the position of the adverb :—

Happily he did not die. He did not die *happily*.
At length he wrote to her. He wrote to her *at length*.

8. Position of Adverb at beginning of sentence.—An adverb or adverbial phrase, which expresses an important or leading qualification, can with great propriety and force be placed at the beginning of the sentence, though in the usual grammatical order it would stand after the verb or at the end of the sentence :—

> *With a great sum* obtained I this freedom.—*New Test.*
> *Never, not even under the tyranny of Laud,* had the condition of the Puritans been so deplorable as at that time.—MACAULAY.
> *For the sake of your fame, for the sake of the civilisation you have attained,* stifle not defenceless wretches in caverns.—JERROLD.

The same principle applies to the position of adverbial clauses :—

> *Though I speak with the tongues of men and of angels, and have not charity,* I am become as sounding brass or a tinkling cymbal.—*New Test.*

9. Position of "only."—It is a very common error to put the word "only" in its wrong place. It sometimes happens that the meaning as well as the force of a sentence depends on this adverb being placed before the word that it is intended to qualify :—

> Sir George added that England would remain a world-power *only so long as* it held command of the sea.—*Daily Express*, p. 5, Sept. 7, 1900. (This is much better than saying "would only remain.")
> Russia is willing to act in concert with the other powers *only until* order has been restored in China and no longer.—*Daily Telegraph*, p. 9, July 7, 1900. (This is much better than saying "is only willing," etc.)
> He looked forward to a time when all our main cables would *only touch* British territory, and would be adequately protected from an enemy.—*Ibid.* p. 6, Sept. 7, 1900. (Here the order is so bad that it alters the sense. It should be "would touch only British territory.")
> Lord H. has proclaimed that he and the section which he represents will *only* be bound by decisions that suit themselves.—*Church Gazette*, p. 674, April 8, 1899. (Say, "will be bound only by decisions," etc.)
> It was *only* when the party had driven some little distance that he bethought him that it might be useful to the officials, etc.—*Daily Telegraph*, p. 5, Aug. 3, 1900. (Correct.)
> The British Government has officially acknowledged that Germans in Samoa can be prosecuted for punishable offences *only* by German courts.—*Ibid.* p. 10, April 17, 1899. (Correct.)
> A Belgian journal denounced England a few months back for having acted as she did on behalf of Belgium in 1830 *only* from egotism

and personal interest.—*Fortnightly Review*, p. 759, Nov. 1900. (Correct.)

Peace could have been had easily and comfortably by self-effacement, but we could have held our own *only* by the methods adopted.— *Spectator*, p. 790, June 1, 1901. (Correct. If *only* were placed before "held," the sense would be different.)

Even that however can succeed *only* if the societies will take it up as a great social, and not as a political, movement.—*Ibid.* p. 790, June 1, 1901. (Correct.)

The difference is so great that it can be explained *only* by wide differences in the origin of the quondam slaves, who belonged originally to at least four unconnected tribes.—*Ibid.* p. 791, June 1, 1901. (Correct.)

10. Position of "even."—Equally important is the position of "even" :—

Forty per cent of the volunteers cannot possibly bind themselves to attend camp *even once* in two years.—Quoted in *Spectator*, p. 453, March 21, 1903. (Correct. The force of the sentence depends upon *even* being placed immediately before *once*.)

Correct, improve, or justify the following sentences :—

1. The announcement is such as to, if it were possible, still more confirm us in our resolve of doing our duty in the present emergency.— Quoted in *Times*, Feb. 22, 1900.

2. The Allies will only be able to test the reality of the apparent awakening of the fighting spirit in China, when they are in a position to carry on their operations upon ground permitting the evolution of flanking tactics.—*Daily Telegraph*, p. 9, July 18, 1900.

3. Mr. John Morley, M.P., attended on Saturday night at Oxford the annual dinner of the Palmerston Club, of which he is honorary president.—*Ibid.* p. 7, June 11, 1900.

4. It is worth while to briefly note the scope and character of their operations ; for these vary considerably.—*Ibid.* p. 7, April 24, 1900.

5. It leads the reader who seeks to understand the real bent of Ruskin's sympathy astray.—Quoted in *Review of Reviews*, p. 247, March 1900.

6. If the Government thought it right to publicly censure a General, the only logical outcome was to supersede him.—Quoted in *Daily Telegraph*, p. 7, May 5, 1900.

7. He had already made strong representations to the imperial government to refrain from sending the prisoners to St. Helena without success.—*Ibid.* p. 7, March 30, 1900.

8. Finally the great Duke taught us by his recognition of the value of sea-power, that the opportunity of Great Britain lies in war in her capacity to prepare in secret those over-sea expeditions, which, etc.— *Fortnightly Review*, p. 826, Nov. 1899.

9. At Paris I only found a different view in regard to the South African war in the house of a well-known Parliamentarian and honorary member of the Cobden club.—*Ibid.* p. 33, July 1900.

10. The legend lives and will live in the picturesque pages of

Macaulay, whose dangerous gift it was to equally take captive his readers whether he were right or wrong.—*Ibid.* p. 1042, June 1900.

11. I told Count Mouravieff that I had been asked to speak by Mr. Francis in the hall of the British American Church. — *Review of Reviews,* p. 541, June 1899.

12. The new Ministry has decided to wholly adopt Mr. Sch——'s proposals regarding the treatment of the rebels.—*Daily Telegraph,* p. 10, June 30, 1900.

13. Our motives will be those which have guided for many generations past English governments in their dealings with the colonies.— Quoted in *Daily Telegraph,* p. 10, May 30, 1900.

14. The actor will only be alarmed for the decline of his prestige when he finds his act small and degraded in the eyes of his honest fellow-countrymen.—*Fortnightly Review,* p. 745, May 1900.

15. Mr. K. proposes to continue the working parties for the sale of work in June, for the Lad's Brigade, until the end of April.—*Ealing Guardian,* p. 6, April 8, 1899.

16. Lessons are only attended to there in the morning.—*Literature,* p. 262, March 31, 1900.

17. A month ago it is reported that M. Delcassé was only restrained at the eleventh hour by the intervention of the Premier from formally raising the question of the date of our retirement from Egypt.—*Review of Reviews,* p. 312, April 1900.

18. To what purpose does he receive an income of between three and four thousand a year ? It is to perform the functions of a bishop, including the answering of such questions as can be only asked in the House of Lords.—*Church Gazette,* p. 86, May 13, 1899.

19. I fear that the dead whom he seeks, and cannot succeed in finding, have come to life in him again violently.—*Literature,* p. 420, June 2, 1900.

20. The Canadians and Queenslanders stood the test of marching long distances through heavy sand with little rest very well indeed.— *Daily Telegraph,* p. 9, May 22, 1900.

21. Clause 74 provides that questions arising out of the Federation Scheme itself should only be referred to the proposed Supreme Court of Appeal established under the Federation Scheme in Australia.— *Review of Reviews,* p. 445, May 1900.

22. Canon MacColl hints that these Protestant Associations are as much likely to injure a candidate as they are to benefit him.—*Church Times,* p. 91, July 27, 1900.

23. As is well known, he has only been able to maintain his position at all owing to the support of the President, acquired through his grotesque servility.—Quoted in *Daily Telegraph,* p. 11, April 24, 1900.

24. If students will remember that Mr. Dent's primers are nothing more than primers, they will only get good out of them.—*Daily Mail,* p. 3, April 20, 1900.

25. She detested him, because she had deluded herself, with the usual equanimity of an injured woman.—WHITTY, *Friends of Bohemia,* ch. xxiii. p. 188 (H).

26. People ceased to wonder by degrees. — Mrs. OLIPHANT, *Chronicles of Carlingford,* ch. vi. p. 75.

27. The leaders of the cotton trade will ensure that the true char-

acter of the cotton crop shall be known to themselves and to all others concerned both early and accurately.—*Spectator*, p. 364, Sept. 22, 1900.

28. It has caused even, wonderful to relate, our evangelical brethren to see that if they do not wake up they will simply dream themselves all away.—*Church Gazette*, p. 178, June 3, 1899.

29. The Home Office has practically decided to in any case issue a licence to Mrs. D. to open the grave at Highgate.—*Daily Telegraph*, p. 7, March 2, 1900.

30. The emperor only embraced the Reform movement when the helplessness of the old system was tragically borne in upon him by the humiliation of the Treaty of Shimonosaki.—*Fortnightly Review*, p. 515, Sept. 1900.

31. It is only possible to proceed with what is properly to be considered technical education after certain subjects which must be regarded as fundamental and absolutely essential have been thoroughly mastered.—*School World*, p. 368, Oct. 1900.

32. He (Domitian) did not fail to persecute Christians, because he had no inclination to do so, but because there were none in Rome during his reign to persecute.—REBER, *Christ of Paul*, p. 241.

33. There is a sort of suspicion among quiet Germans, especially in the non-industrial provinces, that he wishes to pose as a redresser of the world's wrongs—a suspicion which we entirely believe to be unjust. —*Spectator*, p. 737, Nov. 24, 1900.

34. May I remind him that my original letter was only occasioned by a portion of your article of November 3rd ?—*Ibid.* p. 745, Nov. 24, 1900.

35. Sir H. M., who had only been made acquainted with the intentions of the Minister on the day before that on which the Premier introduced the Resolution, protested that the price proposed to be taken for the railway was far too low.—*Ibid.* p. 795, Dec. 1, 1900.

36. To rigidly enforce the Public Health Acts would merely result in throwing thousands of people out into the streets ; and that would create a crisis compelling the Council to act.—*Fortnightly Review*, p. 972, Dec. 1900.

37. Washington was deliberately made, it did not grow, in more senses than one.—*Spectator*, p. 963, Dec. 29, 1900.

38. The advocates of rifle clubs in general, and Dr. Conan Doyle in particular, are spoken of as if they were a set of criminal lunatics who ought to be at once put into strait-waistcoats.—*Ibid.* p. 6, Jan. 5, 1901.

39. It is not the purpose of this paper to consider whether the training which can be given to the auxiliary forces is sufficient to fit them to successfully oppose men fully trained on the recognised modern lines.—*Fortnightly Review*, p. 314, Feb. 1901.

40. I end as I began by imploring the House to seriously consider the essentially unbusiness-like system under which the military forces of the Crown are now administered.—Lord WOLSELEY, quoted in *Daily Telegraph*, p. 6, March 5, 1901.

41. Even if we are fortunate enough to receive and reward very excellent designs, they can only at present be erected in such parts of England as are not cursed with by-laws which render one of the most available of building materials illegal.—*Spectator*, p. 346, March 9, 1901.

42. We should believe that Europe, bewildered by the absence of an objective, weary of an expenditure without result, and at heart ashamed of a slaughter which advances no whither, would acquiesce in this result, accepting the *status quo ante* without demur, but for one serious doubt.—*Ibid.* p. 792, Dec. 1, 1900.

43. They had already proclaimed that the attack of skirmishers in line was simply adopted, both by ourselves and by the Federals, because neither we nor they knew better.—*Ibid.* p. 522, April 13, 1901.

44. Running down a boat into the surf, they leaped in and dashed through the breakers, amidst the cheers of those on shore.—*Stories and Fables for Composition*, p. 104.

45. In a few minutes, impelled by the strong arms of these gallant men, the boat flew on and reached the stranded ship, catching her on the top of a wave.—*Ibid.* p. 104.

46. In our opinion the bicycle is too freely used for the common welfare ; and the public do not seem fully alive to the accidents to which its use gives rise.—*Daily Mail*, p. 4, April 22, 1901.

47. By reducing the cost of ocean-travel the Morgan Syndicate expects to increase the number of passengers on the Atlantic ferry vastly. —*Daily Express*, p. 1, April 30, 1901.

48. You seem to think that orders have only gone abroad because those who gave them did not understand their business.—*Ibid.* p. 5, June 1, 1901.

49. His Majesty has arranged to personally receive a number of distinguished visitors at the Castle to-day.—*Ibid.* p. 5, June 1, 1901.

50. The Fashoda incident never reached a dangerous point in France. Mr. Delcassé settled it before the public understood that the national dignity was involved with a skill for which mankind owes him more gratitude than some patriots are willing to concede.—*Fortnightly Review*, p. 1027, June 1901.

51. This would have meant a great expenditure of money, and we honestly do not see the duty.—*Spectator*, p. 906, June 22, 1901.

52. It was then the law of all Catholic countries that an ecclesiastic should only be handed over to the secular arm after having been found guilty, degraded from his sacred office, and stripped of his religious or sacerdotal habit.—*Ibid.* p. 970, June 29, 1901.

53. Any one who is interested in the question of the reform of the Italian University system will find an exhaustive study of the measure which is being advocated by Professor Buccelli, the present Minister of Public Instruction in Italy, in *La Reforme Sociale.*—*Review of Reviews*, p. 79, Jan. 1899.

54. Summing up, the Lord Chief Justice said he did not like to hear of a late officer in the army writing letters which contemplated the payment of money to public officials, nor of a firm of traders receiving such a communication and continuing to do business with the man who wrote it without a remonstrance.—*Daily Telegraph*, p. 8, June 19, 1901.

55. The sea off the West Coast is to a great extent studded with small islands and points of rock which must necessarily, in the fogs which there prevail, particularly in winter, render the approach extremely hazardous for vessels.—*Spectator*, p. 387, Sept. 21, 1901.

56. The great metropolitan hospitals have recognised its value by

offering to Oxford and Cambridge students only special scholarships on condition that they have completed the earlier—that is, the theoretical —part of their medical studies at the universities.—*Daily Telegraph*, p. 9, April 8, 1902.

57. It is certainly the tax most open to objection, and therefore the tax which ought to be the first to go under improved circumstances.— *Spectator*, p. 828, May 31, 1902.

58. It will be a war on sea instead of on land largely, and we do not know much about sea-warfare of late years.—Quoted in *Daily Telegraph*, April 15, 1898.

59. At Trefriw in Wales is to be seen a danger-board which states: "Notice to cyclists—This hill is dangerous by order of the authorities." While they were in the vein they might as well have ordered it to be safe.—*Daily Telegraph*, p. 7, Aug. 26, 1899.

60. Subtle, proud, daring, resolute, and an accomplished hypocrite, she disguises a long-cherished hatred of her husband, resulting from the sacrifice of her daughter at Aulis, under a cloak of love-sick affection.—Paley's *Æschylus*, p. 320.

61. The Dutch Government is resolved to set its face against any demonstrations, nor will it permit Mr. K. to establish a centre of political intrigue against a friendly power in Holland.—*Daily Telegraph*, p. 9, Oct. 25, 1900.

62. According to the same correspondent, the British Consul at Marseilles has made an investigation, together with a police official, as to the incident which took place yesterday.—*Ibid.* p. 9, Nov. 24, 1900.

63. It has too often been our habit in dealing with the Chinese to forget the crimes committed by them on the first appearance of repentance.—*Blackwood's Magazine*, p. 289, Aug. 1900.

64. The writer contemplates the possibility of the conversion of the four hundred millions of China into a military people with dread.— *Review of Reviews*, p. 290, March 1901.

65. Political bitterness only yields the palm to religious.—*Educational Review* (Madras), p. 59, Feb. 1900.

66. He seldom took up the Bible, which he frequently did, without shedding tears.—Knowles, *Life of Fuseli*, vol. i. p. 389 (H).

67. His last journey was to Cannes, whence he was never destined to return.—Mrs. Grote, *Life of George Grote*, ch. xxix. p. 245.

68. I was informed that the troubles with the students had only a political importance in so far as it had awakened new ideas among the workmen.—*Daily Mail*, p. 5, April 15, 1901.

69. We are informed by the Cunard Company that the shaft was practically a new one, only having been fitted a little over a year ago. —*Daily Telegraph*, p. 9, March 5, 1902.

70. But I do not believe that Aristotle will prevail, as you do. The growth of the Aristotelian spirit will soon call out a corresponding growth of the Platonic.—*Spectator*, p. 86, Jan. 17, 1903.

71. The portrait of President Roosevelt, specially taken for *The World's Work*, gives one side of the character of the man portrayed— namely, his strength and tenacity—with wonderful exactness.—*Ibid.* p. 135, Jan. 24, 1903.

72. The laws of this country are not contained in fewer than fifty folio volumes.—Paley, *Morals* i. 4.

73. Surprise was felt in the House of Commons at the fact that the Land Values Bill was only rejected by a majority of thirteen, despite the opposition of the Government to the measure.—*Daily Telegraph*, p. 10, March 28, 1903.

74. The salt-merchants, the grocers, the confectioners conspired together to adulterate the articles in which they dealt in a thousand ways.—ALISON, *History of Europe.*

75. Hence the despotic state will be generally successful, if a contest occurs, in the outset.—*Ibid.*

76. I have written the history of the Mar-Prelate Faction in *Quarrels of Authors*, which our historians appear not to have known. —D'ISRAELI, *Curiosities of Literature.*

77. One species of bread, of coarse quality, was only allowed to be baked.—*Ibid.*

78. The sublime Longinus in somewhat a later period preserved the spirit of ancient Athens.—GIBBON, *Decline and Fall.*

(e) *Prepositions.*

1. Two words with every Preposition.—The function of a preposition is to show what one person or thing has to do with another person or thing. To denote these two persons or things there must be at least two words accompanying every preposition. The governed word is that which depends on the preposition, and is called its Object. The other, which may be called the principal or governing word, is that on which the preposition itself depends.

The Object of a preposition is always a noun or a noun-equivalent, *i.e.* a word or combination of words which is made to do duty for a noun :—

Listen to *what I say* . . . . (*Noun-clause.*)
He has gone from *here* . . . . (*Adverb.*)

The principal or governing word may be either a noun, or an adjective, or an adverb, or a verb ; and the verb may be either Finite, or Infinitive, or a Participle :—

A *bird* in the hand . . . . (*Noun.*)
Short of money . . . . (*Adjective.*)
Adversely to my interests . . . (*Adverb.*)
He *sat* on the grass . . . . (*Verb.*)

2. Position of Object.—The general and almost invariable rule for the position of the Object is that the Object is placed immediately after its preposition. This rule is so commonly observed in practice that there is no need to give any examples.

Note.—When the Object is a Relative or Interrogative pronoun, the preposition may be placed after it :—as, "*Whom* are you looking *for* ?" "This is the man *whom* I was looking *for*." If the Relative takes the form of *that*, the preposition is always placed after it :—as, "This is the man *that* I was looking *for.*" We have also the familiar phrase, "All the world *over.*"

3. Position of the governing word.—(*a*) If the governing word is a noun, an adjective, or an adverb, the preposition, with its object, is almost always placed immediately after it, as in the examples given above :—

A bird in the hand	(*Noun.*)
Short of money	(*Adjective.*)
Adversely to my interests	(*Adverb.*)

But we cannot always avoid separating a preposition from its governing word. In such an example as the following the separation is inevitable, and because it is felt to be inevitable, it produces no ill effect in point either of clearness or euphony :—

> Both of these new books answer to the *demand*, very natural when taste is chaotic and literature voluminous, *for* some guidance in discriminating between good and bad.—*Literature*, p. 160, Feb. 24, 1900.

There is no excuse, however, for such a misplacement as the following :—

> One of the combatants was unhurt, and the other sustained a wound in the arm of no importance.—Quoted in *Punch*, Oct. 5, 1872. (Say "sustained in the arm a wound of no importance.")

(*b*) If the governing word is a verb, the preposition with its Object may be placed either before or after it,—more usually after. But in either case it must be placed near enough to its governing word to prevent ambiguity or an unpleasing effect :—

> On these two commandments hang all the law and the prophets.— *New Test.* (Here the preposition with its Object is placed before the governing word "hang." It receives emphasis from standing first.)
>
> In 1238 Henry gave him his sister Eleanor, widow of the eldest son of William Marshall, the Regent, in marriage.—*Short History of England*, p. 100. (Here "in marriage" is placed after "gave"; but it is too far off. Say "gave him in marriage.")

4. Several Prepositions dependent on the same word.— When the governing word has several prepositions (each followed by a separate Object of its own) depending on it, it is sometimes convenient to put one of the prepositions with its object first :—

> (1) Herod is bound, body and soul, by an overwhelming passion to his haughty and beautiful wife.—*Fortnightly Review*, p. 180, Jan. 1901.

There is an awkwardness in placing "passion" before "to," and in placing "to" so far away from "bound." To avoid this say :—

To his haughty and beautiful wife Herod is bound, body and soul, by an overwhelming passion.

(2) The action of Germany in storing a quantity of coal on one of the islands of the Farson group has caused considerable irritation in Constantinople. The Porte has suggested the creation on the same island by the Ottoman Admiralty of a coaling station, which would replace the German station, and to which all the other Powers would have access.—*Daily Telegraph*, p. 10, Oct. 26, 1900.

In the second sentence three different prepositions, each followed by a separate Object of its own, are dependent on one word, "creation." The effect is bad. The sentence might be recast thus :—

The Porte has suggested that a coaling station, which would replace the German one, and to which all the other Powers would have access, should be created on the same island by the Ottoman Admiralty.

5. Preposition at end of sentence.—As a general rule a preposition should not be placed at the end of a sentence. It is not strong enough to stand in a place of so much emphasis and importance :—

Bishop J. A. M'Faul, writing on "Catholics and American Citizenship," maintains that American citizens, because they are Catholics, are discriminated *against.—Review of Reviews*, p. 384, Oct. 1900. (Say "do not receive equal treatment.")

The first duty of an agitator is to be sincere, and want of sincerity is a charge that the agitators against alien immigration have certainly laid themselves open *to.—Spectator*, p. 364, March 7, 1903. (Since *that* as a Relative cannot have a preposition placed before it, we must say, "a charge *to which* the agitators against alien immigration have laid themselves open.")

This precaution, however, does not hold good when the verb is "a prepositional verb," *i.e.* when the preposition and the verb have become so closely associated in idea or usage as to form a compound, which can be used in the Passive voice :—

He dislikes being laughed at.

Correct, improve, or justify the following sentences :—

1. The substantial aid the Colonies are giving us show how welcome would be to their forces a more complete union with our own.— *Fortnightly Review*, p. 492, March 1900.

2. Such a camp would afford an opportunity for giving a different kind of instruction and training, but one no less valuable perhaps, from that which is given in the schoolroom.—*Review of Reviews*, p. 611, Dec. 1899.

3. In 1238 Henry gave him his sister Eleanor, widow of the eldest son of William Marshall, the regent, in marriage.—*Short History of England*, p. 100.

4. It is also to be borne in mind that the construction of a railway through at present waste land could lead to great developments; for the natural resources of the territory are great.—*Review of Reviews,* p. 580, Dec. 1899.

5. Four experienced and well-known officers have been appointed to fill the chief diplomatic positions at respectively Vienna, Madrid, Brussels, and Rio de Janeiro.—*Daily Telegraph,* p. 6, Aug. 8, 1900.

6. An Egyptian army, led and officered by Englishmen, had, after some years and a series of difficulties, freed Egypt and the Soudan, and restored a territory which was formerly given up to barbarism to civilisation.—Quoted in *Daily Telegraph,* p. 11, Nov. 1, 1899.

7. We can still, with every hope of success, combat the obtaining by the London United Tramways Company of a monopoly.—*Middlesex County Times,* p. 9, Oct. 21, 1899.

8. In a recent number of *Literature* the discovery at Florence was announced of a series of documents bearing on the family of Dante.—*Literature,* p. 319, Sept. 30, 1899.

9. In the same number is an important plea for the social emancipation of woman from the pen of A. Lusignoli.—*Review of Reviews,* p. 592, Dec. 1898.

10. It is impossible to omit mention in this connection of the curious devices often adopted to encourage drinking of wine.—*Fortnightly Review,* p. 260, Aug. 1899.

11. As regards the sale of liquor, I hold that very different restrictions and regulations are demanded from those which prevail.—Quoted in *Daily Telegraph,* p. 5, Aug. 29, 1899.

12. Medical men in the parish of Marylebone are greatly concerned at the appearance during the last few weeks of excessively hot weather of numerous cases which indicate sickness coming within the description of English cholera.—*Ibid.* p. 7, Aug. 7, 1899.

13. Lord Stanhope will call attention to the effect on the operation of the Sugar bounties of recent legislation in India.—*Ibid.* p. 7, July 20, 1899.

14. There was a tremendous rush on Saturday to take excisable articles out of bond, and there were in consequence numerous applications for loans to bankers.—*Ibid.* p. 8, March 5, 1900.

15. At the Royal Dublin Society's Cattle Show the £100 cup presented to the Society for competition in the Shorthorn bull class by Her Majesty the Queen was won by Mr. Armstrong.—*Ibid.* p. 6, April 19, 1900.

16. Men are not encouraged by such an incident as the shooting of the son of a field-cornet who tried to induce some of the Federals in the senior state to surrender by an irreconcilable named C.—*Ibid.* p. 10, June 22, 1900.

17. It was with the approval of Mr. Balfour and Mr. Chamberlain that the Secretary to the Local Government Board withdrew the schedule fixing a maximum rate of interest from the Money-lending bill.—*Daily Telegraph,* p. 9, June 28, 1900.

18. The Italian nation would have been jarred to the very soul by any outbreak round the corpse of its murdered sovereign of the disastrous feud between the Vatican and the Quirinal, which vitiates the whole political life of the Italian kingdom.—*Ibid.* p. 4, Aug. 10, 1900.

19. Referring to Peel's robbing his opponents, by timely conversion to their views, of their well-earned triumph, Mr. Birrell remarks as follows.—*Review of Reviews*, p. 464, May 1899.

20. The force sent at so much expense and with so many difficulties to conquer to Rhodesia has a further part to play in the operations.—*Daily Telegraph*, p. 9, Sept. 12, 1900.

21. One could not help coveting the privileges they enjoyed for one's sister.—Miss EDWARDS, *A Winter with the Swallows*, ch. xiv. p. 236 (H).

22. There is a very strong movement now on foot among the Federal farmers against the intimidation that has sent hundreds and probably thousands of farmers, who were tired of the war, and had taken the oath intending to keep it, back to the front.—*Daily Telegraph*, p. 10, Sept. 18, 1900.

23. Having read in Dr. Gerhard the admirable effects of swallowing a gold bullet upon his father.—SOUTHEY, *The Doctor*.

24. In theory every knot of increased speed above twenty knots gives an approximate reduction in the time of the voyage of seven hours.—*Daily Telegraph*, p. 8, Dec. 26, 1899.

25. Mr. Yeats has an overdose of symbol. His "Cloths of Heaven" are too much embroidered with, to mundane eyes, inscrutable insignia.—*Literature*, p. 439, April 29, 1899.

26. The axis will shift, therefore, of many sins and of great offences.—*Fortnightly Review*, p. 571, Oct. 1900.

27. In the House of Assembly to-day Mr. M. submitted a motion deprecating the publication by the Imperial Government without his knowledge of a Blue-book containing his letter to Mr. De W., an alleged rebel.—*Daily Telegraph*, p. 9, Oct. 10, 1900.

28. Most of the people (except the Mashonas and Matabeles) among whom I have travelled I have formed some attachment to.—Quoted in *Review of Reviews*, p. 359, Oct. 1900.

29. It needs nothing but the presence of the conquering white man, decked in his shoddy clothes, armed with his gas-pipe gun, his Bible in his hand, schemes of benevolence deep-rooted in his heart, his merchandise (that is, his whisky, gin, and cotton cloths) securely stored in his corrugated iron sheds, and he himself active and persevering as a beaver or red ant, to bring about a sickness which exterminates the people, whom he came to benefit, to bless, and to rescue from savagery.—*Ibid.* p. 400, Oct. 1900.

30. Europe desires to see weakened the non-warlike influence over China of Russia, which has increased of late enormously.—*Daily Telegraph*, p. 9, Oct. 24, 1900.

31. That the power for mischief of the Federals is far from being at an end is apparent from the latest despatch from Lord Roberts.—*Ibid.* p. 8, Oct. 25, 1900.

32. I was less able to praise the sort of fiction we Americans imagine ourselves to have surpassed the remnant of the Anglo-Saxon world in. —*Literature*, p. 473, May 6, 1899.

33. The governor has been invested with a broader control over the entrance to and residence at the fortress-town of strangers, whether of British or alien birth.—*Daily Telegraph*, p. 8, Nov. 8, 1900.

34. The truth in all fulness, he would argue, is the one thing

M

an historian is concerned about.—GRAHAM, *Victorian Literature*, p. 213.

35. I was awoke at three o'clock on Sunday morning by a concert of a very unusual kind to my ears, and tempted by the unwonted strains I stole down into the garden.—Sir RICHARD OWEN, quoted in *Victorian Literature*, p. 469.

36. It is contended that the Emperor should return to his own again, and that all business should be transacted with Li-Hung-Chang and the other plenipotentiaries under his sole authority. — *Daily Telegraph*, p. 7, Nov. 16, 1900.

37. Very much more proof will be required of that fact than the prevalence among the tenant-farmers of the province of the feeling that they have been less liberally dealt with for a year or so than they used to be.—*Spectator*, p. 738, Nov. 24, 1900.

38. These people have done their best to degrade the tone of public life to as low a level as it had sunk to in the days when corruption and jobbery permeated every fibre of the body politic. —*Daily Telegraph*, p. 9, Nov. 28, 1900.

39. The people of the Punjab are now paying the inevitable penalty for the rains and floods that covered the country with water during the monsoon months in the shape of a severe visitation of autumn fever.—*Pioneer Mail*, p. 8, Nov. 2, 1900.

40. I do not pursue the matter except to say that I saw the line taken on many occasions of imputing disloyalty and want of patriotism to men quite as loyal and patriotic, though differing from themselves in opinion, on the other side.—Quoted in *Daily Telegraph*, p. 10, Dec. 7, 1900.

41. The Mayor (of Cape Town) has been called upon to decide in what way the services can be utilised of men unable, owing to urgent business reasons, to devote their whole time to operations in the field.—*Ibid.* p. 7, Jan. 4, 1901.

42. The island of Zanzibar and the island of Pemba have an area of about one thousand square miles between them, with a population of some 200,000.—*Daily Express*, p. 4, Jan. 30, 1901.

43. Professor B. D. of Owens College has expressed the opinion that coal measures would be found under the county of Kent in various publications.—Quoted in *Daily Telegraph*, p. 5, Feb. 14, 1901.

44. The Macedonian propaganda has now assumed too large dimensions, and too strongly influences the popular opinion, for it to be suppressed arbitrarily.—*Ibid.* p. 8, Feb. 22, 1901.

45. Whatever they (foreigners) take in hand can only be a success, provided native sentiment and prejudices are studied and shown consideration for.—*North American Review*, p. 71, Jan. 1901.

46. When they are working in association, opportunities for the exchange of remarks occur, and these they are not slow to avail themselves of.—*Fortnightly Review*, p. 564, March 1901.

47. There is a business aspect in libel to a newspaper. It sometimes pays to have libels in newspaper columns.—Quoted in *Daily Telegraph*, p. 7, March 27, 1901.

48. Perhaps the most pleasing feature in the more recent aspects of South African questions has been the recoil upon the engineers of

the anti-Milner cabal of their own machinations.—*Ibid.* p. 7, March 29, 1901.

49. All the enthusiastic descriptions of the wild horses in the pampas or in the steppe can be paralleled (parallelled ?) by the pictures drawn by delighted hunters and travellers, men well used to see and judge the comparative beauty of animals, of the wild zebra.—*Spectator,* p. 651, May 4, 1901.

50. The rule obtained by the suspended District Superintendent of Police, Noakhali, to quash the proceedings instituted against him for perjury, forging, and using as genuine a forged document by the Sessions Judge, came in for hearing at the High Court, Calcutta, yesterday.—*Pioneer Mail,* p. 10, May 3, 1901.

51. The Master of Baliol said it was very difficult to disconnect anything relating to the war with South Africa from politics.—*Daily Telegraph,* p. 9, June 26, 1901.

52. The classical game of whist, which to be master of was an intellectual distinction, the terror of beginners, the wonder of observers, is now only indulged in by a few antiquated fossils, etc.—*Fortnightly Review,* p. 153, July 1901.

53. The limitation compels him to reject several pieces of superior merit to those he has included.—*Standard,* p. 2, Sept. 16, 1901.

54. Directly, it leads to the diverting of money needed to strengthen and enlarge the capacity of the existing trade connection ; indirectly, it results in the withdrawal from a personal supervision of the business of the younger and more active members of the firm.—*Spectator,* p. 386, Sept. 21, 1901.

55. To-day, forty-three years ago, the death took place in Vienna of Baron Ward, an extraordinary man, who had been Prime Minister at the Court of Parma.—*Daily Telegraph,* p. 10, Sept. 24, 1901.

56. He is necessarily dependent upon books like De Quincey's *Essays* or Lamb's *Letters,* which are probably familiar to most of his readers, for his materials.—*Spectator,* p. 452, Oct. 5, 1901.

57. Five bodies of armed men—Russian, German, Anglo-Indian, French, and Japanese—are standing on the same ground, with little to do, with no enemy whom they all fear, with no fully acknowledged Commander - in - Chief, and with internal jealousies, arising from differences of nationality, of discipline, and of pay, of the most pronounced description.—*Ibid.* p. 448, March 30, 1901.

58. All manner of reports are coming from Spain, the general drift of which is that the Carlists intend to protest against the assumption of power by the young King, who comes of age next year, by a serious rising.—*Ibid.* p. 502, Oct. 12, 1901.

59. We are justified from the extraordinary effect produced by the little and still uncompleted line to Kunlon on trade with the Shan States and Zimmé in assuming that when railways are built into Yunnan the trade with Western China will go up by leaps and bounds.—BOULGER, *Fortnightly Review,* p. 690, Oct. 1901.

60. We hear it used every day to throw doubt on the latest marvels of science by the unscientific.—*Spectator,* p. 663, Nov. 2, 1901.

61. We have often spoken before of the unfair advantages which papers which are registered as newspapers have over papers not so

registered in the matter of postal rates.—*Literature*, p. 262, March 11, 1899.

62. I and others have been in conversation during the later developments of the crisis with the Liberal Ministers who have been silent.— *Daily Telegraph*, p. 5, Oct. 3, 1899.

63. A pronounced taste for table-turning and for the invocation of the spirits of defunct celebrities has just brought a respectable dressmaker, who retired from business a few months ago on a comfortable income of £300 a year, into sad trouble.—*Ibid.* p. 11, Dec. 10, 1901.

64. Mr. A. C. Morton objected at the City Corporation meeting to 200 guineas being spent on decorations for Mr. Chamberlain's visit.— *Daily Express*, p. 1, Jan. 31, 1901.

65. The *National Review* is chiefly remarkable for a long, carefully developed, and most able proposal of a scheme for the reconstruction of South Africa, by "Johannesburg."—*Spectator*, p. 521, April 5, 1902.

66. I find it impossible to censure Mr. Rhodes's participation in the circumstances which led to the Raid on moral grounds.—IWAN MÜLLER, *Lord Milner and South Africa.*

67. The cordon has been drawn, which is, if possible, to prevent the raiders now retiring before the great British force which is working through the eastern portions of the colony from the north from breaking away southwards.—*Daily Telegraph*, p. 10, Oct. 11, 1900.

68. On this side of the Channel we are ready to let many bygones be bygones, because of the Queen's visit to, and the great reception she received in, Ireland.—*Ealing Gazette*, p. 8, March 26, 1900.

69. The alteration secured that every scheme should provide for the appointment by the Council, on the nomination, where it appeared desirable, of other bodies, including associations of voluntary schools, of educational experts and persons acquainted with the needs of the various kinds of schools in the area for which the Council acted.— *Spectator*, p. 927, Dec. 13, 1902.

70. When she prattles about herself and her admirers, she makes the reader blush for the shamefacedness she evidently does not even guess at the lack of.—*Ibid.* p. 155, Jan. 31, 1903.

71. Shut out by the sterility of the soil and the variable nature of the climate, where storms of rain and snow, attracted by the cold summits of the Alps, are frequent, from the labours of agriculture, they dwell in the mountains with their flocks and herds only in the winter and spring.—ALISON, *History of Europe from Fall of Napoleon.*

72. Indeed, were we to judge of German reading habits from these volumes of ours, we should draw quite a different conclusion to Paul's. —CARLYLE, *Miscellanies.*

73. Hence he considered marriage with a modern political economist as very dangerous.—D'ISRAELI, *Curiosities of Literature.*

74. The Canadian Pacific Railway Company has inaugurated a scheme for pensioning its old servants of an unique character.—*Lloyd's Weekly News*, p. 8, April 5, 1903.

(f) Correlative Conjunctions.

Correlative conjunctions, *i.e.* conjunctions which go in pairs, should be made to occupy corresponding positions, so that each member of the pair shall stand before words of the same or a similar part of speech or having the same functional value in the sentence. The misplacement of such conjunctions "produces the same ill-balanced effect as would a pair of crookedly hung pictures" (Hodgson). What is still worse, it might possibly produce obscurity.

(1) *Not . . . but :*—

A wise physician endeavours not to cure diseases, but to prevent them. (*Infinitive mood.*)
Objections were raised not to his having spent the money, but to his having done so without leave. (*Preposition followed by gerund.*)

(2) *Not only . . . but also, but :*—

This not only amused, but enlightened them. (*Verb.*)
He was not only sad, but disgusted. (*Adjective and Participle.*)
All his work was done not only with zeal, but also with judgment. (*Preposition followed by noun.*)

(3) *Not more . . . than :*—

I am not more amused than (I am) surprised. (*Verb.*)

(4) *Both . . . and :*—

Tired out both in mind and in body. (*Preposition.*)
Tired out in both mind and body. (*Noun.*)

(5) *Either . . . or, neither . . . nor :*—

They have worked either stupidly or lazily. (*Adverb.*)
This wall was built either crookedly or of bad material. (*Adverb and adverbial phrase.*)
Neither James nor I saw it. (*Noun and pronoun.*)

In the following sentences the position of the conjunctions is correct :—

On the other hand, the desire of the French for the Alliance springs, as we have shown above, from the very nature of the people,— which neither has changed nor will change.—*Spectator*, p. 272, Aug. 31, 1901.
They should take note not only how powerful was the national movement, but how that movement was stimulated. — *Ibid.* p. 462, Oct. 6, 1900.
The attack of skirmishers in line was adopted both by ourselves and by the federals, because neither we nor they knew better.— *Ibid.* p. 522, April 13, 1901.

They show, too, that he who rows not only may read, but generally does read. The discipline of training suits neither the dissipated nor the idle.—*Ibid.* p. 519, April 4, 1903.

In the following sentences the conjunctions are not properly placed :—

It is neither the duty of Germany to recognise it nor to dispute it.—*Spectator,* p. 37, Jan. 10, 1903. (Say, "neither to recognise it nor to dispute it.")

Fuseli made this observation not only in reference to the physiognomic cast of David's countenance, but his face was also disfigured by a hare-lip.—KNOWLES, *Life of Fuseli,* vol. i. p. 258 (H). (This cannot be corrected by a mere change of order. Say, "in reference not only to the physiognomic cast of David's countenance, but also to the disfigurement of his face by a hare-lip.")

For God sent not his Son into the world to condemn the world, but that the world through him might be saved.—*John* iii. 17. (Say, "sent his Son into the world not to condemn the world, but that the world," etc.)

Correct, improve, or justify the following sentences :—

1. The Greek language had obtained such a vogue in Rome itself, that all the great and noble men of the city were obliged not only to learn, but ambitious everywhere to speak it.—MIDDLETON'S *Life of Cicero,* vol. i. p. 94.

2. The English dramatists are truer to the substance of things, to universal human nature, while the French seem to be in great part an imitation, having root neither in the soil of France nor Athens.—C. D. WARNER, *The People for whom Shakespeare Wrote,* p. 173.

3. There has just died at Clapham a gentlewoman, whose demise will not only be regretted by all those who knew her, but by every constable throughout the metropolis.—*Daily Tel.* p. 10, Oct. 18, 1900.

4. The leaders of the opposition neither have the spirit nor the time to bring home to the mind of the general elector how much he will have to pay for his whistle.—*Review of Reviews,* p. 334, Oct. 1900.

5. In the Democratic platform, therefore, we find trusts not only severely denounced, but a remedy for the evil suggested.—*Ibid.* p. 356, Oct. 1900.

6. The voter is either becoming a Nationalist or a Socialist.—*Daily Express,* p. 4, June 18, 1901.

7. Morally either the war is just or unjust, either the methods are civilised or barbarous. — Lord ROSEBERY'S *Letter, Daily Telegraph,* p. 9, July 17, 1901.

8. As destitute of the constructive power of the masterly Piedmontese as of the inspired idealism of Mazzini, Crispi was neither among the architects nor the prophets of the unification of Italy.—*Daily Telegraph,* p. 6, Aug. 12, 1901.

9. He is here not only aloof from actualities—giving hardly one practical illustration throughout the book—but his manner is throughout too much that of the academic essayist.—*Literature,* Jan. 1900.

10. Was not the admission of the Government that they were ignorant of the state of unpreparedness not only a condemnation of them but of the agent on the spot, who now we were told to implicitly trust?—*Mr. Morley's Speech,* quoted in *Daily Telegraph,* p. 10, Nov. 1, 1901.

11. Instead, we had neither the pluck for the renunciation nor for the maintenance of our rights, but contented ourselves with such verbal poultices as those contained in the two Conventions.—*Spectator,* p. 687, Nov. 9, 1901.

12. He has been nearly five years Commander-in-Chief, and yet he has waited till now to speak out concerning matters in regard to which he had not merely a perfect right to speak, but in regard to which he had a positive duty to speak.—*Ibid,* p. 231, Aug. 25, 1900.

13. The Japanese are known to be most successful in teaching their convicts not only trades, but in making many of them good artists in *cloisonné* and other work.—*Ibid.* p. 943, Dec. 14, 1901.

14. Herr Ridder declared that Prince Henry had violated the Monroe Doctrine in seizing as representative of the Emperor not one spot of ground, but in capturing and making his own all Americans. —*Daily Telegraph,* p. 9, Feb. 28, 1902.

15. Yet of women I should imagine it is truer than of most people; for while they accept either the position of tyrant or slave towards the other sex, they are always critics to their own.—*Ibid.* p. 6, Jan. 28, 1903.

16. You are not obliged to take any money which is not gold or silver; not only the halfpence or farthings of England, but of any other country.—Swift.

(g) *Miscellaneous Examples.*

Correct, improve, or justify the following sentences :—

1. He has the misfortune when returning to Royston to protect his villagers to fall foul of Kirke's "lambs," who pursue him into the very grounds of Drayton Manor.—*Daily Telegraph,* p. 11, June 8, 1900.

2. I am convinced that the vital interests of those who have to live in South Africa and who are at present our enemies will, as well as those on our side, demand that there shall not be two dissimilar antagonistic systems in that which nature and history have decided shall be *one* country.—*Ibid.* p. 5, April 13, 1900.

3. In spite of all his efforts and entreaties he could not get successive Ministries, which trembled at the bare thought of the hereditary enemy, to move.—*Ibid.* p. 8, Aug. 8, 1899.

4. When this prevails in Madras schools, the centre of education, worse will be the case for Mofussil village schools.—*Educational Review* (Madras), p. 63, Feb. 1900.

5. He is the educated native, who can neither go forward nor back, who has left his old beliefs, and finds no place or comprehension in the new.—*Daily Telegraph,* p. 11, June 1, 1900.

6. Their loyalty is not worth any moment a clear day's purchase. —*Ibid.* p. 6, July 20, 1900.

7. These agents profess to already detect signs that England is

getting utterly weary and sick of the struggle.—*Ibid.* p. 9, July 7, 1900.

8. As the leading and consistent champion of the oppressed, I trust you will permit me in your columns to advocate the cause of humanity towards helpless animals.—*Ibid.* Jan. 6, 1898.

9. Outside the immediate theatre of war there is no place that looms so prominently on the horizon of the affairs of the world perhaps as Delagoa Bay.—*Pearson's Weekly*, p. 708, April 28, 1900.

10. According to a usually reliable authority it is estimated that about one-eighth of the canal only will have to be wholly artificial, and that only two locks will be needed.—*United Service Magazine*, quoted in *Review of Reviews*, p. 138, Feb. 15, 1899.

11. Dr. Walker, who is already known as the translator of Ostwald's *Outlines of Physical Chemistry*, also is a lecturer of great experience.—*Literature*, p. 134, Feb. 10, 1900.

12. In the House of Peers the Earl of S. denounced the imputations contained in a question put by —— regarding the dismissal of a Ceylon official as a gross abuse of Parliamentary privilege.—*Daily Telegraph*, p. 8, June 30, 1899.

13. The British North Borneo Company have decided to immediately construct a railway from Gaya to Tinon, a point ninety miles in the interior.—*Ibid.* p. 3, Jan. 27, 1900.

14. Charles Villiers of late years enjoyed the distinction of being the oldest member of the House of Commons, and only died in 1898.—HUNTER's *Short History of England*, p. 435, ed. 1898.

15. Behind them stood great Berlin houses, and behind these was another imperial policy than the policy of imperial England.—Quoted in *Review of Reviews*, p. 156, Feb. 15, 1899.

16. Political bitterness only yields the palm to religious.—*Educational Review* (Madras), p. 59, Feb. 1900.

17. So well is the impracticability of the scheme of settlement recognised even by the conciliationists themselves, that none of them has ventured to explicitly champion it.—*Fort. Review*, p. 844, May 1900.

18. They are confronted every morning with the, to them, insoluble problem of obtaining a single day's material existence.—*Daily Telegraph*, p. 8, Sept. 14, 1900.

19. The Queen opened the new and handsome buildings of the University of London in Burlington Gardens on Wednesday, in the designs and execution of which Mr. Pennethorne is thought to have surpassed himself, with a ceremonial of some pomp.—*Spectator*, p. 601, May 14, 1870 (H).

20. He seldom took up the Bible, which he frequently did, without shedding tears.—KNOWLES, *Life of Fuseli*, vol. i. p. 389 (H).

21. They flocked down here, not before, however, destroying their guns and ammunition.—*Daily Telegraph*, p. 9, Sept. 26, 1900.

22. To this force Gordon was attached, and he remained there (at Tientsin) until the Chinese government having sufficiently complied with treaty obligations, headquarters were moved to Shanghai in the spring of 1862.—*Fort. Review*, p. 379, Sept. 1900.

23. This movement is too far more intensely a patriotic movement than that of which we have recently witnessed the outburst in Peking.—*Ibid.* p. 516, Sept. 1900.

24. In both cases, however, both Israelites and Boers were mistaken. Neither Palestine nor the Transvaal belongs either to the Israelite or the Boer.—Quoted in *Spectator*, p. 409, Sept. 29, 1900.

25. The cordon has been drawn which is, if possible, to prevent the raiders now retiring before the great British force which is working through the eastern portion of the colony from the north from breaking away southwards.—*Daily Telegraph*, p. 10, Oct. 11, 1900.

26. Such an attack, provided the neutrality of Belgium and Switzerland were not violated, could only be accomplished by breaking through the line of French fortresses.—*Review of Reviews*, p. 347, April 1900.

27. The searching reforms which are required can only be carried through by Secretaries who have the energetic support of a Premier with his intellect and his time unemployed by departmental duties.—*Spectator*, p. 609, Nov. 3, 1900.

28. It would be the possible advent to power in France of a "Nationalist" Ministry which would call on Russia to do something to prove the reality of her alliance that would precipitate trouble.—*Ibid.* p. 651, Nov. 10, 1900.

29. There was a renewal of the gale in the channel yesterday, and it is feared that the whole crew have been lost of a vessel which went ashore on the Sussex coast.—*Daily Express*, p. 1, Nov. 13, 1900.

30. We cannot reiterate too often, that in modern days the true analogy of the prophets are the journalists of the most immoderate style.—RENAN, *History of Israel*, vol. iii. p. 285.

31. In free trade she (Japan) finds the means of repaying her indebtedness to the western nations,—especially to the United States which first introduced her into the family of nations,—who imbued her with the spirit of modern civilisation. — Quoted in *Daily Telegraph*, p. 10, Nov. 21, 1900.

32. W. H. W. pleaded guilty to a charge of bigamy, having married Miss H. C. H., a hospital nurse, from whom he obtained a considerable amount of money and jewellery, while his wife was alive.—*Ibid.* p. 4, Dec. 11, 1900.

33. It was plain that the "new woman" meant a too violent departure from what must under any circumstances be the normal type of womanhood, to last.—*Spectator*, p. 838, Dec. 8, 1900.

34. There remains a very copious supply of creditable literature in the autumn lists to be dealt with.—*Fort. Review*, p. 10, Dec. 28, 1900.

35. On the whole it may be said that the change from anonymous to signed articles has followed the course of most changes. It has not led to one half either of the evils or of the advantages that its advocates and its opponents foretold.—MORLEY, *Fortnightly Review*, p. 110, Jan. 1901.

36. What were, so to speak, the ground plan of that marvellous character, the inherent qualities that composed the man, I may be allowed to quote from a work of my own, etc.—*Fortnightly Review*, p. 132, Jan. 1901.

37. But we are aware from the rising of the curtain of the seeds of inevitable tragedy already ripening in the characters and circumstances set before us, without the need of any external fate or hovering prophecy at all.—*Ibid.* p. 180, Jan. 1901.

38. Herod is bound, body and soul, by an overwhelming passion to his haughty and beautiful wife.—*Ibid.* p. 180, Jan. 1901.

39. Mr. H. said that the accident at Liverpool had been caused through the Board of Trade regulations as to guard wires not having been complied with.—*Middlesex County Times*, p. 2, Feb. 9, 1901.

40. A little German book for instance appeared the other day intended to present us in a not unhandsome light, and approved in sober circles across the Rhine as a wholesome corrective of pan-German prejudice.—*Fortnightly Review*, p. 346, Feb. 1901.

41. In the first place there must be no doubt as to the extinction as sovereign independent states of the late Republics ; that is to say, of their annexation to the Crown.—*Daily Telegraph*, p. 9, Feb. 20, 1901.

42. India, which is still of all England's possessions the largest customer for her goods, imported goods from England to the value of fully $156,000,000 ; but she only sent goods to Great Britain—and those to a large extent manufactured goods, and therefore less profitable,—to the value of $136,000,000.—LUSK, *North American Review*, p. 107, Jan. 1901.

43. To those acquainted with the conditions under which competing industries are carried on to-day, it is well known that almost an inappreciable difference in the price paid by the consumer means prosperity or ruin to the producer.—*Empire Review*, p. 208, March 1901.

44. As a Minister the Sovereign has a right to demand from Lord Palmerston that she be made thoroughly acquainted with the whole object and tendency of the policy to which her consent is required.—Quoted in *Fortnightly Review*, p. 428, March 1901.

45. Sir Henry Burdett considered that ground landlords should be compelled, when they dishoused to rebuild, to rehouse the inhabitants, as corporations were compelled to do.—*Daily Telegraph*, p. 6, March 20, 1901.

46. Holland was drawn into the league against England, while she contended against the right of searching neutral vessels for enemy's goods, asserted by England, and of vital importance to a maritime state in war with continental powers.—GOLDWIN SMITH, *United Kingdom*, vol. ii. p. 219.

47. Sir Henry traced our decline in trade to the present method of education, in his article of which the following is an abstract.—*Daily Express*, p. 3, Feb. 1, 1901.

48. On the other hand, we have a fuller and more systematic account of the part played in the war by the foreign auxiliaries of the Boers, nearly nine thousand in all, including six thousand Afrikanders, than has been previously supplied anywhere else.—*Spectator*, p. 603, Nov. 3, 1900.

49. As I write I can think of several cases of families where the breadwinner has come back drunk and ill-treated his wife without coming under the notice of the police with a regularity that is appalling.—Quoted in *Spectator*, p. 423, March 23, 1901.

50. Attic speech dominated the whole Greek world for centuries, with some small exceptions wrought artificially by literary men, such as the pastorals of Theocritus.—*Empire Review*, p. 264, April 1901.

51. I have had a feeling for some little time past that I at any rate, and perhaps the other guests in a lesser degree, was in a false

position, which it was necessary that I should explain.—Quoted in *Daily Telegraph*, p. 10, April 18, 1901.

52. Two of the greatest men, who through this last century have dealt with the finances of this country, have considered coal to be on a different footing to other matters.—*Ibid.* p. 11, April 19, 1901.

53. It will be well to utilise the time which must elapse before any of the works of peace can be undertaken in the Transvaal and Orange Colonies in carefully considering how best to carry them out.—Quoted in *Spectator*, p. 564, April 20, 1901.

54. He knows enough of the three R's to conduct the business of his large farm creditably, but until lately he did not know enough beyond what was necessary for this to enable him to appreciate, as he does to-day, the relative positions of the late Republics and Great Britain.—*Ibid.* p. 564, April 20, 1901.

55. It is obvious that a few such deals would menace the commercial sovereignty of the seas which is the real condition of our wealth and power and empire as it has never been menaced yet.—*Daily Telegraph*, p. 8, May 1, 1901.

56. One would think the coal-industry was a struggling industry desperately fighting for its life to hear the outcry.—*Daily Express*, p. 4, May 3, 1901.

57. Cromwell stands out from the chaos of abuse and eulogy which two hundred years have heaped on him as a living man, whose nature can be intelligently understood, and not as a monster of darkness or an impeccable saint.—*Spectator*, p. 622, April 27, 1901.

58. There can be little doubt that our military authorities would find themselves compelled to mobilise the three army corps at home supposed to be available for foreign service with the least possible delay.—*Fortnightly Review*, p. 702, April 1901.

59. If they work more, they must give up more time to their military duties, to which most of them give up quite as much time as they can afford already.—*Ibid.* p. 705, April 1901.

60. The most startling announcement made by the Secretary of State consisted in his statement that in future officers would only be given high commands at home if fit to command in the field.—*Ibid.* p. 705, April 1901.

61. Human nature could not bear such a hardship, and the men themselves provide another meal at about seven o'clock, when the hammocks are piped down, the character of which depends upon the depth of their purses.—*Ibid.* p. 718, April 1901.

62. She is an exceedingly wide-awake young lady, this "little woman," who adorns the pages of *Rosa Amorosa*, except in the matter of her terms of endearment.—*Daily Telegraph*, p. 11, May 8, 1901.

63. A feeling of the greatest unrest exists in official circles with respect to a revival of the Nihilist conspiracy which the students' disturbances have given vital force to.—*Daily Express*, p. 1, May 8, 1901.

64. The public mind has gathered with reluctance, from the proceedings in the House of Commons, a disappointing sense of the profound unreality and uselessness of the entire discussion.—*Daily Telegraph*, p. 8, May 15, 1901.

65. Of course I can give you an explanation for so doing as far as lies in my power.—*Ibid.* p. 11, May 18, 1901.

66. The soldier should use the time not spent in shooting and in (a very much reduced) drill, in producing his own food and clothing. —*Review of Reviews*, p. 457, May 1901.

67. The most interesting thing about the many letters from missionaries, who have barely escaped with their lives, which are published in this volume, is the entire absence of any vindictive feeling against the Chinese as a whole or even those who were most active in persecuting.—*Ibid.* p. 503, May 1901.

68. Of course, everybody knew (Mr. M. included) that Lord Milner referred, as the verbatim report of his address says, to "his Majesty's Government."—*Daily Telegraph*, p. 8, June 17, 1901.

69. There is scarcely a point at which according to received religious ideas man's life was in special contact with Heaven's purposes where the electricity of Shakespeare's all-expressive genius had not penetrated. —Sir E. RUSSELL, quoted in *Literature*, p. 323, April 28, 1900.

70. M. Ribot recalls the fact that the Comte de Mun tried to do something of the kind some years ago, and that, so far from being encouraged, he was begged to desist from his efforts by the heads of the French Episcopate.—*Review of Reviews*, p. 586, June 1901.

71. The secret of class-unpopularity is class-exemption, the fact that its members escape the liabilities which fall on other men merely by reason of their belonging to the class.—*Spect.* p. 116, July 27, 1901.

72. A telegram from Naples to this morning's Paris papers announces the arrival there, after forty-three years spent as a convict on Devil's Island, of Gomez, one of the four men condemned here with Orsini in 1858 for the attempt on the life of Napoleon III.—*Daily Express*, p. 1, Aug. 3, 1901.

73. Issues of graver importance than most people seem to be aware of are involved in the fresh compact that has just been arrived at between the Belgian Parliament and the Government of the huge African territory known as the Congo Free State, with reference to the ownership and administration of that territory.—H. R. FOX BOURNE, *Fortnightly Review*, p. 294, Aug. 1901.

74. The terrible repression which he authorised in Sicily demonstrated the lengths to which when resisted fury could carry him, and his foreign policy all through was evidence of his megalomania.— *Spectator*, p. 211, Aug. 17, 1901.

75. He would be commissioned to form a government for the sole purpose of maintaining the nation's position in the world, without any regard whatever to party traditions, and without any legislative programme.—*National Review*, March 1900.

76. He was a saint indeed, not a hermit of asceticism, combining piety, meekness, humility, simplicity, with active benevolence and virtue.—GOLDWIN SMITH, *United Kingdom*, i. p. 48.

77. There are few men in Australia, except those who live in the great cities, who are not used to horse-exercise, either for pleasure or for business.—*Daily Telegraph*, p. 7, Feb. 2, 1900.

78. He knows his subject; he has seen the country where this drama was played with his own eyes; he has spent time without stint in studying what has been recorded about it.—*Spectator*, p. 561, Oct. 19, 1901.

79. A fire broke out yesterday morning in the basement of the house of Mr. Vickers, chairman of the great engineering firm at 35 Park Street, Grosvenor Square.—*Daily Telegraph*, p. 8, Oct. 25, 1901.

80. He makes the religion and the irreligion of the people he loves and pities, their virtues and their vices, the prejudices which have eaten into their brains and their receptiveness on certain points, equally clear, and the result is that we know the Malay of the Peninsula as we know any one of the peoples of Europe that has attracted us.—*Spectator*, p. 598, Oct. 28, 1901.

81. We do not propose here to draw a comparison between the intrinsic or operating value of the work respectively put into these British and American engines.—*Engineering*, p. 653, Nov. 8, 1901.

82. Even when in prison the same flippant tone permeated the conversation and letters of hundreds of ladies and gentlemen who were fully aware that they were on the eve of losing their heads.—*Fortnightly Review*, p. 997, Dec. 1901.

83. Now isn't that a good deal nicer and more life-like than saying that the art of acting is diminishing every day, and bids fair to disappear entirely, as Mr. Mansfield does ?—Letter in *New York Herald*, June 1902.

84. Mr. Russell had innocently alluded to his wife having stayed with Lady Merton in the course of the conversation, and had politely expressed his regret at not having been able to accompany her.—R. BAGOT, *Casting of Nets*, chap. xiv. p. 213.

85. After the cordial welcome I and my comrades, strangers as we are, have received at your hands, I should like to say a few words, if without breaking the rules of the Order I may do so.—MARIE CORELLI.

86. The person about whom gathered almost as much interest as about the prisoner himself, Lizzie's appearance in the witness-box caused a profound sensation.—Mrs. LYNN LINTON, *Lizzie Larton*, vol. iii. p. 283.

87. He ended with an eloquent appeal to "all who think that the loss of empire would be for this country in the future to lead a meagre life and to have mere paltry ambitions" to vote for Mr. Gerald Balfour's motion.—*Spectator*, p. 822, Nov. 29, 1902.

88. The best system of sanitation should be carried out in our universities, where the sons of many who devote time and means to the bettering of the conditions of life of others are brought up, where medicine in all its branches is taught, and which are great centres of progress and civilisation.—*Ibid*. p. 790, Nov. 22, 1902.

89. The addition of two distinctly pacifically-disposed states, such as Belgium and Holland are, to the Dual Alliance, would tend to strengthen its purely defensive character. — *Nineteenth Century*, p. 1030, Dec. 1902.

90. This is to be accounted for, according to the opinion of initiated persons, by a certain fatigue of the Sultan, who finds the burden of centralisation too great for him.—*Daily Tel.* p. 9, Nov. 23, 1901.

91. Throughout the whole of the north-east of the Soudan trade and industry are reviving surely, but no doubt slowly.—*Ibid.* June 28, 1898.

92. We should be inclined to believe that the Parliamentary

Republic had become a solid institution in France, likely to last as long as Constitutional Monarchy in our own country or the Federal Republic in America, but for two disturbing facts.—*Spectator*, p. 930, Dec. 13, 1902.

93. There may appear to be a certain inconsistency in such a bequest as that of Mr. Nobel, who left the millions which he had gained by perfecting a deadly instrument of destruction to advance the cause of universal peace ; but it is a kind of inconsistency which need not be discouraged.—*Ibid.* p. 934, Dec. 13, 1902.

94. For the ten years 1891-1900 the London rate was below that of any of the great towns of Europe or of New York, except Brussels, Amsterdam, Copenhagen, Stockholm, and Berlin, and in 1901 was lower than that of any except Brussels, Amsterdam, and Stockholm. —*Daily Telegraph*, p. 9, Jan. 2, 1903.

95. The Malays are Asiatics of the Asiatics, with no desire for Western civilisation, and with a rooted conviction, which they still entertain, that they are, being Mahommedans with a past, the highest and most qualified people on the earth.—*Spect.* p. 978, Dec. 20, 1902.

96. Now, when the long foreseen crisis is upon them, indifference has given way to equally unreasonable panic, and Continental statesmen dream of fighting the unwelcome preponderance of wealth and power which has silently passed to the democracy of the West by anti-American Federations.—*Ibid.* p. 456, March 21, 1903.

97. I must not, however, disguise the fact that there are many funny things to Western eyes in a Japanese play.—*Daily Telegraph*, p. 5, March 28, 1903.

98. I have heard this great student accused for neglecting his official duties ; but it would be necessary to decide on this accusation to know the character of his accusers.—D'ISRAELI, *Curiosities of Literature.*

99. The beaux of that day used the abominable art of painting their faces as well as the women.—*Ibid.*

100. That great original, the author of *Hudibras*, was being censured for exposing to ridicule Sir Samuel Luke under whose roof he dwelt in the grotesque character of his hero.—*Ibid.*

101. Wolsey left at his death many buildings which he had begun in an unfinished state, and which no one expects to see complete.— HALLAM, *Literature of Europe.*

102. I have now and then inserted in the text characters of books that I have not read on the faith of my guides.—*Ibid.*

103. Leo Baptista Alberti was a man who may claim a place in the temple of glory he has not filled.—*Ibid.*

104. There is a copy in the British Museum ; and M. Raynouard has given a short account of one that he had seen in the *Journal des Savans* for 1826.—*Ibid.*

105. You must make haste and gather me all you can, and do it quickly, or I will and shall do without it.—JOHNSON, *Letter to Boswell*, 1774.

106. This immense empire (Russia) is inhabited by a patient and indomitable race, ever ready to exchange the luxury and adventure of the south for the hardships and monotony of the north.—ALISON, *History of Europe.*

CHAPTER IV.—ERRORS IN PREPOSITIONS.

It was stated in section (*e*) of Chapter III. that "the function of a preposition is to show what one person or thing has to do with another person or thing,"—in other words, to express some relation between them. The first point then about which the writer must be on his guard, is to see that the preposition used expresses the relation required by the sense.

But this is not the only difficulty. Prepositions must suit not only the sense intended by the writer, but the idiom imposed by custom. Thus in speaking of a death as caused by a disease, we say, "He died *of* fever," but in speaking of death as caused by something else, we say, "He died *from* hunger." Both prepositions denote cause ; but one is suitable to one context, and one to another. Many similar examples could be given. "I cannot see the matter *in* the same light as you" : "I cannot see the matter *from* your point of view." It would be against idiom to say, "from the same light as you," or "in your point of view."

A few peculiarities in the use of prepositions may be here noted :—

1. **At, in.**—"At" relates to a small extent of space or time ; "in" to a wider extent :—

The end is *at* hand (very close).
The work is *in* hand (being done, stage of completion unspecified).
He will start *at* six o'clock *in* the morning.
Dundee and the Highlanders utterly defeated a royalist army *at* Killiecrankie *in* Perthshire.—HUNTER's *Short History of England*, p. 311.

2. **With, by.**—"With" relates to the instrument employed for doing a thing or to the mode of doing it. "By" relates to the doer of an action or to the cause by which an effect is produced :—

175

His lordship was received *with* loud and prolonged cheering *by* a large gathering of spectators.—*Daily Telegraph,* p. 8, May 31, 1901.

They are never alone that are accompanied *with* noble thoughts.—Sir P. SIDNEY.

He was accompanied *by* two carts filled with wounded rebels.—MACAULAY.

How often has he stricken you dumb *with* his irony !—LANDOR.

Note.—Sometimes it is a debatable point whether we should use *by* or *with.* In the sentence last quoted *with* is certainly correct, as it expresses what the context requires—the instrument or manner, not the agent. But if we turn the sentence into a Passive form, we might say either *by* or *with* :—

How often have you been struck dumb *by* or *with* his irony !

After the word "begins," the use of *by* or *with* depends upon the context :—

(1) He begins *by* or *with telling* a tale of country life.
(2) The book begins *with* a tale of country life.

In (1) " by telling " denotes agency, and "with telling" denotes the manner of beginning. Both make sense, and both are in accordance with idiom.

In (2) *with* is indispensable, and *by* would be wrong.

3. Between, among.—As a general rule "between" is used in reference to two things, and " among" in reference to more than two :—

A and B agreed *between* themselves to share the profits.
A, B, and C agreed *among* themselves, etc.

But "between" can be used for more than two things or persons, to denote some reciprocal action or relation : [1]—

A friendly intercourse is opened *between* the most distant lands.—BUCKLE, *History of Civilisation,* vol. i. chap. 10.

In spite of the constantly increasing intercourse *between* the most remote parts of the world, etc.—JENKS, *History of Politics, Temple Primers,* p. 6.

England has earned her supremacy in Arabian waters by honest attempts to put a stop to the slave trade, in accordance with

---

[1] In the *Oxford Dictionary,* under the word BETWEEN, the following remarks are given : " This word is sometimes said of more than two, when it is desired to mark the participation of all the parties more definitely than it can be done by *among.* It is still the only word available to express the relation of a thing to many surrounding things severally and individually, *among* expressing a relation to them collectively and vaguely. We should not say, The space lying among three points ; or, A treaty among three powers ; or, The choice lies among three candidates : or, To insert a needle among the closed petals of a flower."

the treaties *between* the Powers.—*Spectator*, p. 493, Oct. 13, 1900.

The recent fighting has led many people to reconsider the whole question of the relations *between* the Cape, the Imperial Government, and the natives.—*Review of Reviews*, p. 147, Feb. 1898.

These events were succeeded by the remarkable league *among* the three powers.—PRESCOTT, *History of Mexico*, i. 128. (Change *among* to *between*.)

4. Beside, besides.—The former means *by the side of*, and hence sometimes *outside of*. The latter means *in addition to* :—

He came and sat *beside* me (= by my side).
Your answer is *beside* (= irrelevant to) the question.
Besides (= in addition to) advising he gave practical help.

5. By, since, before.—These are all used for a *point* of time, not for a *period* or *space* of time :—

You must be back *by* four o'clock.
He has been here *since* four o'clock.
He did not get back *before* four o'clock.

6. In, within.—The former denotes the close of a period ; the latter some period short of the close :—

He will return *in* (= at the close of) a week's time.
He will return *within* (= at some period short of) a week's time.
All this progress was jeopardised, when Lord Salisbury undertook to evacuate Egypt *in* two years' time. Happily the Sultan refused to ratify the convention.—*Spectator*, p. 628, Nov. 3, 1900.

7. Before, for.—When the sense relates to *future* time, " for " is used to denote a space of time, while " before " is used to denote a point of time.

The sun will not rise *for* an hour.
He will stay here *for* a month.
The sun will rise
The sun will not rise } *before* six o'clock.

8. Of (in the sense of apposition).—This use of " of " can be traced back to the Tudor period.

The frail sepulchre *of* our flesh.—SHAKESPEARE. (= Our flesh, the frail sepulchre.)
One day, however, M. discovered that his urchin *of* a nephew (= his nephew, the urchin), who had attained the respectable age *of* seven (= the respectable age, seven), did not know how to read or write.—*Nineteenth Century*, p. 822, May 1900.

Examples of the uses of Prepositions.—The preposition by which a word is followed depends, as has been shown, partly

N

upon the requirements of the context (*i.e.* upon the meaning that the writer intends to express), and partly upon idiom or usage. The following sentences will exemplify their usage :—

Abatement. There is no abatement *of* the fever so far. He allowed no abatement *from* the price that he asked.

Abhor. Such an act is abhorrent (repulsive) *to* my feelings. I have a great abhorrence (detestation) *of* such deeds.

Abound (followed by *in* or *with*, but *in* is the more idiomatic). Men abounding *in* natural courage.—MACAULAY. A faithful man shall abound *with* blessings.—*Proverbs* xxviii. 20. Her entertaining book abounds *with* good stories and good illustrations.—*Spectator*, p. 118, Jan. 26, 1901. A faithful man shall have abundance *of* blessings.

Accompany. He accompanied his speech *with* a bow. He was accompanied *by* two carts filled with wounded rebels.—MACAULAY.

Accord (followed by *with* or *to*). Thy actions *to* thy words accord. —MILTON. My heart accordeth *with* my tongue.—SHAKESPEARE. He acted in accordance *with* rule. According *to* him every person could be bought.—MACAULAY.

Account. I cannot account *for* (explain) this circumstance. I am not accountable *to* you *for* my actions.

Adapted. He chose the calling best adapted (suited) *to* his taste. Streets ill adapted *for* (unfit for) the residence of wealthy persons.— MACAULAY.

Adhere. We must adhere (stick) *to* this plan. He is an *adherent* (follower) *of* mine.

Admit. You cannot be admitted *to* the manager to-day (person). You cannot be admitted *into* the manager's office (place). Your conduct admits *of* no excuse (leaves no room for any excuse).

Admonish. He was admonished *of* his faults (the faults were brought to his notice). He was admonished (cautioned, reproved) *for* his faults (on account of his faults). He was admonished (warned) *against* that danger.

Advantage, advantageous. You *have* the advantage *of* me. You *took* advantage *of* my mistake. You gained an advantage *over* me. This is very advantageous *to* me.

Affection. He has an affection *for* her. He is affectionate *to* or *towards* her.

Affinity. The English language has an affinity *with* German. There is an affinity *between* English and German.

Agree. I do not agree *with* you (person). I do not agree *to* that proposal. Agreeably *to* your wishes I have come back.

Alien. (The sense of differing *from* passes imperceptibly to repugnant or opposed *to*. Hence both prepositions are used after *alien*.) This uncouth style, so alien *from* genuine English.—H. REED, *English Literature*, ix. 294. Popery is alien *to* the climate and *to* the races of the Western world.—I. TAYLOR, *Fanaticism*, vi. 177. Methods which are alien from the best traditions of English journalism have been employed.—*Daily Telegraph*, p. 9, March 27, 1901.

Alternate. Day alternates *with* night. This plan is an alternative *to* that.

Ambition. I have no ambition *for* that distinction. I am not ambitious *of* that distinction.

Analogy. Analogy of one thing *with* or *to* another. Analogy *between* two or more things. This is analogous *to* that.

Angry. Be not grieved nor angry with yourselves (person).— *Genesis* xlv. 5. Wherefore should God be angry *at* thy voice (thing)? —*Ecclesiastes* v. 6.

Annoyed. I was annoyed *at* his remarks (thing). I am annoyed *with* you (person).

Anxious. I am very anxious *for* his safety. I am anxious *about* the result (to know what the result is or will be).

Application. He gave much application *to* study. He made an application *for* that post. What you say does not apply (is not applicable) *to* this case.

Apt. He is apt (expert) *at* mathematics. He is apt *to* make mistakes.

Ashamed. I am ashamed *of* him. Shame *at* his conduct was felt by all.

Aspire. Vague aspirations *after* military renown. Men aspire *after* or *to* distinction.

Astonish. I was astonished *at* his appearance (Passive). He astonished me *by* his appearance (Active).

Attend. You did not attend (pay attention) *to* him. He was required to attend *on* the committee (to be in readiness when he was wanted).—CLARENDON.

Authority, authorise. He has no authority *over* me. He is a great authority *on* that subject. He is my authority *for* that statement. He authorised me *to* do this.

Avert, averse. He endeavoured to avert evil *from* his country. Averse (hostile, opposed) *to* pure democracy.—BANCROFT, *History of the United States*, i. 277. There was a vague rumour that French generals were not averse *from* declaring war against us.—*Daily Telegraph*, p. 8, Dec. 29, 1900. This side is not averse *to* any drastic development of administrative action.—*Spectator*, p. 650, Nov. 10, 1900. He was not averse *from* a moderate quantity of good, sound, fruity port.—*Gentleman's Magazine*, p. 261, Sept. 1878. An aversion *to* a standing army in time of peace.—LECKY, *England in the Eighteenth Century*, iii. A state *for* which they have so great an aversion.— ADDISON. Adhesion to vice and aversion *from* goodness.—ATTERBURY. Lord Cromer is a great servant of the State, and is profoundly averse *from* plunging into the arena of party politics.—*Fortnightly Review*, p. 822, Nov. 1900. Averse *from* any interference with the liberty of even a dangerous personage.—*Daily Telegraph*, p. 9, Nov. 9, 1900.

Note.—*From* is always used after the verb "avert"; *from, to,* or *for* may be used after the noun "aversion," and *from* or *to* after the adjective "averse." See above the parallel case of **Alien**.

Aware, alive. I was not aware *of* that fact. I was not alive *to* that fact.

Beg. He begged a favour *of* me ("beg" Trans.). He begged *for* a favour ("beg" Intrans.).

Beneficence, benevolence. Beneficence *to* the poor. Benevolence *towards* the poor.

Betray. He betrayed the city *to* the enemy (gave it up treacherously). Genius often betrays itself *into* great errors (falls unconsciously into).

Blest. Blest *with* good health. Blest *in* his children.

Blind. Blind *of* one eye. Blind *to* one's own faults.

Blush. A man blushes *at* his own faults, and *for* any person who has committed a fault.

Borrow. He borrowed money *of* or *from* me.

Bound. He is bound *in* honour to pay his debt. He was bound *by* a contract. The ship was bound *for* Jamaica. (*N.B.* The last is not from "bind" like the two first, but stands for M.E. *boun*, prepared.)

Break. Thieves broke *into* the house. He broke himself *of* the habit. He broke *through* (got clear of) restraint. He broke the news (ill news) *to* her. He broke (dissolved partnership) *with* him.

Bring. This matter must be brought *to* light. The matter was brought *under* notice.

Buy. This was bought *of* me (person). This was bought *from* A.'s shop (place).

Call. Let us call *on* him (visit him at his house). Let us call *to* him (shout to him). Let us call *for* him (send some one to fetch him). This calls *for* (requires) no comment. This was quite uncalled *for* (not required or justified by the circumstances).

Capable, capacity. He is not capable *of* improvement. He has no capacity *for* improvement.

Care. I do not care *for* (have no liking for) this person or this thing. He took no care *of* his money. He takes no care *about* his dress. He is careful *of* his comfort. He is careless *of* or *about* the consequences (takes no thought of).

Cause. What is the cause *of* this noise?[1] Is there any cause *for* this noise?

Caution. Take every caution *against* error. He is cautious *of* offending (is cautious not to offend).

Chafe (*at, with, against*). He will chafe *at* the doctor's marrying my daughter.—SHAKESPEARE. The troubled Tiber chafing *with* her shores.—SHAKESPEARE, *Julius Cæsar*, i. 2. She too is strong, and might not chafe in vain *against* them.—BRYANT, *The Ages*, stanza 34. (*N.B. At* is the most common, and *with* the least.)

Charge. I charge him *with* (accuse him of) this crime. I charge you *with* this duty (impose it on you). I charge this sum *to* you (look to you for payment).

Claim. I have this claim *on* or *against* you (person). I have a claim *to* this (thing).

Clothed. Clothed *in* fine linen. Clothed *with* shame.

Come. I came *across* him or it (accidentally met). This will soon come *into* fashion. How did you come *by* (obtain) this? This comes *of* (results from) talking. This comes (amounts) *to* forty.

---

[1] It frequently happens in English that a noun, when preceded by *the*, is followed by *of*; and that when preceded by *a*, *any*, or *no*, it is followed by *to*. Cf. *the* slave or victim *of* vice; *a* slave or victim *to* vice.

Commence. I commence *by* remarking. I commence *with* the remark.

Communicate. I wish to communicate *with* you in this matter (Intrans.). I wish to communicate this matter *to* you (Trans.).

Compare. We compare one kind of fruit *with* another (here the things compared are of similar kind). We compare genius *to* a lightning-flash (here dissimilars are compared metaphorically).

Complain. We complain (verb) *of* a person or a thing. But if we make a complaint (noun), the complaint is *against* a person and *about* a thing.

Concerned. Concerned *at* or *about* some mishap. Concerned *for* some one's safety. Concerned *in* some business.

Concur. I concur *with* him (person). I concur *in* your opinion (thing).

Confer. I confer this gift *upon* you (Trans.). He conferred *with* me *on* that point (Intrans.).

Confide. We confide a secret *to* any one (Trans.). We confide *in* some one's honour (Intrans.). I am confident *of* success.

Conform. A rule *to* which experience must conform.—WHEWELL. By our conformity *to* God.—TILLOTSON. The end of all religion is but to draw us to a conformity *with* God.—Dr. H. MORE. (*To* and *with* are equally common after the noun. *To* is more common after the verb.)

Consequent, subsequent. Consequent *upon* (resulting from) his going. Subsequent *to* his going.

Consist (*of* or *in*). To indicate the parts which unite to compose a thing, we use *of ;* as, The land would consist *of* plains and valleys.— BURNET. To indicate the true nature of a thing, or that on which it depends, we use *in ;* as, Our safety consists *in* a strict adherence to duty.

Contemporary. He was contemporary *with* me (adjective). He was a contemporary *of* mine (noun).

Contrast. This picture is a great contrast *to* that (noun). This picture is contrasted *with* that (verb).

Converted. He was converted *to* Christianity (mental change). Moses' rod was converted *into* a serpent (physical change).

Correspond. Atterbury began to correspond directly *with* the Pretender (write letters *to* him). — MACAULAY. None of Sidney's sonnets correspond *to* the Shakespearian type (are of the same metrical form).—SYMONDS.

Count. I count *on* this (confidently expect). This counts *for* nothing (is worth nothing).

Cut. The stick was cut *in* pieces or cut *to* pieces. The apple was cut *in* half (divided).

Deal. He did not deal well *by* his servants (did not treat them well). He deals (trades) *in* fish. He dealt *with* the subject of politics (wrote or spoke on politics). The Jews had no dealings (intercourse of any kind) *with* the Samaritans.

Decision. The decision (settlement) *of* some dispute. The decision (judgment pronounced) *on* a case. Let us decide *on* that plan.

Delight, delighted. I take a delight *in* him. I am delighted *with* him.

Demand. He demanded a shilling *of* us (verb). There is no demand *for* this article (noun).

Dependent. He is dependent *on* your help. He is independent *of* your help.

Derogate. Such a fault derogates *from* your reputation (verb). Such a fault is derogatory *to* your reputation (adjective).

Descended, descendant. A. is descended *from* B. A. is a descendant *of* B.

Die. He died *of* some disease. He died *from* overwork. He died *with* horror at the thought. They fell by the roadside and died *by* fire and sword.

Differ, different, indifferent. This fact differs *from* that. I differ *with* you in opinion. I differ *from* you in character. My plan is different *from* yours (less accurately "*to* yours"). He is indifferent *to* my troubles (unconcerned about them).

Disappointed. I was disappointed *of* that (something not obtained). I was disappointed *in* that (something obtained). I was disappointed *with* him (person).

Disgusted. Disgusted *with* him (person). Disgusted *at* or *with* the result (thing).

Disparagement. It ought to be no disparagement *to* a star that it is not the sun.—SOUTH. Your disparagement *of* my abilities offends me.

Disqualified. He is disqualified (does not possess the required qualifications) *for* that post. He is disqualified *from* competing (debarred from competing by want of some necessary condition).

Duty. I have done my duty *by* him (an equal or inferior). Forgetting his duty *to* God, his sovereign lord, and his country (one greater or superior).—HALLAM.

Embark. They embarked *on* the "Simla" *for* Alexandria (literal). He has embarked *in* a new business (metaphorical).

Enamoured. He soon became enamoured *of* or *with* her. (Used for either person or thing. *Of* is the more common.)

Encourage, discourage. He encouraged me *to* proceed ; but you discouraged me *from* doing so.

Enter. I cannot enter *into* your views. He has entered *upon* a new project.

Entrust. I cannot entrust any one *with* this. I cannot entrust this *to* any one. (These mean the same thing.)

Envy. I feel no envy *at* your success. I am not envious *of* your success.

Equal. I am not equal *to* you. I am not on an equality *with* you.

Exception. He took exception *to* the place of their burial.—BACON. I will answer what exceptions they can have *against* (=*to*) our account. —BENTLEY. She made an exception *of* those two cases.

Excuse. He was excused (pardoned) *for* his fault. He was excused (released) *from* attendance. (The *from* is sometimes left out.)

Exult. Do not exult *over* a defeated enemy. Do not exult *in* the misfortunes of another.

Fail. He failed *in* his attempt. He failed *of* his purpose.

Fall. He fell *under* A.'s displeasure. He fell *into* a mistake. He fell *among* thieves. They fell *on* (attacked) the enemy.

False. He was false *to* his friends, because he was false *of* heart.

Familiar. This subject is familiar *to* me. I am familiar *with* this subject. (These sentences mean the same thing.)

Feed. They fed the cow *with* grass (Trans.). The cow fed *on* grass (Intrans.).

Fight. They fought *against* all difficulties (thing). They fought *with* or *against* their enemies (person). They fought *for* a good cause.

Fill, full. He is filled *with* pride. He is full *of* pride.

Fond, fondness. Fond *of* money. Fondness *for* money.

Fruitful. Though his mind was fruitful *of* resources, his work was fruitless *of* results.

Furnish. He furnished the hungry *with* food. He furnished food *to* the hungry. (These sentences mean the same thing.)

Genius. He has a genius *for* mathematics (abstract noun). He is a genius *in* mathematics (common noun).

Glad. I shall be glad *of* his assistance. He that is glad *at* calamities shall not be unpunished.—*Proverbs* xvii. 5.

Glance. He glanced *at* the letter (momentary and incomplete). He glanced *over* the letter (rapid, but continued till the whole letter was read).

Grieve. I cannot help grieving *for* him (person). We had much grief *at* or *for* or *over* that matter (thing).

Hardened. He was hardened (inured) *to* misfortune. His mind was hardened *against* pity.

Hatred. I have a hatred *of* or *for* such persons, such conduct. His methods were hateful (odious, repulsive) *to* me.

Heir. He is the heir *to* that property. He is the heir *of* his uncle.

Hope, hopeful.—We hope *for* better things (verb). There is no hope *for* or *of* better things (noun). He is hopeful *of* success.

Impatient. Impatient *of* reproof (unable to endure reproof). Impatient *for* payment (eager to receive payment).

Impress. Impress an idea *on* some one. Impress some one *with* an idea.

Indebted. Indebted *to* some one *in* a large sum ; *for* his kindness.

Indignant. Indignant *with* a person. Indignant *at* something done.

Indulge. He indulged (Trans.) himself and them *with* a glass of wine (a single thing). He indulged himself *in* idleness (habit). He indulged (Intrans.) *in* a glass of wine.

Influence. He has no influence *over* or *with* me (person). He has no influence *on* my judgment (thing).

Interest. I take great interest *in* that subject. He has no interest *with* me (has no claim on me for help). Interest *on* this loan is charged *at* 4 per cent.

Intrude. Do not intrude *on* a man's privacy. He intruded *into* my private garden.

Invest. He has been invested *with* a title, or *with* authority. His money is invested *in* railways.

Join. To join *in* a game. To join this *with* or *to* that.

Jump. He jumped *at* (eagerly accepted) the offer. He jumped *to* the conclusion (came to it without sufficient evidence).

Jurisdiction. Jurisdiction *over* a certain province or area. He has no jurisdiction *in* this suit (the suit cannot be heard in his court).

Kick. Kick *against* (resist) authority. Wherefore kick ye *at* (scorn) mine offering which I have commanded ?—1 *Samuel* ii. 29.

Labour. He labours *under* a difficulty ; *for* the public good ; *in* a good cause ; *at* some particular work.

Lay. Lay facts *before* a person ; lay a sin *to* one's charge (accuse one of it) ; lay a person *under* an obligation.

Lend. To lend money *at* high interest. To lend money *on* good security.

Level. This surface is level *with* that (adj.). The walls were levelled *with* the ground (verb). He levelled his gun *at* the bird.

Liable. Liable *to* error (might fall into error). Liable (responsible) *for* payment.

Libel. His conversation is a perpetual libel *on* all his acquaintance. —SHERIDAN, *School for Scandal*, i. 1. He wrote a libel *against* A.'s character.

Liking, dislike. I have a liking *for* her, and a dislike *to* him.

Live. Live *for* riches ; *by* honest labour ; *on* a small income ; *within* one's means.

Look. Look *after* (watch, superintend) some business. Look *at* a person or thing. Look *into* (examine closely) a matter. Look *over* (examine roughly or cursorily) an account. Look *through* (examine carefully) an account. Look *for* (search for) something lost.

Make. He made *away with* (purloined) the money. This does not make *for* (conduce to) happiness. He made *up to* (approached with caution) some one. (In all these instances *make* is used Intransitively.)

Marry one person *to* another (said of the father or the clergyman).

Martyr. A martyr *to* (great sufferer from) rheumatism. A martyr *in* or *for* a certain cause.

Meddle (*in* or *with*). He is always meddling *with* other men's affairs. The civil lawyers have meddled *in* a matter that belongs not to them.—LOCKE.

Moved. Moved *at* the sight ; *by* his entreaties ; *with* pity ; *to* tears.

Murmur (*at* or *against*). The Jews then murmured *at* him.—*John* vi. 41. His disciples murmured *at* it.—*John* vi. 61. The children of Israel murmured *against* Moses and *against* Aaron.—*Numbers* xiv. 2.

Need. There is no need *of* or *for* assistance. We are in need *of* (not *for*) assistance.

Neglect, neglectful, negligent. He showed no neglect *of* duty. He was negligent *in* doing a thing ; negligent or neglectful *of* his duties (things) ; neglectful *of* his friends (persons).

Oblige. I am much obliged *to* you (indebted). This is obligatory *on* you (incumbent as a duty).

Offend. He offended *against* the rule. This was an offence *against* morality. He took offence *at* what I said. He was offended *with* me. My words were offensive *to* him.

Originate. This originated (had its origin) *in* jealousy (thing). This originated *with* him (person).

Overcome (p.p.). He is overcome *with* fatigue. He was overcome *by* their entreaties.

Overwhelmed. He was overwhelmed *with* grief. The boat was overwhelmed *by* the waves.

Parallel (*to* or *with*). Honour runs parallel *with* the laws of God. —ADDISON. This line is parallel *to* that.

. **Part.** He owned that he had parted *from* the duke (left the company of the duke) only a few hours before.—MACAULAY. It was strange to him that a father should feel no tenderness at parting *with* an only son (seeing him or letting him go). He has parted *with* all his property (sold, lost, or given away).

Pass. To pass *from* one thing *into* another ; to pass *for* (have the reputation of being) a clever man ; to pass *over* (omit) a page ; to pass *by* a man's door.

Perish. To perish *by* the sword ; to perish *with* cold.

Play. To play *at* football ; to play *on* the piano ; to play tricks *with* one's health.

Point. To point *at* the winner ; to point *to* a certain fact, result, place, etc.

Ponder (*on* or *over*). To ponder *on* or *over* a question.

Possessed. Possessed *of* wealth (=possessor *of* wealth). Possessed *with* an idea (having the mind occupied with an idea).

Precedence. He has precedence *of* you. (We do not say "precedence *to* or *above*").

Preference. Preference *for* learning *to* or *above* wealth.

Preparatory, preparation. Preparatory *to* going. Preparation *for* going.

Prevail. To prevail *on* (persuade) a person to do something. This argument prevailed *with* me (had more effect on my mind than any other). He prevailed *against* or *over* (defeated) his adversary.

Pride, proud. He takes great pride *in* his wealth (noun). He prides himself *on* his wealth (verb). He is proud *of* his wealth (adj.).

Proceed. To proceed *with* a business already commenced ; to proceed *to* a business not yet commenced ; to proceed *against* (prosecute) a person.

Profuse. Profuse (liberal) *to* many unworthy applicants, the ministers were niggardly to him.—MACAULAY. He was very profuse *of* or *in* his praises.

Provide, provident. To provide *for* the future ; *against* the evil day. To provide oneself *with* something. He is provident *of* his money, *of* the future.

Provoke, provocation. Do not provoke me *to* anger. Provocation *to* anger. There was no provocation *for* such an angry letter.

Pursuant, pursuance. In pursuance *of* this inquiry (in following out this inquiry). The conclusion which I draw, pursuant *to* the query laid down.—WATERLAND.

Qualified, disqualified. He is qualified *to* compete ; but you are disqualified *from* competing.

Ready. Ready *for* a journey ; ready *at* arithmetic ; ready *in* his answers ; ready *with* an answer.

Reconciled. Reconciled *to* a position ; reconciled *with* an enemy.

Reckon. I cannot reckon *on* that (confidently expect). To reckon *with* (settle accounts with) a person.

Regard, regardful. I have a great regard *for* him. With regard (reference) *to* that matter. His first regard was *for* his own interests. Regardful *of* his interests.

Rejoice. To rejoice *at* the success of another. To rejoice *in* one's own success.

Relation. He is a relation or relative *of* mine. He is related *to* me. I have had no relations *with* him (I have had nothing to do with him). This is not relative (relevant) *to* the subject in hand.

Requisite. Requisite *to* happiness. Requisite *for* the purpose.

Respect. I have no respect *for* him. With respect *to* (concerning) this question we cannot make up our minds. In respect *of* age (in point of age) he is senior to me. We gain much and concede nothing in respect *of* our commercial interests.—*Daily Telegraph*, p. 8, Oct. 23, 1900. It was not a failure in respect *of* (in point of, as regards) the feeler it put out.—*Fortnightly Review*, p. 736, Nov. 1900.

Responsible. We are responsible *for* our actions. You are responsible *to* your employer.

Result. What is the result *of* the examination (noun)? It resulted *in* failure (verb). The one thing resulted *from* the other.

Run. To run *after* (eagerly follow) new fashions ; to run *at* (attack) a cat ; to run *into* debt ; to run *over* (read rapidly) an account ; to run *through* (spend rapidly) one's money.

Satisfied, satisfaction. Satisfied (convinced) *of* a fact. Satisfied (contented) *with* a little. I expect some satisfaction (compensation or redress) *for* that loss. I feel great satisfaction (pleasure) *in* or *at* your improvement.

Search. The search *for* or *after* happiness is the great problem of life. In search *of* happiness we often go wrong.

Secure (*from* or *against*). Secure *from* harm ; secure *against* attack.

See. We must see *about* (consider) this matter ; see *into* (investigate) the matter ; see *into* (carefully examine) the matter ; see *to* (attend to) the matter. I saw *through* (understood) his motive.

Seek (*after* or *for*). Most men seek *after* or *for* happiness.

Sensible, sensitive, insensible. I am very sensible *of* (fully appreciate) your kindness. She was too sensitive *to* abuse and calumny (too much affected by abuse and calumny).—MACAULAY. I am insensible *to* pain, while you are sensible *of* it.

Set. To set *about* (begin working at) a business. To set *upon* (attack) a traveller. To set (Trans.) a person *over* a business (place him in charge of it).

Sit. To sit *over* a fire. To sit *under* an imputation.

Slave. A slave *to* avarice. The slave *of* avarice. (*To* is preceded by *a*, and *of* by *the*. See footnote in p. 180.)

Slow. He is slow *of* hearing ; slow *at* arithmetic ; slow *in* making up his mind.

Smile. To smile *at* (treat with contempt) his threats. Fortune smiled *on* (favoured) him.

Solicitous, solicit. He was solicitous *of* or *for* advice (anxious to get advice).—CLARENDON. Enjoy the present, and be not solicitous *about* the future (concerning).—JEREMY TAYLOR. I solicited him *for* his help.

Speak. To speak *of* a subject (briefly). To speak *on* a subject (at greater length).

Speculate. To speculate *in* shares. To speculate *on* some point in science or history.

Stand. To stand *against* (=withstand, resist) any one. To stand *by* (support) a friend. To stand *on* ceremony (make a great point of). To stand *to* (maintain) one's opinion.

Stare. To stare *at* a person. To stare one *in* the face.

Subject. This is *the* subject *of* inquiry. This is *a* subject *for* inquiry.

Suited. This is suited *to* the occasion. He is suited *for* a post.

Sympathy, sympathise. I have no sympathy *with* or *for* him. I sympathise *with* (not *for*) you.

Take. He takes *after* (resembles) his father. I took him *for* a spy (considered him to be a spy). Do not take *to* (commence the habit of) gambling.

Talk. To talk *of* or *about* a thing (casually or cursorily). To talk *over* a subject (to discuss it more seriously and more fully).

Taste. I have had a taste (experience) *of* hard work. I have no taste (liking) *for* mathematics.

Think. To think *of* or *about* a thing (casually). To think *over* a subject (consider more seriously).

Tired. Tired *of* doing the same thing (desirous of change). Tired (fatigued, wearied) *with* work.

Trespass. In the time of his distress did he trespass (sin) yet more *against* the Lord.—2 *Chronicles* xxviii. 22. To trespass *on* some one's time. To trespass *in* some one's house.

Trust (noun), **distrust.** My trust *in* you is greater than my distrust *of* him.

Trust (verb). To trust a man *with* money. Merchants were not willing to trust (entrust) precious cargoes *to* any custody but that of a man-of-war.—MACAULAY. I trust *to* your honour (Intrans.). Trust *in* (have confidence in) the Lord, and do good.—*Psalm* xxxvii. 3.

Use. We have no use *for* that. What is the use *of* that? There is no use *in* that.

Versed, conversant. He is well versed *in* mathematics. He is conversant *with* mathematics.

Vexed. He is vexed *with* me (person). Vexed *at* this (thing).

Victim. *A* victim *to* oppression. *The* victim *of* oppression. Cf. p. 180.

View. *In* view *of* these facts. *With* a view *to* doing something.

Wait. To wait *at* table (do the duties of a waiter). To wait *on* (attend) a person. To wait *for* a person or thing.

Warn. To warn a person *of* his danger. To warn him *against* a fault or *against* another person.

Wary. He was wary (cautious) *in* his own schemes. He was wary *of* (kept his eyes on) another's schemes.

Correct, improve, or justify the following sentences:—

1. I am not in favour of closing all public-houses, but I hold that very different restrictions and regulations are demanded to those which prevail.—Quoted in *Daily Telegraph*, p. 5, Aug. 29. 1899.

2. The degree of civilisation which they (the Mexicans) had reached, as inferred by their political institutions, may be considered perhaps not much short of that enjoyed by our Saxon ancestors.— PRESCOTT, *History of Mexico*, i. p. 39.

3. I told Count Mouravieff that I had been asked by Mr. Francis to speak at the hall of the British-American church.—*Review of Reviews*, p. 541, June 1899.

4. In fact it is every day more clear that the friendly understanding between all the Powers, without exception, must remain intact until the settlement be made.—*Daily Telegraph*, p. 7, Sept. 17, 1900.

5. These are seen of all thinking men, who feel that it is time our administrative system should be properly and effectively overhauled. —*Ibid.* p. 5, Sept. 17, 1900.

6. To any one who has noted the numerous parallels which this remarkable dialogue offers to passages in our Sacred Scriptures, it may seem strange that I hesitate to concur to any theory, which explains these coincidences by supposing that the author had access to the New Testament.—MONIER WILLIAMS, *Indian Wisdom*, quoted in *Bible Parallels*, p. 287.

7. Is she to be forced to renounce that Church into whose maternal bosom she has doubtless long since felt rest and holiness ?—KINGSLEY, *Westward Ho!* ch. xiv. p. 240.

8. The Roumanian reply began by taking cognisance of the expression of Bulgaria's willingness to prosecute the blackmailers.—*Daily Telegraph*, p. 8, Aug. 28, 1900.

9. My contention is that this picturesque old park should be placed in a different category to such public spaces as Lammas Park.— *Middlesex County Times*, p. 6, Aug. 18, 1900.

10. But the funeral of the king was attended by the minimum of religious recognition.—*Daily Telegraph*, p. 4, Aug. 10, 1900.

11. Lord Salisbury has now in his disposal the whole future of South Africa.—*Fortnightly Review*, p. 248, Aug. 1900.

12. Praxiteles is said to have definitely given the character of sensuality to Venus, who had previously floated between several ideals of beauty.—LECKY, *History of Rationalism*, vol. i. p. 271.

13. In the expansions of the heart the Eternal City (Rome) always takes precedence before all other Italian towns.—Quoted in *Daily Telegraph*, p. 8, Aug. 2, 1900.

14. He is looked upon as a great authority on these questions, and will assist to examine scientifically a number of these questions.— *Ibid.* p. 9, Aug. 8, 1900.

15. As the author's name is not sufficiently known to his fellow-countrymen, he has taken care to begin by a short account of himself. —*Literature*, p. 65, July 28, 1900.

16. Mystery has ever been the study of those who in science and art, in philosophy and literature, have not been satisfied merely to observe and portray the trivial facts and realities of life.—*Fortnightly Review*, p. 899, June 1900.

17. No moral teaching, he said, was much good without a religious basis.—*Daily Telegraph*, p. 9, June 22, 1900.

18. The credit of being first into Pretoria will no doubt rest with French and his cavalry.—*Daily Express*, p. 1, May 31, 1900.

19. The Russian forces will have accomplished all we aim for, before we can take a real hand at the game.—*Ibid.* p. 4, June 19, 1900.

20. The province again suffered from heavy storms accompanied by thunder and lightning.—*Ibid.* p. 1, June 13, 1900.

21. The future of Sikhism as an independent creed depends, according to the learned judges, on its votaries' rebelling from the authority of Hinduism.—*Pioneer Mail*, p. 22, May 18, 1900.

22. Unfortunately the ceremony was not unattended by disagreeable incidents.—*Daily Telegraph*, p. 4, Aug. 10, 1900.

23. The writer deals with Anglican worship, and is inclined to slur over difficulties by a benevolent vagueness.—*Literature*, p. 405, May 26, 1900.

24. Their grievances grew apace, and their impatience with the injustice to which they were treated increased with years.—*Review of Reviews*, p. 370, Oct. 1899.

25. The Premier said that the Government had nothing to reproach themselves with, and urged that the Dreyfus affair should be finished with as soon as possible.—*Daily Telegraph*, Jan. 13, 1899.

26. When the Church is done squabbling about rubrics, perhaps it may find time to raise the ethical standard.—Quoted in *Church Gazette*, p. 83, May 6, 1899.

27. The *Humane Review* is a shilling quarterly published by E. B. It aims to represent "the ethics of humaneness."—*Review of Reviews*, p. 481, May 1900.

28. It is evident to Mr. Dicey that from three to five years the administration of the new provinces must remain in military hands.—*Ibid.* p. 450, May 1900.

29. Two-thirds of his time, he often ruefully declares, was devoted to the acquisition of a superficial knowledge of Latin and Greek, which has not been the least use to him in his after-life.—*Review of Reviews*, Character Sketch of Pearson.

30. The race-struggle thus set in motion has been a greater enemy of agriculture than the want of water.—*Fortnightly Review*, p. 853, May 1900.

31. This prospect certainly contributed in no small measure to secure the Federals the sympathy of the whole of Europe.—*Ibid.* p. 797, May 1900.

32. Mr. B. defended the landlords, who, he submitted, were often to be more commiserated with than the tenants.—Quoted in *Daily Telegraph*, p. 7, May 18, 1900.

33. The Government propose to break in upon the solemn contract entered into between themselves by the Australian colonies.—*Ibid.* p. 7, May 15, 1900.

34. Dr. Schmidt, the famous German philologist, has died from injuries received by being run over.—*Daily Express*, p. 1, May 16, 1900.

35. As well as doing its utmost to save human life, the Bombay Government had endeavoured to save cattle by establishing camps, etc. —*Homeward Mail*, p. 660, May 14, 1900.

36. Café life in Vienna seems very different to the proceedings of an English coffee-house.—*Daily Express*, p. 3, May 14, 1900.

37. The result will be much the same in either alternative.—*Daily Telegraph*, p. 9, May 10, 1900.

38. One source of the ancient gods was from deified ancestors.— Professor HENSLOW, in *Church Gazette*, p. 111, May 13, 1899.

39. We know how successful has been the federation of provinces to form the Canadian Dominion.—*Daily Telegraph*, p. 9, April 28, 1900.

40. The efforts of the English force were directed on silencing the biggest of the enemy's cannons, but its fire was not turned on their artillery.—*Ibid.* p. 7, April 26, 1900.

41. The honour of England's name has been dear to them, and loyalty to Queen and country has inspired them to a lofty heroism which is beyond all praise.—*Ibid.* p. 9, April 23, 1900.

42. I look back to a time when different sentiments to those which now prevail existed.—*Ibid.* p. 10, May 9, 1900.

43. An ancient privilege to be attained to by a process of drawing corks during a certain period of time on the river steamboats.—*Ibid.* p. 5, May 2, 1900.

44. It is a singular proof of the independence of the poet's literary and social character upon his theological proclivities that the Roman Catholic family of Th. were among his most intimate and best cherished friends.—*Times Weekly*, p. 4, April 27, 1900.

45. Mr. S. had proceeded far enough in the labour of collecting materials to be struck by the gross injustice produced by much well-meaning legislation.—*Literature*, p. 332, April 28, 1900.

46. He had said that he would rather enter the grave than into Parliament.—*Daily Telegraph*, p. 6, April 30, 1900.

47. In theory every knot increased speed above twenty knots gives an approximate reduction of seven hours in the time of the voyage.— *Ibid.* p. 8, Dec. 26, 1899.

48. These advices allude to the mystery of the whereabouts of the Japanese fleet, the movements of which are veiled with the greatest secrecy.—*Ibid.* p. 7, April 19, 1900.

49. It would appear that these blacks, who can thrive for days on Indian corn and water, are not averse at times from the luxuries of civilised diet.—*Ibid.* p. 5, April 19, 1900.

50. In a few days afterwards both generals were recommended to make as many treaties as possible with tribal chiefs.—*Review of Reviews*, p. 377, April 1900.

51. All their acts should aim to conquer aversion deeply rooted in such prejudices.—*Ibid.* p. 375, April 1900.

52. Next to a church surely the most disgraceful place to pick pockets in is at a cricket-ground during the game.—*Daily Telegraph*, p. 9, July 5, 1899.

53. So far as Europe is directly concerned, the political and economic advantages resulting from the Siberian railway are of comparative insignificance to the latest project of the Russian Government —the establishment of naval and commercial communication between the Baltic and the Black Seas.—*Fortnightly Review*, p. 899, June 1899.

54. There was no applause during his address, nor that of Baron de Staal.—*Daily Telegraph*, p. 7, May 19, 1899.

55. In furnishing the new hotel comfort has not been sacrificed for splendour.—*Ibid.* p. 7, June 7, 1899.

56. That splendid old veteran had commenced his advance, the ultimate success of which he (Lord George) was very confident.—*Middlesex County Times*, p. 3, Feb. 17, 1900.

57. The dismissal of the summons without costs seems to be a kind of admission that the vestry did its best, although it was not much use.—*Daily Telegraph*, p. 10, Feb. 26, 1900.

58. I think the republics would not be averse from that principle.—*Ibid.* p. 11, March 5, 1900.

59. Sir W. H. quoted statistics with a view of showing that we were not the unexampled drinkers of the world.—*Ibid.* p. 8, March 28, 1900.

60. Few people, I imagine, who have had the least experience of English schoolboy life, could read without disgust at the travesty of the English public schoolboy there presented.—*Literature*, p. 154, Feb. 17, 1900.

61. The radical and German parties have been prevented by the adjournment to take any decisive attitude against Slav aspirations.—*Daily Telegraph*, p. 10, March 28, 1899.

62. Indeed one would be perilously near ceasing to be a believer by returning to such sacredotalism, types, and Jewish ceremonial.—Letter in *Ealing Guardian*, p. 6, May 13, 1899.

63. Our scanty sources of knowledge (about the Hanyfs of Mecca) do not warrant us to draw any conclusion as to their creed and religious attitude.—*Church Gazette*, p. 31, April 29, 1899.

64. They were enthusiasts dominated with one idea; but domination by one idea is often, if not usually, the equivalent of monomania.—*Ibid.* p. 40, April 29, 1899.

65. The pamphlet is written with the view of showing that there is less treachery on the one side than on the other.—*Ibid.* p. 40, April 29, 1899.

66. If religious persons would but visit these places of amusement, and see for themselves instead of relying so much on mere hearsay, they would be able to warn men more effectually on the danger of such places.—*Ibid.* p. 104, May 13, 1899.

67. It is deeply engrained in the popular mind with the foreign rites of the Italian mission to this country.—*Ibid.* p. 122, May 20, 1899.

68. It was enjoined that the people should once in the year, at the time accustomed, with the rector, vicar, or curate, walk about the parishes.—*Ibid.* p. 75, May 6, 1899.

69. I came to ask if you could not come down to-night to preach. I am suffering with a severe cold.—SHELDON, *In His Steps*, p. 75.

70. The attitude assumed by the Bishop will, as they think, give strength to the agitation which is now in progress with a view of compelling episcopal or other action.—*Daily Telegraph*, p. 10, May 6, 1899.

71. In a sermon on the anniversary of the English Church Union Dr. Cobb professed his inability to appreciate 'the difference of the Church *of* England and the Church *in* England.—*Church Gazette*, p. 254, June 24, 1899.

72. To their operation many of the working classes owe their independence from parish relief.—*Daily Mail*, p. 2, April 14, 1900.

73. Milner used to come down to the office usually late, invariably accompanied by an umbrella with an extraordinary eagle's head as its handle.—*Review of Reviews*, p. 20, July 1899.

74. One of the prison warders said that he went to the constable's aid and assisted to convey the prisoner inside the gaol.—*Daily Telegraph*, p. 12, Aug. 26, 1899.

75. It was published in successive parts, long intervals between each period of publication.—ANSTER, *German Literature*, p. 158 (H).

76. It is now proposed to extend the test-paper scheme by affording heads of schools with the means of testing the standard of knowledge attained in their classes.—*School World*, p. 306, Aug. 1899.

77. They have filled the European press with statements that the attempt on his life was arranged by himself with the object to get the Radical leaders into his clutches.—*Review of Reviews*, p. 138, Aug. 1899.

78. Two bottles which contained poison were found by the deceased.—*Daily Chronicle*, p. 7, Aug. 22, 1899.

79. Annual subscriptions will be thankfully received by the matron, of whom also full particulars respecting the home can be obtained.—*Advertisement of Children's Hospital*, in Weston-super-Mare.

80. We might desire, with him, for Euclid to be abolished in favour of some other scheme of geometry.—Quoted in *School World*, p. 278, July 1899.

81. That is the object of the Primrose League,—this mutual constant intercourse with all classes with each other,—and therefore it has been a success.—Quoted in *Daily Telegraph*, p. 8, May 19, 1899.

82. He was for years virtually French Ambassador at London.—*Review of Reviews*, p. 330, Oct. 1899.

83. But he is painfully surprised by the total exclusion of stimulants from University Clubs.—*Ibid.* p. 405, Oct. 1899.

84. The date of the "New Race" in Egypt was first put three or four thousand years B.C.—*Ibid.* p. 491, Nov. 1899.

85. Our past losses can easily be made good with a display of resolution at home and of due precaution at the front.—*Daily Telegraph*, p. 6, Dec. 18, 1899.

86. I am writing to say that for some years I have suffered much with neuralgia and indigestion.—*Ibid.* (*Adv.*), p. 5, Feb. 1, 1900.

87. He insisted in regarding the Petition as a seditious document.—*Short History of England*, p. 303.

88. Natural historians tell us that no fruits grew originally among us besides hips and haws, acorns and pigments, with other delicacies of the like nature.—ADDISON, *Spectator*, No. 69, para. 5.

89. This stroke of prerogative was about the last piece of mischief done the country by a strictly pious and moral king.—GOLDWIN SMITH, *United Kingdom*, vol. ii. p. 306.

90. Imperfect as institutions were, the nation, comparing them with those of other countries, was on the whole content with them, and was averse from revolution.—*Ibid.* vol. ii. p. 272.

91. Above all, the oligarchy of Protestant landowners was at heart conscious what, if the arm of Great Britain were withdrawn, its fate would be.—*Ibid.* vol. ii. p. 225.

92. Delighted by the magnificent welcome they received from the

people of Portsmouth, the officers and men of Her Majesty's cruiser " Powerful " were overjoyed yesterday morning, etc.—*Daily Telegraph*, p. 4, April 13, 1900.

93. He quickly finds that even this speck on the face of the globe, inhabited by an idyllic community, is connected, though by slender ties, to the great world outside.—*Review of Reviews*, p. 533, Nov. 1899.

94. She shocked him by her pious austerity, and ended by being superseded in her queenly influence by Madame de Pompadour, the true Queen of France, who understood the king's character better.— *Literature*, p. 209, March 10, 1900.

95. He was rather sorry that the managers of the Prince of Wales's Fund were rather adverse from inquiry, maintaining that their functions were purely administrative.—*Daily Telegraph*, p. 6, Oct. 17, 1899.

96. They outnumbered the French thirty to one, and were certainly not inferior to them in natural valour.—GOLDWIN SMITH, *United Kingdom*, vol. ii. p. 205.

97. Pitt had compared the union of Newcastle with Fox to that of the languid Saône to the impetuous Rhone.—*Ibid.* vol. ii. p. 191.

98. The clause in favour of the King of Scots might be quoted as implying a connection on his part to the English monarchy, which his own attitude towards John seems to suggest.—*Ibid.* vol. i. p. 139.

99. All the correspondents unite to praise the magnificent marching of the English foot-soldiers. —*Daily Telegraph*, p. 9, March 14, 1900.

100. Her Majesty's message to the Lord Mayor shows by how much the love and enthusiasm of London supported the aged sovereign through the fatigues of her progress.—*Ibid.* p. 9, March 9, 1900.

101. Mr. Goschen replied that the Government could not see their way to devote a ship for Antarctic discovery.—*Ibid.* p. 6, March 9, 1900.

102. She writes that they are indolent, fanatical, and intolerant to all creeds except their own, and especially to the Catholic faith.— *Ibid.* p. 10, Feb. 26, 1900.

103. Our men assisted to bury the dead on the enemy's side yesterday.—*Ibid.* p. 10, March 1, 1900.

104. The announcement is such as to still more confirm us in our resolve of doing our full duty in the present emergency.—*Ibid.* p. 9, Feb. 22, 1900.

105. The action began at six in the morning by a heavy cannonade, to which the enemy replied feebly.—*Ibid.* p. 9, Feb. 20, 1900.

106. Sir M. Bhownagree inquired what arrangements had been finally concluded between Her Majesty's Government, the Government of India, and the University of London, for taking over the Imperial Institute buildings.—*Ibid.* p. 6, Feb. 20, 1900.

107. Looked at in this point of view, we cannot refuse to regard them as organisms of some peculiar and amazing kind.—S. SMILES, *Industrial Biography*, p. 298, ch. xv. (H).

108. The truth about humanity is rarely anything save humiliating. —Quoted in *Literature*, p. 163, Feb. 24, 1900.

109. He begins his paper by the following figures.—*Review of Reviews*, p. 145, Feb. 1900.

110. No government will venture to restore Baluchistan or Chitral or the army of Kashmir to the condition it was a few years ago.—*Ibid.* p. 156, Feb. 1900.

111. I am privately informed that the approaching visit of the Shah to the Russian capital will prove to be pregnant of disagreeable surprises for England.—*Standard,* p. 5, March 10, 1900.

112. There must be a very different spirit of energy and concentration than has prevailed since the retirement of Mr. Gladstone.—*Fortnightly Review,* p. 458, Sept. 1900.

113. So far as wounds are concerned, the results of this war have not borne out the forecast made of the effect of the new long-range arms of precision ; but in respect to disease the old experience has been reproduced.—*Ibid.* p. 493, Sept. 1900.

114. The experience of this and former wars concurs in demonstrating the supreme importance of health preservation in the maintenance in efficiency of an army in the field.—*Ibid.* p. 494, Sept. 1900.

115. War cannot but be accompanied by much physical and moral suffering.—*Ibid.* p. 494, Sept. 1900.

116. Worshippers of Buddha venerate serpents. "This animal," says Mr. Wake, "became equal in importance as Buddha himself."— DOANE, *Bible Parallels,* p. 356, ch. xxxiii.

117. Staff and generals have not the counters to play the game of war.—*Daily Express,* p. 1, Oct. 2, 1900.

118. It was undoubtedly a curious and interesting experiment, but not the most obstinate pessimist, while deploring the principle involved, could find anything at which to protest.—*Fortnightly Review,* p. 634, Oct. 1900.

119. There was nothing different to the old days, except that the rooms looked bare and lacked the background of colour and brilliancy. —*Ibid.* p. 634, Oct. 1900.

120. There is no abatement of the demand for ices, even when the ground is covered by snow several degrees whiter than the composition they sell.—Quoted in *Daily Telegraph,* p. 9, Oct. 15, 1900.

121. There are at present at Regent's Park a museum, lecture theatre, and small library and herbarium.—*Daily Telegraph,* p. 10, Oct. 20, 1900.

122. At what time was Linus, the successor of Peter, made Bishop of Rome ? The last trace we have of him, he was with Paul in Rome in the fall (autumn) of A.D. 65.—REBER, *Christ of Paul,* p. 257.

123. What use (if any) is the historical novel to the practical teacher ?—FEARENSIDE, in *School World,* p. 404, Nov. 1900.

124. I am assured here that Don Carlos has made advances to the Vatican, with a view of gaining the Church over to his cause.—*Daily Telegraph,* p. 7, Nov. 5, 1900.

125. The financial position of the Association is not so satisfactory as your Committee could desire, but this is largely accounted for in consequence of the war and the unusual number of deaths arising chiefly from the prevailing epidemic.—*Report of Ealing Conservative Association,* 1899.

126. No one would accuse the representative of an English newspaper as an Irishman desirous of exaggerating the distress and grievances of his country.—*Report of Dillon's Speech,* Feb. 10, 1898.

127. It is difficult to imagine a rougher experience than that involved by his attempt to carry out the adventurous project of reaching Paris from New York by land.—*Times Weekly*, p. 92, Feb. 11, 1898.

128. At any other time and in any other person such an exhibition might have been conducive of pity.—*Windsor Magazine*, p. 258, Aug. 1898.

129. With the view of extending the length of the child's school-life, we petitioned the Education Department to enable us to raise the exemption-standard from the Sixth to the Seventh.—*Fortnightly Review*, p. 795, Nov. 1900.

130. The worship and legend of an effeminate hero like Sandan appear to have spread by means of an early diffusion of the Semitic stock, first to the neighbourhood of Tarsus in Cilicia and afterwards to Sardis in Lydia.—*Ibid.* p. 826, Nov. 1900.

131. His belief of revelation was unshaken ; his learning preserved his principles ; he grew first regular, and then pious.—BOSWELL's *Life of Johnson.*

132. Captain Mahan is sparing with praise ; the good words he has for Roberts, French, Baden-Powell, and other commanders are therefore the more significant.—*Daily Express*, p. 4, Nov. 15, 1900.

133. Mr. Chamberlain and his party spent the whole morning in the Forum, showing great admiration at the recent discoveries, which are of interest to the whole of the civilised world.—*Daily Telegraph*, p. 9, Nov. 21, 1900.

134. At different times the Unitarian College was located at York, Manchester, and London, and is now finally fixed at Oxford.—*Spectator*, p. 712, Nov. 17, 1900.

135. I was much struck by the quiet contempt with which he spoke of the recent achievements of the British arms.—*Review of Reviews*, p. 453, Nov. 1900.

136. It has always seemed to me that here is the key to the unfortunate state of affairs between jailer and prisoner at St. Helena.—Quoted in *Spectator*, p. 747, Nov. 24, 1900.

137. At the time that he resigned from the army Mr. B. took one position which has brought down upon him unceasing criticism from one New England anti-Imperialist.—*Review of Reviews*, p. 437, Nov. 1900.

138. The incident ended by Leigh Hunt recovering the money.—*Ibid.* p. 469, Nov. 1900.

139. He was in essence a Calvinist, *minus* the Calvinist's grasp upon the personality of the Deity.—*Ibid.* p. 492, Nov. 1900.

140. Sir A. C. was a man of varied experience, with the highest character of scrupulous honesty.—*Ibid.* p. 497, Nov. 1900.

141. This last rebuff administered to the revered head of the defunct republic will be felt as a painful blow against the sentiments of the German nation.—Quoted in *Daily Telegraph*, p. 11, Dec. 4, 1900.

142. I saw the line taken of imputing disloyalty and want of patriotism to men quite as loyal and patriotic, though differing in opinion to themselves.—*Ibid.* p. 10, Dec. 7, 1900.

143. W. H. W. pleaded guilty to bigamy, having married Miss

H. C. R., a hospital nurse, while his wife was alive.—*Ibid.* p. 4, Dec. 11, 1900.

144. Lord S. urged that the Colonials would hardly thank them for setting forth that they were to be treated differently to the rest of Her Majesty's troops.—*Ibid.* p. 6, Dec. 11, 1900.

145. The Housing Committee recommended that the resolution be passed, and, it is important to note, backed up their recommendation by the following words :—etc.—*Fortnightly Review,* p. 974, 1900.

146. The Council do approve of action being taken under Part III. of the Act with a view to the purchase of land and the erection of dwellings thereon, and also with the view of purchasing or leasing houses already built.—Quoted in *Fortnightly Review,* p. 979, Dec. 1900.

147. I never cease to mourn the lost companionship of my dear friend, with whom for so long I still went coupled and inseparable.—*Ibid.* p. 1020, Dec. 1900.

148. Alderman Sir W. T. expressed his dissent to the opinion of Mr. Stuart that the education afforded in Germany was better than that given in England.—*Daily Telegraph,* p 8, Dec. 20, 1900.

149. I remember her standing with her feet quite apart and her legs akimbo, challenging me upon some political question, by which and her appearance I was much astonished and a little frightened.—*Temple Bar,* "Life of Mrs. Grote," Dec. 1900.

150. The incorrigible loafer at present escapes unwhipped of justice, because he is mixed up with honest workmen on the look-out for a job.—*Review of Reviews,* p. 561, Dec. 1900.

151. Hence has arisen the rivalry, to the existence of which the English nation has been hitherto oblivious.—*Daily Express,* p. 4, Jan. 2, 1901.

152. Beyond them stretch the several centuries in which the order of the succession was almost constantly disliked or disputed, and reigns were often commenced with trouble or terminated by calamity.—*Daily Telegraph,* p. 6, Jan. 25, 1901.

153. This being the case, the Monthly Reviewer concludes by the following well-weighed words of warning.—*Review of Reviews,* p. 56, Jan. 1901.

154. Being landed at Havannah and plunged into a life of dissipation as the hanger-on of a public billiard-room, he developed at twelve years old into a pert boy without reverence or fear.—*Spectator,* p. 143, Jan. 26, 1901.

155. What use, he argues, is the national cry for an extension of our naval forces, if there be no extension of our foreign trade for them to protect ?—*Daily Express,* p. 3, Feb. 1, 1901.

156. In exercising her gift of sympathy, the Queen gained greatly owing to the fortunate circumstances of her own domestic life.—*Spectator,* p. 160, Feb. 2, 1901.

157. She had a pain across the shoulders, and suffered most severely with rheumatism.—*Middlesex County Times,* p. 3, Feb. 9, 1901.

158. Numerous complaints had been received of a woman calling herself Nurse Watkins, who had obtained goods from tradesmen by means of worthless cheques.—Quoted in *Daily Telegraph,* p. 5, Feb. 14, 1901.

159. He had the courage to stand up before the Grand Old Man and tell him to his face that other things beside the supposed wrongs of the Christian subjects of the Porte claimed the earnest attention and devotion of Englishmen.—*Fortnightly Review*, p. 227, Feb. 1901.

160. It may well be doubted whether the civilisation of the Highlands could have been begun, or if begun, would have been attended by success, but for the power of the sword.—*Daily Telegraph*, p. 4, Jan. 22, 1901.

161. General Wood has been instructed to impress the Convention with the necessity for adopting a satisfactory declaration as to the future relations of the United States and Cuba.—*Ibid.* p. 9, Feb. 23, 1901.

162. It must also be remembered that our prestige was gained under totally different conditions of naval warfare to those which prevail to-day.—*Empire Review*, p. 54, Feb. 1901.

163. The proceedings terminate by the king drinking to the champion's health out of a gold bowl, which the knight carries away with him.—*Spectator*, p. 274, Feb. 23, 1901.

164. People in this country have become familiar to the idea that the British nation is determined to set its house in order after the experience in South Africa.—*Daily Telegraph*, p. 9, March 11, 1901.

165. All Northern Siberia is covered by wood, but it is too far off for export.—*Spectator*, p. 343, March 9, 1901.

166. When she leaves the prison, at the completion of her sentence, the money is handed over to some responsible person or to one of the Prisoners' Aid Societies to be expended for her benefit.—*Fortnightly Review*, p. 564, March 1901.

167. Mr. W. said that possibly the interposition of the right honourable gentleman was with a view of indulging in a cheap sneer at his expense.—Quoted in *Daily Telegraph*, p. 6, March 13, 1901.

168. Such an army would be ready for any sacrifice, any suffering or hardship, and would exhibit a different sort of courage to that displayed by "mercenaries."—*Ibid.* p. 9, March 13, 1901.

169. From the standpoint of the interests of Germany there can be no doubt as to the desirability of the existence of good relations with England, and previous governments would presumably have more energetically opposed the present querulous opposition of England, which springs for the most part from persons who do not clearly know what they are aiming at.—Quoted as a translation from a Berlin newspaper in *Daily Telegraph*, p. 10, March 14, 1901.

170. There is no reason which can be stated why a fire once started should not consume a capital city, as one nearly did in Chicago.—*Spectator*, p. 382, March 16, 1901.

171. Mr. Abbott predicts that in four years hence neither Imperialism nor silver will be an issue (in a general election), but that the question of monopoly will occupy the field.—*Review of Reviews*, p. 283, March 1901.

172. To learn to see and observe with the pleasant inducement of sport is one way, and perhaps as good as any other. But it is not the only way. In this country it nearly always begins by a taste for field sports, even of the humblest kind.—*Spectator*, p. 454, March 30, 1901.

173. The (South African) native of to-day is very different to the native of past generations.—*Empire Review*, p. 288, April 1901.

174. This might seem at first sight to indicate that the black man is unsusceptible towards the disease.—*Ibid.* p. 359, April 1901.

175. This agreement was greeted by laughter in the House of Commons, and it would appear that commercial men generally have failed to accept it seriously.—*Daily Telegraph*, p. 9, April 12, 1901.

176. There is one possible solution to which he is oblivious.—*Review of Reviews*, p. 374, April 1901.

177. The Romance nation of the West is sympathetic to the Slavonic ideal, and chivalrously plants civilisation in Asia in the same spirit as do the Russians.—*Fortnightly Review*, p. 618 April 1901.

178. There for all practical purposes the matter might have ended by a unanimous vote, which could have truly represented the feelings of the nation.—*Daily Telegraph*, p. 9, May 10, 1901.

179. The estimated cost of the docks is about twelve million dollars. Labour-saving machinery is to be employed, such as the English trades unions object to the use of by employers.—*Ibid.* p. 9, May 15, 1901.

180. Cabinet Scandal in France : French Minister accused with abuse of office.—*Daily Express*, p. 1, May 16, 1901.

181. He begins by the paradox that while in some of her actions England outrages the sentiments of justice and of pity which are innate in all hearts, in others she increases our pride in belonging to the human race.—*Ibid.* p. 490, May 1901.

182. I know that we never shall want for support for a firm policy in the city of London.—Quoted in *Daily Telegraph*, p. 10, Nov. 14, 1901.

183. But there are two things in this book which I cannot pass by even a cursory notice without special mention.—*Review of Reviews*, p. 499, May 1901.

184. There is not a man or woman familiar with the character and traditions of Tommy Atkins, who is not aware that he would at any time go half starved himself rather than women and children should want for anything he could supply.—*Daily Telegraph*, p. 8, June 18, 1901.

185. I never heard the olde song of Percy and Duglas (the Ballad of Chevy Chase), that I found not my heart moved more than with a trumpet.—SIDNEY.

186. It is indeed not the "superior respectability and decency" to which temperance reformers are likely to object, but to the creation of licensed houses in districts which have hitherto been free from them.—*Spectator*, p. 914, June 22, 1901.

187. Sir E. G. ended by a vigorous attack on the Government, and by declaring that he and his friends, whatever might happen, would never join them.—*Ibid.* p. 43, July 13, 1901.

188. In these countries the educational system had been settled on exactly those lines which the Liberal party would like to see it settled in England.—Quoted in *Middlesex County Times*, p. 5, July 20, 1901.

189. The violent moral of his practical conclusion is quite out of keeping with this frame of mind, which makes a different, and a less

pardonable, inconsistency than that of mutually contradicting hypotheses impartially entertained.—*Spectator*, p. 126, July 27, 1901.

190. For himself at no period of his career has money for money's sake ever seemed matter of concern. The majority of clerks at decent wages live as luxuriously.—*Ibid.* p. 152, Aug. 3, 1901.

191. It goes without saying,—or rather the outside nations are never tired of insisting as an incontestable fact,—that the Jameson Raid was prompted and organised by the Secretary of State for the Colonies.—*Fortnightly Review*, pp. 329, 330, Aug. 1901.

192. The death of your daughter would have been a blessing in comparison of this.—JANE AUSTEN, *Pride and Prejudice*, ch. xlvii.

193. After having enjoyed practical immunity from smallpox for several years, London is now threatened by a serious outbreak.—*Daily Telegraph*, p. 10, Aug. 28, 1901.

194. The list of cities taken by Sheshonk commences by the north and is composed of lists of former conquests, which the adulatory writer ascribes to Sheshonk.—RENAN, *History of Israel*, Book IV. ch. i.

195. "Jane Eyre" as a story lacks in life and animation.—E. J. MATHEW, *History of English Literature*, 1901.

196. On Friday there will be an address by Lord Rosebery, to which follow luncheon at the Guildhall, service at the Cathedral, conversazione at the college, and illuminations.—*Daily Telegraph*, p. 11, Sept. 18, 1901.

197. Continued resistance can therefore lead to no other result save that the people of this country will be in a worse condition, both morally and materially, by delaying the inevitable termination.—*Ibid.* p. 10, Sept. 17, 1901.

198. A German field-officer declares that nothing done by the British in South Africa can compare to the severity of the methods used by the Germans in France.—*Daily Mail*, p. 1, Sept. 25, 1901.

199. Certainly, the Boer prisoners now in Bermuda are enjoying an ideal prison life. They want for nothing to make them comfortable and happy, so far as men in captivity can be happy.—*Daily Telegraph*, p. 10, Sept. 26, 1901.

200. It may safely be remarked that the scheme (to be completed in two more volumes) does not want for comprehensiveness.—*Spectator*, p. 525, Oct. 12, 1901.

201. But the examination of Professor Saintsbury's book ought to throw some light upon the nature and meaning of literary criticism, and at least one can attempt to avoid bearing false witness of it.—*Fortnightly Review*, p. 599, Oct. 1901.

202. The successful advance of the field-marshal into the heart of the enemy'ε country will so dishearten them as to make them relax their final preparations of resistance.—*Daily Telegraph*, p. 10, June 5, 1900.

203. Under the outrageous treatment of the white peoples the idea of unifying the yellow peoples is pretty certain to become audibly and visibly operative before many years.—H. G. WELLS, *Fortnightly Review*, p. 912, Nov. 1901.

204. His decision was appealed from, on the contention that before it was given he refused to admit evidence of a previous conviction.—*Daily Telegraph*, p. 8, Nov. 20, 1901.

205. This is to be accounted for, according to the opinion of initiated persons, to a certain fatigue of the Sultan, who finds the burden of centralisation and the decisive management of all State affairs in the Palace too great for him.—*Ibid.* p. 9, Nov. 23, 1901.

206. Mr. W. Jones, M.P., amidst tremendous disorder charged the police with partisanship by ejecting Liberals from the building, but the officer in charge denied the truth of the accusation.—*Ibid.* p. 10, June 24, 1901.

207. The result is that the tenants and servants of all kinds to be found about them are a finer stamp of men to those in similar positions elsewhere.—*Man*, No. 132, p. 163, Nov. 1901.

208. Equally certainly Druids were there at this late date, though discredited of the Pictish king and his people.—*Fortnightly Review*, p. 692, April 1900.

209. President Hadley writes a level, flowing style, but never aspires at epigram.—*Spectator*, p. 879, Dec. 7, 1901.

210. There is one that will think herself obliged to double her kindness and caresses of me.—ADDISON, *Spectator*, No. 409.

211. From this coalition, and not from the spirit of its own laws and institutions, he attributed the harsh and ungenerous treatment of our fallen enemy.—*Autobiography of Mr. Fletcher*, p. 374 (H).

212. The greatest masters of critical learning differ among one another.—ADDISON, *Spectator*, No. 321.

213. 'Tis my humble request you will be particular in speaking to the following points.—*Guardian*, No. 57.

214. When England depends, after this war, upon her developed strength and consistent policy, she will no longer want for friends.—*Daily Telegraph*, p. 5, April 18, 1900.

215. Italy will be specially careful not to endanger her good relations with England, who would naturally prefer Italy as a neighbour in Egypt instead of France.—*Ibid.* p. 10, Jan. 9, 1902.

216. His tenure of the Foreign Office during a trying time has been marked with tact and discretion.—*Ibid.* p. 10, Jan. 14, 1902.

217. The company was compelled by the promoters, three months after the issue of the prospectus, to change its bankers, with a view of stopping the company's credit.—*Ibid.* p. 5, Jan. 16, 1902.

218. This inspired so much apprehension into printers that they became unwilling to incur the hazard of an obnoxious trade.—HALLAM, *Literature of Europe*, vol. ii. p. 266.

219. So far it would seem the Cobdenites are justified of their protests against efforts to destroy or counteract this particular form of Protection.—*Daily Telegraph*, p. 8, March 7, 1902.

220. St. Vincent is covered by ashes and dust that have destroyed all the herbage and growing provisions and fruit.—*Ibid.* p. 8, May 24, 1902.

221. Do you suppose that it would be a pleasant thing to see myself forced to allow my children to be brought up in another creed to my own?—R. BAGOT, *Casting of Nets*, ch. viii. p. 108.

222. It takes a very high rank among the biographical literature of the year, we will venture to add, of the century.—*Spectator*, p. 703, Nov. 8, 1902.

223. A friendship **among** persons of different sexes seldom takes place in this country.—SYDNEY SMITH, *Memoir*, vol. i. p. 131 (H).

224. It must at least be supposed that the author had other sources of information from those which we have, and that to us it may well have the value of an original.—RENAN'S *Life of Jesus* (tr. W. M. Thomson), appendix, p. 271.

225. Neither English nor Dutch in the old Colony can be oblivious to this consideration, which has been pressed upon them very clearly by Mr. Chamberlain.—*Spectator*, p. 284, Feb. 21, 1903.

226. It was on the support of France and England that they looked for their only effectual aid.—ALISON, *History of Europe from Fall of Napoleon*.

227. It is owing to his advice that the general plan of this campaign, afterwards so admirably carried into execution by Barclay, is to be ascribed.—*Ibid.*

228. Alphonsus ordered a great fire to be prepared, into which, after His Majesty and the public had joined in prayer for heavenly assistance in this ordeal, both the rivals were thrown into the flames.—D'ISRAELI, *Curiosities of Literature*.

229. To the 365 days in the year he has prefixed to each an epistle dedicatory.—*Ibid.*

230. It is to this last new feature in the supposed Game Laws, to which we intend to confine our notice.—SYDNEY SMITH, *Essays*.

231. The conversations of men of letters are of a different complexion with the talk of men of the world.—D'ISRAELI, *The Literary Character*.

232. The Italian universities were forced to send for their professors from Spain and France.—HALLAM, *Literature of Europe*.

233. Such were the difficulties with which the question was involved.—ALISON, *History of Europe from Fall of Napoleon*.

234. The accounts they gave of the favourable reception of their writings with the public.—FRANKLIN, *Essays*.

235. Napoleon sought to ally himself by marriage with the royal families in Europe, to ingraft himself to an old imperial tree.—CHANNING, *Essay on Napoleon*.

236. William Cobbett was a popular, but inconsistent political writer, who wrote upon momentary impulse.—Mrs. FOSTER, *Handbook of European Literature*.

237. We were at first inclined to imagine that there was, after all, no reason to fear the German Government proposing that we should take any share in the Baghdad Railway, or, if it did, of our Government listening for a moment to such perilous propositions.—*Spectator*, p. 520, April 4, 1903.

238. He (William II.) is restrained neither by Ministry nor Legislature.—*Daily Telegraph*, p. 11, April 16, 1903.

CHAPTER V.—ERRORS IN CONJUNCTIONS.

(a) Co-ordinative Conjunctions.

1. "And."—Avoid the common mistake of beginning a fresh sentence with *and.* It is the province of this conjunction to add one word to another word or one clause to another clause. It follows from this principle that *and* ought not to be made the first word of a fresh sentence.

> The horrors of the cholera or the plague must be diminished at almost any cost. *And* the cost, *i.e.* the suffering inflicted by these experimental inoculations, can hardly be set against the value of a preventive serum.—*Literature*, March 3, 1900. (Cancel *and.*)
>
> The other measures for increasing the capitulation grant are all to the good. *And* after a long debate the Government are entitled to say that, etc.—*Daily Telegraph*, p. 9, Feb. 20, 1900. (Cancel *and.*)
>
> No other method was suited for a work of reference which is meant to endure. *And* on the whole the editors have scored a success. —*Ibid.* p. 11, Feb. 21, 1900. (Cancel *and.*)
>
> They intermarried until the whole state became one vast family, and with this intermarriage their intellects grew debased. *And* thus they gradually lost much that makes man manly and attractive.—Quoted in *Review of Reviews*, p. 143, Feb. 1900. (Cancel *and.*)
>
> For my part I predict that the man of the twentieth century will be more muscular than the man of the nineteenth. *And* certainly for one evil which the bicycle now provokes, it will yield us a hundred benefits in time to come.—*Ibid.* p. 259, March 1900. (Cancel *and.*)
>
> A similar train of reasoning would justify the absence of clothing, and of tooth-brushes, and of soap. *And* as to the customs of our ancestors there are those who teach that these respected forerunners of our noble selves lived up trees, etc.—*Morning Leader*, p, 7, March 21, 1900. (Cancel *and.*)

Note.—In the Authorised Version of the Bible a fresh sentence very frequently begins with *and.* See, for example, *Genesis*, ch. i. But this is no guide as to modern idiom.

2. **"And which," "and who," "or who,"** etc.—Avoid the common mistake of using the conjunctions *"and"* or *"or"* to connect a Relative clause with some word or words going before, in which no Relative occurs. It is the province of *and*, no less than of other co-ordinative conjunctions, to join *similar* words or *similar* clauses; *i.e.* words or clauses which stand in the same relation to the other parts of the sentence. "The effect of such ill-balanced sentences is like that which would be produced by coupling together in a pair a pony and a full-grown horse. To amend them one must make either both or neither of the clauses Relative, just as with the pair one might substitute either a horse for the pony or a pony for the horse" (Hodgson). (This subject has been alluded to already in Chap. II. (*d*) 12.)

(1) Another form of civilisation might exist, *which* might suit them better, *but which* they are not allowed to develop freely.— *Spectator*, p. 798, Dec. 1, 1900.

Here the balance is correct. Two Relative clauses are connected by *but*, and since the case of the Relative is not the same in each clause, the *which* is rightly repeated.

(2) One of its most powerful exponents was George Whitfield, brought up at a public-house, *and who* lived among Bristol colliers.—*Daily Telegraph*, p. 10, Nov. 26, 1900.

Here a Relative clause is connected by *and* to the participle "brought up." Say, "who was brought up at a public-house and lived among Bristol colliers."

(3) The India Office had other experts to consult quite as good as he, *and in whose* judgment they had more confidence.— *Review of Reviews*, p. 497, Nov. 1900.

Say, "who were quite as good as he, and in whose judgment," etc. Or, cancel the *and*.

(4) Jacko, the regimental monkey of the City Imperial Volunteers, *and which* went through the whole of the South African campaign, has been removed to the Zoological Gardens, Regent's Park.—*Daily Telegraph*, p. 8, Nov. 10, 1900.

To preserve the balance, either cancel *and* before *which*, or cancel *which* after *and*, and say, "Jacko, which was the regimental monkey, and went," etc.

3. **"Both . . . and."**—If the conjunction *both* is used, take care that it is followed by its proper correlative *and*, and not by any other conjunction such as *"as well as"*:—

Both in London *as well as* in the country generally there was great excitement about the relief of Mafeking. (Change *as well as* to *and*.)

4. " Or " for " and."—In negative sentences or clauses we use *or* in preference to *and* for joining words or phrases :—

> He had no book *or* slate with him, when he started for school.

This is equivalent to " He had no book *and* he had no slate." We see how *or* has come into use for *and* in negative sentences, if we rewrite the above sentence as follows :—

> He had not *either* a book *or* a slate with him, when he started for school.

Even when the sentence is affirmative, we sometimes use *or* as almost equivalent to *and*, the alternative force of *or* being so weak as to render the conjunction Cumulative rather than Alternative :—

> Such trades as those of leather *or* carpentry *or* smith's work flourish best in large cities.
>> Their strength *or* speed *or* vigilance were given
>> In aid of our defects.—COWPER.

Note.—The Plural form given to the verb "*were* given," though of questionable accuracy, was no doubt due to the sense of plurality suggested by the cumulative sense of *or*.

5. " But."—While it is the province of *and* to add one statement to another by way of continuation or supplement, it is the province of *but* to set one statement against another by way of opposition or contrast :—

> It was not the boy's first offence, *and* there was a grave breach of discipline in the attempt to foment sedition and persuade scholars to desert their duties.—*Daily Telegraph*, p. 9, April 17, 1899.

Here two reasons are given for punishing the boy : (1) it was not his first offence ; (2) he had committed a grave breach of discipline. The second statement adds force to the first by continuing the same line of argument. The two statements therefore are rightly connected by *and*. Suppose, however, we cancel the word *not ;* we must then change *and* to *but*, or the combination will make nonsense :—

> It was the boy's first offence ; *but* there was a grave breach of discipline, etc.

Here the second statement is placed in antithesis to the first: "True, it was the boy's first offence ; *but* he had committed a grave breach of discipline in what he did, and we cannot pardon him."

6. " Though," " but."—These two conjunctions are both Adversative, because both set one statement against another. The former, however, is Subordinative, while the other is Co-ordinative. Hence *though* represents the weaker clause, and *but* the stronger one.

(1) It was the boy's first offence ; *but* there was a grave breach of discipline in what he did, and we cannot pardon him.

(2) *Though* it was the boy's first offence, there was a grave breach of discipline in what he did, and we cannot pardon him.

These two sentences mean precisely the same thing. The only difference is that the former is Compound, the latter Complex. Observe, that in (1) the stronger and more emphatic clause is that following *but*, and therefore in (2) this same clause has been made the Principal clause, to which the clause beginning with *though* is subordinate.

7. "But" confounded with "and."—Since the province of *but* is so entirely distinct from that of *and*, care must be taken not to use the one where we ought to use the other. The confusion, however, is sometimes met with.

(1) The outside costume of a clergyman is not a matter of much or any importance, *and* I think there would be a strong barrier to break down before we could do away with it.—Quoted in *Church Gazette*, p. 109, June 3, 1899.

Here the *and* should be displaced by *but*, as there is evidently an antithesis between the first clause and the second.

(2) Cathartic Pills do more harm than good. Carter's Little Liver Pills do only good, *but* a large amount of it.—*Advertisement, Daily Telegraph*, May 1, 1899.

The last clause, since it is meant to continue what is stated in the preceding one, should have been preceded by *and*, not by *but*. The real opposition is between Cathartic Pills and Carter's Pills. The advertisement therefore should have been worded thus :—"Cathartic Pills do more harm than good. *But* Carter's Liver Pills do only good, *and* a large amount of it."

8. "Either . . . or," "neither . . . nor."—As these are correlative pairs, care must be taken (1) that *either* is followed by *or* and *neither* by *nor* ; (2) that each member of the pair is placed before words of the same part of speech or of the same function. (The latter point has been dealt with already in Chap. III. (*f*).)

(1)   The world, which seems
To lie before us like a land of dreams,
So various, so beautiful, so new,
Hath really *neither* joy, *nor* love, *nor* light,
Nor certitude, *nor* peace, *nor* help for pain.
                        MATTHEW ARNOLD, *Dover Beach.*

(2) The Moriscos became *neither* clergy, *nor* monks, *nor* nuns ; they did not go into the army.—*Spectator*, p. 482, Oct. 5, 1901.

(3) It was *neither* by superior numbers, discipline, organisation, *or* enlightenment, that the leaders of the Confederate army hoped to prevail.—*Fortnightly Review*, p. 663, April 1900.

The first two sentences are correct. There are three faults in the third : (*a*) *neither* is followed by *or ;* (*b*) the conjunction is not repeated before each noun ; (*c*) the word "superior" is intended to qualify each noun, but this is not obvious from the construction. The sentence can be rewritten thus :—

> It was not by superiority in numbers, discipline, organisation, or enlightenment that the leaders of the Confederate army hoped to prevail.

9. Confusion between "or" and "and." — Since it is the province of *or* to express an alternative or choice, and of *and* to express addition and continuation, care must be taken not to use the one where we ought to use the other. Such confusion, however, is sometimes met with.

> Some of her poems have appeared already in volumes written singly *and* in collaboration with her sister Louisa, to whom a touching reference is made in the preface.—*Literature*, p. 351, May 5, 1900.

Since the same volume could not have been written both singly by one author and in collaboration with another, *and* should be displaced by *or*.

10. Confusion between "or" and "if." — We can say "little, or nothing"; we can also say "little, if anything." These two phrases mean the same thing. But we are not entitled for that reason to mix them together, and say "little, if nothing," as is sometimes done.

> Little, if nothing, was done after the meeting was closed.

11. "Or never," "if ever."—Another instance of confusion between *or* and *if* occurs in using the phrase "seldom or ever," as if this were equivalent to "seldom or never." It is right to say "I have seldom, *if ever*, heard of it," which written out in full means "I have seldom heard of it, if indeed I have ever heard of it at all." It is equally right to say, "I have seldom *or never* heard of it," which means the same thing as the preceding. But we sometimes meet with the phrase "seldom *or ever*," which has no meaning, and has evidently resulted from a confusion between the two.

> Those who walk in their sleep have *seldom or ever* the most distant recollection that they have been dreaming at all.—SYDNEY SMITH, *Moral Philosophy*, Lect. ii. p. 75 (H).

12. "Or" in an interrogative sentence.—In questions (direct or indirect), if the noun following *or* is meant to be contrasted with the noun preceding it, put an article (if possible) before the second noun, and if a preposition has been used before the first noun, repeat it before the second :—

Has he gained a prize or scholarship? (Insert *a* before *scholarship.*)
Tell me whether he influenced you with promises or threats.
(Insert *with* before *threats.*)

Correct, improve, or justify the following sentences :—

1. Both amongst the people here, as well as among members of the
court, the news of the relief of Mafeking has been hailed with great
rejoicing.—*Daily Telegraph,* p. 10, May 21, 1900.

2. The short and final truth is that England has not one firm
friend in Europe, and perhaps in the world.—*Ibid.* p. 5, April 13,
1900.

3. Behind the Japanese workman, on whom the wealth of the
nation rests, are an illimitable resource, a tireless patience.—*Ibid.*
p. 11, June 14, 1900.

4. All was quiet in Ladysmith yesterday. From a point close to
the hospitals the enemy could see all the positions of the British
garrison, and there was little sign of active resistance, evidently on
account of want of ammunition.—*Ibid.* p. 9, Feb. 22, 1900.

5. They (the Hooligans) do not rob, and appear to be actuated by
a mixture of violent brutality and boyish delight in hurting some-
body.—*Spectator,* p. 514, Oct. 20, 1900.

6. They only slightly damaged the railroad, but did not succeed
in cutting the telegraph wires.—*Daily Telegraph,* p. 9, July 3, 1900.

7. In fact, neither in his teaching or example is it possible, if we
regard him as a mere man, to attribute to any particular parts a
distinct, or distinctive, and a permanent authority.—*Fortnightly
Review,* p. 287, Feb. 1900.

8. We derive neither greatness, sublimity, nor depth from un-
ceasingly fixing our thoughts on the infinite and the unknown.—
Ibid. p. 919, June 1900.

9. The last recourse to pistols or swords in a controversy is neither
an evidence of the highest wisdom, the truest courage, nor the firmest
belief in Christianity itself.—Dr. Madden's *Life of Lady Blessington,*
ch. iv. p. 106.

10. Cruelty with some of the larger and fiercer beasts may be
necessary, and, if not cruelty, what we may without prejudice term
extremely rigorous handling.—*Fortnightly Review,* p. 387, March
1900.

11. A long time ago I said that Great Britain might sustain
checks in the Transvaal, and that she could not be vanquished.—
Quoted in *Daily Graphic,* p. 2, Feb. 19, 1900.

12. Neither at Berlin or at St. Petersburg is there the least
desire to precipitate these contingencies,—certainly not on the part of
Russia.—*Fortnightly Review,* p. 302, Aug. 1900.

13. Mr. Harry O'Brien is neither a deep philosopher or a vivid
artist.—*Ibid.* p. 873, Dec. 1898.

14. Miss Corelli has been engaged on this novel for some years,
and her work was interrupted by her dangerous illness of two years
ago.—*Literature,* p. 357, May 5, 1900.

15. Neither in State nor in Church, neither in policy nor in arms,
in morals, in literature, or in art, did the civilisation of the New

Rome equal or even approach the Catholic Feudalism.—Quoted in *Literature*, p. 49, July 21, 1900.

16. Mr. Chaplin pointed out that upon the whole the quality of the London water was admirable, and that little, if nothing, was left to be desired upon that point.—*Daily Telegraph*, p. 9, March 30, 1900.

17. Nine shots in the minute is rapid work, and I have seen ten shots fired in the time, and every shot hit the ring.—Quoted in *Review of Reviews*, p. 152, Feb. 1900.

18. When we ask for the result of this great strategic movement, we learn that it has been brilliantly carried out, but that they have neither captured an enemy, a waggon, nor a cannon.—*Ibid.* p. 407, May 1900.

19. I never saw a similar operation more quickly, more quietly, nor more methodically performed in any English dockyard.—*Engineering*, p. 462, April 6, 1900.

20. There has always been more or less of a latent feeling that eventually Canada would become a part of the United States, either by gravitation, annexation, conquest, or voluntary action of the people.—Quoted in *Daily Mail*, p. 4, April 11, 1900.

21. Marvellous as have been the achievements of Egyptian administration during the last twelve years, neither the English public, the Egyptian people, nor the administrators themselves are content with the present administration of affairs.—*Fortnightly Review*, p. 937, June 1899.

22. How lucky then that neither the Cabinet, the Unionist party, the House of Commons, or the Press had the faintest conception of the hornet's nest we were about to stir up.—MANSE, *National Review*, Jan. 1900.

23. When an attempt was made to bring the Bible home to the peasants, and translated into the Russian language, the simple folk were not able to read.—*Church Gazette*, p. 138, May 20, 1900.

24. He was a young man of much ability, and who gave much promise of a brilliant political career.—*Daily Telegraph*, p. 9, May 17, 1900.

25. This was a good while ago ; but instead of his hurrying back to let her know how he had got on, she saw nor heard no more of him till quite recently, when, etc.—Quoted in *Daily Telegraph*, p. 12, Nov. 6, 1900.

26. The adulteration of food generally occurs in some wholesome form. Margarine is an excellent food-substance, though it is not butter ; the potato is very nourishing, but it should not be found in bread.—*Ibid.* Aug. 27, 1898.

27. Throughout the whole of the north-east of the Soudan trade and industry are reviving surely, but no doubt slowly.—*Ibid.* June 28, 1898.

28. All these things have won him the admiration and affection of colonists everywhere. And they have helped to give him a reputation in this country greater than that enjoyed by any of his predecessors in the Colonial Office.—*Fortnightly Review*, p. 749, Nov. 1900.

29. Had his other friends been as diligent and ardent as I was, he

(Johnson) might have been almost entirely preserved. As it is, I will venture to say that he will be seen in this work more completely than any man who has ever yet lived. And he will be seen, as he really was ; for I profess to write, not his panegyric, which must be all praise, but his life, which, etc.—BOSWELL'S *Life of Johnson.*

30. Neither Ezekiel, Jeremiah, Deuteronomy, or the ancient prophets ever allude to Aaron as the stem of the true priesthood.—RENAN, *History of Israel,* vol. iii. p. 344.

31. There has been a rise of at least five per cent in the cost of all kinds of provisions : hence the halfpenny mug of tea, coffee, and cocoa is threatened.—*Daily Telegraph,* p. 9, Nov. 21, 1900.

32. The existence of neither France, Germany, nor Russia depends on a mighty navy equal at least to the fleets of two other Powers.—*Daily Express,* p. 4, Nov. 22, 1900.

33. Nothing can be finer than the spectacle of this ruined lady setting forth with her young children to seek another fortune in Russia. And how she found it, and with what splendid endurance she faced disappointments, is clearly told in the last chapter of an interesting book.—*Spectator,* p. 751, Nov. 24, 1900.

34. It (their choice) ought not to be limited either to antiquated fictions, social claims, or private regard, but ought only to be influenced by considerations of public interest and personal fitness.—Quoted in *Daily Telegraph,* p. 10, Nov. 27, 1900.

35. The general feeling of ship-owners was that the administration of the Port of London and the docks should be in the hands of an authority constituted for this purpose, and which should have powers to impose such dues either on ships, on river craft, or on goods, as would appear necessary for the purpose of raising a sufficient revenue.—Quoted in *Daily Telegraph,* p. 6, Nov. 28, 1900.

36. A few words about the late Government House, which I built on the St. Loo estate, may not here be out of place, if only for the enlightenment of those misinformed, or who possess no knowledge of the actual facts.—*Pioneer Mail,* p. 20, Nov. 9, 1900.

37. Neither in China, Persia, Egypt, South Africa, nor Newfoundland is there any reason why a firm policy should provoke war.—*Daily Express,* p. 4, Dec. 4, 1900.

38. They ought to have saved us from sensualism and metaphysics, and they ran us aground on both reefs.—*Women of the Renascence,* quoted in *Spectator,* p. 807, Dec. 1, 1900.

39. Mr. J. R. in putting the resolution to the vote declared that he agreed neither with its wisdom, policy, nor expediency.—*Spectator,* p. 875, Dec. 15, 1900.

40. He speaks foolishly of "the common English prejudice against Paul Jones," and a little thought might have convinced him that the prejudice which he denounces is far too rare.—*Ibid.* p. 54, Jan. 12, 1901.

41. We are much too apt to assume that what is sauce for the goose is sauce for the gander. And the application of Western methods to Oriental peoples is fraught with difficulties and dangers.—*Ibid.* p. 94, Jan. 19, 1901.

42. Steam will rapidly be replaced by electricity, and with much better results both in economy, speed, and safety.—*Review of Reviews,* p. 70, Jan. 1901.

43. The Victorian age, the longest, the greatest, and the noblest in our annals, closes ; and we begin not only a new century, but a new reign, under entirely new and different conditions. And the Victorian epoch closes in storm.—*Spectator*, p. 128, Jan. 26, 1901.

44. Though she gave its true weight to ceremonial, she never fell into the vice of kings, and attached an undue importance to the trivialities of royal pomp.—*Ibid.* p. 160, Feb. 2, 1901.

45. Neither officially nor unofficially, formally nor informally, has any member of the Opposition been asked his advice.—*Daily Telegraph*, p. 9, Feb. 6, 1901.

46. In almost all the colonies except New South Wales the territorial revenue was in fact largely given back to the people by reason of the railway communications established, and which at present did not in all the states pay interest on the capital invested in them.— Quoted in *Commerce*, p. 1005, Dec. 19, 1900.

47. We are far from making a bogey of any economic doctrine, but granted certain industrial conditions and Protection becomes suicidal. —*Spectator*, p. 196, Feb. 9, 1901.

48. The only troops for which I am called upon to answer, on this or any other occasion, are the troops commanded by British officers, and who serve the King.—Quoted in *Daily Telegraph*, p. 7, Feb. 15, 1901.

49. The late Professor Max Müller wrote an interesting essay on fortuitous and rational coincidences.—*Ibid.* p. 10, Feb. 16, 1901.

50. He has written all this, because he has come across a manual of drill, of which he understands neither the scope, the aim, the application, nor the contents.—*Fortnightly Review*, p. 302, Feb. 1901.

51. He devoted even more attention to the collection of medals and coins, collected by him since his earliest boyhood, and which has made of him one of the most expert numismatists in Europe.—*Ibid.* p. 500, March 1901.

52. Let neither partiality or prejudice appear, but let truth everywhere be sacred.—DRYDEN.

53. It was an entirely new creation, uninspired by any previous work, but which gave birth to many others, having furnished the plot to six theatrical pieces.—*Memoir of Bernardin de St. Pierre*, p. xxxiii., *Paul and Virginia*, ed. 1879.

54. The two peoples, the most inventive and to whom we owe many of the implements of marine warfare that are our defence, have investigated this new type of warship.—*Fortnightly Review*, p. 720, April 1901.

55. A week after the cyclone had wrought such havoc, and my office was beset with people who had nothing to claim but everything to hope, I was informed by the private secretary that a lady, her husband, and her son would take no refusal, but insisted on seeing the governor himself.—*Empire Review*, p. 386, May 1901.

56. This faith, which, it is urged, is neither mind-cure, faith-cure, mesmerism, nor hypnotism, has spread over the civilised world.— *Daily Telegraph*, p. 9, May 31, 1901.

57. The Powers could not even create, as allies have repeatedly created, a commander-in-chief. Nobody thought Count von Waldersee unworthy of that position, nobody objected to his appointment, and nobody would obey him except as a momentary act of grace.— *Spectator*, p. 828, June 8, 1901.

58. Austria has made an alarming step towards disintegration, a step long dreaded, and which now threatens to be inevitable and near. *Fortnightly Review*, p. 109, June 1901.

59. Happily the late Queen has been succeeded by a son brought up in her school, thoroughly reverencing her character and her mode of action, and who himself has stepped carefully in the footsteps by which she expressed her constitutional attachment to the institutions of the country over which she ruled.—Lord SALISBURY, *Daily Telegraph*, p. 10, June 27, 1901.

60. Upon one thing everybody was agreed—namely, that the principal business of the statesman, the philanthropist, and the good citizen of the United States at the present time and for the immediate future must be the task of public education. But it was not content to rest there, and adopted resolutions calling for the publication and distribution of its proceedings, and more particularly for the appointment of a standing board of seven members to enter upon an active campaign on behalf of the improvement of educational conditions in the South.—Dr. SHAW, *American Review of Reviews*, p. 569, June 1901.

61. The Czar is a man of sincere and pacific mind, but he is neither paladin or prophet.—*Fortnightly Review*, p. 1036, June 1901.

62. A great City meeting was held at the Guildhall in support of the South African policy of the Government—a gathering described by the Lord Mayor as neither party nor political, but "fully and completely patriotic."—*Daily Telegraph*, p. 8, July 11, 1901.

63. He shows that the Homeric shield was not derived from Phœnicia, or Egypt, Libya, Persia, or Assyria.—*School World*, p. 306, Aug. 1901.

64. Rest assured that where British officers and men are, there you will find neither outrage, cruelty, nor wanton bloodshed. Whatever sounding tongue-clappers may shout to the contrary in Britain's disparagement, neither Tommy nor his officer is guilty of either small meannesses, nor are they ever brutal.—*Daily Telegraph*, p. 8, Aug. 19, 1901.

65. An express train has been thrown over a railway bridge in the southern Portuguese province of Algarve, and completely wrecked. Many passengers have been killed and injured.—*Daily Express*, p. 1, Sept. 10, 1901.

66. A guard from this kilted regiment defended the train at Naboomspruit on July 4 till all had been killed and wounded.—*Daily Telegraph*, p. 6, Sept. 13, 1901.

67. A lad of eighteen, named Henry Bagster, and who for the past year has been a pest to the authorities at Victoria Station, was brought before Mr. Horace Smith at Westminster, on charges of begging and assaulting Police-constable White, a railway officer.—*Ibid.* p. 5, Sept. 24, 1901.

68. That this jealousy will produce war we do not, however, believe. The Powers want trade, not territory, and another war with China, and will arrange a method in which competition, however fierce, will not lead to blows.—*Spectator*, p. 861, June 25, 1901.

69. She (Mrs. Lynn Linton) represented the modern English girl as "neither tender, loving, retiring, or domestic."—Quoted in *Fortnightly Review*, p. 510, Sept. 1901.

70. The necessity of trying to repair all losses at the expense of the peasantry taxed to the point of torture, and whom further pressure would make mad, might not be the worst evil.—*Fortnightly Review*, p. 1037, June 1901.

71. The enemy were severely shelled, and their casualties are believed to have been twenty killed, wounded, and prisoners.—*Daily Telegraph*, p. 9, Oct. 17, 1901.

72. It must require a large number of men to deal effectively with them, and there is no reason for alarm at the apparently slow progress, but rather cause for deep satisfaction that so many, week after week, are being put out of action.—*Ibid.* p. 7, Oct. 28, 1901.

73. But both for good or evil, the sea and the seafaring life exercise a potent influence on character.—*Spectator*, p. 605, Oct. 26, 1901.

74. Though a good many reports have reached us, they are not sufficiently detailed, sufficiently complete, nor in some cases sufficiently well authenticated to warrant the expression of an opinion on the whole case.—*Engineering*, p. 653, Nov. 8, 1901.

75. The statement was incorrect, as any one acquainted with American engines, and who has seen the engines in question, will recognise.—*Ibid.* p. 653, Nov. 8, 1901.

76. But the fact remains that his war experience is neither recent nor large, while the army is now full of general officers who have had an experience both wide, long, and recent.—*Spectator*, p. 749, Nov. 16, 1901.

77. The old cannon captured at Cabul, and which were more dangerous to those who fired them than to those at whom they were aimed, with a few of our own guns which were considered too troublesome to take back to India, were the niggard contribution of the British army to our new friend and ally.—*Fortnightly Review*, p. 750, Nov. 1901.

78. In a society so pre-eminently free from religious prejudice, but which from force of custom and tradition was condemned to publicly assist at ceremonies they scoffed at in private, the Masonic Lodges presented a sort of neutral ground.—*Ibid.* p. 998, Dec. 1901.

79. The educational authority of the future if this bill should pass, and which would have to supervise not only the primary, but secondary and technical education, and, of course, raise a somewhat heavy rate for the purpose, should be the rating body for the district, and no other body.—Quoted in *Daily Telegraph*, p. 10, April 10, 1902.

80. The many miles of path at present tar-paved, and which by Resolution of the Council it has been decided to supersede with stone, will take all the stone which may be manufactured for some years to come.—*Middlesex County Times*, p. 7, May 4, 1901.

81. A petty constable will neither act cheerfully or wisely.—SWIFT'S *Free Thoughts*.

82. The kingdoms of Anahuac were in their nature despotic, attended with many mitigating circumstances unknown to the despotisms of the East.—PRESCOTT, *History of Mexico*, i. 23.

83. It has been already mentioned how Sir Hone Popham pro-

ceeded from the Cape of Good Hope to Buenos Ayres, and the disastrous issue of that expedition.—ALISON, *History of Europe.*

84. He was neither an object of derision to his enemies or of melancholy pity to his friends.—JUNIUS'S *Letters.*

85. There are few scenes more affecting, nor which more deeply engage our sympathy.—D'ISRAELI, *Calamities of Authors.*

86. The experienced commander will not deem such aids to patriotic ardour of little importance, and willingly fan the harmless vanity of the young aspirant.—ALISON, *History of Europe.*

(b) Subordinative Conjunctions.

1. "**Against.**"—Avoid using this preposition as if it were a conjunction. By an ellipsis for "against *the time when*" its use as a conjunction was once common, but is now rare and practically obsolete.

> And they made ready the present *against* Joseph came at noon.— *Gen.* xliii. 25. (Say, "against the time when Joseph would come at noon.")
>
> Some say that ever *'gainst* that season comes
> Wherein our Saviour's birth is celebrated,
> This bird of dawning singeth all night long.
> *Hamlet*, i. 1, 158.

Note.—Writers of fiction sometimes use *against* as a conjunction to express a colloquialism that has survived only among the less cultured classes :—

> Throw on another log of wood *against* father comes home.—*Pickwick Papers.*

2. **Except, without, save.**—Avoid using these prepositions as if they were conjunctions equivalent to "unless." As prepositions these words could of course be followed by a Noun-clause introduced by "that"; and, through the omission of "that," they were once used as conjunctions by the best writers. But this use of them is becoming more and more uncommon; and it is better now to say "unless."

> I will not let thee go, *except* thou bless me.—*Gen.* xxxii. 26.
> He may stay him : marry, not *without* the prince be willing.— *Much Ado about Nothing,* iii. 3, 86.

Note.—These words, though not now used as conjunctions in the best prose-compositions, are still met with in colloquial prose and in poetry :—

> You know my uncle declared he would not suffer me to return *without* my mamma desired it.—SIDNEY BIDDULPH, vol. iv. p. 276 (H).
>
> *Save* they could be pluck'd asunder, all
> My quest were but in vain.—TENNYSON, *Holy Grail.*

I needs must break
These bonds that so defame me : not *without*
She wills it.—*Ibid., Lancelot and Elaine.*

3. "**But**."—This is another preposition, which, like the four already described, acquired a conjunctional force. This force it has retained to the present day. The full expression, *but that*, is often reduced to *but*. The chief uses of *but* or *but that* are the following :—

(*a*) In the sense of "except that." The clause going before is negative. Here the conjunction usually takes the form of *but*.[1]

> A new lease cannot be granted nor an old one altered, *but that* the Charity Commissioners must take six months to investigate the matter.—*Daily Telegraph*, p. 6, May 16, 1900.
> It rarely happens *but that* in the course of the week two or three charges of violent assaults or robbery are heard in the court in question.—*Ibid.* p. 5, Aug. 29, 1901.
> Nothing would satisfy Sir George, *but* he must go into the den.—Steele, *Guardian*, No. 146.
> There never was a reform yet propounded *but* some one pronounced it forthwith to be chimerical, extravagant, and Utopian.—*Daily Telegraph*, p. 11, Dec. 1880.
> Never dream *but* ill must come of ill.—Shelley.
> Let no man dream *but that* I love thee still.—Tennyson.

(*b*) In the sense of "were it not that" : introducing a consideration or reason to the contrary. The clause going before is affirmative. Here the conjunction takes only the form of *but that*.

> He would be wholly a Christian *but that* he is something of an atheist.—Earle, *Microcosm*, xlvi. 66.
> I too would be content to dwell in peace,
> *But that* my country calls.—Southey, *Joan of Arc*, i. 359.

(*c*) In the sense of "if not." The clause going before may be either affirmative or negative. Here the conjunction takes only the form of *but*.

> No one may take the man *but* he have authority from the Sheriff.—*St. German's Doctor and Student*, p. 278.
> It is ten to one *but* my friend Peter is among them.—*Spectator*, No. 457.
> Beshrew me *but* I love her heartily.—Shakespeare, *Merchant of Venice*, ii. 6, 52.

---

[1] In the *Oxford Dictionary* (see Bur, II.) it is said that *but that* in this sense is obsolete. The examples quoted, however, from the *Daily Telegraph* show that this assertion is not correct.

It will go hard with her *but* she will contrive somehow so to twist and turn it, as to give it individuality.—*Fortnightly Review,* p. 856, Nov. 1900.

(*d*) In the sense of a negative relative "that not." The clause going before is negative. Here the conjunction takes the form of *but*, which may either stand alone or be followed by a pronoun in the Third person. It usually stands alone.

We cannot conceive of any portion of matter *but it* is either hard or soft.—H. MORE, *Inmost Soul*, p. 66.

There was scarce a plantation near me *but* had some of them.—DE FOE, *Colonel Jack*, p. 290.

Hardly one of the Frenchmen round, *but* looked on Hereward as a barbarian Englishman.—KINGSLEY, *Hereward*, ch. xli. p. 495.

There is no man, whatever his opinions may be, *but* would say that the absence of Mr. John Morley would be a loss to the Liberal party.—Quoted in *Daily Telegraph*, p. 8, Nov. 16, 1900.

(*e*) After verbs of doubt, fear, question, etc., the clause going before is negative. Here the conjunction takes the form either of *but*, or *but what*, or *but that*, or simply *that*.

We have no doubt *but* it will yet spring up.—LIVINGSTONE, *Travels*, i. 19.

There is no doubt *but that* the Russian crown has always intended to round off the gradual occupation that is certain to result ultimately in the annexation of Manchuria.—*Daily Telegraph*, p. 10, March 31, 1900.

When they showed that they were worthy of him, they need not fear *but that* they would obtain his leadership.—*Spectator*, p. 699, Nov. 17, 1900.

I am not certain *but what* the Medical Officer would have to transmit his orders to them through the Sanitary Inspector.—*Ealing Guardian*, p. 2, March 10, 1900.

There is no doubt *but that* the British people will be anxious enough to be trained in the use of the rifle.—*Daily Express*, p. 4, May 17, 1900.

There can be no doubt *that* the spirit of economic discontent is very widespread.—*Spectator*, p. 649, Nov. 10, 1900.

There is no question *but* the King of Spain will reform most of the abuses.—ADDISON.

4. "But" for "than" or "when."—Avoid the error of using *but* for *than* after "no sooner," or for *when* after "scarcely," "hardly," "not."

Hardly was Charles dead, *when* the publication of *Eikon Basilike* (the Royal Likeness), which professed to have been written by Charles himself, produced a reaction in his favour.—RANSOME, *History of England*, p. 253. (Correct.)

No sooner do the bells leave off *than* the diligence rattles in.—BROWNING. (Correct).

Philoclea *no sooner* espied the lion *but* she ran to the lodge-ward.—
SIDNEY'S *Arcadia.* (Wrong. Change *but* to *than.*)

Nor had we received him on board half-an-hour, *but* we put out to
sea.—DE FOE, *Voyage Round the World*, p. 208. (Wrong.
Change *but* to *when.*)

He had *scarce* rubbed his eyes *but* Darius fled.—H. MORE. *Exp.
Dan.* ii. 35. (Wrong, change *but* to *when.*)

5. "As," "than."—*As* is used after an adjective in the
Positive degree to denote some kind of equality, while *than* is
used after an Adjective in the Comparative degree to denote
some kind of inequality. The same conjunction therefore will
not do duty for two adjectives, one of which is Comparative and
the other Positive.

(1) Will it be urged that the four Gospels are as old or even older
than tradition ?—BOLINGBROKE, *Philosophical Essays*, iv. 19.

Say, "as old as tradition or even older." The words "than tradition" can easily be understood after *older.*

(2) The majority of them established another doctrine *as* false in
itself, and if possible *more* pernicious to the Constitution,
than that on which the Middlesex election was determined.—
JUNIUS'S *Letters.*

Say, "as false as that on which, etc., and if possible more pernicious
to the Constitution."

**6. "Other than," "other from," "other but," "other
except."**—After the adjective *other* (which is by etymology a
kind of Comparative), the only word that can be correctly used
for contrasting one thing with another is *than.* The prepositions
from, but, except in such a connection are wrong.

Other foundation can no man lay *than* that is laid.—1 *Cor.* iii. 11.
(Correct.)

When he took the reins (of government) the army was being
exploited for *other* ends *than* its own dignity.—*Spectator*, p. 613,
Nov. 3, 1900. (Correct.)

He had no *other* object *but* to get back his money. (Change *but* to
than. Or cancel *other*, and leave *but* as it is.)

He had *another* reason *from* what he professed. (Change *from* to
than. Or change *another* to *a different.*)

7. Misuse of "other than."—The phrase *other than*, when
it is not used for contrasting one thing with another, is inappropriate. It must not be substituted for *other besides*, as it conveys
an entirely different sense.

(1) *Other* persons *than* he were at fault.
(2) *Other* persons *besides* him were at fault.

The meaning expressed by (1) is, that not he, but others were at fault. The sense expressed by (2) is, that not only he, but others besides him were at fault.

8. "As" for "that."—Avoid using *as* for introducing a Noun-clause after "say," "know," "think," etc. This is now avoided by all good writers, and is heard only in the southern dialect or among the less cultured classes.

> I don't know *as* you'll like the appearance of our place.—Mrs. STOWE, *Dred*, xi. p. 100. (Change *as* to *that*.)

9. "Like" for "as."—Avoid using the adjective *like* as if it were a conjunction equivalent to *as :*—

> *Mr. L.* : The (brewing) trade has all gone to pieces. I don't know what the people drink now. They don't seem to drink beer *like* they used to.—Quoted in *Daily Telegraph*, p. 6, Oct. 19, 1900. (Change *like* to *as*.)

10. Like as, the same as.—Equally objectionable and scarcely less common are the phrases *like as, the same as*, where *as* alone would express all that is wanted :—

> It looks *like as* if it were going to rain.
> He took a seat in the carriage *the same as* you did.

11. Directly, immediately.—These two adverbs should not be used as conjunctions. When they are accompanied by *that*, as "immediately that," "directly that," they make a conjunctional phrase equivalent to "as-soon as," but even then they are not good substitutes for "as soon as."

> The question of how we stand becomes vital *immediately that* the limitation of demand forces commercial nations to trench more deeply upon the livelihood of others.—*Daily Telegraph*, p. 9, Nov. 22, 1900.
> *Directly* he stopped, the coffin was removed.—DICKENS. (Say, *as soon as*.)

12. "Once."—This adverb ought not to be used as a con-junction equivalent to "if once" or "when once." The custom has been springing up very recently in journalism, but is not sanctioned by literature. The four examples given below show how *once* is correctly used, either by itself as an adverb, or in connection with *if* or *when*.

> He defeated them, and, *once* having started them on the run, he pursued them across a hill which they might easily have held. —*Daily Telegraph*, p. 10, July 7, 1900.
> The report, however, *once* on the wing, was carried like the city dust into all ears.—*Ibid.* p. 9, May 18, 1900.
> We have no means of preventing the rush of a mobile French force upon London, *if once* they could succeed in evading the Channel fleet.—*Review of Reviews*, p. 448, May 1900.

> *When once* they realise that they have been thoroughly defeated, they will give up all notion of further resistance.—*Fortnightly Review*, p. 861, May 1900.

In such examples as the following, all of very recent date and seen only in journalism, *once* is incorrectly used as a Subordinative conjunction :—

> They would follow their leader *once* their seats in the House were secure.—*Daily Express*, p. 1, Sept. 28, 1900.
> Other things had to be attended to *once* the enemy were got rid of. —*Daily Telegraph*, p. 8, Sept. 3, 1900.

Note.—This conjunctional use of *once* appears to have arisen from a misunderstanding of the construction exemplified in such a sentence as the following :—

> *Once* get into a tangle of that description, and weeks and months must elapse before it is possible to emerge from it.—*Daily Telegraph*, p. 11, Nov. 8, 1900.

Here *once* is correctly used as an adverb, not as a conjunction. The verb *get* is in the Imperative mood. One of the uses of the Imperative is to express a condition; so that *once get* is equivalent to *if you once get*. From the use of *once* with the Imperative mood to express a condition, an idea seems to have sprung up that *once* can be used with the Indicative mood for a similar purpose.

13. "And that," "or that," "but that."—Such phrases should not be used to introduce a Subordinate clause, unless another Subordinate clause similarly introduced by *that* has been expressed already. Even then the repetition of *that* in the second Subordinate clause may not be necessary. (Compare the parallel case of *and which*, ch. ii. (*d*) 12 ; and see (*a*) 2 in the present chapter.)

> (1) We believe the freedom and happiness of a people are not the result of their political institutions, *but that* their political institutions are in a great degree the result of their own temper and aspiration. — PURNELL, *Literature and its Professors*, p. 267 (H).

To give this sentence its proper balance a first *that* must be inserted after "believe."

> (2) The treaty is said to have received some modification in its passage through the Foreign Affairs Committee, and that these modifications are likely to be adhered to by the Senate.— *Manchester Examiner*, May 24, 1872 (H).

This is a worse sentence than the preceding. The first part must be rewritten thus :—"It is said *that* the treaty has received," etc.

14. Moment, instant, time, way, reason.—If such nouns are followed by a Subordinate clause, it is better that they should be accompanied by some conjunction as *that*, or by some conjunctive adverb as *when*, *why*, etc., according to the context :—

> The *instant that* Fitz-Eustace spoke,
> A sudden light on Marmion broke.—SCOTT.   (Correct.)

> The *moment* they saw their own privileges and emoluments taken from them, they (the bishops) changed their minds about the duty of passive obedience.—BUCKLE, *History of Civilisation*, vol. i. (Say *the moment that*, or still better, *as soon as*.)

> There was not the slightest doubt that that was the *reason* they had got into financial difficulties.—*Middlesex County Times*, p. 6, Oct. 20, 1900. (Insert *why* after *reason*.)

15. Now.—This adverb should not be used (in prose) as a conjunction unless it is accompanied with *that* :—

> Why should he live, *now* nature bankrupt is ?—SHAKESPEARE.
> But, O the heavy change, *now* thou art gone,
> *Now* thou art gone, and never must return !
> MILTON, *Lycidas*, 37, 38.

16. Notwithstanding.—This preposition should not be used as a conjunction, unless it is accompanied with *that* :—

> These days were ages to him, *notwithstanding that* he was basking in the smiles of the pretty Mary.—W. IRVING.   (Correct.)

17. Provided.—This participle (an elliptical form for *it being provided*) may be used as a conjunction either with or without *that*. It is not correct, however, to use *providing* as an equivalent, though the custom has been springing up of late in journalism.

> *Provided that* nothing in this Act shall prejudice the right of any person whatever.

> *Provided* British rule is reasonably fair and just, they will not be slow to recognise its manifold advantages.—*Fortnightly Review*, p. 861, May 1900.

> There is every desire to give the preference to British firms, always *providing* that the Government's requirements be reasonably met.—*Daily Express*, p. 5, May 13, 1901. (Change *providing* to *provided*.)

18. Slipshod use of " that."—Instead of repeating the conjunction used in the preceding clause, some writers have a habit of introducing a subsequent clause by *that*, as if *that* could be used as a general hack for any purpose whatever. This practice should be avoided.

> Far distant be the day *when* the measured walk along the Trumpington Road takes the place of the manly exercise of the cricket-ground and the river, or *that* lectures multiply while sports decrease.—*Quarterly Review*, vol. lxxiii. p. 100.

Even when there is no preceding clause, and therefore no other conjunction, we sometimes find *that* carelessly used for *though, if, when, whether*, etc. :—

> On the other hand, it may be doubted *that* M. Berthet's elaborate and long-winded descriptions are sufficiently interesting to command the attention of the average British novel-reader. —*Daily Telegraph*, p. 7, Aug. 11, 1900. (Change *that* to *whether*.)
>
> There is not a great journal in the world which would not give him five thousand a year as editor, and not a public man who would not doubt in his heart *whether*, if he ruled England, England were safe. (Correct.)—*Spectator*, p. 736, Nov. 24, 1900.

19. "Different than."—Avoid the error of using *than* for *from* after the adjective "different":—

> He took up a *different* kind of occupation *than* what he had been used to before. (Change *than* to *from*.)

20. "Prefer than."—Avoid the error of using *than* for *to* after the verb "prefer."

> Above all, it should *prefer* to leave a point untaught *than* to teach it in a way that must be unlearned.—LATHAM, *English Literature*. (Wrong. Say, "prefer leaving a subject untaught to teaching it," etc.)

21. "No sooner than," "as soon as."—These two conjunctional phrases mean the same thing, except that what is the Principal clause with the former becomes the Subordinate clause with the latter, and *vice versâ*.

Principal Clause.	*Subordinate Clause.*
He had no sooner heard the news,	than he wept aloud.
He wept aloud	as soon as he heard the news.

22. "Since."—This conjunction denotes present time dating back to some past event. It is therefore followed by a Past Indefinite tense, and preceded by some form of Present tense.

> I have been in such a pickle *since* I *saw* you last.—SHAKESPEARE, *Tempest*, v. 1, 282.
>
> We know the time *since* he *was* mild and affable.—SHAKESPEARE, *2 Henry VI.* iii. 1, 9.

Note 1.—In Indirect oration the verb, which in Direct oration would be in the Present tense, is changed to the corresponding Past tense, provided that the reporting verb is in a Past tense :—

> I *have* not seen you *since* you wrote last.
>
> He told me that he *had* not seen me since I wrote last.

Note 2.—When *since* is used as an adverb, it is preceded by a verb in the Past Indefinite tense :—

I *took* this house four weeks since.

When it is used as a preposition it is preceded by a verb in the Perfect tense :—

I *have* not seen him since Monday last.

• **23. "After."**—When this word is used as a conjunction in reference to some event that is expected to happen in future time, it is not followed by any form of Future tense, but by some form of Present tense :—

After I *am risen* again, I will go before you into Galilee.—*Matthew* xxvi. 32. (Authorised Version, 1611.)

After I *am* raised up, I will go before you into Galilee.—*Matthew* xxvi. 32. (Revised Version, 1885.)

Note.—It is interesting to notice, however, that in Wiclif's version of the same passage, the Future tense is used with *after :*—"After that I *shall* rise again, etc."

24. "Before."—This conjunction, like the preceding, even when it refers to future time, is not followed by a Future tense :—

Before this treatise *can* become of use, two points are necessary.— SWIFT.

Verily I say unto thee, that this night, *before* the cock *crow* twice, thou shalt deny me thrice.—*Mark* xiv. 30.

Note.—In Old English one of the regular uses of the Present tense, whether Indicative or Subjunctive, was to denote Future time no less than Present. The use of the Present tense after the conjunctions *after* and *before,* even when Future time is referred to, appears to be a survival of the Old English idiom.

25. Omission of "that."—The omission of the conjunction *that,* though commonly met with, should not be practised without caution. Most sentences would be improved in clearness and euphony, if the conjunction were not omitted.

Then let the Board look to the medical officer that they approved, and it is between them the blame rests.—*Ealing Guardian,* p. 2, March 10, 1900. (Insert *that* after "them.")

26. Omission of Copulative verb after certain Conjunctions.—After the conjunctions *when, though, if, while, till,* the verb and subject following may be understood, provided that the subject has been expressed already in the Principal clause. (See Chap. I. (*b*) 6.)

He sprained his foot, *while* walking in the dark (*i.e. while he was* walking). (Correct ; because the subject *he* is expressed in the Principal clause.)

If a good singer, it is possible to earn a fairly good livelihood. (Wrong. Say, "If a person is a good singer," etc.)

The German Kaiser apparently wants to push German trade, *while* "protecting" Prussian squires.—*Spectator*, p. 610, Nov. 3, 1900. (Correct.)

Canning and Wellesley, when in retirement, occupied themselves in translating the odes and satires of Horace.—SMILES, *Character*, p. 119, chap. iv. 1879. (Correct.)

27. Conjunctions to be used after "fear," "doubt," "hope."

—The verbs "fear," "hope," and their equivalents have some *fact* for their object, while the verb "doubt," representing a phase of mind distinct from both, has some *alternative* for its object. Evidently then "that" is the proper conjunction to be used after the former, and "whether" after the latter. But we sometimes see "that" wrongly used after "doubt," where "whether" should have been used.

In the evening milder conditions prevailed, and it seems now doubtful at this stage of the season *that* the frost will be able to maintain its grip.—*Daily Telegraph*, p. 10, Feb. 11, 1902. (Change *that* to *whether*.)

28. "Equally . . . as."

—These are not true Correlatives. When *as* is used as a conjunction to denote equality of degree, it should be preceded by *as* in an affirmative clause, or by *so* or *as* in a negative one :—

To our mind, for reasons which we shall presently show, it is *equally* wonderful that he (Josephus) should talk of Essenes, under the idea of a known, stationary, original sect among the Jews, *as* that he should not talk of the Christians.—DE QUINCEY, *Edited by Masson*, vol. vii. p. 108. (Substitute *as* for *equally*.)

Correct, improve, or justify the following sentences :—

1. Except this be the the case, what possible basis is there for such an appeal?—*Daily Telegraph*, p. 6, April 19, 1900.

2. Scarce had I left my father, but I met him.—ADDISON, *Cato*, iv. 4.

3. Now this miracle, with those that have been already mentioned, has as authentic an attestation, and even more so, as any of the Gospel miracles.—DOANE, *Bible Parallels*, p. 270.

4. In getting the bill ready *against* it was necessary.—WALPOLE, *George II.*, II. iii. 79.

5. This project, I need hardly say, was a very risky one ; for we had bound ourselves to stop for nothing once the light out.—HALDANE, *Blackwood's Magazine*, p. 175, Aug. 1900.

6. He had no other fault but that of being too short.—STEELE, *Guardian*, No. 143.

7. By the strict law of the Church in England the right of hearing

confession is equally vested in every baptized layman as it is in every ordained priest.—Quoted in *Church Gazette*, p. 68, May 6, 1899.

8. The new Japanese minister has hardly been twenty-four hours in this country, but he has already laid his finger upon the weakness of the "Concert."—*Daily Telegraph*, p. 7, July 7, 1900.

9. The publican shut his shutters in the sunshine against service commenced.—THACKERAY, *Vanity Fair*, liv. 454.

10. You will never attain to my age without you keep yourselves in breath with exercise and in heart with joyfulness.—Sir P. SIDNEY.

11. In these musings upon one of the most tragic and desolate of human themes, the ex-Premier reveals another mood from those in which his readers have met his magnetic mind before. — *Daily Telegraph*, p. 7, Nov. 2, 1900.

12. No other but such a one as he.—COLERIDGE.

13. Therefore I say to you that I will not leave here save ye bear me away by force.—Dr. BINION, *Quo Vadis?* chap. i. p. 193.

14. He had not gone many steps more but he saw his brother.—*Secrets of Invisible World*, 236.

15. Those who believe in the immortality of the soul generally quit life with fully as much, if not more, reluctance, as those who have no such expectation.—J. S. MILL, *Three Essays on Religion*, p. 120.

16. There needed no more but to advance one step.—STEELE, *Guardian*, No. 143.

17. That the Fop should say as he would rather have such-a-one without a groat than me with the Indies.—STEELE, *Spectator*, No. 508.

18. We Russians do not look upon China as a field for the investment of capital, like others do, because we have not enough capital for our own country.—Quoted in *Fortnightly Review*, p. 590, Oct. 1900.

19. We should make no mention of what concerns ourselves, without it be matters in which our friends ought to rejoice.—STEELE, *Spectator*, No. 100.

20.   Scarce have I arrived
But there is brought to me from your equerry
A splendid richly-plated hunting dress.

            COLERIDGE, *Piccol.* I. ix.

21. It has no literary pretensions, except the total absence of all pretension may pass for one in these days of abundant conceit.—Miss MITFORD, *Letters and Life*, vol. i. p. 150 (H).

22. The troops have set out with four days' supplies, so that looks like as if we were going no further than Ladybrand.—*Daily Telegraph*, p. 11, May 15, 1900.

23. Hardly had this storm subsided than another was stirred up by the students from the French provinces.—*Ibid.* p. 5, Aug. 8, 1900.

24. By our jurisdiction the prisoner is not necessarily regarded as guilty upon his arrest, whereas he is, immediately he is arrested, not regarded as innocent.—*Ibid.* p. 10, Sept. 3, 1900.

25. Once, however, we depart from this teaching, our relations towards the lower animals assume a totally different aspect.—*Fortnightly Review*, p. 383, March 1900.

26. Pleasure is nothing else but the intermission of pain.—SELDEN, *Table Talk*, p. 159.

27. Do you know my Lord Bishop of St. Asaph's handwriting? Not as I know of.—*Trial of Bishops*, p. 55.

28. Circuitous are the ways of the Chinese Government, and high-sounding dignities are used, like embassies to the Mongols were in the days of the Stuarts.—*Daily Telegraph*, p. 11, June 11, 1900.

29. But this does not make it the less trifling, or hinder one nowadays from seeing it to be trifling directly we examine it.— ARNOLD, *Literature and Dogma*, ch. v. p. 142.

30. Once they became emancipated, they could not keep the Sabbaths, living amidst the Christian environment.—*Daily Telegraph*, p. 7, Aug. 13, 1900.

31. They may find themselves between two fires, and be eventually hemmed in like their co-nationalists are at Colesberg.—*Ibid.* p. 9, Feb. 8, 1900.

32. No sooner did they acquaint my brother, but he immediately wanted to propose it.—FIELDING, *Tom Jones*, vi. 5, 72.

33. The Belgian expedition has scarce returned to Europe after two years of exploration than three more expeditions are announced.— *Review of Reviews*, p. 268, Sept. 1900.

34. The term itself is both negative and positive in the same way the Ten Commandments are.—*Church Gazette*, p. 206, June 10, 1899.

35. I don't know as I am any worse than the rest of the men around me.—SHELDON, *In His Steps*, p. 64.

36. Accordingly, as soon as they sallied out, and that the gold-laced hat of the captain was seen rising like Hesper above the dewy verge of the rising ground, the clash of the bell was heard from the old moss-grown tower.—SCOTT, *Heart of Midlothian*, ch. xliv. para. 31.

37. The Hollander censor watches the English prints of Johannesburg like a cat watches a mouse.—*Daily Express*, p. 4, May 16, 1900.

38. His day of domination is over the moment peace is declared, and no one understands this better than he.—*Daily Telegraph*, p. 9, May 22, 1900.

39. The bakehouse buildings are situated but a short distance from the prison wall, and once he was out of the door of the bakehouse and round the corner it was difficult for any one within the prison to detect his subsequent movements.—*Ibid.* p. 9, Nov. 5, 1900.

40. He frankly admitted the existence of the evils complained of, and that this state of things had become worse since the amalgamation of the companies.—*Ibid.* p. 8, Nov. 1, 1900.

41. You did wisely and honestly too, notwithstanding she is the greatest beauty in the parish.—FIELDING.

42. The English farmer is crippled and discouraged by the obstacles that prevent his rising in his business of agriculture, the same as other men do in trade and manufactures.— *Church Gazette*, p. 202, June 10, 1899.

43. Even providing the British were eventually victorious, about which he had the gravest doubts, the termination of the present conflict before Christmas was, he asserted, impossible. —*Daily Telegraph*, p. 6, April 13, 1900.

44. Whether his legs had expanded with his years, or that the

longitude of his trousers had shrunk by reason of repeated washings, remains an insoluble problem.—J. C. YOUNG, *Memoirs of C. M. Young*, vol. i. ch. ix. p. 334 (H).

45. Chilo thinks that Lygia goes intentionally to different places of worship than those frequented by Pomponia.—Dr. BINION, *Quo Vadis?* ch. xv. p. 136.

46. There is a general impression in Pretoria that once those commandoes are destroyed as a force in being, the war will be over.—*Daily Telegraph*, p. 9, July 4, 1900.

47. The American admiral has been ordered, now shooting has begun, to act in concert with the other Powers.—*Daily Express*, p. 1, June 19, 1900.

48. We venture to doubt that the popularity, which the intrinsic merits of this book may win for it in this country, will to any considerable extent be due to the time in which it is written.—*Daily Telegraph*, p. 7, Aug. 11, 1900.

49. Colliery proprietors then urged that it would be much more satisfactory if the Admirality contract for the year was made at the time other annual contracts came in.—*Ibid.* p. 7, Oct. 31, 1900.

50. Of this, however, we may be sure that he has, like every capable General does, put himself in imagination in his enemy's place.—*Ibid.* p. 9, Dec. 11, 1899.

51. Which Nicias had no sooner notice of, but he embarked his troops.—GOLDSMITH, *History of Greece*, i. 265.

52. This loan could not be effected, notwithstanding the Minister of Finance did his utmost to oblige the Bank of England.—*Daily Express*, p. 1, May 21, 1900.

53. They sympathise with British subjects who have been ill-treated, and consider that it is the duty of Government to interfere, providing they do not interfere effectually.—*Daily Telegraph*, p. 7, May 12, 1900.

54. It must remain fixed for the latter end of April, unless any very bad weather should set in, or that you can fix with agreeable travelling company.—*Life of George Grote*, ch. i. p. 3.

55. It is some years since she has been seen in classical parts.—*Daily Telegraph*, p. 9, Oct. 1899.

56. We were fully prepared, once Lord Roberts was across the Vaal, to hear that Johannesburg had fallen.—*Middlesex County Times*, p. 5, June 9, 1900.

57. When camping out in uncivilised parts, the pot has to be supplied by the gun.—*Fortnightly Review*, p. 385, March 1900.

58. He also commends the President that he has not pressed his case with all the force it derives from absolute legitimacy.—*Review of Reviews*, p. 375, Oct. 1899.

59. "The second series," he says, "will be issued like the first was issued, and the last, if it ever appears, must be published by subscription."—*Literature*, p. 583, Dec. 17, 1899.

60. People claim the existence of certain treaties between the Nicaragua Government and the different states in Europe will stand in the way of early action.—*Daily Telegraph*, p. 9, Feb. 6, 1900.

61. We take it upon ourselves to reassure Mr. Tennyson that even after he shall be dead and buried as much sense will still remain as

he has now the good fortune to possess.—Quoted in *Church Gazette*, p. 159, May 27, 1899.

62. In the broad interests of the Dominion it will be necessary to have state-control of the railways in the same way all the other states and colonies now administer their own lines.—*Fortnightly Review*, p. 555, April 1900.

63. Immediately the retreat of the enemy was perceived, General H. ordered a portion of his troops to advance in pursuit.—*Daily Telegraph*, p. 9, May 7, 1900.

64. There is not a man whose fighting value,—providing he has escaped disease and serious wounds,—will not have been vastly increased by reason of his practical knowledge of the requirements of active service.—*Ibid.* p. 7, June 11, 1900.

65. Once it had been said in the name of Tsar Nicholas that Russia would act in concert with the other Powers to restore order in China, no Minister, however great his authority, had power to alter the decree.—*Ibid.* p. 10, June 30, 1900.

66. As it is nearly thirty years ago that the coal supplies in the United Kingdom were reported on, the Government are to be asked to consent to the appointment of another Royal Commission.—*Ibid.* p. 9, Feb. 26, 1900.

67. Hardly was Edward dead than a struggle began for the possession of the reins of power.—RANSOME, *History of England*, p. 162.

68. He might suggest, however, to him and to others that once they began a career of violence it was the inevitable result that others would go further than what was originally intended.—*Daily Telegraph*, p. 11, July 10, 1900.

69. An Anglican cleric is bound to obey his bishop or go away and set up for himself, like Dr. Parker has done in the City Temple.—Quoted in *Literature*, p. 45, Jan. 14, 1899.

70. He would be altogether detestable only that we are bound to remember in his excuse that Emma did treat him in a truly maddening style.—*Nineteenth Century*, p. 815, May 1900.

71. Before the war his reputation was that of a very able and honest politician. But once the war commenced, he soon made his mark.—*Daily Telegraph*, p. 8, May 19, 1900.

72. When five-eighths of a mile from the ground, various manœuvres were carried out.—*Ibid.* p. 7, Oct. 22, 1900.

73. The situation is critical in Gujerat, Baroda, and Rajputana, which are unsown, and no fodder of any description available.—*Ibid.* p. 7, July 31, 1900.

74. It is now about twenty years that our influence in Beluchistan has been supreme throughout that region.—*Nineteenth Century*, p. 773, May 1900.

75. It is urged upon us that there are no material compensations for our sacrifices,—that once the mines are exhausted, South Africa will prove worthless to us as a colony.—*Fort. Review*, p. 848, May 1900.

76. All I wish to point out is both the British and the Dutch colonists, however much they may differ upon other questions, are absolutely in accord upon this general principle.—*Ibid.* p. 865, May 1900.

77. Such an attack, providing the neutrality of Belgium and Switzerland were not violated, could only be accomplished by breaking through the great line of French fortresses.—*Review of Reviews*, p. 347, April 1900.

78. It is doubly significant, because coming not from a Manning, but from a Vaughan.—*Ibid.* p. 237, Sept. 1899.

79. Previous to the time the work began the bare houses looked like those of the Noah's ark village.—*Ibid.* p. 466, May 1899.

80. In illustration of this I wish to do like my friend, the Moulvi, said to you :—"*give two examples.*"—Quoted in *Educational Review*, Madras, p. 79, Feb. 1900.

81. They know that Dreyfus's friends will be prepared to prove his innocence once the Exhibition is over.—*Daily Express*, p. 5, May 17, 1900.

82. His many friends are hoping that once his financial affairs have righted themselves he will justify the great hopes which were formed of him at Harrow and Balliol.—*Ibid.* p. 4, May 17, 1900.

83. Once the great mass of the people had learned to regard State-support in old age as their normal prospect and inalienable right, it would be impossible, without producing a social revolution, to recede.—*Review of Reviews*, p. 255, March 1900.

84. It is hoped that diplomacy may discover a convenient formula, and once the matter has been settled with Germany, it is expected that similar conventions will be entered into with other countries.—*Spectator*, p. 560, Oct. 27, 1900.

85. Once Japan has made good her foothold upon the American continent, it would not be easy to forecast the issue of so suggestive an event.—*Ibid.* p. 560, Oct. 27, 1900.

86. It would entail the destruction of the French fleet, and once the French fleet is gone, Germany has no fear of the French army.—*Daily Mail*, p. 4, April 20, 1900.

87. The military plan which was to be put into action once the rounding up of the enemy had fairly begun, was to penetrate and pulverise the enemy's lines, etc.—*Daily Telegraph*, p. 11, May 14, 1900.

88. And once the railway communication was cut the result would manifest itself in scarcity of food-supplies, disease, and laxity of discipline.—*Ibid.* p. 7, Feb. 20, 1900.

89. He objected to the measure, because once they commenced to fix the price of an article there was no telling where the principle would end.—*Ibid.* p. 4, March 23, 1900.

90. As these rebels are the very lowest type of the enemy, they are not likely to give much trouble once they are confronted by white troops.—*Ibid.* p. 9, March 10, 1900.

91. But once the electors changed their views, it was marvellous how rapidly politicians were converted.—*Ibid.* p. 11, May 1, 1900.

92. The excitement caused by the arrests at Johannesburg subsided once it had been clearly shown that Imperial officers were not concerned with the movement.—*Ibid.* p. 9, May 17, 1900.

93.   But scarce were they hidden away, I declare,
         Than the giant came in with a curious air.—HOOD.

94. Air, when carefully tested, is found to contain something else than nitrogen and oxygen.—GEIKIE.

95. We were no sooner sat down (seated), but after having looked upon me a little while, she said, etc.—ADDISON, *Spectator*, No. 7.

96. Men and women who have no object or aim than amusement.—*Daily Telegraph*, p. 8, Feb. 16, 1898.

97. Competent authorities doubt that the enemy will make a stand on the Drakensberg at this season of the year, when the highlands are covered with snow.—*Ibid.* p. 9, June 13, 1900.

98. Mr. Conger reports that the missionaries are safe up to the present ; but he doubts that the protection promised by the Chinese Government will ensure their permanent safety.—*Ibid.* p. 10, June 12, 1900.

99. I doubt that you will find that promotion by seniority prevails in any of the great armies of Europe to the extent that it does with us.—*Ibid.* p. 6, Jan. 31, 1900.

100. If I had applied for a licence to open an hotel, there might have been reason that I should move my shop elsewhere.—Quoted in *Middlesex County Times*, p. 6, March 17, 1900.

101. How could I hear such words, how could I meet such looks, from any other man but he ?—Mrs. CRAIK, *The Ogilvies*, ch. x.

102. They say that the moment the tax is imposed, publicity is inevitable.—*Spectator*, p. 613, Nov. 3, 1900.

103. The Armenians cannot be detached from Turkey like Bulgaria was.—*Daily Telegraph*, p. 7, Nov. 8, 1900.

104. What that support is to be and on what conditions, our generals and diplomatists will hammer out, once they have freed themselves from the initial rivalries, jealousies, and misunderstandings.—*Fortnightly Review*, p. 738, Nov. 1900.

105. We could never have looked for anything from them on this subject than criticism, and it might even be censure.—*Ibid.* p. 754, Nov. 1900.

106. As to the time, however, the United States should enter upon their new career, that is a matter for the American people and their political guides, and upon this Englishmen have never thought of offering an opinion.—*Ibid.* p. 789, Nov. 1900.

107. Scarcely had the echoes of the Diamond Jubilee died away than an International Women's Congress pressed our achievements upon a slightly wearied world.—*Ibid.* p. 850, Nov. 1900.

108. Judging by results, he considered that the claims of non-literate technical education among the industrial classes to be greater than those of literary education as imparted in primary schools.—*Times of India*, p. 17, Aug. 25, 1900.

109. Hardly has one awakened than one of the girls of the hotel brings into the room a portable native stove.—*Daily Express*, p. 4, Nov. 14, 1900.

110. We very much doubt that the Imperial President of the Boxer movement has been at the place assigned.—*Daily Telegraph*, p. 8, Nov. 19, 1900.

111. He repudiated the idea that the present disorders arose from the German occupation of Kiao-Chau ; for similar disorders had occurred long before the name of Germany was hardly known in China.—*Ibid.* p. 10, Nov. 20, 1900.

112. It was the morning that the Coxey procession was about to

enter the Capitol grounds, and Mr. B. and I stood on one of the Capitol steps to watch the event.—*Review of Reviews*, p. 432, Nov. 1900.

113. Once they began something, it was natural that Germany's output of ore should be quadrupled and America's quintupled in five-and-twenty years.—Quoted in *Review of Reviews*, p. 465, Nov. 1900.

114. Neither Liberal nor Tory Viceroy, or Liberal or Tory Secretary of State for India, has done anything else but pass him as if he were a mere crank uttering wild and whirling words.—*Ibid.* p. 497, Nov. 1900.

115. But once a stock is made there is no difficulty in keeping up the supply, as the different brewings mature in rotation.—*Daily Telegraph*, p. 7, Dec. 6, 1900.

116. Providing the Home Secretary does not punish him for being out at that time in the morning, he will come forward and say what he has seen.—Quoted in *Daily Telegraph*, p. 5, Dec. 6, 1900.

117. Americans are cleverer in their generation, and know that once Time makes a mark in a face, it is not easily obliterated.—*Ibid.* p. 11, Dec. 6, 1500.

118. A strong police force was quickly upon the scene, and the sepoys retired from the fight immediately they heard that the police had been sent for.—*Pioneer Mail*, p. 2, Nov. 2, 1900.

119. He purposes to show the Yankees the comeliest stage-women in Great Britain, much in the same manner that he introduced to London the American burlesque belles in the "Belle of New York."—*Daily Express*, p. 5, Dec. 13, 1900.

120. A peculiarly instructive fact is that, during the years Part III. of the Act was in abeyance, the Council's zeal for sanitation steadily declined.—*Fortnightly Review*, p. 972, Dec. 1900.

121. Providing that no charge be placed on the County Rate, the Council do approve action being taken under Part III. of the Housing of the Working Classes Act, 1890.—Quoted in *Fortnightly Review*, p. 979, Dec. 1900.

122. I have ordered a new habit against the time I visit you, so as to travel with all possible comfort.—*Ibid.* p. 1024, Dec. 1900.

123. But once he pins himself down to the definite historical romance, or to the problems of a known and well-ascertained society, his sense of fact hampers him at every turn.—*Ibid.* p. 1033, Dec. 1900.

124. Immediately the British guns came into action the enemy, as usual, retired, moving in the direction of Henning.—*Daily Telegraph*, p. 9, Dec. 29, 1900.

125. General C. demands an inquiry, and it is gradually becoming known that others than General C. are making the same demand.—*The Sun*, p. 2, Jan. 3, 1900.

126. Of this great measure it has been well said that on the morning it received the Royal assent the Irish tenant exchanged serfdom for freedom.—*Fortnightly Review*, p. 2, Jan. 1901.

127. The use of large armaments, it must be remembered, is not so much to win victories but to make thoughts of war discouraging and to avoid it altogether.—*Ibid.* p. 30, Jan. 1901.

128. A further resolution was adopted, suggesting that a survey of all schools in England other than elementary should be conducted

by the State, as an aid to organising Secondary education, providing that no delay is incurred thereby.—Quoted in *Daily Telegraph*, p. 8, Jan. 11, 1901.

129. These flats are fitted with every modern comfort and sanitary improvement; and as the operation has already occupied three years, and is not yet completed, fully one-third are now occupied.—*Ibid.* p. 3, Jan. 17, 1901.

130. He knows that once the rayahs get the bit between their teeth it is all up with the supremacy of the Osmanli.—*Spectator*, p. 94, Jan. 19, 1901.

131. Once his character for contemptuous arrogance is established, the great farmer may say truthfully enough to the landlord's agent, "I hear no complaints about the cottages."—*Continental Review* for Jan. 1901 ; quoted in *Review of Reviews*, p. 53.

132. Did you give him the £1 as a free gift or as a loan? *A.* As a free gift, like I have given him before.—Quoted in *Daily Telegraph*, p. 6, Feb. 14, 1901.

133. By Allah, O my masters, we have fallen into grevious calamity, and I see no method of delivery from the inscriptions wherewith we are tormented, except we expedite these accursed engines.—RUDYARD KIPLING, *Fortnightly Review*, p. 216, Feb. 1901.

134. The Chinese were aware that their government was corrupt, but they preferred to be governed, however badly, by a people of their own race than by aliens.—Quoted in *Middlesex County Times*, p. 5, March 2, 1901.

135. But once he is convicted, let us have done with this stupid and ignorant system of measuring his sentence by his latest offence.—*Nineteenth Century*, Feb. 1901.

136. Never, continues this expert, did the economic prosperity of Great Britain reach so vigorous a development than in the days when, abandoning an aggressive policy, she contented herself with an army and a navy sufficient for the protection of her colonial territory and her mercantile marine.—*Review of Reviews*, p. 186, Feb. 1901.

137. Very few people know anything about this security, and the majority care less, providing the tip which has been spread about comes off.—*Daily Telegraph*, p. 4, March 9, 1901.

138. The Cabinet was formed in 1880, and the Duke of Argyll has stated that when formed Mr. Gladstone did not contemplate further Irish Land legislation.—*Fortnightly Review*, p. 399, March 1901.

139. There existed a firm belief that the new king would turn out Saracco and his ministry, and appeal to the younger forces, which alone can save the nation and the dynasty, because not bound by agreements previously contracted.—*Ibid.* p. 499, March 1901.

140. Considerable doubt is expressed that such a treaty could have been negotiated in the space of a fortnight, and the belief is entertained that the negotiations must have been proceeding a long time prior to Feb. 8.—*Daily Telegraph*, p. 10, March 19, 1901.

141. I have occasionally met the poet in St. John Street when there were no other guests but Erskine, Terry, George Hogarth, and another intimate friend or two.—LOCKHART'S *Life of Scott*, abridged edition, p. 400.

142. In days gone by, when yeomen received little else but dis-

encouragement, and were subjected to no small amount of ridicule, recruiting was mainly dependent on showy uniforms.—*Empire Review*, p. 257, April 1901.

143. We want a Pauper Immigration Act to prevent people landing, something like the Americans have.—Quoted in *Daily Telegraph*, p. 10, April 15, 1901.

144. It is arranged that the Chinese shall live separate from the other workmen, and shall be worked in gangs in different parts of the mines to the Kaffirs.—*Daily Telegraph*, p. 9, May 22, 1903.

145. In the event the board decides to extend the strike, it will probably confine it, for a time at least, to the mills of the Sheet Steel Company.—Quoted in *Daily Telegraph*, p. 9, April 18, 1901.

146. It is interesting to note that the very year the poet's father was bailiff was the first in which the corporation had entertained actors at Stratford.—*Ibid.* p. 11, April 22, 1901.

147. Of course the fatal facility, with which indirect taxes can be raised and no one seems much the worse, is one of their dangers, and, as we believe, a great danger.—*Spectator*, p. 556, April 20, 1901.

148. For my part I prefer the opinion of Mr. Gladstone in his earlier than his later years.—Quoted in *Daily Telegraph*, p. 6, May 3, 1901.

149. He had the charm of speaking on apparent terms of equality with whomsoever he might be addressing, providing the conversation was with one towards whom he was not ill-disposed.—*Review of Reviews*, p. 401, April 1901.

150. Mr. Brodrick has deliberately taken measures which can have no other effect but to injure the recruiting for the only force which we can employ in any part of the world.—*Fortnightly Review*, p. 701, April 1901.

151. The Viceroy throughout our interview spoke with the utmost frankness and earnestness, and at the close impressed on me his opinion that, once England and Japan agreed upon the policy to be followed, the present difficulties would vanish, and a permanent settlement would be achieved.—Quoted in *Daily Tel.* p. 10, May 15, 1901.

152. He found what he expected to find, and wrote home that he could hear the sparrows and nightingales singing like they did in Castile.—*Spectator*, p. 691, May 11, 1901.

153. The apparent difficulty between these two sets of bodies, which is largely one of devolution, will probably right itself once the province of the County Council has been clearly understood.—*Fortnightly Review*, p. 826, May 1901.

154. Are not the rights of conscience of the Sectarian equally respectable as those of the Secularist in the eyes of the State?—*Ibid.* p. 827, May 1901.

155. Providing the same qualities distinguish our merchants in the future, we may confidently hope that in any development of China's vast natural resources Great Britain will play a conspicuous part.—*Empire Review*, p. 390, May 1901.

156. It is obvious, of course, that Russia having a railway through Manchuria to Port Arthur cannot be content, without she has security for its safety.—*Ibid.* p. 396, May 1901.

157. I am aware that the subject is full of difficulty, but I feel

that once a scheme of this kind were started the sense of the majority would be favourable to it.—*Ibid.* p. 411, May 1901.

158. Moreover, it is inconceivable that a needle-eyed, perspicacious advocate like Sir E. C. has always proved himself to be, should drop the theory of conspiracy in his closing remarks, after alluding to it in his opening.—*Daily Telegraph*, p. 7, May 27, 1901.

159. It is this insularity even when away from home which goes far to justify the assertion that travellers are not necessarily many, because trains and hotels are full and comfortable.—*Empire Review*, p. 550, June 1901.

160. He cannot resist the force which urges him to produce a book immediately he arrives in England.—*Ibid.* p. 550, June 1901.

161. The contrast between the seminary and the barrack is evidently not so unfavourable to the former as Radicals and Bishops alike expected, and there are other motives which determine men to enter the priesthood than the wish to escape conscription.—*Spectator*, p. 178, Aug. 10, 1901.

162. There is a certain class of people who prefer to say that their fathers came down in the world through their own follies than to say that they rose in the world through their own industry and talents.— WINWOOD READE, *Martyrdom of Man*, p. 392.

163. Once loose and flabby ideas are allowed to prevail in the matter we shall find our politics and our party system at the mercy of the men with the long purses, who prefer, as they say, to stand outside and above party.—*Spectator*, p. 242, Aug. 24, 1901.

164. We were not much more than a quarter of an hour out of our ship but we saw her sink, and then I understood for the first time what was meant by a ship foundering in the sea.—DE FOE, *Robinson Crusoe* (Chandos Classics), p. 10.

165. It (the water buffalo) can tow barges along canals and streams, sometimes walking in the shallow water by the banks, like the horses did in the lower Thames before the tow-path was made.—*Spectator*, p. 279, Aug. 31, 1901.

166. I had no sooner stepped down on the firm ground, but I plainly saw it was a terrible earthquake; for the ground I stood on shook three times.—DE FOE, *Robinson Crusoe*, p. 71 (Chandos Classics).

167. The production of books in English, except the author be a wealthy amateur, rests finally upon the publishers. — *Fortnightly Review*, p. 734, Oct. 1901.

168. Least of all is the loss of any human creature considered irreparable in the unchanging continent where immemorial systems survive the generations of mankind like the sea its bubbles.—*Daily Telegraph*, p. 9, Nov. 8, 1901.

169. Dr. Sidgwick, trained in an English school of philosophy, and pouring out volumes which had most other merits save those of brilliancy and profundity, desired to effect compromises between rival systems.—*Ibid.* p. 8, Aug. 30, 1900.

170. The whole set will occupy less room than the reports from 1866 onward, and so it will be possible for the practising barrister to have in his chambers a complete treasury of English decisions. But the work will be interesting to others than the professional lawyer.— *Spectator*, p. 740, Nov. 16, 1901.

171. We only wish that Mrs. Dudeney, who writes so well, would not say of her heroine that she was "not *very moved*," or make Boaz Boylett wonder why his dead wife Christobel "had never watched and tended their child *like* this odd gardener girl had done."—*Ibid.* p. 806, Nov. 23, 1901.

172. Will it be urged that the four Gospels are as old or even older than tradition ?—BOLINGBROKE, *Philosophical Essays*, iv., Sect. 19.

173. In order, even though blind, to believe that Saturn has a belt, I need but make a series of inferences based on actual experience of the statements of men in general and of astronomers in particular, to give me a rational proof of the truth of the statement.—Quoted in *Middlesex County Times*, p. 7, April 26, 1902.

174. I only know that the subject which the noble lord has brought forward is one of the most thorny and difficult which can be submitted to any legislative assembly, and I am extremely doubtful that any exhortations will have for their result in either House a satisfactory clue to the labyrinth of our marriage laws.—House of Lords, *Daily Telegraph*, p. 7, May 6, 1902.

175. In common with many youths of all times, of whom Lyly was one, he was scarcely out of "nonage," to use his own word, than he wanted to impart to his fellow-men his experience of a life, for him just begun, and to teach them how to behave in a world of which he knew only the outside.—*English Novel in the time of Shakespeare*, by Jusserand, p. 148, Ed. 1899, Fisher Unwin.

176. Mr. W. P. Reeves discusses Mr. Wise's Industrial Arbitration Act, which is of interest to others than the inhabitants of New Zealand.—*Spectator*, p. 537, Oct. 11, 1902.

177. Scarcely had the vast successes of the German forces showed the astonishing efficacy of the system that sent them forth, than Alexander (the Czar) set himself to imitate it.—*Nineteenth Century*, p. 846, May 1878.

178. The reason they discover no new laws of nature like gravitation, the correlation of forces, the causation of disease, and so on, is that intellect as such deals not with things uncoupled and disjoined, but with their relations and connections when united as parts of a living whole.—*Fortnightly Review*, p. 1015, Dec. 1902.

179. Being a thing of continued movement, trade always requires a force somewhere in the background to keep it going, like our locomotive its coals ; and industrial supremacy involves this force.—*Ibid.* p. 78, Jan. 1903.

180. They want to dig like the gardener digs, and plant "just like him," and they take an infinite amount of pains when they think it worth while to take any.—*Spectator*, p. 991, Dec. 20, 1902.

181. Innumerable trap-doors lay concealed in the bridge, which the passengers no sooner trod upon but they fell through them into the tide and immediately disappeared.—ADDISON, *Spectator*, No. 159.

182. He saw that the reason why witchcraft was ridiculed was because it was a phase of the miraculous.—LECKY, *History of Rationalism*, i. 126.

183. When on the eve of departure, he desired his wife, who was at the time pregnant, that if she brought him a son, to place a tower on the church.—THORPE, *Northern Mythology*.

184. To a mind like yours there is no other road to fame but by the destruction of a noble fabric.—JUNIUS's *Letters.*

185. They have no other standard on which to form themselves except what chances to be fashionable.—BLAIR's *Lectures on Rhetoric.*

186. A history now by a Mr. Hume, or a poem by a Mr. Pope, would be examined with different eyes than had they borne any other name.—D'ISRAELI, *Curiosities of Literature.*

187. You may infuse the sentiment by a ray of light, no thicker, nor one thousandth part so thick, as the finest needle.—WILSON, *Recreations of Christopher North.*

188. This does not so much seem to be owing to the want of physical powers, but rather to the absence of vehemence.—ALISON, *Essay on English Theatres.*

189. Scarcely had he uttered the fatal word than the fairy disappeared.—SOANE, *New Curiosities of Literature.*

190. To our mind it is equally wonderful that he (Josephus) should remember the imaginary, as that he should forget the real.—DE QUINCEY, *Edited by Masson,* vol. vii. p. 108.

PART II.

CHAPTER VI.—ANSWERS TO EXAMPLES IN CHAPTER I.

(a) *Verb and Subject* (pp. 12-24).

1. Change *hangs* to *hang*. But the Singular *is* in the main clause is defensible; for the non-repetition of the article before "position" shows that the two nouns "position and influence" are intended to express jointly a single idea. Both are qualified by "the rightful." The single idea thus expressed corresponds with the Singular noun "the vital question," which is the complement to the verb "is." If the writer had wished to distinguish "position and influence" he would have said, "The rightful position and *the rightful* influence of laymen *are* the vital *questions*," etc.

2. Change *are* to *is*. This error exemplifies the snare of what has been called attraction.

3. Change *has* to *have*.

4. Change *seem* to *seems*.

5. Change *as me* to *as I am*. "As" is a form of Relative used after "such"; we cannot say "such as me am." (In Hodgson's *Errors in the Use of English*, p. 158, the phrase *as me*, provided there is an Objective case going before, is declared to be right, on the ground that "conjunctions connect nouns and pronouns in the same case." This view is untenable for two reasons—(1) *as*, when it is preceded by *such*, is not a conjunction, but a Relative; (2) even if it were a conjunction, it is not Co-ordinative, but Subordinative; and the rule quoted by Hodgson applies only to the former.)

6. Say *it passes* for *passes*. The omission of *it* as Subject of "passes" is against usage, though the real Subject is "to predict."

7. Change *is* to *are*, since "tracts" is the antecedent of "that."

8. Change *is* to *are*, since "all" is Plural. The words "each and" should be cancelled, since they create a grammatical difficulty, and their sense is implied already in the word "successively."

9. Change *were* to *was*.

10. Say, "a keen sense of disappointment and chagrin is felt."

11. Change *is* to *are*. Say, "much pumping and much repairing of machinery are," etc.

12. Change *whom* to *who*, since "who" is the Subject of the verb

"had paid." "He alleged" is parenthetical, and should have had a comma before and after it.

13. There is no Subject to the verb "divides." Say, *than what divides*, or *than that which divides*.

14. Change *were* to *was*, since "neither" is Singular.

15. Change *are* to *is*. This is another example of the snare of attraction; see (2).

16. Here *are* might be admitted by some, on the ground that "score" is a noun of Multitude implying plurality. Most persons, however, would prefer *is*.

17. Change *teach* to *teaches*. Attraction again; see (2).

18. Change *is* to *are*. But the sentence could be improved by saying, "Not only England, but the world is to be congratulated," etc. This is evidently what the writer had in his mind.

19. Change *is* to *are*. Here *are* is certainly wrong, since "number" in this place is a Common noun, not a Collective noun used distributively.

20. There is no Subject to the verb "have fallen." The sentence must be recast. "The rainfall, extending, etc.—the Darling river, has varied in quantity from one inch to one and a half."

21. It does not sound well to use "meeting" as a Noun of Multitude. Recast the sentence thus:—"In an influential meeting held at Herschel his constituents were," etc.

22. Change *has* to *have*.

23. Change *lie* to *lies*.

24. Change *is* to *are*. On the force of the repetition of the article see (1).

25. Change *seem* to *seems*.

26. Change *me* to *I*. *I* is needed as Subject to the verb "have" understood.

27. *Was* is grammatical; but it would be more idiomatic to say *were*, since plurality is obviously intended. "Number" is here Distributive rather than Collective.

28. This is grammatical and defensible, since the clause "Where a British, etc.—new markets," may be regarded as a Noun-clause, Subject of the verb "lies." Nevertheless it would sound better to say, "The direction in which a British merchant could do much towards opening up new markets lies," etc.

29. Change *were* to *was*, since "news," though Plural, is always followed by a Singular verb.

30. Change *whomever* to *whoever*.

31. Here *are* is admissible, since "variety" is a noun of Multitude implying plurality. Nevertheless it would be rather better to say, "many and various places," etc.

32. Change *is* to *are*.

33. Say, *To aim at public and to aim at private good*, etc.

34. Change *is* to *are*. But it would sound better to leave the verb as it is, and say *rancour coupled with arrogance*.

35. Change *are* to *is*. Here a plural verb is out of place, since "force" is used in a Collective, not a Distributive sense.

36. Change *is* to *are*. Or say, *What is contained in it* for *its contents*, and leave the verb "is confirmed" as it stands.

37. Here *were* is defensible, since "series" might be Plural, and not Singular.   Probably, however, the writer intended "series" to be Singular, in which case *were* must be changed to *was*.

38. Change *whom* to *who*.   "We were led to believe" is parenthetical, and should have had a comma before and after it.

39. Change *form* to *forms*.   "Tribe" is here Collective.

40. Say, *as legacies of war realise themselves*, etc.

41. Change *are* to *is*.   "Body" is evidently Collective in this sentence.   In the clause "though it is a small one," change *it* to *the navy*.

42. Change *is* to *are*.

43. Change *do* to *does*.   Attraction again ; see (2).

44. Change *were* to *was*.   See (19).

45. Change *Oxford* to *The Oxford players*.

46. Cancel *which*, since the Subject is "illuminations."   The sentence as a whole is a bad one.   Say, "In all their rejoicings the ancients used fires ; but the fires were intended merely to burn their sacrifices, and as most of their sacrifices were performed at night, the illuminations," etc.

47. Change *is* to *are*.   But the sentence requires to be entirely recast : "So far as the Council is concerned on the one hand, and the Sanitary Inspector on the other, the Council must obey the official, even though the official may be wrong ; but in this case the Council has its remedy."   *Council* is not here a Noun of Multitude.

48. Change *whom* to *who*.   "I presume he would have us believe" is all parenthetical.   The punctuation is misleading : there must be a comma after "believe," and none after "presume."

49. Change *was* to *were*.   The context shows that "cab" and "horse" are to be understood, not as a collective whole, but as separate objects.

50. Change *methods* to *method*.

51. Change *is shown* to *are shown*.

52. Change *have* to *has*.   Attraction again ; see (2).   The sentence would be more suitably worded :—"Realisable securities of the worth (value) of half a million pounds have been," etc.

53. Change *raise* to *raises*.   Attraction again.   What the writer had in his mind was :—"The numerous small French posts present in Egyptian territory raise," etc.

54. Say, *The ivory procured in Dar Fertit*, etc.

55. Here the construction is confused.   Say either "half of which has," or "half of whom have."

56. Change *narrative* to *narratives*.

57. Change *have* to *has*.   The writer has allowed himself to be misled by the conjunction "and."   "Have got to be" is a bad phrase.   It would be better to say "is regarded" or "must be regarded."

58. Correct ; but the order of the words could be improved.   Say, "who think that intrigue and the odour of sanctity are inconsistent." Or say, "that the odour of sanctity is inconsistent with intrigue."

59. Change *has* to *have*.   "Riches," though originally a Singular, is now universally used as a Plural.

60. Since "rarely" is more negative than positive, *dare* is defensible.   We always say, "He dare not,"—never "He dares not."   But

the mood is wrong. The "should" ought to have been followed by "would." "He would rarely dare to allow," etc.

61. Change *suffer* to *suffers*. "Quality" is the antecedent of "which."

62. Here *lies* is correct, since "head" and "front" stand for the same thing and have only one article.

63. Place *were* after "teaching," and place *was* after "attitude."

64. Change *has* to *have*. Another instance of attraction.

65. Change *does* to *do*, since "which" has two nouns for its antecedent. Or we may consider "merits" the antecedent. In either case *which* is plural.

66. It would be better to say, "The sight of the clerical costume and countenance does not," etc.

67. Change *has* to *have*. Here "which," the Subject, has four antecedents.

68. Change *leaves* to *leave*.

69. Say, *The evidence of Picquart and that of Bertulus contain*, etc. The verb "contains" was put in the wrong number, because the Subject had been defectively worded.

70. Change *is* to *are*.

71. Change *makes* to *make*.

72. Change *appear* to *appears*.

73. Change *has* to *have*.   •

74. Here *is* might be defended on the ground that the sum amounting to "two-thirds" represents a collective whole. Yet *are* would sound better and is better grammar. *Are*, however, should be changed to *were*, so that the tense may correspond with that of "received."

75. Here *was* might be defended on the ground that "splendour and grace" stand for the same thing. But, as there is no article going before, the construction is of questionable accuracy. Leave out *splendour and*, which are superfluous.

76. Change *lie* to *liest*.

77. Change *distinguishes* to *distinguish*. (It is curious that such an obvious false-concord should have been published throughout the length and breadth of the British empire by the promoters of the sale of the *Century Dictionary*. The article, it will be observed, is carefully expressed three times, and yet the verb is made singular.)

78. Change *frown* to *frowns*.

79. Change *and the study* to *coupled with the study*. Otherwise *is* must be changed to *are ;* but this would not suit so well the Singular complement "guarantee."

80. Change *were* to *was*. Attraction again.

81. Change *was* to *were*.

82. Correct. Three constructions are possible, all meaning the same thing :—

    (a) The spiritual and the temporal ruler appear.

    (b) The spiritual ruler and the temporal ruler appear.

    (c) The spiritual and temporal rulers appear.

But the following construction would give a different sense ·—

    The spiritual and the temporal rulers appear.

This would imply a plurality both of spiritual rulers and of temporal rulers.

83. Insert *wisdom* after "sacred." Here the repetition of the noun is necessary, since there is no article.

84. Say, "The wantonly destructive and vindictive spirit shown by the enemy," etc.

85. Change *have* to *has.* It is curious that the writer should first have said *have* and then *is* for the same Subject, "set." *Had* in the next clause should be changed to *has,* to make the sequence of tenses correct.

86. Change *were* (the second one) to *was,* and *are* to *is.* The Subject "number" is here a Common noun, not a Collective noun used distributively.

87. There is no Subject to "was." Say, "one cause, as we have seen, was that almost every nation," etc.

88. Change *was* to *were.*

89. Change *have* to *has.* Attraction again ; see (2).

90. Insert *the* before *world,* or make "world" plural. See (82).

91. Change *whom* to *who.* The commas show that "he says" is parenthetical.

92. Change *were* to *was.* Attraction again.

93. Change *have* to *has.* But it would be better to change *the flower* to *the best,* and leave the verb plural. The noun understood after "best" will then be "forces."

94. Say, "There was a spirit of dulness and stiffness."

95. Say, "The same degree of affection, devotion, and happiness exists."

96. Here *is* is correct, because "thirty years" stands for a collective period of time. The sentence, however, would be better worded, "A period of thirty years is not a long one," etc.

97. Change *is* to *are,* and repeat the article. The sentence will stand thus :—"There are at present in Regent's Park a museum, a lecture-theatre, and a small library with an herbarium attached."

98. Change *a part* to *some.*

99. There is no proper Subject to *knew.* Say, "He stated that men like himself, who were behind the scenes, knew," etc.

100. Change *is* to *are.* The repetition of the article makes the change indispensable.

101. Insert *Company* after "Railway."

102. Change *were* to *was.*

103. Insert *be* after *will.* At present the verb is incomplete. But the words *there will be sure to be* have an awkward sound. Say, "There will certainly be a special race-meeting," etc.

104. Say, "than any that have yet been placed," etc. The verb cannot be Singular, since three distinct things are named. *Him* must be changed to *them,* since the antecedent is "those."

105. Change *Oxford* to *the Oxford players ;* and insert *players* after "Scottish."

106. Change *are* to *is.* Or say, "there are a great many rumours," etc.

107. Say, "Jewish progress and Christian progress both owe," etc. The noun must be repeated for the reasons given in (83).

108. Change *is* to *are.* The £150,000 is here used distributively, not collectively, as the context shows.

109. Here *do* might be in the Subjunctive mood after "if." Never-

theless it will sound better to say "does." The verb, whatever its mood may be, must be Singular.

110. Change *secure* to *secures*.

111. Change *furnish* to *furnishes*. The Subject is "edict." If "with" is changed to "and," the verb will remain "furnish."

112. Change *are* to *is*.

113. Change *is* to *are*. The article should have been repeated before "determination" and before "energy."

114. The phrase "all manner of things," in the sense of "all kinds of things," though now almost obsolete, was once common, and apparently on the principle of attraction it was followed by a Plural verb. Though we must allow this sentence to pass, we cannot commend it. It would be better to say "all kinds of things."

115. Change *not me* to *not I*.

116. Change *is* to *are*. An adjective preceded by "the" can stand for a Singular noun only when it is intended to denote some abstract quality.

117. Change *have* to *has*. Another example of attraction.

118. Say, "of a quantity and *a* quality that *demand*," etc. The article must be repeated before "quality," since two very distinct things are intended.

119. Change *whom* to *who*, since *who* is needed as Subject of the verb "were." The sentence "he observed" is parenthetical, and should have had a comma before and after it. Change the second *who* to *and*.

120. *Has* is here correct, since "fourteen degrees" represents a collective unit. Nevertheless the sentence would sound much better if the Complement and the Subject were made to change places :—" On one or two nights at Davos the lowest reading was fourteen degrees," etc.

121. Change *has* to *have*. "Which" the Subject has here two antecedents, and these make it Plural.

122. Change *whom* to *who*. "They believed" is parenthetical.

123. There is no proper Subject to the verb "have joined." Change *under a thousand men* to *not even a thousand men*.

124. Change *strike* to *strikes*. The conjunctions "neither . . . nor" are not Cumulative.

125. Change *proves* to *prove*.

126. Change *has accorded* to *have accorded*.

127. Change *was* to *were*. There is no reason here to consider "£200" or "£300" as a Collective unit. The context shows that these sums were intended to be distributed amongst many different persons.

128. Either omit *moral and*, or change *and* to *or*.

129. Change *bonâ fides* to *bona fides;* or better still, substitute the English phrase "good faith" for the Latin one. *Have* must be changed to *has*.

130. Change *is shown* to *are shown*.

131. There is no proper Subject to the verb "has been selected." Say, "some spot outside Buckingham Palace has been selected."

132. Change *whom* to *who*. "He considered" is parenthetical.

133. There is no proper Subject to the verb "can." Say, "That

this person should accuse us of want of knowledge can only create," etc. Substitute "as I have studied and know them" for "as I have and do."

134. Insert *together* after *who*. This will show that "who" has both of the preceding nouns for its antecedent, although they are separated by "or."

135. Change *is* to *are*, and insert *the* before "note."

136. Change "the legal twelve miles" to "the legal limit of twelve miles."

137. There is no Subject to the verb "remain." Insert "the said letters" so as to supply the needed Subject.

138. Change *was* to *were ;* or say, "Great was the disappointment and great the anger," etc.

139. Change *whom* to *who*. "They believed" is parenthetical, and should have had a comma placed before and after it.

140. Change *are* to *is*. Another example of attraction.

141. Change *seems* to *seem*. The repetition of the article "a" leaves no doubt as to what the number of the verb should be.

142. Change *or* to *and*.

143. The Subject is not sufficiently distinct. Say, "an area of no less than 400,000 square miles has laughed," etc.

144. Change *is* to *are*. See remarks under 141. It sounds awkward, however, to say, "There are a Christian and a criminal," etc. This can be avoided by saying—"There is a mixture of Christian and criminal," etc.

145. Change *have been given* to *has been given*. The first part of the sentence could be improved thus : "The number of books of this character that have been published within the past few years is so extraordinary," etc.

146. Change *fall* to *falls*. The writer has allowed himself to be misled by the three nouns immediately preceding the verb.

147. Here the plural *were* is correct, since the repetition of *the* before the phrase "Orange River Colony" shows that two distinct colonies are intended.

148. Here the construction is obviously confused. First we have "the alarm and indignation" followed by a Singular verb "is," then "that fear and anger" followed by a Plural verb "have proved." Let *is* be changed to *are*.

149. Change *were* to *was*. Attraction again.

150. Say, "the attitude of unions and that of employers both become intelligible."

151. Change *were* to *was*. The Subject is the Noun-clause "What had, etc.—of Israel." The comma after "Judges" should be cancelled. The sentence might, however, be reconstructed thus : "The circumstances which had characterised the epoch of the Judges and led to the defeats of Israel were the want of precaution and the inferiority of arms."

152. Change *was* to *were*.

153. There is no proper Subject to the verb. Say, "not even 2 per cent of the population hold," etc.

154. Change *have their* to *has its*. The Singular force attaching to the word "each" is so great that the verb following must be Singular.

155. There is no Subject to the verb "should have been pursued." Insert *which* after *course*. The sentence is—"The conciliatory course which, as Mr. A. H. contends, should have been pursued, etc.—was actually pursued."

156. The Singular verb *retains* is correct, but *their* must be changed to *its*.

157. Change *constitute* to *constitutes*. The Subject is "history."

158. Here *was* might be defended, because the two Subjects relate to a single act. The writer would have done better, however, if he had said, "The Act for disestablishing and disendowing the Irish Church," etc.

159. Change *the major part* to *most of the Norfolk lakes*.

160. Say, "has the qualities to make itself irresistible," etc.

161. Change *are* to *is*. Another instance of attraction.

162. The word "all" implies plurality. But it sounds so awkward to say "all the news are good," that the sentence had better be recast : —"for now we get nothing but good news of our armies."

163. Change *were* to *was*. Another example of attraction.

164. The last sentence should be rewritten thus :—"Granted this, then the heavy man and the heavy horse have no longer any reason of their being." *Raison d'être* is not English, and it is not every reader who knows what it means. Anyhow it is Singular, and should not have been followed by *have*.

165. Change *were* to *was*. Attraction again.

166. Say, "the total number of men captured last week in South Africa was three hundred and twenty-five."

167. The *us* is obviously wrong. Say, "The difficulty that we, or rather those among us who," etc.

168. Change *do* to *does*.

169. Say, "The obstinate maintenance of an alien church and that of an alien land-law are," etc.

170. Change *is* to *are*, since the antecedent of *which* is plural.

171. Change *whomsoever* to *whosoever*   It would be better to say, "to any one who."

172. Say, "the doctrine of the true function of," etc.

173. Change *have* to *has*. "Council" is here Collective : the Council was acting in its corporate capacity.

174. It will sound better to say "neither his life nor his works throw," etc. The original is quite correct ; but it sounds better in such instances to put the Plural last.

175. There is no verb for "jury." Say, "the jury having given their verdict, surely that verdict must be respected," etc. The comma after "jury" must be cancelled, since "jury" is Nominative absolute.

176. Change *cuts* to *cut*. The context shows that "obsolescence" and "destruction" are not intended to express a single idea. The article "the" should be repeated before "destruction."

177. Change *are* to *is*. "Force" is evidently here Collective.

178. Change *has* to *have*, since "I" is the nearest Subject.

179. Change *are* to *is*. The proper wording would be, "the Government of Germany, in contrast with that of England, is opposed," etc.

180. *Was* might be allowed to pass, since "strength and unity,"

preceded as they are by a single article, might be regarded as a single idea. But if this is to be conceded, *result* must be changed to *results*. Otherwise the construction is mixed.

181. Change *were* to *was*.

182. Properly speaking, the Relative clause should be—"that loves his friend,"—since *man*, not *I*, is the antecedent of "that."

183. Change *appear* to *appears*.

184. Change *were* to *was*.

185. Change *has* to *have*.

186. Change *has* to *have*. But even with this change the sentence is a bad one, and should be rewritten thus :—"Among the sovereigns of modern Europe, Alexander, Emperor of Russia, is the one who has left," etc.

187. Change *were* to *was*.

188. Change *bear* to *bears*.

189. Change *come* to *comes*.

190. Change *were* to *was*, or change *with* to *and*.

191. Change *with* to *and*. It would not suit the sense to change *were* to *was*.

192. Change *is* to *are*. Repeat "the" before "precision."

193. As the article has been given twice, this sentence is defensible ; see remarks under (2). It would be better, however, to insert *know-ledge* after *abstract*. The verb in any case must be Plural.

194. Insert *freedom* after *political*. Since there is no article, the insertion is indispensable.

195. Change *coincides* to *coincide :* the verb must certainly be Plural, since it has two Subjects connected by *and*. The article must be repeated before *historical ;* the repetition is indispensable, since two different kinds of analysis are here alluded to. These two changes make the sentence admissible. But the sentence might be further improved by mentioning *analysis* twice.

196. Change *literature* to *literatures*, and *that* to *these*.

197. Change *furnish* to *furnishes*.

198. Say, "a reduction of some 400 or 500 millions in our expenditure has taken place."

199. Change *dispels* to *dispel*.

200. Here *the Germans* is pendent. The sentence can be recast thus :—"As to the Germans of the present day, there are who opine that, although greatly superior to their ancestors, they are still distant," etc.

201. *It* is here pendent, and must be cancelled.

(b) *Miscellaneous* (pp. 30-40).

1. Change *ye* to *you*.

2. "Accused" is pendent or unattached, *i.e.* there is no noun or pronoun which it can qualify ; for it is difficult to make it qualify *her* in the phrase "the example of her reign." The sentence had better be recast :—"Accused as she was of, etc.—titles, she has been held to furnish by her reign a striking example of the evil of," etc.

3. Cancel the superfluous *he*, and place a comma after *projector*. The word "projector" cannot here be in the absolute construction, because it is the Subject of "left."

4. Change *thee* to *thou*.

5. Change *society* to *men*. "Society" is not a fit antecedent for "whom."

6. Say, "were very far from entitling him," etc. ; or say, "did not at all entitle him." The preposition "from" cannot be left pendent,—without an Object.

7. Say, "in preparation for their removal." *Preparatory* as it stands is a pendent adjective,—having no noun to qualify.

8. Change *their* to *his*. The antecedent to *his* is "every one."

9. Change *except he* to *except him*. (Insert "that" after "now.")

10. Change *and she* to *and this woman*. "She" is bad grammar, and "her," though correct grammar, would not sound well.

11. Say, "him alone can I trust."

12. *Unlike* is left pendent. Say, "It was not necessary for him, as it was for North, to," etc.

13. Change *agreeable* to *agreeably*.

14. Change *having regard to* to *regard being had to* or *considering*. *Considering* is well established as an "impersonal absolute"; the same cannot be said for *having*.

15. Say, "by selling them than by keeping them." Or cancel the superfluous words "or works," and leave *it* as it was.

16. *Agenda* is Plural. Say, "list of agenda."

17. Change *when ironing* to *when you are ironing*. "Ironing" must not be left pendent. Such a phrase is correct only when there is some noun to which the participle can be referred.

18. Change *me* to *I*.

19. Change *when camping* to *when one is camping*. See remarks under (17).

20. Change *absorb* to *absorbing*.

21. Change *as it really is* to *as they really are*.

22. Three mistakes in three lines. Say, "This party *has* stopped at no language, however strong, against those *whom* it considers the authors of the war, and *who* are at all events," etc.

23. Change *who* to *whom*.

24. Say "as fish are wont to do." There is no antecedent to "their."

25. Change "we Britishers" to "us Britishers."

26. Change *he* to *him* in both places.

27. "The enemy being completely frightened." This is an example of the "Gerundive use of Participles," and is therefore defensible. Yet this use is rare, when the phrase is made the Subject of a verb. Say, "but the state of utter fright to which the enemy were reduced on the 15th July seems to have frightened them."

28. Say, "when you are drying in the open." See (17).

29. Change *which* to *whom*. *Which* cannot be a Relative to "millionaire."

30. "Weighing" is here pendent or unattached. The sentence can be put right by inserting the words "he considered that" before the words "the war."

31. The first *who* is right ; the second should be *whom*.

32. Change *who* to *which*.

33. Change *thee or Venus* to *thou or Venus*.

34. Change *their* to *his*. The antecedent is "any one."

35. Here *which* is mentioned only once, although it is first used as an Indirect object, and then as a Direct one. This is not good English. Say, "some details *to which* we have allowed, etc., and *which* it would pain us to miss," etc.

36. *Than whom* is quite correct, *whom* being in the Objective case governed by "than," which is here a preposition, not a conjunction. "Than whom" means "by the side of whom," where "by the side of" is a preposition, or rather a prepositional phrase, equivalent to "than."

The best grammarians are agreed that "than" can be used as a preposition in certain contexts. Thus Abbott, in *How to Parse*, p. 278, says, "*than* in this phrase (and sometimes in others) has assumed the force of a preposition." Mr. Sweet, the highest living authority on English grammar, makes a very distinct pronouncement (*New English Grammar*, vol. i. § 380):—"In fact, *than* governs an Objective case like a preposition in such a construction as—

> Beelzebub, than whom,
> Satan except, none higher sat.—MILTON.

Bain, on the other hand, is vague and indecisive. He says (*Higher English Grammar*, p. 315, ed. 1896):—"The Objective occurs where the Nominative is expected. . . . Perhaps *whom* is the uniform usage, 'than *who*' seldom or never occurring." Such treatment is very unsatisfactory and feeble. If *who*, not *whom*, is to be "expected," we have a pendent Nominative,—a Nominative that has no verb for its subject,—which is absurd.

Mason (*English Grammar*, § 478, ed. 1891) is equally delusive :— "No satisfactory syntactical explanation can be given of the use of *whom* after *than*. There is not the slightest necessity for regarding *than* as a preposition." Yet he adds, "At the same time it is to be observed that, as the sentence stands, it would be impossible to fill up the ellipsis so as to make *who* the Subject of a finite verb."

Since it is impossible to show that *whom* ought to be a Nominative *who*, we must accept the fact pointed out by Mr. Sweet that it is an Objective governed by the preposition *than*.

37. Say, "by any one reflecting." *Reflecting* as it stands is pendent or noun-less.

38. Change *using* to *to use*. "Using" is pendent.

39. Change *than that* to *than those*.

40. *As thee* should have been *as thou*.

41. Say, "The invention, if we may assume that it has been made, gives," etc. There are two slight defects in the sentence as it stands : (1) *assuming* is hardly established as an impersonal absolute, like "considering," "concerning," "regarding"; (2) it is not a good construction to make *it* a Subject and *invention* an Object.

42. Change *acting as he did* to *by the plan on which he acted*. Here "acting" is pendent or noun-less.

43. Change *who* to *whom*.

44. Change *guides, protects, saves* to *guide, protect, save*. These are all violations of concord.

45. Change *simultaneous* to *simultaneously*. The adverb "simultaneously" will qualify the verb "moved."

46. There is no clear antecedent to "his own." Change *the slave-mind* to *the mind of the slave.*

47. Say, "It will be a long time before the railway begins to pay."

48. Here "partisan," a noun, is qualified by "less," an adverb, which is bad grammar. Say, "he is less of a partisan than," etc.; or "has less of the partisan spirit."

49. For "the least optimist" say "one who is least optimistic." *Optimist* is a noun, and *least* is an abverb. An adverb cannot qualify a noun.

50. For "the almost impossibility" say "the practical impossibility." An adverb must not be made to qualify a noun.

51. Here the adverb "sufficiently" is made to qualify the noun "admirers." For "to be sufficiently his admirers" say "to admire him sufficiently."

52. Change *the far ago dates* to *the remote dates.*

53. Change *considering* to *all things considered* or *on the whole.* "Considering" may, it is true, be used as an impersonal absolute; but if so, it must have some Object placed after it.

54. For *instead* say *instead of this.*

55. *I and thou.* These are pendent Nominatives. Either say *me and thee ;* or change the construction and say "between ourselves."

56. Say, "whatever he did and whatever he was." *Whatever* as it stands is made to do duty first as an Objective and then as a Nominative. It must therefore be repeated.

57. Say, "this difficult pass of six or seven miles"; or say, "these six or seven miles of," etc.

58. *Than whom* is correct. See remarks in (36).

59. Say, "If the ordinary courts fail." *Failing* is pendent.

60. *Than me* is defensible, being of the same construction as *than whom* in (58) and (36). It is also very commonly used, even in the best ranks of society. Bain (*Higher Eng. Grammar,* p. 315) admits, "It has in its favour this authority of an extensive, if not predominating, usage." In the example given in the text we can say either "you know it better *than me*" or "you know it better *than I do.*" Both are good grammar, and both constructions occur in Greek, Latin, and French. In the former *than* is a preposition, in the latter a Subordinative conjunction. The former construction, however, should be avoided in any contexts, in which it may give rise to an ambiguity. There is no ambiguity in "you know it better than me." But "you know him better than me" should be written "you know him better than I do"; otherwise it might mean "you know him better than you know me."

61. Change *their own* to *the Church's own* or *its own.*

62. "Business" is here intended to qualify "age." But the construction is grammatically awkward, besides being ambiguous in sense. Say, "This is essentially a busy, a practical age"; or say, "an age of business, an age of practical work."

63. The absolute construction "she having great possessions" is out of place here, because *Sylvie* and *she* occur in the sentence already. The sentence should be reconstructed—"to the intense chagrin of the holy Monsignori, who had cast wistful eyes on her great possessions."

64. Change *relative* to *relatively.* An adverb is here indispensable.

65. Change *who has* to *who have.*   The antecedent is "myself."

66. Change *themselves* to *himself.*

67. There is no antecedent to "they."   Change *they hold* to *it holds.*

68. Change *knoweth* to *knowest.*

69. Change *who* to *which.*

70. Say, "If a girl is a good tennis-player," etc.

71. Change *is it him?* to *is it he?*

72. Say, "while he was holding," etc.

73. Change *not alone* to *not only.*

74. Change *extraordinary* to *extraordinarily.*

75. *Hampered* is pendent, *i.e.* it has no noun to qualify. The sentence can be reconstructed thus:—"To make living and real personages of the men of past ages, in doing which the writer must be hampered with the necessity," etc.

76. Change *is* to *are.*

77. Say, "which has not its representative in this club."

78. Change *genius* to *geniuses.*

79. Change *are* to *is.*

80. After "truth" insert *told,* and cancel the comma.   "The truth told simply, literally, and in all fulness."

81. Change *independent* to *independently;* or say, "no account being taken of literary abilities," etc.

82. Change *exist* to *exists.*

83. The participle "having been reproached" is pendent or un-attached. Say, "considering that it has been reproached," etc.

84. Change *which latter* to *the latter of whom.* The antecedent of "whom" is "Red Indians."

85. Correct. But it would sound rather better to say "very un-equally matched in resources."

86. Reconstruct : "An extremely clever boy in every sort of way, he had many accomplishments." Boy, as it stands in the original, is pendent, unless it can be considered in apposition to *his.*

87. The first part of the sentence is bald, and the second *who* is wrong. Reconstruct thus : "We all know that this is not a defence of purity, but an attack on one man,—who has made his power felt throughout the country, and whom," etc.

88. Change *days of long ago* to *former days.*

89. Change *their* to *his.*

90. Change both the *whos* to *which.* The second one is superfluous.

91. Here *having resumed their attire* belongs grammatically to "Miss Cusack and Miss Ranssom" ; but it belongs in sense to "three claimants." Say, "When these had resumed their attire."

92. *Once arrived* is pendent or unattached. Say, "when once the relief has arrived." *Would be meted* should be changed to *will be meted.* There is no justification for putting the Future into a Conditional form, when the verb going before is Indicative, *i.e.* Assertive.

93. For "no use me describing" say "no use in my describing."

94. Change *and have* to *and which they have.* Or reconstruct thus : "which the father and mother have been dreading for the last ten years and have at last incurred."

95. Change *strata* (Plural) to *stratum* (Singular).

96. Change *root-and-branch* to *radical*. A noun can do the work of an adjective, when it is used attributively, but not when it is used predicatively.

97. Change *making every allowance* to *when every allowance is made for them*. "Making" as it stands is pendent or noun-less. It looks as if it were meant to qualify "Government."

98. Change *consistent* to *consistently*. Even then the sentence is not a good one. Say, "as homelike as is consistent with school-work."

99. We cannot use a Plural *are* with a Singular subject "to stuff." Say, "To make an apple-pie bed, to roll a guest in the snow, or to stuff up his dress-coat pockets with sticky sweets—these are among the pranks," etc. It is tautological to say "among some of the pranks."

100. "Speaking" is here pendent, or noun-less. Say, "Speaking as a South African, I can hardly say," etc.

101. On the wrong use of "having regard" see (14). Reconstruct thus: "His chief argument is that in the punishment of habitual criminals regard should be had to their past offences, and not merely to the present offence."

102. Cancel the superfluous *they*.

103. Reconstruct thus:—"The eloquence of Mr. J. R. I., however, like that of Mr. S., suffers," etc.

104. This very involved sentence may be reconstructed thus:— "Conversation is not allowed; but when the members are working in association, opportunities for the exchange of remarks do occur, and of these opportunities they are not slow to avail themselves."

105. Change the second *who* to *whom*.

106. Say, "still more schools of science and commerce"; or say, "still more scientific and commercial schools." The construction *science and commercial* is bad.

107. *But she*, though ungrammatical (*but* being a preposition), is well established by usage and must be tolerated.

108. Change *who* to *whom*, since *whom* is Object to the verb "wanted." But the sentence is very awkwardly worded. Reconstruct thus:—"I asked whom I should name, when questioned as to the persons that were to see the ship, and they said *the owners*."

109. Change *these* to *this*.

110. Change *bitter* to *bitterly*.

111. Change *which do not* to *which does not*.

112. Say, "who the men were with whom he was acting."

113. Say, "that he or any *other* man should not be estimated beyond *his* deserts."

114. Change *they . . . they* to *he . . . he*. "Everybody" cannot be antecedent of *they*.

115. Change *herself* to *she herself might be*; and insert *what* after "than," this being needed as Object of the verb "harboured." In the sentence as it stands there is no noun or pronoun with which "liberal" can be made to stand in predicative relation.

116. Change *if I was her* to *if I were she*.

117. Change *their* to *its*.

118. Change *dreadful* to *dreadfully*.

119. Change *Irish discontent* to *the discontent of the Irish*. *The Irish* is needed as antecedent to "their." Also change *was* to *were*. As there is a Subjunctive going before, there should be a Subjunctive following.

120. *Taking* is here pendent, though it looks as if it were meant to qualify "yokel." Say, "The said widower having taken unto himself," etc.

121. *Which* is here made to do double duty, firstly as Object of "to," and secondly as Object of "dislikes." Say, "which the average individual, being a stranger to such things, utterly dislikes."

122. *Walking* is here pendent. Say, *to any one walking*.

123. Change *feeling thus* to *if he felt thus*. "Feeling" is pendent. ("To have produced" should be changed to "to produce," the Present form of the Infinitive being sufficient after the Past tense, "was.")

124. Here there are two mistakes in less than two lines. Say, "longer and more heavily manned than those of the Danes."

125. Say, "but in only four cases was the accident sufficiently serious," etc.

126. Change *as them* to *as they are*. According to Hodgson, from whom this example is taken (*Errors in English*, p. 158), *as them* is correct, because there is an Objective ("Rosicrucians," "fanatics") going before, and "conjunctions connect nouns and pronouns in the same case." But this rule applies only to Co-ordinative conjunctions, whereas *as* is Subordinative.

127. Reconstruct thus :—"Each of the sexes should keep within its particular bounds : each should content itself with exulting within its own province."

128. Here "regardless" is pendent. It looks as if it qualified "priests." Say, "no regard being paid by the police to the fact that," etc.

129. Change *whom* to *who*. "He knew" is parenthetical. It is strange that such an obvious blunder should occur in a book intended for general use in schools and issued by the Clarendon Press.

130. Change *whomsoever* to *whosoever*. Nevertheless the construction, though now made grammatical, sounds awkward. Say, "of any power that had command of the sea."

131. There is a perpetual habit in these days of using the adverb *quite* to qualify nouns ; which is, of course, ungrammatical. In many instances the *quite* is superfluous, in others it is unmeaning, in others, where it is wanted, it could easily be replaced by an adjective. In the present example *quite* is unmeaning. *Quite* signifies "completely," "perfectly." There is no sense in saying "perfectly a small crowd." *Quite* must here be cancelled.

132. Change *these* to *this*.

133. Change *and* to *or*.

134. *Betrothal and marriage*, being in this instance the result of a single bargain, express a single idea, and hence *which is based*, though it has an awkward sound, is grammatically correct. The awkwardness can be removed by saying, "The ceremonies connected with the contract of betrothal and marriage, which is based," etc.

135. Change *love* to *loves*, since "Sornia" (Third person) is the antecedent of "who."

136. Change *he* to *him*, and *she* to *her*. The change is required by the rule, that nouns or pronouns in apposition must be in the same case. Nevertheless *he* and *she* seem to give more point to the sentence than *him* and *her*. We might say, "the man softened by her tears, and the woman receiving his devotions with effusion."

137. *Than he* is correct, because the verb "was" can be understood after it. Hodgson (*Errors in English*, p. 158) says that *than he* should be *than him*, because "than" is a conjunction and as such must have the same case after it as before it. The rule quoted, however, does not apply to Subordinative conjunctions, of which "than" is one. Nevertheless, *than him*, had it so been written, would have been defensible for the reasons stated in (36) and (60). In fact, it would have been better had the writer said either *than he was* or *than him*. To say *than he* is neither one thing nor the other.

138. Change *marvellous* to *marvellously*.

139. Change *have placed themselves* to *has placed itself*.

140. *Rising* is here pendent. Say, "He rises early, and a day of labour," etc.

141. Since "those" (the Subject of the sentence) is the antecedent, *ourselves* and *our* should be changed to *themselves* and *their*.

142. Change *require* to *requires*. It would be better, however, to retain *require* and change *or* to *and*.

143. Here *and* is made to connect an adjective "useless" with a noun "folly." Say, "is useless and foolish."

144. *Happening* is here pendent. Say, "as they happened."

145. Say, "having root neither in the soil of France nor in that of Attica."

146. Change *following* (which is here pendent) to *in accordance with*.

147. Change *whom* to *who*. Otherwise there is no Subject to the verb "is."

148. Change *taking care* to *care being taken*. "Taking" is pendent.

149. Change *who* to *that* or *which*. *That* is preferable since *which* has been used already in the same sentence.

150. Say, "and which were excellent food." In the sentence as it stands there is no Subject to *were*. Also place *which* before "I had taken."

151. Change *suitable* to *suitably*.

152. *Other* is here a pendent adjective. Change it to *otherwise*.

153. *It* is here a pronoun without an antecedent. Change *it* to *sleep*.

154. It is better to regard "save" as a preposition and change *he* to *him*. "Thy shores are empires changed in all save *thee*" (BYRON). Nevertheless, *save he* might find some persons to defend it on the ground that this was originally an absolute construction = he being save or safe, *i.e.* he being excepted.

155. Change *their* to *his*.

156. Change *their* to *his*. This change has to be made four times.

157. The second *which* is pendent, having no antecedent. It must be cancelled. The sentence will then be correct.

158. *Who* is here a pendent Nominative, having no verb to which it can be the subject. Say, "who, desirous of entering Bristol on an ass, found, as Hume informs us, that all Bristol," etc.

159. Change *she* to *her*. The apposition as it stands is wrong.

160. Change *I* to *me*.

161. Change *them* to *they*. Say, "as they are." *Should* should be changed to *shall* to make the moods agree.

162. Change *as him* to *as he was*.

163. *Than him* is defensible, since after an Intransitive verb like *becomes* there can be no ambiguity in the sense, and *than* can be used as a preposition, as in the phrase *than whom*. Those who deny that *than* can ever be used as a preposition may appease their consciences by saying *than he is* or *than he was*.

164. *Which* is here a pendent Relative, having no antecedent. Cancel it, and rewrite as follows :—"that the invention of notes in literary history has been produced."

165. Change *whom* to *which*.

166. *Ignorant* is here a pendent adjective, having no noun for it to qualify. Say, "though the speaker may be entirely ignorant," etc.

167. Cancel *and climate*. Or rewrite as follows :—"The climate of Scotland and the soil, even where it is susceptible of cultivation, are incomparably less favoured, etc., than those," etc.

168. *Joined* is a pendent participle, having no noun to which it belongs. Change *joined to* to *and*.

169. Here *weighing* has no noun to which it belongs. Change it to "if we weigh."

170. The use of the Possessive *their* in connection with a Participle or adjective is defensible perhaps, though it is not recommended. Say, "Sensible that, as they had not hanged Josephus at first, it was now become," etc.

CHAPTER VII.—ANSWERS TO EXAMPLES IN CHAPTER II.

(a) *Nouns* (pp. 44-46).

1. The Possessive case in such a word as "audience," though becoming more and more common in the daily press, is not at present sanctioned by literature. Say "The power of a theatrical audience to sustain its attention is," etc.

2. Change *an ass* to *asses*.

3. Change *great warriors* to *very warlike*. Or say, "were much addicted to war." We cannot speak of races as warriors. This is mixing up a Collective noun with a Distributive or Common one.

4. Change *Germany's Kaiser* to *The Kaiser*, or *The Emperor of Germany*. "Germany's" is objectionable for the reason stated in (1). Another objection is that "Germany's" is tautological, Germany being the only country in which the Emperor is called Kaiser. Reconstruct the last part of the sentence thus :—"with deep regret and with much sympathy for," etc.

5. *Pair* is a Collective noun, and does not match with the Distributive phrase "each other." Say, "The two bore each other," etc.

6. Say, "the federation of the great island-continent."

7. Change *prisoner* to *prisoners*.

8. Correct. "The Duke of Orleans" may be regarded as a kind of compound- or phrase-noun, and as it relates to a person, the Possessive case is not inappropriate. It would, however, be more correct to say *Orleans's* than *Orleans'*.

9. Say, "to the reputation of Lord Roberts and to that of Lord Kitchener." Or make *reputation* Plural. Two distinct reputations are referred to.

10. In the last part of this sentence there is a great deal of confusion between the Singular and the Plural. Say, "that, like the lamb of the fable, they have been worried by the British wolf."

11. Change *low types* to *men of low type*. "Settlers" is a Common noun, and "type" is an Abstract one ; the one should not be predicated of the other.

12. Change *French* to *French's*. When *separate* possession is implied, as it is here, the possessive *'s* must be given to both nouns.

13. Say, "when the last theatrical success of the London season," etc.

14. Here the repetition of the Possessive form in "St. Thomas's

252

and "St. Bartholomew's" is quite correct, since the properties of the three hospitals denoted are separate from one another. So far, so good. But "property" (Singular) is awkward. Say, "the properties belonging to St. Bartholomew's, St. Thomas's, and the Bridewell Hospitals respectively are exempt," etc. Observe the insertion of the word "respectively."

15. Change *these speeds* to *these rates of speed.* "Speed," being an abstract noun, should not be pluralised without necessity.

16. Change *province* to *provinces,* since two distinct provinces are referred to. Or say, "the province of reason and that of emotion."

17. Change *policies* to *policy,* since the context shows that the policy referred to was one, not two.

18. Change *tune's* to *tune.* By this change "having been derived" becomes a participle instead of being a verbal noun or gerund. This is called "the Gerundive use of participles."

19. "Church" is a Collective noun, and "few" is a Distributive adjective. The two therefore do not match. Say, "and the church at the time was numerically small and easily managed." Observe that *was* has been inserted, to fit the Subject "church."

20. Change *Music's firm hold* to *The firm hold of Music.*

21. Say, "between the danger of foreign and that of civil war"; or say, "between the dangers of foreign and of civil war." In the latter, observe that *danger* has been pluralised and that *of* has been repeated. The repetition of the preposition shows that two distinct kinds of danger are referred to.

22. Say, "in which American criticism and German criticism were directed," etc. The change is necessitated by the word "equal." One criticism is declared to be equal to the other. Or say, "in which American criticism was directed as severely as German against the same fault."

23. Change *the couple* (Collective) to *the two* (Distributive).

24. Change *nearer neighbours* to *a nearer neighbour.*

25. Change *a failure* to *failures.*

26. "Among the legislation" is an awkward phrase. Say, "Among the legislative measures."

27. It is not good English to say "is alike essential," etc., when only one thing ("existence") is given as Subject. Say, "Malarial germs and mosquitos are alike," etc. The word "existence" is superfluous.

28. Insert the word "respectively" after *Camorra.*

29. Change *excessive heats* to *excessive degrees of heat.* See remarks in (15).

30. Say, "indicate two widely different ranks," or say, "indicate a wide difference of status." The noun *status* is not met with in the plural.

31. We cannot speak of peoples or nations (Collective) being either waiters or travellers (Distributive). *And who* is objectionable, since there is no *who* going before. Moreover, *who* is not a correct form of Relative for such an antecedent as "peoples" (= nations). Reconstruct thus:—"Among peoples which are not actually subject to British or American rule, and do not abound either in waiters or in commercial travellers, the inducements," etc.

32. Change *book's faults* to *faults of the book*.

33. Change *Joshua* to *Joshua's*.

34. Insert *of one* after *name*.

35. Change *the strange contrasts which exist* to *the strange diversity that exists*.

(b) Adjectives, including Articles (pp. 51-55).

1. Say, "for their respective candidates." Also insert *with* before "Liberals." The repetition of the preposition gives additional point to the distinction between Conservatives and Liberals.

2. Cancel *the* before *pictures*.

3. Insert *the* before *more objectionable*. The Comparative is here used in a selective sense.

4. Say, "from all the thoroughfares," etc. "Whole" is used in a Collective sense, and should not be made to qualify a Distributive plural.

5. Cancel *the* before *French*. When a language is spoken of, no article is used before the Proper name.

6. Here *little* (= not much) is quite correct. *A little* would have been wrong. It would be rather better, however, to say "one another" than "each other," since more than two shires are referred to.

7. Say, "The whole fleet was taken." *Of their ships* is superfluous, and *were* is wrong.

8. Insert *by the* after *and*:—"is shown by the Metropolitan Railway and by the Metropolitan District Railway." This removes ambiguity.

9. Say, "either by the military or the civilian shots." The repetition of the article gives additional point to the distinction between "military" and "civilian."

10. Change *a historic* to *an historic*. On account of the accent being on the second syllable of "historic," the initial *h* is silent. In talking we invariably say "an 'istoric." What we say in talking, we should repeat in writing. On the other hand, we must write *a history*, not *an history*, because in "history" the accent is on the first syllable and the *h* is sounded. (The tense of the verb is not quite what it should be. The sense requires that *is* should be changed to *has been;* otherwise there is no point in adding the clause, "even if its events be yet completed.")

11. Cancel *other*:—"any man but (= except) him." If "other" is retained, then *but* must be changed to *than*. According to an anomalous idiom *but he* must be allowed to pass. Yet it is better to say *but him*.

12. Change *either* to *any* or *any one*. "Either" applies to two things only.

13. Change *something* to *anything*. The word "rarely" has a negative force, and is not followed by "something." Perhaps, however, what the writer meant to say was this:—"Although I rarely read your journal without finding something with which," etc.

14. Insert *the* before "Unionist." See remarks in (9).

15. Change *less* to *fewer*.

16. Change *an ambition* to *another ambition*

17. Here *other* should be cancelled. Or the words *of any other friendly state* could be rewritten—"of any other state, that is on a friendly footing with himself."

18. Change *an united* to *a united*.

19. Say, "We have in the Pacific three complete naval stations,—the China station, the Pacific, and the Australian." The article must be repeated before each adjective, in order to denote the three distinct stations. If *China* is to be used as an adjective, it must have the noun placed immediately after it.

20. Say, "All nations were blended," etc. Or say, "Every nation was blended with every other nation."

21. Insert *other* after "all."

22. Say, *both the one and the other*.

23. Insert *others* after "all."

24. Reconstruct thus:—"Every morning our scouts and patrols got in touch with the enemy, and each side saluted the other with a shot or two."

25. Insert *other* after "every."

26. Say, "all the coal-carts had been," etc. See (4).

27. Change *all the Powers* to *all the other Powers*.

28. Cancel *a* before "figure." This article is implied already in *no* (A.S. *ne* "not" and *án* "one").

29. Insert *the* before "progressive" and before "rash."

30. Insert *the* before "tribal" and before "mystical." The noun "slave" does not sound well in the middle of all these adjectives. Change it to "servile."

31. Insert *the* before "greatest."

32. Insert *a* before "crying wrong."

33. Change *a habitual and an accepted fact* to *an habitual and accepted fact*. For an explanation of *an* before "habitual" see (10). The repetition of *an* before "accepted" is wrong, because it implies that two facts are intended instead of one.

34. Change *frontier* to *frontiers*. Or say, "the British and the French frontier."

35. Cancel *the* before "Jews."

36. Insert *other* after "any."

37. *One another* would be rather more appropriate than *each other*, since more than two Powers are spoken of.

38. Say, "Most of the casualties were among Russians and Japanese."

39. Say, "all the other Governments."

40. Say, "as all other nations put together."

41. Cancel *a* before "patient." See remarks in (33).

42. Say, "the ministers were not altogether satisfied with one another."

43. Change *an ubiquitous* to *a ubiquitous*. See (10).

44. Say, "The court finds that the prisoner is not guilty of any of the charges, and honourably acquit him of all."

45. Change *an eulogy* to *a eulogy*.

46. Insert *the* before "lower."

47. Change *the lion, tiger, or bear* to *the lion, the tiger, and the bear*. The grammar of the sentence requires that *or* should be

changed to *and*. Say, "if these qualities could be used" : *they* as it stands appears to have the same reference as *their*, whereas it really refers to "qualities."

48. Say, "into all the disasters." Or say, "into the whole subject of the disasters."

49. The articles are here used very inconsistently. Say, "the loved and *the* loathed, spendthrift and miser, king and beggar," etc. The participles and adjectives must all have articles placed before them : the nouns do not require them.

50. Change *each other* to *one another*. The words will have more point if we say, "in very much the same or in precisely the same social circle."

51. Insert *on the* before "logical."

52. The construction is confused. Say, "A pacificator of the bold and intuitive temper which characterised the Earl of Durham." Or say, "A pacificator of bold and intuitive temper, like the Earl of Durham."

53. Say, "the Transvaal and the Orange River Colony." Since *colony* is singular, the article must be repeated.

54. Change *a heroic* to *an heroic*. See (33).

55. It is better to repeat *the* before "liberal." This is the proper construction, although the sense in this case happens to be clear already.

56. Say, "as resident war-correspondent." When a noun is used as an adjective, the noun qualified by it should be placed immediately after it.

57. Say, "from every other man in the world."

58. Insert *the* before "Native."

59. Insert *other* after "any," and *what* after "as" :—"an extent as great as what any other statesman has enjoyed."

60. Say, "the editor and the publisher," since two distinct men are intended.

61. "Were the more intolerable." See remarks in (3).

62. Say, "the learned and the ignorant, the temperate and the debauched."

63. Cancel *the* before "helpful." The second *the* is worse than useless.

64. Insert *the* before "wild." Or say, "between tame buffaloes and wild."

65. Insert *other* after "any."

66. Say, "English is as much the language of the German-American as of the Anglo-American, and the former is as good a citizen of the United States as any man could be."

67. Insert *other* after "any."

68. Insert *other* after "any."

69. Insert *else* after "anything."

70. Insert *other* after "most."

71. Change *hundreds of great men* to *hundreds of other great men*.

72. Change *any one* to *any other person*.

73. Say, "enters deeper into the soul than any other vice."

74. Here *coal* is used as an adjective before "strike," which is quite legitimate, but it should be repeated before "famine," as it is intended to qualify this noun also. Say, "and the coal-famine."

75. Say, "in any other European or in any American State."

76. Insert *those between* between "and" and "Germany."

77. Cancel *the* before "most."

78. Insert *the* before "Treasurer." Chancellor and Treasurer are not one person.

79. Insert *of* before "England." Or say, "of France and England respectively."

80. Change *only* to *alone*. This change removes ambiguity.

81. In these two lines there are four mistakes : (1) change *excellence* to *excellences*, plurality being implied by the adjective "various"; (2) insert *the* before *French;* (3) change *the most* to *the more;* (4) substitute "afforded the more admirable example" for "were the most admirable example."

82. Change *others* (which is wrong in this context) to *professions*.

(c) *Comparison of Adjectives* (pp. 57-59).

1. Say, "than any of the *other* Powers." Since *we, i.e.* England, is a power, the word "other" is necessary.

2. The construction is confused. Say, "as deserving as any man he had ever known." Or say, "the most deserving of all men," etc. It is not clear which of these two the author intended.

3. Insert *other* after "any."

4. The construction is confused. Say, "Mr. Stanley was the first to slaughter the natives," etc. He could not have been one of his own predecessors.

5. Change *others* to "countries."

6. *Chiefest* is not a proper Superlative. The sense attaching to the word "chief" is not one that admits of degrees of comparison.

7. Change *more universal* to *more general*. Universality admits of no degrees. Cancel the comma after "income," and cancel *to be.* These may remain however, if we recast the sentence as follows :— "if every wife had a separate income,—the said income to be at her independent disposal."

8. Say, "a shorter memory than any other distinguished politician." Or say, "the shortest memory of all distinguished politicians."

9. Change *than Bismarck* to *to those possessed by Bismarck*. "Than" is not used after Latin comparatives. A change of order, too, is desirable :—"of abilities far inferior to those possessed by Bismarck."

10. Change *stronger* to *strongest*. Here there is no comparison between two nations in particular.

11. Change *most* to *more*.

12. Change *of any paper* to *of all papers*. Even with this change the sentence is a bad one. Say, "has of late years risen to a circulation as widespread as that of any other paper in Great Britain."

13. Such a phrase as "more impossible" is open to the same objection as "more universal" in (7). If the phrase is retained, it should be accompanied with some apology. "Mr. Bock's humour is of course more impossible, if such a phrase may be allowed, to transfer," etc.

14. See above, under (6).

S

15. Change *latter* to *last*. There is no point in saying that too much of a thing has been condemned, since "too much" implies already something to be condemned. Say, "The last, when used beyond a moderate quantity, has been condemned long ago."

16. Change *most* to *more*.

17. Change *latter* to *last-named*.

18. Say, "as more obscure than any of her sisters."

19. Change *of all others* to *of all churches*.

20. Change *strongest* to *stronger*.

21. Change *latter* to *last*.

22. Say, "the steepest that I had ever climbed."

23. Change *latter* to *last*.

24. Change *former* to *first*.

25. Say, "the elevation in death to which the last attained."

26. Change *latter* to *last*.

27. The construction is confused. Say, "with a heartier welcome than what he usually accords to men who are not his own subjects." Or say, "with a hearty welcome such as he accords to few men who are not his own subjects."

28. Change *the most* to *the more*.

29. Say, "the most extensive of all the Anglo-Saxon states"; or "more extensive than any other Anglo-Saxon state."

30. Say, "hath admitted fewer corruptions than any other."

31. The sentence contains a confusion between two different constructions. Say, "The vice of covetousness is of all vices the one which enters deepest into the soul"; or say, "The vice of covetousness enters deeper into the soul than any other."

32. Change *deeper* to *too deep*.

33. Say, "less offensive than that of any other of the French generals," etc.

34. Say, "the likeliest of all"; or say, "likelier than any other."

35. Change *universal* to *widely diffused*.

36. Change *others* to *sciences*.

37. Say, "The event, which most of all the Orleans party ardently desired to avoid."

(d) Pronouns (pp. 68-78).

1. Say, "a long sword which was slung in a belt and bumped ceaselessly," etc. The *which* need not be repeated after "and," because the two verbs are connected by "and" and have the same Subject.

2. Correct. The first *which* is Object of the verb "rules." The second is Subject of the verbs "loves" and "reveres." Under such circumstances *which* is rightly repeated after "and"; for it cannot be in two different cases at once.

3. *That* cannot do duty at once for a Demonstrative and a Relative pronoun. Insert *which* after "that." (The insertion is not absolutely necessary, because in English the Relative is often understood. The sentence, however, is much improved by the insertion.)

4. After "same" it is more idiomatic to use *that* than *who*.

5. Cancel *and which are*. On the impropriety of *and which* see (1).

6. Change *who* to *as*. After "such" the Relative *who* is not used.

7. Insert *as those* between "mind" and "manifested."

8. The repetition of *who* is awkward and misleading. Reconstruct thus:—"He feared there was no man among us, who, having borne that responsibility, could truthfully," etc.

9. Correct. *But* is often used in the sense of *who not* or *which not*. The use of a Demonstrative pronoun such as "he" after *but* is optional.

10. Say, "the pace *at which* our men can move." Though the Relative is often understood in English, it should never be omitted when the context requires that a preposition should be placed before it.

11. Cancel *he*. If the comma is retained after "returning" (which is not necessary), a comma must be inserted after "clerk."

12. Change *himself* to *he*, or say *he himself*. *Himself* should not be used as Subject of the verb, unless it is backed by some noun or by some other pronoun.

13. *But who*, in such a sentence as the present, is as faulty as *and which* described in (1). Say, "who retire by rotation, but are eligible for re-election." The *who* after "but" need not be retained, since the *who* going before is the Subject of both verbs, "retire" and "are."

14. Say, "There are others who must have foreseen and felt the need of reform ; and these can take up the question." Or say, "There are others—men that must have foreseen and felt the need of reform— who can take up the question."

15. Say, *he himself*. See (12).

16. Say, "Four of them kicked one another, and in one instance very severely."

17. Change *one's* to *my*. *One's* cannot have "I," or in fact any pronoun, except "one" for its antecedent.

18. Say, "nothing is raised by the right honourable gentleman, which has not been touched," etc. ("Touched on" would be more appropriate here than "touched.")

19. Say, "with those of the Loyal Laymen's Union."

20. Say, "which clearly defines how the men were employed, and which did not escape the attention of your auditor." In examples (1) and (13) it has been pointed out that the Relative need not be repeated after *who* or *which*, when it is the Subject (or Object) of two or more verbs connected by "and" or "but." Here, however, it is better to repeat the *which* after "and," because the two clauses express entirely distinct actions, one of them has its verb "defines" in the Present tense, while the other has its verb "did not escape" in the Past.

21. Correct. The repetition of *which* after "and," though not indispensable, is appropriate for the reason stated in (20).

22. Say either, "who was late so haughty and reserved, and whom," etc. Or cancel *and* before "whom."

23. The construction and concords are both confused. Say, "as it has been from every *other* sect which conceives it to be its duty to spread its faith."

24. Say, "and not to those of a life hereafter."

25. *Their* makes a bad antecedent to "whose." Say, "the responsibilities of those men, whose," etc.

26. *But which* must not be retained unless it is preceded by a *which*. See (1) and (13). Here its retention is necessary, because *which* is needed as Object of "dwell upon." Say, "and next of a matter which is perhaps irrelevant, but which," etc.

27. Insert *in which* after "way." See remarks in (10).

28. Reconstruct thus:—"Those, whom faint-hearted Liberals assumed to be wedded to the cramping doctrines of the Manchester school, are, as it turns out, the very people who," etc.

29. It will improve the sentence, if the two nouns "advantages" and "Acts" are separated by the insertion of the Relative *that* or *which*.

30. It will improve the sentence to insert *which* or *that* after "problem." See (29).

31. Cancel *which is.* Then follows an extraordinary mixing up of pronouns. Say, "the signing of which by the purchaser entitles the next of kin to claim £200, if the purchaser should happen to be killed on the railway with the coupon in his or her pocket."

32. Change *the way* to *in the way in which.*

33. "He made so great a show of mistrusting his own judgment and esteeming the judgment of any person with whom he happened to be conferring at the time, that he seemed," etc.

34. "No one, who has studied the question, would see without reluctance," etc.

35. Change *as* to *which.*

36. The antecedent "outburst" is at too great a distance from its Relative *which*, and the phrase *and which* is inappropriate, since there is no *which* going before. The sentence may be reconstructed thus :—
"Almost equally fine is the petulant outburst of temper, when at last Jane opposes his wishes,—an outburst which Emma humanely cures by pointing," etc.

37. Change *as* to *that.*

38. *They* is a bad antecedent to *which.* "Would they (the Colonies) be with us, if those considerations that guided us in the path in which we had embarked were sordid" (unworthy of a great nation). (There is some confusion of metaphor, however, between *path* and *embarked.* Say, "the path in which we had decided to go.")

39. Say, "but the Queen's character is inadequately drawn."

40. Change *who* to *which.*

41. Say, "measures which are still unready and may not prove satisfactory."

42. Here *and which* should stand, because there is a *which* going before, and because each Relative clause contains a distinct and separate statement of its own. The verb, however, should not be Plural. Change *were* to *was.*

43. Apparently the writer intends *but which* to be a continuation of "nominal." If so, the sentence can be reconstructed thus :—"The Sultan would lose the hold which he has had hitherto over other Moslems, but which even now is only nominal and is always growing weaker."

44. Change *their* to *his.*

45. Say, "when he himself was in office." See (12).

46. Change *who* to *as.*

47. Say, "the speed at which the ship travelled." See (10).

48. Change *which imputes* to *imputing*.

49. Say, "no ships of our own with which to catch these German ships." (The sentence is faulty on other grounds. Change *is this safe?* to "can we consider this to be safe?" By means of this change there is a pronoun, "we," with which "remembering" can be construed. At present there is nothing.)

50. It would be better to insert the Relative *that* after "ingenious way."

51. Insert *in which* after "way."

52. "Among the cases which have been pending against Her Majesty's Government there is not a single one, in which," etc.

53. Cancel the second *he*.

54. Insert *in which* after "way." ·

55. Say, "among whom and among whose predecessors," etc.

56. Say, "It was the popular interest excited by their sacrifices in Russia itself, which led," etc.

57. "Those gentlemen who were loudest in denunciation of Government were the very ones who were least willing," etc.

58. "Of those 670 gentlemen who walked last Monday, and who could boast themselves to be M.P., there is not a single one who," etc. "Initials" is here the wrong word to use, since M.P. comes after the name, not before it. Say, "to that honourable and responsible title."

59. Cancel *he*, and put a comma after "ascetic." Change *in its belief* to *in his belief in Buddhism.*"

60. "I have a shyness of disposition that looks like pride, though it is not, which," etc. (The phrase "household domestics" is tautological. Say, "house-servants.")

61. *Who have, and who has:* the juxtaposition is intolerable. "Captain L. is one of those who have broken with Mr. Gladstone's Irish policy, and he has not concealed," etc.

62. Here *which, and which* have different antecedents. The first relates to "everything," the second to "sentence." "That sentence was right and tactful, as is everything which the Commander-in-Chief says, and it will please," etc.

63. Insert *whom* after "people." The insertion is indispensable, since the next clause begins with *and who*.

64. *Whose, whose, who!* "The class whose labour is most exhausting and unremitting, and whose pay and food are of the scantiest, is the very one that never tires and never complains."

65. Say, "the shy, shrinking girl of the past, who had no ideas, no conception of life, and no opinions of her own, and who was generally," etc. Here the *who* in *and who* is not superfluous. It serves to distinguish the statement made in the first Relative clause from that made in the second.

66. Insert *respective* before Legations. "It was Imperial officers of exceptionally high rank, as denoted by their peacock feathers, who mounted," etc.

67. Cancel *them*.

68. Say, "especially the sort of fiction in which we other Americans imagine ourselves to have surpassed the rest of the Anglo-Saxon world."

69. Say, "which a clergyman announced that he intended to take." The omission of the Relative and of the conjunction in such close proximity has an awkward effect.

70. Cancel *which is*. These words are superfluous and ill-sounding.

71. Insert *in which* after "order."

72. Change *their* to *whose*.

73. "There are now extant writings referred by learned men to the apostolic age," etc.

74. Here "committee" is a Collective noun to the Relative *which*, and a Distributive noun to the Relative *who*. This has an awkward sound. The sentence must be broken up into two—"The whole question, etc.—our columns. This committee will consider," etc.

75. Say, "a thorough Chinaman, who, though he dislikes foreigners, is a Progressive, but has the unique distinction," etc.

76. Change *himself* to *he himself is*.

77. An ambiguously worded sentence. The antecedent of the first *who* is "those," and that of the second is "section." Reconstruct thus: "Apparently among those who paraded the streets in the evening there was an appreciable section which was," etc.

78. Say, "compare his vision with that of a Boer," etc.

79. An awkward and erroneous combination of *which, who*. *Which* has been wrongly written for *who*, since "ally" is the antecedent. "The only support which Mr. Spender found or which rendered the least service to him was that of Mr. Chamberlain, who," etc.

80. Say, "perhaps somewhat nerveless, yet on the whole only a little behind that of Addison."

81. Say, "between the Boer of French and the Boer of Dutch origin."

82. Insert *in which* after "way." Say, "both to the authors of such plays and to the reputation of that sort of poetry."

83. Say, "Mr. Addison's idea of women, according to which the toilet is," etc.

84. The sentence can be reconstructed thus:—"Of the hundreds who, while I sat, were standing around and wandering about my camp, not one carried fewer than three spears, and most of them carried a gun besides."

85. Change *which* to *whom*. "The rising generation" is a standard phrase for "growing boys and girls."

86. Insert *in which* after "business."

87. Here *which* and *him* are applied in the same sentence to the same antecedent. Say, "who often rode on it."

88. Here *he* has "one" for its antecedent, which is impossible. Change *he* to *one*. A definite Demonstrative like *he* cannot have an indefinite like *one* for its antecedent.

89. Here *that* would be better than *which* after such an antecedent as "the same commando."

90. "Who" is not a proper Relative after "such," and *such men*, followed immediately by three nouns ending in *men*, is tautological. The sentence can be put right by cancelling *such men*. It will therefore run—"developed by Scotchmen, Irishmen, and Englishmen, who," etc.

91. Insert *which* after "means."

92. Cancel *it*, and put a comma after "basin."

93. Insert *as that* after "the same agency."   "Agency" need not be repeated, however, after "the same."

94. Insert *in which* after "way."

95. Much confusion here occurs in the use of the Relatives.   "It is a matter of order; but if any member has been named and suspended by me under a mistake, the proper course," etc.

96. Say, "But there are circumstances beyond his control, which are bound," etc.

97. Say, "than that of either of the British works," etc.

98. Reconstruct thus : "The prophets were importunate, proud in their humility, and masters of so much power, that without pleasing them it was hopeless for any one to expect success."

99. Cancel the last word *him*.   The Object of "slew" is *whom*.

100. A sentence with four *ones* in it sounds awkward.   Yet *one* is the only pronoun that can be used in the sentence as it stands.   See remarks in (88).   If we change *when one* to *when the reader*, the pronouns in the rest of the sentence will be correct.   It would be better to say, "he is surprised to find to what a distance he has gone from the object," etc.

101. Here *he* is superfluous after "wonder."   Reconstruct thus :— "The colonial settler, too, with work as hard as a navvy's and continual dangers and risks, eats largely of meat, as we might expect, and where he cannot get it, has an admirable," etc.

102. Insert *that of* after "as."   There is no antecedent to *them*. Say, "who could lead the nation to battle."

103. Cancel the superfluous *who* after "but."   Its presence improves neither the sound nor the sense.

104. One fault in the sentence is the uncertain reference of *it* in "it is economically unsound."   The phrase "the whole of the mining districts" is also objectionable.   Reconstruct thus :—"That this meeting, representing all the mining districts of the nation, hereby enters its protest against the imposition of an export duty on coal, as in our opinion such a duty is economically unsound and highly dangerous to our position as wage-earners."

105. Say "One knows scores of cases of men who, though they never had any military training of any sort, have in the present war greatly distinguished themselves."

106. Change *which* to *whom*.   "Witnesses" here denotes persons, not things.

107. This sentence can be corrected by inserting *had* before "all." Say, "which was drained and had all its ponds," etc.

108. There is no antecedent to *their own;* and in other respects the sentence is slipshod and pointless.   "He counselled Mr. Childers, if bent on making any declaration at all, to confine himself to saying that he would be willing to consider the claims of the Irish to have a legislature of their own, provided that the said legislature restricted itself to local or non-imperial questions."

109. There is no antecedent to *their*.   Change *their relations* to *the relations of Germany*.

110. Say, "other than those which formerly existed."

111. Insert *which* after "dismay." It is better, however, to recon-struct the sentence :—"whether the effect of the anti-reform fiat was dismay or triumph."

112. Insert *which* after "power."

113. Confused construction. Say, "Your disappointment is no-thing to mine; for I had a horse with which I hoped to win the Derby, but which went," etc.

114. *And whom* is here inadmissible, since there is no *who* or *whom* going before. Say, "if the peasants, who are taxed already to the point of torture, and whom further pressure would make mad, these," etc.

115. Change *them* to *those* or *those persons*.

116. Say, "which is sometimes described as magnanimity, some-times as conciliation, and sometimes as humanity, but which," etc.

117. Change *they only* to *those persons only*.

118. Say, "as compared with that of Russia and France."

119. Change *unless myself* to *unless I myself*.

120. Say, "than the highest reading of Thursday last."

121. Say, "whose hardships we deplore and are doing our best to alleviate."

122. Say, "which could not be separated from politics, and which would never," etc. Here the retention of *which* after "and" is desirable, because the two Relative clauses contain two very distinct statements. See remarks in (20).

123. Insert *which* after "woman": otherwise there is no subject to the verb "will become." "There are excellent reasons for antici-pating" is parenthetical.

124. There is no antecedent to *those* unless it is "interests"— "those interests of the smaller interests." Reconstruct thus:—"shall represent only the largest commercial interests, viz. those of Eng-land, Germany, and Japan, or shall also include the smaller ones, viz. those of the United States, France, and others."

125. Say, "would listen to no proposal invented by Craigengelt, which had," etc.

126. There is no antecedent to *their*. Change *management* to "managers."

127. Say, "the Emperor and I," etc.

128. Change the first *who* to *that*.

129. Say, "and many of those who attempted to enter in were men whose patriotism," etc.

130. Change *who* to *which*.

131. Say, "than that of ancient Rome." Cancel *it rested*, which is superfluous.

132. Cancel *other*, which spoils the sense, and say, "have each left a reputation different in kind from that left by any of their con-temporaries."

133. Say, "is that offered by books."

134. Change *are* to *is;* also change *and into which* to *and one into which*.

135. Insert *on which* after "plan."

136. Say, "to make statements like those of Shouvaloff."

137. Say, "to which I have referred in my estimates."

138. Say, "but of which we seek in vain to discover any certain causes."

139. Say, "and whose lives were contemptible."

140. Change *their* to *his*. Insert *what* after "than."

141. Change *which* to *who*.

142. Insert *in which* after "manner."

143. Insert the Relative *that* after its antecedent "madness." This Relative is needed as Subject to the verb "seizes."

144. Cancel *them* before "modified."

145. Say, "few talents to which most men are not born, or which at least they might not acquire."

146. Change *which* to *that* or *as*.

147. Say, "in which God hath before ordained that we should walk."

148. Say, "the temper of mind *in which* he then was."

149. Change *themselves* to *himself*.

150. Insert *which* before "are."

151. Say, "different from that of England or of Scotland." The *of* must be repeated before Scotland, because the system of Scotland differs from that of England.

152. Insert *one* after *and*.

153. Change *his idea* to *the idea of him*.

154. Change *Warburton's* to *Warburton ;* or cancel *that of*.

155. Change *his character* to *the character of him*.

156. Change *equal* to *such*.

157. Change *with* to *as*.

158. Change *the same* to *similar ones*.

159. *The same* is ambiguous, because there is no saying what its antecedent is. It might be "every part" (expressed), or it might be "the creed as a whole" (not expressed). The latter makes the better sense.

160. Insert *that* between *and* and *of*.

161. Insert *those of* between *and* and *to-day*.

(e) *Finite Moods and Tenses* (pp. 82-86).

1. Change *be* to *are*.

2. Change *have been* to *were*. The Present Perfect tense cannot be used in reference to an event that took place twenty-six years before the date of writing, and is spoken of as entirely past.

3. Change *had* to *had had*.

4. Say, "that he has been and is acting," etc.

5. Change *were killed* to *have been killed*. The tense must tally with that of "has been made." The event just completed can be described only by a Present Perfect tense.

6. Change *publish* to *will publish*.

7. Say, "and would never have cared for it at all but for him."

8. Insert *involved* after "have," otherwise the form of the tense is not complete.

9. Change *going on* to *to go on*.

10. Insert *is* before "fixed."

11. Say, "not only could have killed Chilo, but ought to have done so."

12. Insert *be* after "can."

13. Insert *were* after "ships." "Taken prisoners" is a bad phrase to apply to ships. Say, *captured.*

14. Change *were* to *are*, since the previous verbs are all in the Historic Present.

15. Say, "and cookery, unless things are greatly changed, is an unknown art."

16. Insert *there was* after "at least."

17. Change *it does* to *it will.*

18. Say, "of which memory may yet recall the counterpart or which experience may yet discover."

19. Change *be* to *may have been.* The writer has used the Subjunctive mood apparently for the purpose of expressing a doubt, but he has not used the tense required by the context.

20. Insert *were* after "several."

21. Change *do not* to *may not.* Say, "as they have to do at present in South Africa."

22. Change *has lived* to *lived* or *had lived.* "Has lived" would imply that he was still alive.

23. Here *be* is the Subjunctive mood, and this mood is not inappropriate here, since the context shows that there is an uncertainty. The Indicative, however, could have been used with equal propriety and would sound better.

24. *Has got to be regarded* is an ungainly phrase. Insert *it was* after "than." "The absolution, etc., is now regarded more charitably than it was in the days when," etc. (It does not sound well to say "Protestantism was iron instead of putty." It would sound better to say, "Protestantism was as hard as iron instead of being, as it now is, as soft as putty.")

25. Insert *talked* after "have."

26. Change *has lived* to *lived.* The Present Perfect tense implies that he is still alive.

27. Insert *are used* after "products."

28. Cancel *have* before "experienced."

29. Cancel *had* before "proved." The Past Perfect tense would imply that she was dead, while she was still alive, laid up with fever. *Which* must be inserted after "fever."

30. Change *has done* to *did* or *had done.* Either the Past Indefinite or the Past Perfect will here be correct. But the Present Perfect is altogether wrong, because all reference to present time is excluded by the sense.

31. If *has given* is to be retained, *on* must be changed to *ever since.* But if *on* is to be retained, *has given* must be changed to *gave.*

32. Insert *impose* after "does not."

33. Change *was* to *would be.* The participle "being" should be inserted before "well aware."

34. Change *were* to *was.* A Conditional past tense is here wrong, since the blotting out of Venice was an admitted fact.

35. Insert *was* after "intercommunication."

36. Change *are* to *were.*

37. We cannot say "have formerly," since "formerly" refers to past time, and "have" to present. The sentence is very confused in

other respects.   Say, " In the whole journey through these States I scarcely saw a gun or a spear, though formerly I used to sit with hundreds of men standing around, not one of whom carried fewer than three spears and most were also armed with a gun."

38. Insert *think* after " will."

39. We cannot apply a Present Perfect " have founded " to Greece, because the Empire founded by Greece no longer exists.   Cancel *have* and say, " founded at wide intervals apart."   The tenses that follow, " succeeded," " has failed," are perfectly correct.

40. Insert *are* after observations.   (Change *the book's faults* to " the faults of the book.")

41. Change *has been* to *was*.   Say, " far from his going his own way and leaving the queen to follow hers."

42. Change *was* to *would have been*.   No war was made about the Pandjeh incident, and therefore *was* is wrong.   Insert *that* after " and."

43. Say, " than they were before or have ever been since."   The Present Perfect tense *have been* cannot be used with the adverb " before."   It involves a contradiction.

44. Insert *been* after " have," in order to complete the tense.   At present the form is elliptical.

45. Change *is brought* to *will be brought*.

46. Change *has lasted* to *lasted*, and *is* to *was*.

47. Change *the child will be weaned* to *the child will have been weaned*.

48. Change *the result was* to *the result is*.   Here past time and present time are mixed up to the utter confusion of the sense.   Say, " the result is not only an accurate edition of the Sanskrit text, which appeared in 1892, but the present," etc.

49. Change *shall look* to *looks*.

50. Say, *as I am*.

51. For " which I have " say *that I have done*.

52. This sentence is correct, since the verb " has been condemned " is not intended to be qualified by the phrase " eighteen months ago." The sentence might be recast as follows :—" The committee appointed eighteen months ago by the Admiralty and the War Office has condemned cordite in favour," etc.

53. Change *has done* to *did*, and *has met* to *met*.

54. Change *were* to *was*.   The Subjunctive mood is here decidedly inappropriate.

55. Change *is settled* to *has been settled*.   It is the function of the Present Perfect tense to bring some past or completed action into connection with present time.   Such a tense is indispensable when the verb is qualified by the phrase " for some time past," which includes present time as well as past.

56. Insert *is given* after " nothing more."

57. Cancel *is* (which is unnecessary), and add *been* after " has." (*Will be published* (Third person) would be more suitable here than " shall be published " (First person).)

58. Here the Subjunctive *avoid*, as the context shows, is less suitable than the Indicative *avoids* would have been.

59. Insert *arrested* after " has."

60. Say, "as great a wit as he was a preacher," etc.

61. Insert *be* after "**may**."

62. Insert *has been* before "strengthened," and *have been* before "formed."

63. There is no Nominative to *smoothed*. Say, "and his way has been smoothed," etc.

64. Say, "so late as he have done so."

65. Change *has been* to *was*.

66. Cancel *has*, or change it to *had*.

67. Say, "was published in 1822, and is still with us."

68. Cancel *has*.

(f) "Shall," "should"; "will," "would" (pp. 90-94).

1. Change *shall* to *will*.

2. Change *will* to *shall*.

3. Change *should* to *would*. The Future here takes the form of *would*, instead of *will*, because there is a Past Indefinite going before.

4. Change *shall* to *will*.

5. Change *should* to *would*.

6. Change *should* to *would*, since "country" is the nearest of the two Subjects. The words "we and" might be cancelled.

7. Change *shall* to *will*.

8. Change *would* to *should*, since the verb is in the First person.

9. Change *shall* to *will*.

10. Change *should* to *would*.

11. Change *shall mark* to *marks*. Here a Future tense is not required. But if a Future had to be used at all, the form would be *will mark*, not *shall mark*.

12. Here *shall* (in the Third person) is correct, because it indicates the intention or purpose of the publication.

13. Change *shall* to *will*. But the Present tense would be here more suitable than the Future, since futurity is clearly implied by the context.

14. Here a Future tense in any form is out of place. Say, "which it is impossible that Shakespeare wrote."

15. Change *would* to *should*, since the verb is in the First person.

16. The expected answer to this question is :—"No one shall say." This is a confident prediction. *Shall* is correct in the interrogation as in the answer.

17. Change *should* to *would*, since the verb is in the Third person.

18. Change *would* to *should*, since the verb is in the First person.

19. Change *will* to *shall*, since the verb is in the First person.

20. *Shall* is here wrong, since there is no prediction of any kind. Change *shall* to *will*. It would be equally correct, however, to say *should* for *shall*, so as to express a doubtful futurity in the conditional clause.

21. Change *would* to *should*, since the verb is in the First person.

22. Change *shall* to *will*, since the verb is in the Second person.

23. Change *will* to *shall*, since the verb is in the First person.

24. The only *shall* that is correct in this sentence is the first one. This one is correct, because it is meant to express command or

intention. The remainder of the sentence must be rewritten thus :— "so that they *may* or *will* (not *shall*) remain effective, when the interest excited by the present events *will* (not *shall*) have died away and the present outburst of patriotism *will* be a thing of the past."

25. *Will* is here quite wrong, as the very opposite to an intention is meant. Say, "we shall never be prepared."

26. Change *shall* to *will*.

27. Change *will* to *shall*.

28. Change *should* to *would*.

29. Change *shall* to *will*. There is no need, however, of a Future tense in this clause : say, "and the sooner all mankind *becomes* (or *has been made*) acquainted with his doctrines the better will it be."

30. Change *will* to *shall*.

31. Say, "when that General has heard, etc., and has thoroughly considered the military situation, he will report." If a Future is to be used at all in the Adverb-clause, it must be in the form of *will*, not *shall*. But no future is necessary in this context.

32. Change *should have published* to simply *published*. The verb is not here either Conditional or Future. The sentence might be reconstructed :—"Complaint has been made against Mr. Chamberlain for having published," etc.

33. Change *would* to *should*.

34. Change *shall* to *will*.

35. Change *shall* to *will*.

36. Change *will* to *shall*.

37. Change *should* to *would*.

38. Change *shall no longer feel* to *will no longer feel*. The former verb "will be appreciated" is correct.

39. Change *will* to *shall*.

40. Change the first *will* to *shall*. The second *will* is correct.

41. Change *we would be giving* to *we should be giving*.

42. Change *would* to *should*.

43. Change *they should be paying* to *they would be paying*. "Which would be saved" is correct.

44. Change *will* to *shall*.

45. The first *would* (being in the Third person) is correct. The second *would* (being in the First person) is wrong and must be changed to *should*. Change the *would* and the *should* to *will* and *shall*.

46. Change *would* to *should*.

47. Here *should* in "should realise" is correct. It expresses a contingent or doubtful futurity combined with a sense of duty or desirability. This is one of the uses of "should." In the final clause, which expresses an expectation, not a confident prediction, *shall* must be changed to *will*, because the verb is in the Third person.

48. Change *would have* to *should have*, since the verb is in the First person.

49. Change *would show* to *should show*. The verb is in the Third person and therefore *would* might have been expected to be correct. But after *lest* the only Auxiliary verb used to express contingent futurity is "should." This is purely a matter of idiom.

50. Change *we would* to *we should*.

51. Change *you shall* to *you will*. Change *or any* to *if any*.

52. Change *shall succeed* to *succeeds*. After the conjunction "before" the Future is not used. If any Future were used, the Auxiliary would be "shall," not "will."

53. Here is a curious and unaccountable mixture of "would" and "should." The *woulds* are wrong, and the *shoulds* are right, since the verb is in the First person.

54. Change *shall they get* to *will they get*.

55. Change *they should not* to *they would not*.

56. Change the first *shall* to *will*. The second *shall* is correct, since it is intended to express a confident prediction.

57. Change *we will hear* to *we shall hear*.

58. Here *shall* is correct. It expresses the determination of the speaker, and says a great deal more than simple futurity.

59. Here *will* and *shall* are both correct. *Will* expresses intention. The first *shall* expresses simple futurity ; the second *shall* expresses a determination or a promise.

60. Change *is not ready* to *should not be ready*.

61. Change *will* to *shall*.

(g) Sequence of Tense and Mood (pp. 98-103).

1. The sequence "it *is* contrary" is defensible, because the dependent clause states an habitual fact. But if *is* is to be retained, *were* must be changed to *are :* otherwise the sequence of tenses will not be consistent.

2. After the Past tense "trusted," *will* must be changed to *would*.

3. After the Present Perfect tense "have been," *would* must be changed to *will*.

4. Change *were* to *be ;* or (as the Subjunctive is not often used after "provided") change *were* to *is*.

5. Change *remind, can,* and *has* to *reminded, could,* and *had*.

6. Change *can, understand,* and *is* to *could, understood,* and *was*.

7. Change *this is so* to *this was so*.

8. Change *will be* to *would be*.

9. Here *would* is defensible, as it may be intended to express contingent futurity. Some clause such as "if she were provoked" may be understood.

10. Change *will cover* to *covered*, and *be granted* to *should be granted*. There is a promise or order implied in *should*. If we detach the dependent clause from the principal, it will run thus :—"If Mr. S. covers the shed, he shall be granted a licence for five years."

11. Change *is concerned* to *was concerned*. (The past form of the Infinitive, "to have performed," is here correct ; it is equivalent to saying, "he performed, as was fabled, many more.")

12. Change *is* to *was*.

13. Here *could* is not quite suitable : *shall* would be more appropriate, because an order or command is implied by the sense.

14. Change *allow* to *allowed*.

15. Change *dare* to *dared*.

16. Change *have* and *belong* to *had* and *belonged*.

17. The Past tenses coming after "points out" are permissible, if the sense requires it. But Present time is obviously referred to ;

so *were, continued,* and *would* must be changed to *are, continue,* and *will.*

18. Change *will* and *is* to *would* and *was.*

19. Here *has ridden* is correct, because the Subject is "any living man." But *rode* must be inserted after "Bevan." The same verb will not do for both Subjects.

20. Change *occupy* to *occupied.*

21. Change *has* to *had,* and *will* to *would.*

22. Here the sequence *should* and *would* is correct. "Should" in the Third person is here correctly used in the conditional clause, and is correctly followed by "would," which denotes a contingent futurity.

23. Change *is* to *were.* (Change "inveigled" to "having been inveigled.")

24. Change *there should not be* to *there shall not be.* The Past tense is out of place in this connection.

25. Change *has* to *had.*

26. Change *succeeded* to *succeeds* or *may succeed.* The verb cannot be Past, without spoiling the sense.

27. Change *is* to *has been.* The Present Perfect tense brings present time into connection with Past : both are implied by the context.

28. Change *will be* to *would be.*

29. Change *would be* to *will be.* Or, change *have declared* to simply *declared,* and leave ".would be" as it is.

30. Change *he was* to *he is.*

31. Change *bid* to *bade.*

32. Change *might* to *may.*

33. Change *will* to *would.*

34. Change *might* to *may.*

35. Change *will* to *would.*

36. Change *will* to *would.*

37. Change *should* to *shall.* The Past form is not required by the sense, and does not come well after "provides."

38. *Consisted,* though it is in accordance with the general rule as to the sequence of tenses, is not here correct. It should be changed to *consists* (Present tense), because when an habitual or universal fact is asserted in the dependent clause the verb must be in the Present tense in spite of the fact that there is a Past tense in the principal clause.

39. Change *suggests* to *suggested* or *could suggest.* A Present tense cannot be used after a past gerund "having done."

40. Change *is* to *was.*

41. Change *is* to *was.*

42. Change *came* and *would* to *comes* and *will.*

43. Change *deserve* to *deserved.* (*Hanged* would be more appropriate here than *hung.*)

44. Change *would, would,* to *will, will.* After such a strong word as "inevitable," contingent futurity is out of place.

45. Say, "and would have the advantage, very great in France, that few of those who voted for it in the Chambers would be called upon to pay it."

46. Change *skulked* to *skulk.* A Past tense, unless it is required by the sense (which is not the case in this sentence), is not appropriate

in a dependent or relative clause, when the verb in the Principal clause is in the Present Perfect tense.

47. Change *dare* to *dared*.

48. Change *was* to *is* for two reasons—(1) a Past tense, unless it is demanded by the sense, is not appropriate after a Present Perfect tense ; (2) the dependent clause is intended to express a general or fundamental fact.

49. Here *would* is correct, since contingent futurity is implied by the context.

50. Change *has* to *had*.

51. Change *was* to *were*.

52. Change *would* to *will*.   The sense does not require that the sequence of tense should be disturbed.

53. Change *drank, gambled*, and *played* to *drink, gamble*, and *play ;* and change *would* to *will*.

54. Change *will* to *would*.

55. Change *shall* to *should*.   When *if* is used to express a condition or uncertainty, *should* is used in the Second and Third persons no less than in the First.   In the last clause change *should* to *shall*.   A request is made for an order prohibiting the sending of more expeditions, and this request is preceded by a verb in the Present tense, "is inclined."

56. Change *would* to *will*.

57. Change *would, would, would* to *will, will, will*.

58. Change *would be* to *would have been*.

59. Change *has been* to *was*.

60. Change *should* to *will*.

61. Change *has broken* to *had broken*.

62. Change *would* to *will*.

63. Change *are* to *were*.

64. Change *dare* to *dared*.

65. Change *is* to *would be*.

66. Change *can* to *could*.

67. Change *is to prevent* to *was to prevent*.

68. Change *has* and *can* to *had* and *could*.

69. Change *can* to *could*.

70. Change *might* to *may*.

71. Either change *rememberest* to *remember ;* or leave *rememberest* as it is and change *bring* to *bringest*.

72. *Will* is here defensible, because in this clause a general fact is asserted.

73. Change *were it not* to *had it not been*.

74. Change *should* to *shall*.

75. Change *has* to *had*.

76. Change *shall* to *should*.

77. There is nothing wrong in using Past tenses in the dependent clause or clauses, when the principal verb is in the Present tense. But here the change of tense is not only unnecessary, but obstructive to the sense.   Moreover, *were* is in the wrong mood.   Say, "but seem to think that the further their style is from any known model, the more closely will it convey foreign ideas."   Observe the necessary change of *closer* (comparative adjective) to *more closely* (comparative adverb).

78. *Correct.* The *Present* Perfect "has forwarded" is followed by "*shall* be submitted." *Should* would have been out of place, since there is no doubt or contingency about the nature of the proposal offered.

79. Change *will* to *would.*

80. Change *will* to *would.*

81. Change *was* to *is.* The writer appears to have thought that *have made* was a Past tense instead of being a Present Perfect. The change from *was* to *is,* though not grammatically wrong, is required by the sense.

82. Either change *be* to *is ;* or change *are* to *be.*

83. *Arises* is Indicative, while *be* is Subjunctive. Either mood would be correct in this context ; but let the one or the other be used in both clauses.

84. Change *was* to *were,* since the previous verb is *were.*

(h) Infinitive, Verbal Noun, Gerund, Participle
(pp. 113-122).

1. It is better to say *its being found.* But *it* is not absolutely wrong, nor is it very uncommon in such a construction. If *its* is used, "being found" is a verbal noun preceded by a Possessive case. If *it* is used, "being found" must be parsed as a Participle used gerundively.

2. Say, "if they want to do so." It is not good English, even colloquially, to leave a pendent *to.*

3. Here *being contained* stands too far away from its noun "sprinkling." Say, "is fed by the knowledge that a sprinkling of descendants from French Huguenots is contained," etc.

4. Say, "to your explaining." "You explaining" is not absolutely wrong ; but the other is the older and the better construction of the two.

5. Change *to have taken* to *to take.* Past time has been expressed once already in the verb "would not have dared." After this nothing more is needed of the Infinitive than to express the action in its simplest form. The Present, not the Perfect, Infinitive should be used when the action denoted by the Infinitive is simultaneous with that denoted by the Finite verb going before.

6. Say, "used to live." See remarks in (2).

7. Cancel *he.* The absolute construction is inadmissible in this sentence.

8. *Having developed* cannot be used in the absolute construction without the accompaniment of some noun or pronoun. Say, "but since the situation has developed."

9. Say, "attempted to fire." See remarks in (2).

10. Who enjoyed the refreshing cup of tea ? Since "who" is the Subject last mentioned, the phrase *after enjoying* must be taken to relate to "who" ; but the context shows that it relates to "we." Say, "who with kindly hospitable care put us up for the night, after we had enjoyed a refreshing cup of tea."

11. Say, *its being* for *it being.* See remarks in (1).

12. Change *to have made* to the Present form *to make.* See remarks in (5).

T

13. Change *to be taught* to the Active form *to teach.* Or, if the writer prefers to retain the Passive voice, he can say "is much more easily taught." *To be taught* after "easy" cannot be called wrong, but the Passive infinitive is less idiomatic than the Active.

14. Change *it being* to *its being.* See remarks in (1).

15. Cancel *for.* "To save" is here the Gerundial Infinitive expressive of purpose. It is therefore unnecessary to place the preposition "for" before it. This use of "for" was once common, but it has become a vulgarism.

16. The absolute construction "the Castilian," etc., is not quite suitable, when the Subject following, viz. *they,* relates to the same persons as those named in the absolute phrase. A comma should be placed after "Castilian," and the sentence written out in full will be as follows :—"The Castilian, having made his addresses to her and married her, lived in perfect happiness with her for some time."

17. Either say, "prevent his rising," or say, "prevent him from rising." The construction "prevent him rising" is a mixture of these two.

18. Insert *do* after "to." "Just as they used to do of old," etc. See remarks in (2).

19. The absolute construction, "he being then," etc., is out of place here, since its antecedent "Thurlow" is the Subject of the sentence. Cancel *he.*

20. Change *who are to hang* to the Passive form *who are to be hanged.* ("They shall hang" is here defensible, because "shall" can be understood to imply intention or command.)

21. Change the absolute phrase "Dreyfus having been imposed," etc., into a Conditional clause, "should Dreyfus be imposed," etc. A condition is not well expressed by an absolute phrase; "Dreyfus having been imposed" implies more properly past time.

22. Insert *in which* after "place"; or say, "to pick pockets in." The preposition must not on any account be omitted.

23. Change *him being allowed* to *his being allowed.*

24. Change *them* to *their.*

25. Say, "too powerful to be suppressed or ignored." Or say, "too powerful for any one to suppress or ignore."

26. Say, "wanted to have them." See (2).

27. The phrase following "direct result," though not commendable, is not grammatically wrong. Say, "the direct result of the insults thrown upon the army by M. Waldeck-Rousseau."

28. Change *it spreading* to *its spreading.*

29. An ill-constructed sentence. Say, "What happened after the occupation of Germinston, which took place, as we have said, last Tuesday, is still by no means clear."

30. Insert *to be* before "sewn." The sentence requires some readjustment in order to remove the ambiguity of "it." "The waistcoat, on pretence that it needed a button to be sewn on, was handed to Bennett."

31. Only a few Intransitive verbs can form a Past participle such as "knelt." "Knelt" is not one of them. Say, "the retainers who were kneeling."

32. The absolute construction "they considering" is out of place

here, because "some," the antecedent of "they," has just been mentioned. Change *they considering* to "considering as they do."

33. Insert "being" or "having been" after "intervention."
These Auxiliaries should not be omitted in the absolute construction.

34. Change *without insisting* to *without our insisting.* Or say, "if we allowed the present session to pass away without insisting," etc. If "we" is made the Subject of the verb, there is no need to insert "our" before "insisting."

35. Change *by assuring him* to *by an assurance being made to him.* The context does not show who it was that assured him.

36. Say, "Hunger being satisfied." ("*One's* head" must be changed to "*my* head.")

37. Change *them* to *their.*

38. Change *it refusing* to *its refusing.*

39. Change *risen* into a conditional clause, which cannot be well expressed by a Past participle. "The whole prospect might be too much for a possible successor of Napoleon, if in the future such a man should arise in response," etc.

40. Say, "without any great loss to our forces."

41. There is an incongruity in this sentence ; for the first *having* is absolute, while the second one qualifies the pronoun "he." Say, "Accident having opened a new and most congenial career to him, he became a great favourite and useful helpmate to Mr. Nash, and ultimately accompanied his patron to London.

42. Say, "the bringing of a dowry by the wife," etc.

43. Insert *with* after "Secretary." But it does not sound well to end a sentence with a preposition. Say, "not good enough to use for beating the Colonial Secretary."

44. Change *votaries* to *votaries'.*

45. Say, "to do it *in.*" The preposition is indispensable in this construction. The preposition "upon" is rightly placed after the verb "draw."

46. Say, "but his offer was declined." The absolute construction is quite out of place in this sentence. Such a construction can refer only to some previous or simultaneous action, not to a subsequent one.

47. There is an obvious incongruity in this very ill-shaped sentence ; the participle "extending" is used attributively, while the participle "sweeping" is used gerundively, and finally the participle "burying" is used ambiguously. Say, "Two lives have been lost in North-West Clare, where a bog, extending over a number of acres, swept with terrific force over some low-lying land and buried a house."

48. Insert *being* or *having been* after "much."

49. "To create"—"to carry." Both are Gerundial, and they come very near together. For the sake of variety let *to carry* be changed to *for carrying.*

50. Change *be* into *have been,* which is plainly required by the sense.

51. "It having been occupied," etc. Here the absolute construction is wrong, since "Cape," the antecedent of *it,* is the Subject of the verb. Say, "When the Cape, after having been restored to Holland in the peace of 1802, was reoccupied by England in 1806, Sir Hume," etc.

52. The juxtaposition of *he* with *believer*, the latter being in the Objective case, and the former in the Nominative absolute, is not good, since both refer to the same person. Say, "As the Mosaic law is no longer binding, the believer being dead to it with Christ," etc.

53. "Become" is not one among those few Intransitive verbs which can be used in the Past participle. Say, "who had become."

54. Say, "in a way in which they are unable to wield them at other times." A verb must be placed after *to*, and *in which* must not be omitted.

55. Change *it being* to *its being*.

56. "Come." See remarks in (53) in reference to "become." Say, "who had come."

57. See remarks in (52). It is not good to have *wife* (Objective) and *she* (Nominative) in juxtaposition, when both refer to the same person. The absolute construction is here out of place. Say, "in the course of which she reproached him, etc., and alleged," etc.

58. Change *him making* to *his making*.

59. Change *it being* to *its being*.

60. Here the absolute construction is not quite suitable. Say, "He was convinced that his cause, being just, would not be abandoned by God and would triumph."

61. Say, "power to construct and manage refreshment rooms in parks was asked for." In the sentence as it stands it looks as if *for to construct* were to be construed together.

62. Say, "The overseers demand that payment of the Poor Rate shall be made on," etc. The omission of *on* is objectionable.

63. Change *after defending* to *after I had defended*. The gerund "defending" cannot be referred to "which," the Subject. Say, "On the morning of my capture, etc.—the air was raw and damp."

64. Change *you using* to *your using*.

65. Insert *with which* after "food." Or change *to feed the troops* to "for the troops."

66. Change *it being* to *its being*. Or say, "without having it knocked to pieces."

67. Change *he having married* to *since he had married*. *He* has no right to be absolute when it has a Nominative, *W. H. W.*, for its antecedent.

68. Change *being* to *to be*, which is obviously required by the sense.

69. Cancel *they* (which has no right here to be used absolutely with a participle), and change *they finding* to *finding as they do*.

70. Cancel *he* before "being." Here again the absolute construction is out of place.

71. "Having thus fortified Bokh"—who? Say, "The Amir having thus," etc.

72. Insert *having been* before "given."

73. Here *turned*, the past participle of a Transitive verb, is used in an Active sense, which in English is impossible. Say, "her father, who had long since turned over a new leaf, and had for some weeks been," etc.

74. Say, "of a man's committing suicide, or of his being hanged, or of his suddenly going to Timbuctoo," etc.

75. Change *come of* to *sprang from* or *descended from*. The Past participle of "come," as of most other Intransitive verbs, is not used in this way.

76. Change *me being* to *my being*.

77. Change *him asking* to *his asking*.

78. The absolute construction "she having been passed" is out of place here. Say, "Mrs. Botha, having been passed through the British lines, has left," etc.

79. *Without dwelling* is evidently meant by the writer to refer to himself; but by the necessity of the construction it refers to the Subject "he." Say, "Without dwelling upon a most unlucky appointment, believed, etc.—responsible, I must remark that he has," etc.

80. Say, "he did not want to do so."

81. Say, "did not like to do so."

82. Say, "if this is desired": otherwise *desired* will refer to pupils or to examinations.

83. Change *proven* to *which has just proved*.

84. Say either "prevent his undertaking" or "prevent him from undertaking."

85. Change *Mr. Sauer reaching* to "Mr. Sauer's reaching." But the sentence could be rewritten with advantage:—"On reaching King William's Town, where Gordon was in residence, Mr. Sauer at once asked him to accompany him to Basutoland."

86. Insert *I was* after "since."

87. Insert *in which* after "places."

88. Change *you getting* to *your getting*.

89. Cancel *to* before "repeat" at the end of the sentence. *To* is not used after the verb "bid."

90. Cancel *to* after "wanted"; or repeat the verb "do." *Openly* is in the wrong place. Say, "Let the Government do openly what they wanted to do."

91. Here are six words ending in -*ing* used in different ways: and *returned* (Past participle of an Intransitive verb) is wrong. Reconstruct thus:—"As many of the soldiers who have returned from South Africa have been placed on furlough pending their discharge, those who have no document to testify to the characters they bore whilst serving have experienced a difficulty in obtaining employment."

92. After *not likely to* add "marry a servant-maid." Without this addition (which is also needed by the construction), the sense is obscure.

93. Here the absolute phrase "The Company being," etc., is out of place, because Company is the Subject of the verb. Place a comma after "Company," and cancel *it*.

94. *Having decided* is here a pendent participle. *If not too far* is elliptical. Say, "Having decided . . . frequent, we usually return to camp for the night, if the camp is not too far away." "We" is here qualified by *having decided*.

95. Here are three participles belonging to no noun in particular. Apparently they relate to "French Protestants." Say, "Persecuted, forcibly converted, and finally expelled, French Protestants did not feel strongly tied to French Catholics."

96. *When founding.* What verb and Subject can be supplied?

None from the sentence as it stands. Say, ''One of the objects that we had in view when founding,'' etc.

97. *When praising.* This is open to the same objection as the preceding. Say, ''When a thing is being praised, it is either nice,'' etc.

98. *Exciting* and *bringing out* are here gerunds, but there is no Subject to which they can relate. Change them into Verbal nouns, and say, ''the exciting of interest and the bringing out of intelligence.'' To make the sentence more perspicuous, insert the words ''by the teacher'' after ''given.''

99. *In talking.* Who is talking? See remarks in (96) and (97). The sense shows that ''talking'' here refers to *me*, but by the construction it refers to *he*, which makes no sense. Say, ''In a conversation that I had last month in Paris with Dr. Leyds, he told me,'' etc.

100. *Far from going.* See again remarks in (96) and (97). Say, ''far from his going his own way independently of his wife.'' Change *has been* to *had been* or *was*, which is obviously required by the sense as well as by the Sequence of Tenses.

101. Say, ''if they wish to do so.''

102. *Besides supplying.* See again remarks in (96) and (97). Say, ''Not only could electric power be supplied to the gold mines at Kolar, but electric furnaces,'' etc.

103. Change *them* to *their*.

104. The absolute construction beginning with *the Forbidden City* is out of place. Say, ''Pekin herself, the Forbidden City, has been plundered to the bare walls, having suffered especially,'' etc.

105. *To do* might refer either to ''finding'' or to ''grow.'' Say, ''as they were accustomed to grow it.''

106. Here *taking* is used as an Impersonal absolute. This is perhaps admissible. It would be shorter and simpler, however, to say, ''All things considered, it is,'' etc.

107. Change *for it having* to *for its having*.

108. The absolute construction ''he having,'' etc., is out of place here, since *he* relates to the Subject ''J. M. S.'' Make a full stop after ''payment.'' Then say, ''He had been previously convicted,'' etc.

109. *Him, he being,* etc. The absolute construction is here inappropriate. Either cancel *he*; or say, ''when it became necessary to remove this man, who had proved to be too like a mean kind of Eli, the Chamber,'' etc.

110. Change *Assuming* to *If we assume*. There is no antecedent to ''it'' in the clause ''it might be done.'' Say, ''the correction might be made.''

111. Change *the dealer taking* to *the dealer's taking*.

112. *While shooting.* Who is said to be shooting? Say, ''at the time of shooting.'' Place a comma after ''shooting'' and a comma after ''home.''

113. *They assuming.* The absolute construction is here wrong, since it has the same reference as ''who.'' Say, ''who knew nothing of him, but assumed,'' etc.

114. Say, ''were impelled to do so.''

115. *Expressing himself.* A pendent participle. Say, ''while he was expressing himself,'' etc.

116. Say, "I might have been," etc.

117. *After paying.* Who is supposed to be paying? This is not stated. Say, "which will be ample, even after the separate States have been paid their stipulated shares."

118. Say, "we have no need to do so."

119. Add the preposition *on* after "settle."

120. Say, "at his trying to ride," etc. ; or say "at him for trying," etc.

121. Change *that had a mind to* to *that was so minded* (or so inclined).

122. Say, "those that were able to retreat did so as fast as they could."

123. *Introducing reforms.* Say, "of their introducing reforms" (here *their* means "the Sultans'").

124. Change *Rawlinson* to *Rawlinson's.* Cancel *but,* which is superfluous in addition to the phrase "on the other hand." *Admitting* is a pendent participle. Say, "on the other hand, though I admit that," etc.

125. Place a comma after "matter," and cancel *it.*

126. Cancel *I* before "having found," and place it before "came." Since *I* is the Subject of the sentence, it should not be followed by the Absolute phrase "I having found," etc.

127. The gerunds "having approved" and "having encouraged" are left without any noun or pronoun to which the action can be referred. Say, "it was pointed out that so far from the Council's having approved," etc. Or, what is rather better, say, "it was pointed out that this scheme, so far from its having been approved or even encouraged, had as yet had no official recognition."

128. The construction is confused. An absolute construction is connected by *and* to one which is not absolute. Say, "A conspiracy against her having been discovered, and Frederick the Great of Prussia being suspected to be at the bottom of it, she embraced," etc.

129. "Overlooking" is here a pendent participle ; for there is no authority to use it as an impersonal absolute. Change *Overlooking* to "If we overlook."

130. Change *to discover* to *to have discovered.* Here past time is evidently needed for the Infinitive, since the discovery must precede the claim.

131. Insert *being* after "instead of." Change *to be aimed* to the Active voice, Perfect Infinitive, *to have aimed.*

132. Here *speaking* is pendent. Insert *I find that* before "there is an extraordinary concurrence."

133. *Having regard.* Who is having regard? Say, "all circumstances past and present being taken into account." Or say, "regard being paid to," etc.

134. Say, "he was to have embarked." The past Infinitive is here indispensable, because it relates to a plan which was not carried out.

135. The construction is confused : "falling" is used attributively, and "inundating" gerundively. Say, "Owing to an inundation of the fields caused by rain, which fell heavily for five days without a break, the hay crop was ruined."

136. Insert *to be* before "earned." The context shows that the

reference is to future dividends, not to past ones.   For the sake of euphony, *and* should be inserted before "whose object."

137. Say, "it would have been impossible *to treat* him with more consideration," etc.   A Perfect Infinitive after "would *have been*" is both unnecessary and inelegant.

138. Say, "it may assist the reader, if I place," etc.

139. Insert *of* after *contracting*.

140. Insert *the* before *reading*.

141. Change *have made* to *make*.

142. Change *have sent* to *send*.

143. Two blunders : (1) *to* is not used after the verb *see ;* (2) *have predominated* should be changed to *predominate*.

144. Change *inquiring* to *to inquire*.

145. Change *accompanying* to *to accompany*.

146. Cancel *the* before *surmounting*.

(*i*) *Miscellaneous* (pp. 122-129).

1. Say, "Those Canadians and Queenslanders, who were dismounted, stood," etc.

2. Change *shall* to *will*.

3. If *which* is retained, it must be followed by *was*. If *were* is retained, it must be preceded by *who*.

4. Say, "The movable platform, which was imitated from the Chicago model and is one of the features of the exhibition," etc.

5. Say, "through thefts committed by people, whom from their dress and bearing it is almost impossible to detect."

6. Here the verbal noun would be more appropriate than the gerund, because there is no person or persons to whom the action expressed by the gerund can be referred.   Say therefore, "In the furnishing of the new hotel," etc.

7. Say, "all the people have committed," etc.

8. Change *that* to *what :* the former is somewhat ambiguous.

9. Correct.   "The soldier rising," etc., is in the absolute construction.   "The soldier" here means "the feelings or spirit of a soldier," the concrete being used for the abstract.

10. *And who* is here wrong, because there is no Relative clause going before.   Change *and who* to "both of whom."   Say, "their own and your sense" instead of "their sense and your sense," which does not sound well.

11. *They being separated*, etc.   The absolute construction should not be used, as it is here, with another *they* immediately following, and the antecedents "France and Germany" going immediately before.   Say, "between France and Germany in Europe, separated as they are by Alsace-Lorraine, the two countries could at least," etc.   It adds to the point of the sentence to say, "the two countries" for "they," because "they" might more naturally be supposed to refer to "politicians" as the antecedent.

12. *A king at five years old.*   This is a confusion between two distinct constructions—(1) a king five years old, (2) a king at five years of age.   The confusion, though not uncommonly made, had better be avoided.   In this context (2) suits the rhythm better than (1).

13. Here the construction is confused. The Subject of the sentence is "the thief named Meonitz," and therefore *he* must be cancelled. *And the tailor unknown to him* is an absolute phrase improperly connected by *and* with the Subject of the sentence. Say, "the thief named Meonitz, being as unknown to the tailor as the tailor was to him, must have derived," etc.

14. It does not sound well to use *siege* and *field* as adjectives after their noun "artillery." Nor does it sound well to use a Singular verb "was weak," when two distinct artillery forces are referred to. Say, "Both siege artillery and field artillery were weak, till they were," etc.

15. Say, "Some alarmist news about the way in which the lads of the Public Schools battalions are alleged to have suffered from fatigue," etc. The Relative phrase *in which* must on no account be omitted after "way."

16. Correct in all respects. "General Buller tells us" is parenthetical. "And which" is here appropriate—(1) because there is a *which* going before, and (2) because the second *which* introduces a statement quite distinct from that introduced by the first one.

17. "Myself" should not stand as Subject of a sentence, unaccompanied with "I." Say, "I myself and a few comrades with me," etc. ; or "A few comrades with myself," etc.

18. Say, "There are men with whom it is impossible to work," etc.

19. Insert *which* after "ground," for the sake of clearness. Say, "to gain which so many lives were lost."

20. It sounds awkward to use *land-registry* as an adjective to a noun that is immediately afterwards qualified by a real adjective "public" and has already been qualified by another adjective "new." Say, "for building new offices in London to be used for land-registry and other public purposes," etc.

21. We cannot say *there is as yet none of sign*. The sentence must begin with, "That he realises," etc., and end with, "there is as yet no sign."

22. Change *them* to *that*.

23. Say, "almost impossible in all but a few places."

24. *Average intelligent Englishmen* is a bad phrase. Say, "Englishmen of average intelligence."

25. Insert *with the nature* after "especially."

26. *And which* is here wrong, because there is no previous Relative clause to justify its use. If *and* is cancelled, no other alteration is necessary.

27. Change *has never got to be* to *has never become*. "Got to be" is a bad phrase, which need never be used.

28. Cancel *also*, which has been implied already by the phrase "in addition to." There is obviously a confusion in the concluding clause ; what is the Object of the verb "join"? Say, "join one sentence to another by showing the relation between them."

29. Insert *who has* after "a man." *Come* must not be used as a Past participle, but only as part of a tense.

30. Cancel *to* before "creep." This particle is not used after the verb "make."

31. Change *we have got to retain* to "we have no choice but to retain."

32. Change the second *will* to *shall*.   Nothing more than simple futurity is required by the context.

33. Change *old* to *of age*.   See remarks in (12).

34. Change *and* to *so that :* otherwise *should* is inappropriate.

35. Change *Something has got to be done* to *Something must be done* or *Something has to be done.*

36. It would sound rather better to say, "to find this third attempt prove unsuccessful like the previous ones."

37. Say, "enjoyable in the literal sense of the word."   The Possessive form "enjoyment's" should not be used.

38. Change every *shall* except the last to *will*.   It will improve the final clause if *which* is inserted after *that*.

39. Say, "and of which the ringleaders were punished."   The Auxiliary *were* must not be omitted.

40. It would be better to write *one another* than *each other*, because more than two things are referred to.   This, however, is not a rigid rule.   Insert *the* before "most far-fetched"; this insertion is indispensable.

41. Cancel *got*.

42. Insert *to be* after "fiction."

43. Insert *with which* after "nothing."   "Remembering" is pendent.   In order to give it some noun or pronoun, insert "let me ask you" before "is this safe?"

44. Cancel *and* before "which."

45. It would be rather better to say, "built himself."

46. Cancel both the *gots*.

47. *Forwarder* is a bad form of Comparative.   Change to *more forward*.

48. Insert *in which* after "way."

49. *Who, and which.*   Such a connection is altogether wrong. Say, "and who, so long as he can choose his own ground, is as nearly invincible as any that we know of in history."

50. Say, "unknown to any Latin or to any other Teutonic people."

51. Correct.   *Shall* expresses a confident prediction, and this is what the context requires.

52. Say, "the celebration at Ealing."

53. Change *long-ago* (which is not an adjective) to *distant*.

54. Change *let alone* to *much less*.   Nothing but an adverbial phrase can be used with a verb such as "protect."

55. Change *much less* to *though not*.   Or say, "far from being justified, could only be explained by," etc.   The phrase *much less* is not used, unless there is a negative going before.

56. *And in which* cannot be retained, unless a Relative clause is placed before it.   Say, "a scheme which was recommended by Her Majesty's Government, and in which," etc.   It would be simpler, however, to leave the sentence as it is and cancel *and*.   *Should* is here correct, since it expresses something that ought to be or is recommended.

57. Here *but which* is correct, because there is a Relative clause

going before. The *which* after *but*, however, is superfluous, as the sense is perfectly clear without it.

58. Insert *the name of* after "rolls." Change the last *who* to *but*.

59. Change *the Administration's* to *of the Administration*.

60. Change *shall* to *will*.

61. Insert *in which* after "way."

62. "Paul was instructing his countrymen in the mysteries of the new covenant, and was pointing out to them the relation which Christ bore to this new covenant, as compared with that which Moses bore to the old."

63. Insert *built* after "already."

64. Say, "If this is necessary." The conventional phrase, "if necessary," though by no means uncommon colloquially, sounds rather slipshod in written composition.

65. Change *whose ascription* to *the ascription of which*.

66. Change *is* to *has*.

67. Change *save* to *than*. After "else" or "other" we must use *than*.

68. *Ought* must be followed by "to"; but as the construction of the present sentence does not readily admit of this, change *they ought not* to *they should not*. Again, to use *which* and *who* with the same antecedent, "army," is not good English. Say, "which they themselves had invited, and which would always have an excuse for remaining by saying that they were keeping the country peaceful." Observe that "the excuse of remaining" has been changed to "an excuse for remaining."

69. Change *who will include* to *amongst whom will be included;* or say simply *including*.

70. Change *How long* to *How much time*.

71. Reconstruct thus:—"As Mommsen said of France, that she had shaken many empires but founded none, so of Mr. M. it may be said that he has broken up ministries, but has never established one." Observe that "and founded" has been changed to "but founded."

72. The sentence is grammatical. But there is a lack of unity both in the sense and in the construction. Reconstruct thus:—"He found his chief enjoyment in the retired circle of select literary friends; and in the amenities of female converse, which for him had the highest charm, he sought the purest and most refined recreation."

73. *Who, whose, who.* Reconstruct thus:—"It is not the Chinese that are in a hurry to see Pekin evacuated, but the allied foreigners, who are spending between them something like a million a week on their armies and fleets, and whose forces are in constant need of replenishment."

74. Say, "If there is opposition and that opposition is persevered in," etc.

75. Cancel *else*, which is not merely superfluous, but gives a bad construction. The proper word to use after *else* is "than," not "but."

76. Insert *the more* after "or."

77. Say, "and between them they have brought," etc.; or say, "and between the two South Africa has been brought," etc. The construction as it stands is a confusion of both renderings.

78. Reconstruct thus :—"The kind of men to be employed in the Cape Colony will, of course, be very different from that needed for the new territories."

79. Change *before leaving Kumási* to *before the garrison left Kumási ;* or say, *before they left Kumási.* In the original no persons are named to whom the action implied in "leaving" can be referred.

80. The construction is very slipshod. Reconstruct thus :— "Shan-hai-kwan is to be garrisoned by contingents of 500 men, France, Russia, Great Britain, and Germany each furnishing one such contingent, and Italy supplying one company.

81. Change *they endeavour* to *it endeavours.*

82. Change *the man is* to *the man will be.*

83. Say, "without men's thoughts being profoundly affected by questions about capital and capitalists," etc. There is no agent to whom the Active gerund "affecting" can be referred.

84. Change *their* to *his.*

85. Say, "If a comparison is to be made between the blast furnace practice of English and Americans respectively, the state of things existing ten years ago is ancient history." *Ten years ago* is an adverbial phrase, and as such it cannot be made the Subject of a verb. The phrase *in comparing* has the same kind of defect as *before leaving,* which has been corrected in (79), or as *without affecting,* which has been corrected in (83).

86. Say, "wants which the people are acquainted with, and which their national life has developed."

87. Substitute *and* for the second *which,* and cancel the comma after "Ottawa."

88. Change *at twelve years old* to "when he was twelve years old." In the sentence as it stands "old" qualifies "mother," which makes nonsense.

89. The sentence is grammatical as it stands, but could be improved by a few slight changes. "The general feeling, both official and unofficial, is in favour of the reform which Lord Curzon has accomplished and which previous Viceroys contemplated, but did not carry out."

90. Reconstruct thus:—"I believe that of late there have been very few engagements or even skirmishes, in which the number of British soldiers has been largely in excess of that of the Boers, and I believe that in many cases it has been less."

91. Say, "his distinction between the responsibility resting upon the Government and that resting upon the Field-Marshal for the barbarous," etc.

92. Say "or which at least they may not acquire."

93. Insert *the rigour* after "mitigates."

94. Insert *whom* after "beasts."

95. Say, "a history of anything in the world rather than a history of the literature of England."

96. The phrase *some time ago,* which can only be used of something that is past and gone, does not fit the Present Perfect tense "has been transferred." One or other must go. If *some time ago* is retained, then the verb must be "was transferred." If "has been transferred" is to be retained, then *some time ago* must be cancelled.

97. *Nobody hardly* is a double negative. Say "hardly any one tours"; or "there is hardly any one who tours."

98. *Already* does not fit the context. Say *once before.*

99. Here is a double negative. Change *neither . . . nor* to *either . . . or.*

100. Change *hardly* to *just.*

101. Change *essentially a condition* to "an essential condition." An adverb cannot qualify a noun.

102. Insert *solve* after "will."

103. *Preparatory* is a pendent adjective. The writer evidently desires it to be understood in an adverbial sense; but this is grammatically inadmissible. Say, "in preparation for partaking," etc.

104. Change *nor* to *or.*

105. Say, "This principle having been once asserted," etc.; and change *not alone* to *not only.*

106. Change *neither* to *either.*

107. Say, "between the effect of private and that of public measures on personal interests."

108. *Quite* cannot qualify a noun, and yet this misuse of it is very common in journalism. Say, "The chief sensation," etc.

109. Say, "more cheaply and more quickly." *Cheaper* is not an adverb. Change the colloquial or slang phrase *A1* to "perfectly."

110. Say, "and why there was so little before."

111. The sentence is slipshod. Relatives are omitted, and prepositions are placed at the end of clauses: "cause of introducing" is a roundabout phrase. Say, "Meanwhile it introduces ideas, of which we shall not easily get rid, when we realise that we have a past up to which we should strive to live."

112. Say "having arrived."

113. Change *to have transferred* to *if he had transferred.*

114. "At ninety years old" is a questionable phrase. Moreover from its position it looks as if it were meant to qualify *which.* Say, "which, when he was ninety years old or thereabouts, seemed," etc.

115. Say, "with a thousand men fewer than those with whom he had set out."

116. Change *they are* to *it is.* Blair appears to have quarrelled with the well established *it is,* and to have substituted *they are* as an amendment.

117. Change *those* and *their* to *that* and *its.*

118. Rewrite the sentence thus:—"It was only by lavishing his praise that he found himself able to display," etc.

119. Change *retorting* to *to retort.* It would be more idiomatic to say *would be* than *were.*

120. Change *looking* to *to look.*

121. There is no antecedent to *they.* Substitute *their descendants,* which is evidently required by the sense.

CHAPTER VIII.—ANSWERS TO EXAMPLES IN CHAPTER III.

(a) Subject, Object, Apposition (pp. 134, 135).

1. "At Rugby, yesterday morning, took place the death of Mr David B.," etc. Or say, "At Rugby, yesterday morning, died Mr. David," etc.

2. Insert the particle "there" before "remains."

3. "If I mistake not, Brandis finds the inimitable touch of the master in just those scenes," etc.

4. "Little by little rose the number of those," etc.

5. The order can stand, but *to* should be inserted before "whom," because this Indirect object is not placed immediately after its verb.

6. The sentence requires reconstruction :—"During the engagement Major McKenzie nearly fell into a trap laid by a Kaffir. Thorneycroft's Horse, who were treated by another native guide with similar treachery, had an equally narrow escape."

7. Place *their muskets* after "gave in."

8. Place *battalions* after "Russian."

9. Begin the sentence with, "Of all surviving types."

10. "Public opinion, as well as the influence of governing bodies and headmasters, would be," etc.

11. Begin the sentence with, "In the composition of his administrative board." (Insert *the* before the word "Progressive.")

12. Place "his conversion" immediately after *hailed.* (It would improve the sentence to change *they* into *those.*)

13. *From the labours,* etc., belongs to "expect," not to "abolition." It should therefore be placed immediately after "expect."

14. Place *without a struggle* immediately after "resign."

15. *In good time* belongs to "make," not to "necessary." Say, "whose failure to make timely improvements," etc.

16. Insert *there* before "should."

17. "Though he was a graduate of Trinity College, Dublin, he had never, so far as I could gather, received," etc.

18. Say, "needs some grand prize to hearten it."

19. "Suspicion" is needlessly separated from the Noun-clause with which it is in apposition. Begin the sentence thus :—"Among quiet Germans, especially in the non-industrial provinces, there is," etc.

20. Begin thus:—"In a recent number of *Literature* was announced the discovery at Florence of," etc.

21. Say, "When this prevails in the schools of Madras," etc.

22. Begin thus:—"As the leading and consistent champion of the oppressed, you will, I trust, permit," etc.

23. Since "the life of moral emotion" is in apposition with or relates to "the spiritual world," while "the life of movement" relates to "the physical world," the order should be made to tally. Say, "the life of moral emotion and the life of movement."

24. Place "to injudicious competition" immediately after "attributing."

(b) Adjective and Participle (pp. 139-141).

1. The sentence must be recast:—"It was an inferior work, but, as is often the case, the author had a manifest partiality for it and rated it among his best pieces."

2. "These excellent villas to be let, or to be sold either freehold or leasehold."

3. Say, "having arrived at this stage, we know pretty well what we," etc. *Having* must not be omitted before "arrived," and there is no occasion to separate "know" from its Object.

4. Say, "He was not a hermit of asceticism, but a saint indeed, combining," etc.

5. Place *not far distant* immediately after "time."

6. Begin the sentence with, "Having ample leisure for the purpose."

7. The concluding phrase and clause, "having recently inherited the property of a large and valuable tea-plantation in Ceylon, the affairs of which will require her to go out there," should be placed before "is anxious."

8. Say, "Articles dealing with, etc., appear in our page for women." Or better, "In our page for women appear articles dealing with," etc.

9. The sentence must be recast:—"The United States expressed the desire that the questions, etc., should be considered."

10. "Look at it from where one will, one could not but feel how poor in comparison with this natural cathedral was a temple made with hands."

11. Place "much less certainly than he wished for" after "little time"; there should be a comma both before and after it.

12. Place "dealing with various aspects," etc., after "volumes."

13. The phrase "on the 24th July 1899" should be placed at the end of the sentence. If this was not the order intended by the writer, the words "as taking place" are objectless and should be cancelled.

14. Place *alone* after "life." Or say, "It was only ordinary life that she depicted," etc.

15. Begin the sentence with, "First among the episodes of the month."

16. Say, "will have upon them the effect predicted."

17. Say, "and arguments and articles based on these false assumptions have been written by the thousand."

18. Begin the sentence with, "Regarded from the naturalist's point of view."

19. Place "suited to their hearers" after "moral lessons." Say, "in deducing from every-day occurrences moral lessons suited to their hearers."

20. Place "being the only child of a man well-to-do" after "Agnes Stanfield."

21. Say, "a deeper glance."

22. Begin the sentence with, "Disliking controversy."

23. It would be rather better to begin the sentence with, "Compared with several European countries."

24. Place "as hopeless" after "dismisses."

25. Place "for town-defence" after "to form." The last word "alone" might be cancelled ; but if it is retained, it should stand after "firm."

26. Reconstruct thus :—"Eventually the motion was withdrawn on the strength of an inquiry being promised by Lord Salisbury, who regretted," etc.

27. Reconstruct thus :—"Roads at present much more dangerous than the road to Comassie would be made fairly safe by a few convictions."

28. Say, "in events never to be forgotten."

29. Say, "by which alone we can hope."

30. "During the last half-year was effected a reduction," etc.

31. Place "denied to the remainder of mankind" after "knowledge."

32. Say, "that, alone and unassisted, they cannot deal with," etc.

33. Here are three qualifying phrases, all having reference to "article," with the result that the third one is at too great a distance. Reconstruct thus :—"to an article dealing with the causes of the war, which appeared in the September *National Review* from the pen of Sir Edward Grey."

34. Placed "possessed by some barbers" after "knowledge."

35. "Relying," etc., belongs to "party organs." Say, "But relying, etc.—facts, those party organs have deceived and played with you."

36. Reconstruct thus :—"The sitting closed definitely at five o'clock, by which time the matter that had brought so many together had not been practically entered upon."

37. Say, "In the autumn lists a very copious supply of creditable literature remains to be dealt with."

38. Say, "With this small band, closely followed by 4000 men, they advanced against," etc. Even now, however, the construction is questionable ; there is no need of *with* or *they* :—"This small band, closely followed by 4000 men, advanced," etc.

39. Place "burlesque and ridiculous" immediately after "render."

(c) *Pronouns* (pp. 142-147).

1. Say, "my countrymen and I."

2. Say, "For the sake of Herodias, his brother Philip's life."

3. The Relative clause should come after "force." It would be

better, however, to leave the order as it is, and change *which* to *but that it*.

4. Say, "If the Emperor is still alive, it may be found possible to re-establish him on the throne."

5. Begin thus :—"Yesterday, in the House of Lords, Lord Salisbury made a statement, which," etc.

6. Say, "my family and I," etc.

7. Begin thus :—"At Manchester has just been closed an exhibition, which," etc. (Say, "to many persons besides those of the trade.")

8. Place the Relative clause immediately after "meaning."

9. "Object" here means "person." The sentence hangs together very awkwardly and can be reconstructed thus :—"Many people would have been of opinion that the Laird would have done better to transfer his glances to a person who was possessed of charms far superior to Jeanie's, even when Jeanie's were in their bloom, and who began now to be distinguished by all that visited," etc. After "would have done" the Perfect Infinitive "to have transferred" is out of place. The word "superior" should stand immediately before "to."

10. Say, "I with others."

11. Place the Relative clause immediately after "he."

12. Place the Relative clause immediately after "a white city of canvas."

13. Place "by an unscrupulous exploiter of public confidence" after "applied."

14. Say, "and to her the King's large fortune," etc.

15. Begin thus :—"Except sergeants, who were taken up to thirty-five years of age, all men under twenty-one and over thirty, who were considered," etc.

16. Say, "my house and I."

17. Place "of which he does not approve" after "reforms."

18. Say, "the tracks of Rufinus."

19. Place the last Relative clause, "that claim," etc., after "points."

20. Place the Relative clause after "statement."

21. Place the last Relative clause, "which requires," etc., after "Brent."

22. Begin thus :—"The President gave to a German, non-resident in the country, a monopoly of the supply of dynamite, which taxed," etc. End thus :—"the highest price for which it could otherwise have been bought."

23. Place "who observed," with all that follows it to the end of the sentence, after "no one."

24. Cancel the second *which*, and reconstruct thus :—"against the current habit, universal in Government circles, of looking at the colonist as something outside and inferior."

25. *Which* is separated too widely from its antecedent "story." This antecedent must be repeated in the following way :—"wreaked usually on the innocent—the story which we have read so often, and which yet," etc.

26. Here *which leaves*, etc., is too far away from "novel." Say,

"Since seeing that novel, which gave new life to the times of Erasmus, we cannot point to one which leaves," etc.

27. Begin the sentence with, "As he was whiling away the hours of darkness that yet remained." (The Perfect Infinitive "to have been engaged" is here correct, because the time to which it refers is previous to the action expressed by "conjectured.")

28. Cancel "who escaped," which, besides being separated too far from "eleven," is superfluous.

29. The Relative clause is in the wrong place. Say, "His object is to help on the work of the Association, which has been set on foot in the *Nineteenth Century*, for securing," etc.

30. Rearrange thus :—"Trying to fish out the exact state of the chemist's concerns, business men wasted with Mrs. Stern many a half-hour, which they thought," etc.

31. Say "your readers and me."

32. Begin—"You may be interested in the following conversation, which," etc.

33. Say, "my friends and I."

34. Say, "and who, to meet the difficulties of the hour, has plans which he intends," etc.

35. Say, "you and I."

36. There is more than one blemish in this sentence :—"During the last five years I was a director, not of several companies, but of one, and in this one my family and I were largely interested."

37. The Relative clause is in the wrong place. Say, "one of the most remarkable and most pathetic illustrations, which the history of social organisation contains, of human," etc.

38. Place the Relative clause after "Ross."

39. Say, "a defence of the pursuit of wealth as an end,—a defence, which in its want of reserves and qualifications would, we think, have made," etc.

40. Here "I and others" must stand, as we cannot say "others and I." It would be possible, however, to say "others besides myself."

41. Say, "They that complain to their wives are some of the feather-bed soldiers," etc. But *they* should be changed to *those*.

42. Say, "I am one among many thousands who welcome," etc.

43. Reconstruct thus, "Speaking somewhere of the different lights in which all the daily wonders of the world are regarded by different men, Carlyle alludes to the matter-of-fact attitude, which ceases," etc. The sentence is grammatically correct as it stands ; but "which ceases" is rather too far away from "attitude."

44. Place "at Pittsburg" after "creation."

45. Place the Relative clause standing at the end of the sentence immediately after "power."

46. Place "at that early day" after "could." *Then* causes difficulty, as it seems to refer to "at that early day." It means here "in that case." Say, "which in that case would not have struck him in the end like lightning."

47. *Are* should be changed to *is*. Even then both the order of the words and the construction are awkward. Say, "I trust that neither Mr. Chamberlain nor I will say anything which can be taken," etc.

48. Reconstruct thus :—"The great distance at which we now find the buffalo separated from its original home in India." The sentence, as it stands, is not a bad one ; but *which* is a little too far apart from its antecedent.

49. Say, "the chapel and priests' house built by the people of the wholly Christian village of Ta Tien Tze,—built by their own hands and with their own money."

50. "His" should not stand before its antecedent, "Palladio." To avoid this say, "and Vicenza is adorned by the classic architecture of her own son, Palladio."

51. Rearrange thus :—"We are inclined to think that what was largely accountable for the rapid failure of the Lollard movement was a real recognition of the fact that Wycliffism," etc.

52. Say, "He whose work was finished cannot be said to have died prematurely, nor does he who died so full of honours deserve," etc.

53. Begin thus :—"Meanwhile there is here no lack of critics, who," etc.

54. Insert the Relative clause after "one."

55. Say, "We may well ask what is the use of energetic action, if it is not," etc.

56. "Among its cliffs there is a huge cave, where the Mac Somethings to the number of above two hundred men had taken refuge," etc.

57. "Their own" refers to "Boer generals," which should have been mentioned first, but is not given till long afterwards. Say, "until we had from the pens of the Boer generals themselves their own view," etc.

58. According to the position, the pronoun "she" must refer to the nearest noun "Mrs. Jameson," whereas the sense requires that it shall refer to the more distant noun, "Mary Magdalene." Since we cannot change the order of the words, substitute "Jesus" for "He," and "Mary" for "she."

59. Place "of which much notice is taken" immediately after "book."

60. "The same," being here used as a pronoun, ought to be placed after, and not before, its antecedent. It would be better to write—"so long as we are ignorant of these words, would the said words have conveyed."

61. Put *taxes* in the place of *they*, and change *of taxes* to *of them*.

(d) Adverb, Adverbial Phrase, or Adverbial Clause
(pp. 152-157).

1. "The announcement is such as to confirm us still more, if that were possible, in our resolve," etc.

2. Place "only" before "when."

3. Begin the sentence with—"On Saturday night at Oxford."

4. Say, "to note briefly."

5. Place "astray" after "leads."

6. Say, "to censure publicly."

7. Place "without success" before "made."

8. The sentence is not a bad one as it stands ; but it might be

rearranged thus :—"Finally the great Duke, by his recognition of the value of sea-power, taught us that in time of war the opportunity," etc.

9. Insert "only" before "in the house."

10. "Equally" is badly placed besides being rather unsuitable. Say, "to take his readers captive as much when he was wrong as when he was right."

11. Place "by Mr. Francis" after "asked."

12. Place "wholly" after "adopt"; or better still, change "wholly" to "all" :—"all Mr. Sch.'s proposals."

13. Place "have guided" after "past."

14. Place "only" before "when."

15. Place "until the end of April" after "continue." The sentence would be improved by changing the second *for* to *on behalf of.*

16. Place "only" before "in the morning."

17. Place "only" before "at the eleventh hour." The sentence should begin thus :—"A month ago, as is reported, M. Delcassé," etc.

18. Place "only" before "in the House of Lords."

19. Say, "have violently come to life again in him."

20. Place "very well indeed" after "stood."

21. Place "only" before "to the proposed Supreme Court of Appeal."

22. Place "as much" before "as they are."

23. Place "only" between "owing" and "to the support."

24. Place "only" before "good"; or better still, say, "nothing but good."

25. Begin the sentence thus :—"With the usual equanimity of an injured woman."

26. "By degrees" should stand first, or after "ceased."

27. Insert "both early and accurately" after "known."

28. "Wonderful to relate" should stand first.

29. Say "to issue in any case."

30. Place "only" before "when."

31. Place "only" before "after."

32. "Not" must stand before "because." "He failed to persecute Christians, not because he had no," etc.

33. The sentence should begin :—"Among quiet Germans, and especially in the non-industrial provinces, there is," etc.

34. Place "only" after "portion" or after "by."

35. Place "only" before "on the day."

36. Say, "to enforce rigidly."

37. "In more senses than one" should stand first.

38. Say, "to be put at once."

39. Say, "to oppose successfully."

40. Say, "to consider seriously."

41. Place "only" before "in such parts."

42. "But for one serious doubt" should stand first, since it qualifies "believe."

43. Place "simply" before "because."

44. It would be rather better to say, "Running a boat down into the surf."

45. Place "in a few minutes" before "reached."

46. Say, "is used too freely for," etc.

47. Place "vastly" after "increase."

48. Place "only" before "because."

49. Say, "to receive personally."

50. The second of these two sentences should run thus :—"Before the public understood that the national dignity was involved, M. Delcassé settled it," etc.

51. The second clause should be "and honestly we do not see the duty." "Honestly" should stand first, because it qualifies the whole sentence, and not "see" in particular.

52. The sentence should end with "only after having been found guilty."

53. Place "in La Reforme Sociale" after "find."

54. Place "without a remonstrance" after "receiving."

55. Place "must necessarily" before "render." The word "necessarily," however, is superfluous.

56. Place "only" before "on condition."

57. Place "under improved circumstances" before "ought."

58. Place "largely" after "will be."

59. The right order would be :—"Notice to Cyclists by order of the authorities.—This hill is dangerous."

60. Place "under a cloak of love-sick affection" after "disguises."

61. Place "in Holland" after "establish."

62. Place "together with a police-official" before "has made."

63. Rearrange thus :—"In dealing with the Chinese it has too often been our habit to forget, on the first appearance of repentance, the crimes committed by them."

64. Place "with dread" after "contemplates."

65. Place "only" before "religious."

66. "Without shedding tears" is intended to qualify "seldom took up." Reconstruct thus :—"He frequently took up the Bible, but seldom without shedding tears."

67. Place "never" before "to return."

68. Place "only" before "in so far as."

69. Place "only" before "a little," etc.

70. Place "as you do" immediately after "believe."

71. Place "with wonderful exactness" immediately after "gives."

72. Say, "are contained in no fewer than fifty folio volumes."

73. Place "only" before "thirteen."

74. Place "in a thousand ways" immediately after "adulterate."

75. Place "if a contest occurs" immediately after "hence."

76. Begin the sentence with "In the *Quarrels of Authors*."

77. Begin the sentence with "Only one."

78. Say, "a somewhat later period."

(e) *Prepositions* (pp. 159-164).

1. Place "to their forces" after "welcome."

2. Rearrange thus :—"a kind of instruction and training different from, but perhaps not less valuable than, that which is given in the schoolroom."

3. Place "in marriage" after "gave him."

4. Say, "through land at present waste."

5. Place "respectively" last.

6. Place "to civilisation" after "restored."

7. Place "of a monopoly" after "obtaining."

8. Say, "was announced the discovery at Florence of a series," etc.

9. Place "from the pen of A. Lusignoli" after "plea."

10. Place "In this connection" at the beginning of the sentence.

11. Rearrange thus:—"that restrictions and regulations very different from these which prevail are demanded."

12. Reconstruct and rearrange thus:—"During the last few weeks of excessively hot weather medical men in the parish of Marylebone have been greatly concerned at the appearance of," etc.

13. Say, "the effect of recent legislation in India on the operation of the Sugar bounties."

14. Place "to bankers" after "applications."

15. Place "by Her Majesty the Queen" after "presented."

16. Rearrange and reconstruct thus:—"Men are not encouraged by an incident such as that in which a field-cornet's son, who tried to induce some of the Federals in the senior state to surrender, was shot by an irreconcilable named C."

17. Place "from the Money-lending bill" after "withdrew."

18. Rearrange and reconstruct thus:—"The Italian nation would have been jarred to the very soul, if round the corpse of its murdered sovereign there had been any outbreak of the disastrous," etc.

19. Rearrange and reconstruct thus:—"Referring to the incident, in which Peel, by a timely conversion to their views, is said to have robbed his opponents of their well-earned triumph, Mr. Birrell," etc.

20. Place "to Rhodesia" after "sent."

21. Place "for one's sister" after "coveting."

22. Place "back to the front" after "sent."

23. Place "upon his father" after "effect."

24. Place "of seven hours" after "reduction."

25. Say, "with insignia inscrutable to mundane eyes."

26. Say, "The axis of many sins and of great offences will therefore shift."

27. Reconstruct and rearrange thus:—"In the House of Assembly to-day Mr. M. submitted a motion, in which he begged that a Blue-book containing his letter to Mr. De W., an alleged rebel, would not be published by the Imperial Government without his knowledge."

28. Begin the sentence with "to."

29. "To bring about" belongs to "it needs." As the latter is separated from the former by a great number of words, it must be brought near it by repetition. "It needs nothing but the presence, etc. etc., in his corrugated iron sheds, and the man himself active and persevering as a beaver or red ant,—it needs nothing but the presence of such a man to bring about," etc. (Observe that *he himself*, which should have been in the Objective case, has been changed to "the man himself.")

30. Place "of Russia" after "influence."

31. Place "of the Federals" after "power."

32. Say, "the sort of fiction in which we Americans," etc. Final *in* must now be cancelled.

33. Say, "a broader control over the entrance to the fortress-town and the residence there of strangers," etc. Insert *of* before "alien."

34. Say, "the one thing about which an historian is concerned."

35. Say, "of a kind very unusual to my ears." (Change "awoke" to "awakened," the latter being the more correct form of the Transitive verb.)

36. Place "should be transacted" after "plenipotentiaries."

37. Place "of that fact" after "proof."

38. Say, "as low a level as that to which it had sunk."

39. Place the phrase "in the shape of a severe visitation of autumn fever" after "paying," with a comma before and after.

40. Reconstruct and rearrange thus :—"except to say that the line which I saw taken on many occasions was that of imputing disloyalty and want of patriotism to men on the other side quite as loyal and patriotic as themselves, though differing from themselves in opinion."

41. Reconstruct and rearrange thus :—"to decide what use can be made of the services of men unable," etc. Or leave the words as they are and place "can be utilised" at the end of the sentence.

42. Place "between them" after "have."

43. Place "in various publications" after "has."

44. Rearrange thus :—"has assumed dimensions too large, and influences the popular opinion too strongly, to be suppressed arbitrarily." The words *for it*, being superfluous, are cancelled.

45. Say, "and receive consideration." This removes the blemish of a final "for."

46. Place "of" before "these."

47. Begin the sentence with "To a newspaper."

48. Too many prepositional phrases after "recoil." Say, "that the anti-Milner cabal contrived by the engineers has recoiled upon themselves."

49. Place "of the wild zebra" after "pictures."

50. Place "by the Sessions Judge" after "instituted against him."

51. Place "from politics" after "disconnect."

52. Say, "to be master of which."

53. Say, "of merit superior to those."

54. Place "of the younger and more active members of the firm" after "withdrawal."

55. Say, "took place in Vienna the death of," etc.

56. Begin with "for his materials."

57. Say, "arising from differences of the most pronounced type in nationality, in discipline, and in pay."

58. Place "by a serious rising" after "protest."

59. Rearrange thus :—"From the extraordinary effect on trade with the Shan States and Zimmé produced by the little and still uncompleted line to Kunlon, we are justified in assuming," etc.

60. Place "by the unscientific" after "used every day."

61. Place "in the matter of postal rates" after "advantages." Cancel the words "which are."

62. Reconstruct and rearrange thus :—" During the later development of the crisis I have been in conversation, and so have others, with," etc.

63. Place "into sad trouble" after "brought."

64. Begin with "At the City Corporation meeting."

65. Place "by Johannesburg" after "proposal."

66. Place "on moral grounds" after "censure."

67. Reconstruct and rearrange thus :—" The cordon has been drawn, by which if possible, the raiders now retiring, etc., will be prevented from breaking away southwards."

68. The separation of the preposition "to" from its object is awkward. Say, "the Queen's visit to Ireland and the great reception she received there." (The juxtaposition of the words *reception, received*, has a bad sound. Substitute "cordial welcome" for "great reception.")

69. Rearrange thus :—" The alteration secured that on the nomination, where it appeared desirable, of other bodies, including associations of voluntary schools, every scheme should provide for the appointment by the Council of educational experts," etc.

70. Say, "at the lack of which she evidently does not even guess."

71. Place "from the labours of agriculture" immediately after "shut out."

72. Say, "a conclusion quite different from Paul's." (*From* is better than *to* after "different.")

73. Begin the sentence with : "Hence with a modern political economist."

74. Place "of a unique character" (where *an* has been wrongly used for *a*) immediately after "scheme."

(f) Correlative Conjunctions (pp. 166, 167).

1. Say, "were not only obliged to learn it, but everywhere ambitious to speak it."

2. Say, "having root in the soil neither of France nor of Attica."

3. Say, "regretted not only by all those who knew her, but by every constable throughout the metropolis."

4. Say, "have neither the spirit nor the time."

5. Say, "we find not only trusts severely denounced, but a remedy for the evil suggested."

6. "The voter is becoming either a Nationalist or a Socialist."

7. "Morally the war is either just or unjust ; the methods are either civilised or barbarous."

8. Say, "among neither the architects nor the prophets."

9. "Not only is he here aloof from actualities, etc., but his manner throughout is too much that of the academic essayist."

10. Say, "a condemnation not only of them, but of the agent on the spot," etc. (*Who* must be changed to *whom* to make the last clause grammatical.)

11. "Instead, we had not the pluck either for the renunciation or the maintenance," etc.

12. Say, "concerning matters in regard to which he had not merely a perfect right, but a positive duty to speak."

13. Say, "not only in teaching their convicts trades, but in making," etc.

14. Say, "had violated the Monroe Doctrine not in seizing as representative of the Emperor one spot of ground, but in capturing and making his own all Americans."

15. Place *either* between "of" and "tyrant."

16. "You are not obliged to take any money but what is either gold or silver : you need not take any halfpence or farthings, whether of England or of any other country."

(g) *Miscellaneous Examples* (pp. 167-174).

1. Say, "When returning to Royston to protect his villagers he has the misfortune," etc.

2. The phrase "as well as those on our side" should be placed before *will*. Even then the sentence is badly balanced. Say, "I am convinced that the vital interests of those who have to live in South Africa—our enemies as well as our friends—will demand," etc.

3. This sentence might be allowed to pass : but "to move" is rather too far away from "get," and "get" is hardly a fit equivalent to "induce." Say, "In spite of all his efforts and entreaties successive Ministries, which trembled at the bare thought of the hereditary enemy, could not be induced to move."

4. Here *Madras* is first used as an adjective to qualify schools, and then as a noun in apposition to *centre*. Say, "When this prevails in the schools of Madras, the centre," etc.

5. *Neither* is in the wrong place. *He* is too far from its Relative *who*. Say, "The educated native is one who can go neither forward nor back, who has left," etc. Or say, "who can neither go forward nor go back."

6. "Their loyalty is not at any moment worth a clear day's purchase."

7. Say, "to detect signs already." Some persons, however, admit the split Infinitive and see no harm in it, although at present literature is against it.

8. The introductory phrase "as the leading," etc., belongs by position to "I"; but it is intended to belong to "you." Say, "I trust that you, as the leading and consistent champion of the oppressed," etc.

9. Say, "there is no place perhaps that looms," etc.

10. Say, "that only about one-eighth," etc.

11. Say, "is also a lecturer," etc.

12. Say, "denounced as a gross abuse of Parliamentary privilege the imputations contained," etc.

13. Say, "to construct immediately."

14. Say, "and died only in 1898." But the word "only," when used to signify that something happened very recently, is rather colloquial. Say, "and died so recently as in 1898."

15. Say, "and behind these was an imperial policy other than

that of England." "Imperial" is wrongly made to qualify "England." What the writer means is "the imperial policy of England."

16. Place "only" before "to religious."

17. Say, "to champion it explicitly."

18. Say, "with the problem, to them insoluble, of obtaining," etc.

19. Say, "The Queen opened, with a ceremonial of some pomp, the new and handsome buildings," etc.

20. Say, "He frequently took up the Bible, but he seldom did so without shedding tears."

21. Say, "not however before destroying," etc.

22. Say, "he remained at Tientsin till the spring of 1862, when the headquarters were moved to Shanghai, the Chinese Government having by that time sufficiently complied with treaty obligations."

23. Say, "This movement too is far more intensely patriotic than that," etc.

24. Say, "Neither does Palestine belong to the Israelite, nor the Transvaal to the Boer."

25. Place "from breaking away southwards" immediately after "prevent."

26. Say, "could be accomplished only by breaking," etc.

27. Say, "can be carried through only by the Secretaries," etc.

28. "What would precipitate trouble would be the formation in France of a 'Nationalist' Ministry, which would," etc.

29. Say, "that the whole crew of a vessel which went ashore on the Sussex coast has been lost."

30. Say, "that in modern days the journalists of the most immoderate style are the true analogy of the prophets."

31. Say, "her indebtedness to the Western nations who imbued her with the spirit of modern civilisation, and especially to the United States, which," etc.

32. Say, "having married, while his wife was still alive, Miss H. C. H.," etc.

33. Say, "meant a departure, too violent to last, from what must," etc.

34. "In the autumn lists a copious supply of creditable literature remains to be dealt with."

35. Insert *other* before *changes*. Rearrange the remainder thus: —"It has not led to one-half either of the evils foretold by its opponents or of the advantages foretold by its advocates."

36. "What was, so to speak, the ground-plan of that marvellous character,—what were the inherent qualities," etc.

37. Begin the sentence thus :—"But from the rising of the curtain we are aware of," etc.

38. Begin the sentence with :—"By an overwhelming passion." Or say, "To his haughty and beautiful wife Herod is bound," etc.

39. Say, "through non-compliance with the Board of Trade regulations as to guard wires."

40. Begin thus :—"The other day, for instance, appeared a little German book."

41. "In the first place there must be no doubt of the extinction of

the late Republics as sovereign independent States ; that is to say, of their annexation to the Crown."

42. *Only* should be placed after *to the value* :—"to the value of only $136,000,000."

43. Say, "an almost inappreciable difference."

44. *As a minister* should be placed after the words "Lord Palmerston."

45. Say, "that ground-landlords, when they dishoused in order to rebuild, should be compelled to rehouse," etc.

46. Say, "while she contended against the right of searching neutral vessels for enemy's goods,—the right asserted by England and one of vital importance," etc.

47. Begin thus :—"In his article, of which the following is an abstract, Sir Henry traces," etc.

48. The clause "than has been previously supplied anywhere else," should be placed after "account," with a comma before and a comma after it.

49. Say, "the breadwinner, with a regularity that is appalling, has come back," etc.

50. "With some small exceptions, such as the pastorals of Theocritus, wrought artificially by literary men, Attic speech dominated," etc.

51. Change *and* to *with* to make the sentence grammatical ; and rearrange thus :—"For some little time past I have had a feeling that I myself at any rate, with perhaps the other guests in a less degree, was," etc.

52. Say, "on a footing different from that of other matters."

53. Begin thus :—"Before any of the works of peace can be undertaken in the Transvaal and Orange River colonies it will be well to utilise the time which must elapse in carefully considering," etc.

54. Say, "but beyond what was necessary for this he did not, until lately, know enough to enable him," etc.

55. Rearrange thus :—"It is obvious that a few such deals would menace, as it has never been menaced yet, the commercial sovereignty," etc.

56. "To hear the outcry one would think," etc.

57. "From the chaos of abuse and eulogy, which two hundred years have heaped on him, Cromwell stands out as a living man," etc. (Insert "as" before "impeccable saint" in order to place this phrase in antithesis with "a monster of iniquity.")

58. The phrase "with the least possible delay" should be placed after "mobilise."

59. Place "already" after "most of them."

60. Say, "that in future only those officers, who were fit to command in the field, would be given high commands at home."

61. The Relative clause "the character of which depends upon the depth of their purses," should be placed immediately after the antecedent "meal." The order should be,—"at about seven o'clock, when the hammocks are piped down, the men provide themselves with another meal, the character of which," etc.

62. Begin the sentence with :—"Except in the matter of her terms of endearment."

63. "There exists in official circles a feeling of the greatest unrest with respect to a revival of the Nihilist conspiracy, to which the students' disturbances have given vital force."

64. "From the proceedings in the House of Commons the public mind has with reluctance gathered a disappointing sense," etc.

65. "Of course, as far as lies in my power, I can give," etc.

66. "The time not spent in shooting and in drilling—the latter to be very much reduced—should be spent by the soldier in producing his own food and clothing."

67. Place the Relative clause "which are published in this volume" immediately after its antecedent "letters."

68. Say, "everybody (Mr. M. included) knew," etc.

69. "Of the many points at which, according to received religious ideas, man's life was in special contact with Heaven's purposes, there is scarcely one where," etc.

70. Place the phrase "by the heads of the French episcopate" after "encouraged."

71. Place the phrase "merely by reason of their belonging to a class" after "members."

72. "A telegram from Naples to this morning's Paris papers announces the arrival in Naples of Gomez, who with Orsini and three others was condemned in 1858 for the attempt on the life of Napoleon III., and who has spent the last forty-three years as a convict on Devil's Island."

73. "With reference to the ownership and administration of the Congo Free State, issues of graver importance than most people seem to be aware of are involved in the fresh compact that has just been arrived at between the Belgian Parliament and the government of that huge African territory."

74. Say, "the lengths to which fury could carry him, when he was resisted."

75. "He would be commissioned, without any regard whatever to party traditions and without any legislative programme, to form," etc.

76. "He was not a hermit of asceticism, but a saint indeed, combining," etc.

77. "Except those who live in great cities there are few men in Australia who are not," etc.

78. Say, "the country where this drama was played he has seen with his own eyes"; or, "he has with his own eyes seen the country where this drama was played."

79. "At 35 Park Street, Grosvenor Square, the house of Mr. Vickers, chairman of the great engineering firm, a fire broke out yesterday in the basement."

80. "The religion and the irreligion of the people he loves and pities, their virtues and their vices, the prejudices which have eaten into their brains, and their receptiveness on certain points, he makes equally clear," etc.

81. "Respectively" should stand last. But the sentence might be reworded:—"We do not propose to draw a comparison between British and American engines in respect of the intrinsic or operating value of the work put into them."

82. "The same flippant tone permeated the conversation and letters of hundreds of ladies and gentlemen, even when they were in prison and fully aware," etc.

83. Put the clause "as Mr. Mansfield does" after "saying."

84. Begin the sentence with—"In the course of the conversation."

85. Say, "my comrades and I."

86. "The person" is here in apposition with *Lizzie's*. But its distance renders a reconstruction necessary :—"A profound sensation was caused, when Lizzie, about whom gathered almost as much interest as about the prisoner himself, appeared in the witness box."

87. The sentence must be recast :—"He ended with saying that 'the loss of empire would be for this country in the future to lead a meagre life and to have mere paltry ambitions,' and made an eloquent appeal to all those, who think with him in this matter, to vote for Mr. Gerald Balfour's motion."

88. The Relative clause at the close of the sentence is too far away from the antecedent "universities." Rearrange and recast thus :— "The best system of sanitation should be carried out in our universities—the great centres of progress and civilisation, where the sons, etc., are brought up, and where medicine in all its branches is taught."

89. It would be rather better to say, "The addition to the Dual Alliance of two," etc. For the sake of euphony change "distinctly pacifically disposed states" to "distinctly pacific states," which means the same thing and is shorter.

90. Begin the sentence with, "According to the opinion of initiated persons."

91. *Slowly* and *surely* must change places, since *surely* is the more important word.

92. Begin the sentence with, "But for two disturbing facts."

93. The object of the bequest is stated in the wrong order as if it belonged to "perfecting," whereas it really belongs to "left." Say, "who having gained millions by perfecting, etc., left them to advance the cause of universal peace."

94. Say, "below that of New York or of any of the great towns of Europe," etc.

95. Say, "that, being Mahommedans with a past, they are the highest," etc.

96. Place the phrase "by anti-American federations" immediately after "fighting."

97. Say, "that in Japanese art there are many things funny to Western eyes."

98. Say, "but to decide on this accusation it would be necessary to know," etc.

99. Say, "The beaux of that day as well as the women used," etc.

100. Place "in the grotesque character of his hero" immediately after "ridicule."

101. Place "in an unfinished state" immediately after "left." Say, "Wolsey at the time of his death left," etc.

102. Begin the sentence thus :—"Now and then, on the faith of my guides, I have inserted in the text," etc.

103. Say, "a place he has not filled," etc.

104. Say, "has given in the *Journal des Savans* for 1826 a short account," etc.

105. Say, "I shall and will," etc.   The weaker of the two words should be placed first.   In the first person, Future, *shall* is weak and *will* is strong.

106. Say, "to exchange the hardships and monotony of the north for the luxury and adventure of the south."   The words as they stand in the original express the opposite to what the writer meant.

CHAPTER IX.—ANSWERS TO EXAMPLES IN
CHAPTER IV. (pp. 187-201).

1. *To* is admissible after "different," but *from* is better. (The order is bad. Say, "that restrictions and regulations very different from those which prevail are demanded.")

2. Either change *inferred* to *implied ;* or change *by* to *from.*

3. Say, "in the hall." "*At* the hall" would mean at the place where the hall stands, but not inside it.

4. Here "between," though applicable to only two things when it signifies position, is correct, because here it denotes reciprocal action or relation.

5. Say, "by all thinking men."

6. Say, "concur in any theory."

7. Say, "in whose maternal bosom." *Into* is used to express motion, *in* to express rest.

8. Say, "begins with taking." *By* implies agency ; which does not suit the present context.

9. The order is not good, and *to* is less suitable than *from.* Say, "in a category different from such public spaces."

10. Say, "with the minimum of religious recognition."

11. Say, "at his disposal."

12. Say, "among several ideals." *Between* is not here admissible, since it does not in this context signify reciprocal action or relation.

13. Say, "of all other," etc.

14. Say, "will assist in examining." We use the Infinitive after "help," as "help to examine," or "help us to examine."

15. Say, "begin with a short account."

16. Say, "satisfied merely with observing and portraying."

17. Say, "was of much good."

18. Say, "being first in Pretoria." But the phrase is not a good one. Say, "being the first to enter Pretoria."

19. Say, "we aim at."

20. *By* is here admissible, since thunder and lightning may be regarded as agents or active accompaniments ; but it sounds rather better to say, "accompanied with thunder and rain."

21. Say, "rebelling against," or "seceding from."

22. Say, "with disagreeable incidents." *With* here denotes manner or concomitant circumstance.

23. Say, "with a benevolent vagueness."

24. Say, "impatience of the injustice."

25. Cancel *with* after "finished." Substitute "concluded" or "disposed of," either of which is better than "finished."

26. Insert *with* after "done."

27. Say, "It aims at representing."

28. Say, "for a space of from three to five years."

29. Say, "has not been of the least use to him."

30. It would be rather better to say, "a greater enemy to agriculture."

31. Say, "to secure for the Federals."

32. Cancel *with* after "commiserated."

33. *Between* is here admissible, since it denotes reciprocal relation. But the phraseology of the sentence might be improved ; such phrases as "break in upon," "entered into between," are not commendable. "The Government proposes to disturb the solemn contract that the Australian colonies have formed with one another."

34. It would be better to say, "has died *of* injuries received *from* being run over."

35. Substitute *besides* for "as well as."

36. Say, "different from the proceedings."

37. Say, "on either alternative."

38. Cancel *from*. But it would be better to say, "One source of the ancient gods was the deification of ancestors."

39. Say, "in forming."

40. Say, "directed to silencing."

41. Say, "has inspired them with a lofty heroism." Or say, "has aroused them to," etc.

42. Say, "sentiments different from those." The order in the original is bad. Say, "when the existing sentiments were different from those," etc.

43. Cancel *to* after "attained."

44. We cannot say "independence upon," and if we substitute the proper preposition, "of," the sense becomes obscure. The sentence can be recast as follows :—"That the Roman Catholic family of Th. were among the poet's most intimate and best cherished friends is a singular proof that his literary and social character was independent of his theological proclivities."

45. "Struck by the gross injustice" is admissible. But *with* would be equally correct, and would here sound better, since there is another *by* immediately after.

46. Cancel *into*, and say, "than enter Parliament." The form "enter into" can be applied to such nouns as "contract," "agreement," but not to such a noun as "Parliament." Moreover the rhythm of the sentence is destroyed by *into*.

47. Although it is possible to parse "every knot" as an adverbial objective qualifying "increased," it would be better to make "every knot" the subject of the sentence and place a preposition after it :— "In theory every knot of increase of speed above," etc.

48. Say, "veiled in the greatest secrecy."

49. Correct. "Averse" can be followed by *from*, though *to* has become perhaps more common. Etymologically *from* is the more correct, since "averse" means "turned away." Having acquired the sense of "hostile," "opposed," it is now followed by *to*.

50. Cancel *in.* "A few days" is an adverbial objective qualifying the adverb "afterwards."

51. Say, "aim at conquering."

52. Cancel *at.* It would be better to say, "the most disgraceful place in which to pick pockets is a cricket ground," etc.

53. Say, "are insignificant in comparison with the latest project."

54. Reconstruct thus : — "There was no applause during his address or during that given by Baron de Staal." (After "no" we should use *or*, not *nor*.)

55. Say, "sacrificed to splendour."

56. Insert *of* before "the ultimate success." Or leave this phrase as it stands, and change "was very confident" to "confidently expected."

57. Insert *of* before "much use."

58. Correct. See remarks in (49).

59. Either "with a view to showing" or "with the view of showing" is admissible. The former phrase is the one recommended. "The view to showing" is a confusion of both.

60. Cancel *at.* "Travesty" is here the Object of the verb "read."

61. Say, "from taking."

62. There is nothing wrong in the prepositions ; but the order is not good, and it would sound better to say, "By returning, etc., Jewish ceremonial one would be perilously near the state of ceasing," etc.

63. Say, "in drawing."

64. Say, "dominated by one idea." "Domination by one idea" in the next clause is correct, since "idea" is here the agent which dominates.

65. "With the view of showing," though not quite so common as "with a view to showing," is correct. See remarks in (59).

66. Say, "against the danger."

67. Reconstruct thus :—"Its association with the foreign rites, etc., is deeply engrained in the popular mind."

68. Say, "at the time to which the rector, vicar, or curate was accustomed."

69. Say, "from a severe cold."

70. Say, "with a view to compelling."

71. Say, "the difference between the Church *of* England and the Church *in* England."

72 Say, "independence of parish relief."

73. Say, "accompanied with an umbrella." *By* is not appropriate here, since an umbrella cannot be considered an agent. Reconstruct thus :—"accompanied with an umbrella that had an extraordinary eagle's head as its handle."

74. Say, "assisted in conveying."

75. Say, "at long intervals." We cannot say "between each," since "between" implies two things at least. Reconstruct thus :— "at long intervals between every new instalment and the previous one."

76. The preposition *with* can be retained, if "furnishing" is substituted for "affording."

77. Say, "with the object of getting."

X

78. Say, "by the side of the deceased."

79. Say, "from whom."

80. *For* can be placed after the noun "desire," but not after the verb. Reconstruct thus :—"We might share with him a desire for Euclid to be abolished"; or, "We might desire with him that Euclid should be abolished."

81. The sentence is very ill-worded. *That* should be changed to *this*, *mutual* should be cancelled as superfluous, *with* should be changed to *of*, *each other* should be changed to *one another*, and *it*, being of uncertain reference, should be changed to *the League*. The sentence is a good example of slipshod English of the worst type. With the above changes it will stand as follows :—"This is the object of the Primrose League,—this constant intercourse of all classes with one another,—and therefore the League has been a success."

82. Say, "in London," since the area of London is decidedly large.

83. Say, "at the total exclusion."

84. Say, "at three or four thousand years B.C."

85. Say, "by a display,"·since here "display" is the agent, not the instrument or manner.

86. Say, "from neuralgia and indigestion."

87. Say, "on regarding."

88. Say, "except hips and haws."

89. Say, "done to the country."

90. Correct. *From* can be used after "averse," though *to* is perhaps more common

91. It would be rather better, though it is not necessary, to place *of* after "conscious."

92. It would be rather better, though it is not necessary, to say, "Delighted at the magnificent welcome."

93. Say, "with the great world outside."

94. Say, "with being superseded."

95. Say, either *adverse to* or *averse from.*

96. Say, "by thirty to one."

97. Say, "with the impetuous Rhone." "Compare *to*" is correct.

98. Say, "with the English monarchy."

99. Say, "unite in praising."

100. Say, "how much." The *by*, though not wrong, is superfluous besides being unidiomatic.

101. Say, "to devoting."

102. Say, "intolerant of all creeds except their own, and especially of the Catholic faith."

103. Say, "assisted in burying."

104. Say, "to do our full duty."

105. Say, "with a heavy cannonade."

106. *Between* is here appropriate, because it is intended to signify plurality of reciprocal relations.

107. Say, "from this point of view."

108. Say, "anything else than humiliating."

109. Say, "with the following figures."

110. Say, "the condition it was in."

111. Say, "with disagreeable surprises."

112. Change *than* to *from*, and reconstruct thus :—"There must be a spirit of energy and concentration very different from what has prevailed," etc.

113. Say either, "with respect to disease," or "in respect of."

114. Say, "for the maintenance."

115. Say, "with much physical and moral suffering."

116. Say, "to Buddha himself."

117. Say, "with which to play the game of war."

118. Say, "against which to protest."

119. It is rather better to say, "different from the old days."

120. Say, "covered with snow."

121. Say, "in Regent's Park."

122. Some preposition such as *in* must be placed before "the last trace"; otherwise "trace" is a pendent Nominative. Or we can say, "The last trace we have of him is that he was with Paul," etc.

123. Say, "Of what use."

124. Say, "with a view to gaining."

125. Say, "this is largely accounted for by the war." Or say, "this is largely in consequence of the war." The language as it stands is tautological.

126. Reconstruct thus :—"No one would accuse the representative of an English newspaper of desiring, as if he were an Irishman, to exaggerate the distress and grievances of Ireland."

127. Say, "involved in his attempt."

128. Say, "conducive to pity."

129. The phrase "with the view of extending" is admissible, though it would be more idiomatic to say "with the object of extending," or "with a view to extending."

130. Here *of* (the fifth word in the sentence) is used equivocally. Say, "The worship of an effeminate hero like Sandan and the legend concerning him appear," etc.

131. Say, "His belief in revelation."

132. Say, "is sparing of praise."

133. Say, "great admiration for the recent discoveries."

134. Change "at York," "at Oxford," to "in York," "in Oxford."

135. "*By* the quiet contempt" is here as correct as *with*, and *by* sounds better, since *with* comes immediately after.

136. Say, "in St. Helena."

137. Either cancel *from* or change "resigned" to "retired."

138. Say, "with Leigh Hunt's recovering," etc. (Observe the change from "Leigh Hunt" to "Leigh Hunt's.")

139. Say, "grasp of the personality."

140. Say, "for scrupulous honesty."

141. Say, "to the sentiments."

142. Say, "from themselves," and place this phrase immediately after "different."

143. We cannot well say "guilty to bigamy." Say, "to a charge of bigamy."

144. Say, "differently from the rest."

145. Say, "with the following words."

146. Correct. Here the writer has well observed the two phrases, "with a view to the purchase," "with the view of purchasing."

147. We cannot say, "with whom inseparable." The clause can be reconstructed thus :—"with whom for so long I still went coupled in inseparable friendship." Or say, "inseparably coupled."

148. Say, "dissent from the opinion."

149. The difficulty is that "astonished" takes *at* after it, while "frightened" takes *by*. The Relative clause can be reconstructed thus :—"which, added to her appearance, frightened me a little and astonished me more."

150. "Unwhipped of justice" is a bad phrase. We might say, "uncorrected by justice." But it would be better to say, "The incorrigible loafer at present escapes the penalty that he deserves."

151. Say, "of the existence of which."

152. Say, "commenced with trouble or terminated with calamity."

153. Say, "with the following," etc.

154. The proper phrase for "at twelve years old" would be "at twelve years of age." If we use the adjective "old" at all, we ought to say "twelve years old." But this would not suit the rhythm of the sentence.

155. Say, "Of what use."

156. "Gained greatly owing to," etc., is a bad phrase. Say, "the Queen owed much to the fortunate," etc. Or say, "the Queen gained much credit from the fortunate," etc.

157. Say, "from rheumatism."

158. Say, "against a woman."

159. Change *beside* to *besides*.

160. Say, "attended with success."

161. Say, "to impress upon the Convention the necessity."

162. Change *to* to *from* and rearrange thus :—"under conditions of naval warfare totally different from those which," etc.

163. If "terminate" is changed to "are terminated," then "by the king" will be correct, as "king" will here be the agent or doer of the action. But if "terminate" (= come to an end) is to be retained, then *by* must be changed to *with* as showing how, or the manner in which, the proceedings come to an end, not the agent by whom they are brought to an end.

164. Say, "familiar with the idea."

165. Say, "covered with wood." Substitute *the wood* for *it*.

166. Say, "on the completion."

167. Say, "with a view to indulging."

168. Say, "a sort of courage different from that," etc.

169. Say, "opposition to England." (It is not good English to say "opposed the opposition." Say, "set their faces against the opposition.")

170. Cancel *in* before "Chicago."

171. Cancel *in* before "four years hence," or say, "in four years' time."

172. Say, "begins with a taste."

173. Say, "different from the native."

174. Say, "of the disease."

175. Say, "greeted with laughter."

176. Say, "of which he is oblivious."
177. Say, "with the Slavonic ideal."
178. Say, "with a unanimous vote."
179. Say, "object to being made use of by employers."
180. Say, "of abuse of office."
181. Say, "with the paradox."
182. Cancel *for* before "support."
183. Insert *in* before "a cursory notice."
184. Cancel *for* after "want" and insert *that* after "than."
185. Say, "by a trumpet." Insert "by it" after "moved."
186. Cancel *to* before "the creation."
187. Change *by* in both places to *with*.
188. Insert *on* before "which."
189. Say, "which makes an inconsistency different from, and less pardonable than, that," etc.
190. Say, "on decent wages."
191. Insert "on it" after "insisting."
192. Say, "in comparison with this."
193. Say, "threatened with a serious outbreak."
194. Say, "commences with the north."
195. Cancel *in*. Or change "lacks" to "is wanting."
196. *To* is not used after "follow." The writer's only reason for inserting it was to show that the subjects of "follow" are "luncheon," "service," etc. Reconstruct thus:—"an address by Lord Rosebery, to be followed by luncheon," etc. (Another mistake in the sentence consists in using "follow" instead of "will follow.")
197. Substitute "than" for "save."
198. Change *to* to *with*.
199. Cancel *for* after "want."
200. Say, "is not wanting in comprehensiveness."
201. Say, "bearing false witness against it (literary criticism)."
202. Say, "preparations for resistance."
203. Say, "treatment by the white peoples," and reconstruct thus:—"Under the outrageous treatment of the yellow peoples by the white, the idea of unifying the former is pretty certain to become audibly and visibly operative before many years have passed."
204. It is more common to say "appeal against a judgment" than "appeal from one." But we can speak of appealing from one court to another.
205. Either say, "ascribed to a certain fatigue," or "accounted for by a certain fatigue." (The order in the original is bad. The phrase, "according to the opinion of initiated persons," should stand first.)
206. Say, "charged the police with having shown partisanship by ejecting," etc.; or say, "charged the police with partisanship for having ejected," etc.
207. Say, "than those," instead of "to those." It would be rather better to rearrange thus:—"are men of a finer stamp than those," etc.
208. Say, "by the Pictish king and his people." ("Equally certainly" has a bad sound. "It is equally certain that," etc.)
209. Say, "aspires to epigram."

210. Reconstruct thus :— "to double the kindness and caresses to be bestowed upon me."

211. Change "from" to "to."

212. Either say, "differ from one another"; or say, "differ among themselves."

213. Say, "speaking on the following points." Insert the conjunction "that" after "request."

214. Cancel *for* after "want."

215. Say, "prefer Italy to France as a neighbour in Egypt."

216. Say, "marked by tact and discretion."

217. Say, "with a view to stopping."

218. Say, "inspired printers with so much apprehension."

219. Say, "are justified in their protests."

220. Say, "is covered with ashes and dust."

221. Say, "in a creed other than my own"; or, "in a creed different from my own."

222. Say, "among the biographies of the year"; or, "in the biographical literature of the year."

223. Change *among* to *between*.

224. Change *from* to *besides*. "Than" is often used after "other," but here it would not give the sense required by the context.

225. Say, "oblivious of."

226. Either change *on* to *to ;* or change *looked* to *relied*.

227. Cancel *owing*.

228. Cancel *into the flames*, as this has been expressed already by *into which*.

229. Begin the sentence with, "To each of the 365 days."

230. Begin the sentence with, "This last new feature in the Game Laws is the one to which," etc.

231. Say, "of a complexion different from that of the talk," etc.

232. Say, "to send to Spain or France for their professors."

233. Either change *with* to *in ;* or change *involved* to *beset*.

234. Change *with* to *by*.

235. Change *to* to *on*.

236. To prevent the ambiguity of the last four words say, "wrote under the influence of momentary impulse."

237. Cancel the *of* before "our Government listening." The writer appears to have forgotten that the *fear* in a previous clause is a verb, not a noun. The sentence, however, requires to be recast :— "no reason to fear that the German Government would propose that we should take any share in the Baghdad Railway, or, if it did, that our Government would listen for a moment," etc.

238. Insert the preposition *by* before "Legislature."

CHAPTER X.—ANSWERS TO EXAMPLES IN CHAPTER V.

(a) Co-ordinative Conjunctions (pp. 207-213).

1. Change *as well as* to *and*.

2. Change *and* to *or* and cancel the comma after "Europe." If *and* is retained, the wording must be "and perhaps not one in the world."

3. Probably *are* is here a mistake for *is*. But if *are* is to be retained, *and* must be inserted after "resource" and the comma cancelled.

4. Change *and* to *but*.

5. Change *and* to *but*.

6. "Only slightly" signifies "but little," "not much." We could hardly say, "They did not much damage the railroad, but did not succeed," etc. Reconstruct thus:—"They did some slight damage to the railroad, but did not succeed in cutting the telegraph wires." If the first clause, "They only slightly damaged the railroad," is to be retained, then *but* must be changed to *and*.

7. Rewrite as follows :—" In fact neither in his teaching nor in his example is it possible, if we regard him as a mere man, to attribute to any particular parts a distinct, or distinctive, or permanent footing."

8. Insert *nor* before "sublimity," and cancel the commas after "greatness" and after "sublimity."

9. Say, "is evidence neither of the highest wisdom, nor of the truest courage, nor of the firmest belief," etc.

10. After "necessary," change *and* to *or*.

11. Change *and* to *but*.

12. Change *or* to *nor*. For "certainly not" say "certainly there is none." "Not," as it stands, makes a double negative with "neither."

13. Change *or* to *nor*.

14. Change *and* to *though*. The subordinate clause thus produced will qualify the phrase "for some years." The clause ought certainly not to be co-ordinate.

15. Say, "neither in morals nor in literature nor in art," and cancel the commas after "morals" and "literature." For "the Catholic Feudalism" say "that of Catholic Feudalism."

16. Say, "and that little or nothing was left," and cancel the

commas after "little" and "nothing." But if the commas and the "if" are to be retained, then *nothing* must be changed to *anything*.

17. Change the first *and* to *but*.

18. Say, "nor a waggon nor an enemy," cancel the commas, and place "neither" immediately after "captured."

19. Say, "more quickly or more quietly or more methodically." Cancel the commas after "quickly" and "quietly."

20. Say, "either by gravitation, or by annexation, or by conquest, or by voluntary," etc.

21. Insert *neither* before "the Egyptian people."

22. Say, "neither the Cabinet, nor the Unionist party, nor the House of Commons, nor the Press," etc.

23. Cancel *and*. Or retain *and* and say, "and the Bible was translated into." The construction, as it stands, is mixed.

24. Cancel either *and* or *who*. One of these is sufficient.

25. Say, "she neither saw nor heard any more of him."

26. Say, "Margarine, though it is not butter, is an excellent food-substance ; the potato, though it should not be found in bread, is very nourishing." The writer through animadvertence did not attend to the difference between *though* and *but*. Here the context requires *though* in the fourth clause, no less than in the second.

27. Say, "are reviving, slowly no doubt, but surely." The order of the adverbs is wrong, since *but* is required for the more important word or words. If, however, the order of the adverbs is to be retained, then *but* must be changed to *though*.

28. Cancel *and* at the beginning of the second sentence.

29. Cancel *and* at the beginning of the third sentence.

30. Say, "Neither Ezekiel, nor Jeremiah, nor Deuteronomy, nor the ancient prophets ever allude," etc.

31. It would be rather more correct to say, "the halfpenny mug of tea, coffee, or cocoa."

32. Insert *nor* before "Germany."

33. Cancel *and* at the beginning of the second sentence.

34. Cancel *either*. If *either* is to be retained, it must be followed by *or* :—"either by antiquated fictions, or by social claims, or by private regard." ("Only" should be placed after "influenced.")

35. *And which* is wrong :—"in the hands of an authority which should be constituted for this purpose and should have," etc. Or the sentence may stand as it is, provided that *and* is cancelled. Insert *or* before "on river craft."

36. Say, "of those who have been misinformed." After this change has been made, the retention of *who* after "or," though admissible, is not necessary.

37. Say, "Neither in China, nor in Persia, nor in Egypt, nor in South Africa, nor in Newfoundland, is there any reason," etc.

38. Change *and* to *but*.

39. Say, "neither with its wisdom, nor with its policy, nor with its expediency."

40. Change *and* to *whereas*.

41. Change *And* to *Moreover*.

42. Cancel *both*, which is not merely superfluous, but wrong, since three things are here mentioned.

43. Cancel *and* at the beginning of the second sentence.

44. Change *and* to *or*. Cancel the comma after "kings."

45. Insert *neither* before "formally."

46. *And which* cannot be tolerated in this context. Cancel the *and*, which here happens to be superfluous.

47. Cancel *and* before "Protection." If, however, the *and* is to be retained, then change "granted" to "grant." The construction, as it stands, is mixed.

48. *And who* is inappropriate. Say, "troops who are commanded by British officers and serve the King."

49. The phrase "fortuitous and rational," appears through the force of *and*, to imply that these two epithets are intended to be combined in sense, whereas it is clear from the context that they are intended to be separated both in sense and application. Say, "an essay on coincidences which may be either fortuitous or designed (rational)."

50. Say, "neither the scope, nor the aim, nor the application, nor the contents."

51. *And which* is here doubly faulty. There is no Relative clause going before, and *which* has for its antecedent the noun "collection," which stands much too far off, and is not used in quite the same sense. The sentence must be recast:—"He devoted even more attention to the collecting of medals and coins ; and the collection, which he began from his earliest boyhood, has made him," etc.

52. Change *or* to *nor*.

53. Say, "It was an entirely new creation, which was not inspired by any previous work, but gave birth to many others," etc.

54. Say, "who are the most inventive, and to whom we owe many," etc.

55. *And my office* is not here sufficient. Insert "when" between *and* and *my*.

56. Say, "is neither mind-cure, nor faith-cure, nor mesmerism, nor hypnotism."

57. Change *and nobody* to *but nobody*.

58. Say, "a step which has long been dreaded, and which now threatens," etc.

59. Say, "a son who thoroughly reverences her character and her mode of action, and who himself," etc. Here the second "who" is retained, because it introduces a statement entirely distinct from the previous one.

60. The *and* before "adopted," though correct, is weak and unsuitable. Say, "But it was not content to rest there. It adopted resolutions," etc.

61. Change *or* to *nor*.

62. "Neither party nor political" is an awkward combination, because "party" (though used adjectively, as we find by reading on) is a noun, while "political" is a real adjective. The sentence can be reconstructed thus :—"In support of the South African policy of the Government there was held at the Guildhall a great City meeting, described by the Lord Mayor as neither a party gathering nor a political one, but one fully and completely patriotic."

63. Say, "or Libya, or Persia."

64. Insert *nor* before "cruelty." Cancel *either* before "small meannesses."

65. Change *and* to *or* in the last three words.

66. Change *and* to *or* in the last three words.

67. Cancel *and* before "who."

68. The *and* in "and another war," though correct, is weak. Say, "not territory nor another war." There must be no comma after "territory."

69. Say, "neither tender, nor loving, nor retiring, nor domestic."

70. Say, "the peasantry, who are taxed already to the point of torture, and whom further pressure," etc.

71. Say, "twenty, consisting of killed, wounded, or captured."

72. The *and* at the head of the second clause does not fit in with the sense of the previous one. "It must require a large number of men to deal with them effectively. Hence there is no reason for alarm at the apparently slow progress, but rather cause," etc.

73. Change *or* to *and*. Cancel the comma after "evil."

74. Insert *nor* before "sufficiently complete."

75. Say, "any one who is acquainted with American engines and has seen," etc.

76. *Both* cannot be used before three words, "wide, long, and recent." Say, "at once wide, long, and recent."

77. Cancel *and* before "which."

78. Insert *which was* after "society." Place "publicly" after "assist."

79. Cancel *and* before "which."

80. Cancel *and* before "which." Change *supersede* to *pave*.

81. Say, "will act neither cheerfully nor wisely."

82. There are two faults in this sentence : (1) *attended* is pendent, having no noun to which it can refer ; (2) there is need of some adversative conjuction before *attended*. Say, " but their despotism was attended with," etc.

83. Say, "and how disastrous was the issue of that expedition."

84. Change *or* to *nor*.

85. Say, "more affecting or more deeply engaging our sympathy."

86. Say, "but will willingly fan."

(b) *Subordinative Conjunctions* (pp. 222-234).

1. Change *except* to "unless." The Indicative "is" might here be substituted for "be."

2. Change *but* to "when."

3. Say, "has as authentic an attestation as any of the Gospel miracles, and even a more authentic one."

4. Change *against* to the conjunctional phrase "by the time." Or use *against* as a preposition and say "against the time by which it was necessary."

5. Say, "when once the light was out."

6. Cancel "other," or if other is to be retained, change *but* to "than."

7. Cancel " equally," and insert *much* after *as*.

8. There is no error in the use of "but." The sentence might

equally stand thus : "The new Japanese minister, though he has been hardly twenty-four hours in this country, has already laid," etc.

9. Say, "in anticipation of the commencement of service"; or, "in preparation for the commencement," etc. We have no conjunction that can be substituted for "against," the use of which as a conjunction is now obsolete. We could say, however, "against the time when service would commence."

10. Change *without* to "unless."

11. Say, "reveals a mood different from those"; or, "reveals a mood other than those."

12. Change *but* to "than."

13. Change *save* to "unless."

14. Change *but* to "when."

15. Say, "certainly with not less, and perhaps with more, reluctance than those," etc.

16. "Nothing more was needed than to advance," etc.

17. Change *as* to "that."

18. Change *like* to "as."

19. Change *without* to "unless."

20. Change *but* to "when."

21. Change *except* to "unless."

22. Cancel *like*.

23. Change *than* to "when."

24. Change *immediately* to "as soon as."

25. Insert *when* before "once."

26. Change *but* to "than."

27. Change *as* to "that."

28. Change *like* to "as."

29. Change *directly* to "as soon as."

30. Insert *when* before "once."

31. Either change *like* to "as," or cancel *are*.

32. Change *but* to "than."

33. Change *than* to "when."

34. Insert *as* after "way."

35. Change *as* to "that."

36. Cancel *that* before "the gold-laced hat." There should be no comma after "sallied out."

37. Change *like* to "as."

38. Insert *that* after "moment." Insert "does" after "he."

39. Insert *when* before "once."

40. The construction is mixed. We can either say, "He frankly admitted that the evils complained of existed and that the state of things had become worse," etc. Or we can say, "He frankly admitted the existence of the evils complained of and the deterioration of the state of things," etc.

41. Insert *that* after "notwithstanding."

42. Say, "in the same way as other men," etc. Or say, "to the same extent that other men," etc.

43. *Providing* is both wrong in form and gives a wrong sense. The form, if the word is to be used at all, should be, "provided that." But the word here required by the sense is "supposing that," or "assuming that."

44. Change *or that* to " or whether."

45. Change *than* to "from." Or change *different* to "other." The order should be, " to places of worship different from," etc., or "other than," etc.

46. Insert *when* before " once."

47. Insert *that* after " now."

48. Change *that* to " whether."

49. Insert *when* after " time."

50. Change *like* to " as." The order should be, " that he has put himself, as every capable General does, in imagination," etc.

51. Change *but* to " than." The order should be, " of which no sooner had Nicias notice, than," etc. It would be better to insert " received " before " notice."

52. Insert *that* after " notwithstanding."

53. Change *providing* to "provided " or " provided that."

54. Change *that* to " unless."

55. *Since* is correct, but *has been* must be changed to " was."

56. Insert *when* before " once."

57. Either say, "when men are camping out"; or, "to men camping out." No Finite verb with its Subject can be understood after " when " from the context.

58. Insert *for the fact* before " that." Or say, " He also commends the President for not having pressed his case," etc.

59. Change *like* to " as."

60. Insert *that* after " claim."

61. The future tense is rarely used with the conjunction *after*. Say, " after he is dead and buried."

62. Insert *as* after " way."

63. Change *immediately* to " as soon as."

64. Change *providing* to " provided " or " provided that."

65. Insert *when* before " once."

66. This will stand. But it would be simpler to change *ago that* to " since."

67. Change *than* to " when."

68. Insert *when* before " once."

69. Change *like* to " as."

70. Say, " altogether detestable if we were not bound to remember," etc. Or we might retain *that* and change *only* to " except":—" He would be altogether detestable except that we are bound," etc.

71. Insert *when* before " once."

72. Say, " when the troops were five-eighths of a mile," etc. Or, "The troops being five-eighths," etc. The conjunction " when " cannot be retained, unless some Subject and Finite verb are placed after it. Neither Subject nor verb can be understood from the context.

73. Say, " which are unsown, and where no fodder of any kind is available."

74. The construction is mixed. We can say, " It is now about twenty years since our influence became supreme," etc. Or we can say, " The time during which our influence has been supreme, etc., is now about twenty years."

75. Insert *when* before " once."

76. Insert *that* after " is."

77. Change *providing* to "provided" or "provided that."

78. The verb and its subject are not usually understood after "because." Say, "because it comes."

79. Insert *when* after "time."

80. Change *like* to "as."

81. Change *once* to "as soon as," or insert *when* before it.

82-92. Correct in the same way as example (81).

93. Change *than* to "when."

94. Change *else* to "more." Or say, "Some other properties besides," etc.

95. Change *but* to "than."

96. Insert *other* after "aim."

97. Change *that* to "whether."

98. Change *that* to "whether."

99. Change *that* to "whether."

100. Change *that* to "why."

101. *But* cannot be used after "other." Say, "from any other man than him." Here "than" is used as a preposition, to which "him" is the object. Compare "than whom," where the construction is similar. Those who will not admit that "than" can be used as a preposition, notwithstanding the assertions of Sweet and Abbott, may consider that "him" is the object of the preposition "from" carried forward from the previous clause.

· 102. "The moment," though rather commonly used as a subordinative conjunction, might well be changed to "as soon as." Or say, "the moment when."

103. Change *like* to "as."

104. Insert *when* before "once."

105. Change *than* to "but." The sentence is awkward and ill-balanced, and could be reconstructed thus :—"On this subject we could never have looked for anything from them but criticism or even censure."

106. Insert *when* before "the United States."

107. Change *than* to "when."

108. Cancel the conjunction *that*.

109. Say, "No sooner has one awakened than," etc. Or change *than* to "when."

110. Change *that* to "whether."

111. Change "had occurred long before" to "had occurred long ago when." Or change *hardly* to "ever."

112. Change *that* to "when."

113. Insert *when* before "once."

114. *But* is wrong after "else," and the co-ordinative conjunctions at the beginning of the sentence need correction. Say, "No Liberal or Tory viceroy, and no Liberal or Tory Secretary of State, has done anything else than pass him," etc.

115. Insert *when* before "once."

116. Change *providing* to "provided."

117. Insert *when* before "once."

118. Change *immediately* to "as soon as."

119. Say, "in the same manner as that in which he introduced," etc.

120. Insert *when* or *in which* after "years."
121. Change *providing* to "provided."
122. Insert *when* after "time." Or say, "against the time of my visit."
123. Insert *when* before "once."
124. Change *immediately* to "as soon as."
125. Change *than* to "besides."
126. Insert *when* or *on which* after "morning."
127. Change *but* to "as." Or cancel *so much*, and leave *but* as it is. The construction is confused. Substitute "war" for "it" in the final clause.
128. *Other than* is here correct. But *providing* should be changed to "provided."
129. Change *as* to "though."
130. Insert *when* before "once."
131. Insert *when* before "once."
132. Change *like* to "such as."
133. Change *except* to "unless."
134. Change *than by aliens* to "to being governed by aliens."
135. Insert *when* before "once."
136. Change *than* to "as." Or say, "a more vigorous development than in the days," etc.
137. Change *providing* to "provided."
138. Insert *it was* after "when."
139. Insert *they are* after "because."
140. Change *that* after "doubt is expressed" to "whether."
141. Cancel *other*.
142. Change *but* to "than."
143. Insert *what* after like.
144. The conjunctions are correct ; but the final clause should be recast thus :—"shall be worked in gangs in parts of the mine different from those allotted to Kaffirs."
145. The construction is confused. If "in the event" is retained, we must say, "in the event of the board deciding," etc. But we might substitute the conjunctional phrase "in case" for the prepositional phrase "in the event of." The sentence will then run—"In case the board decides," etc.
146. Insert *when* or *in which* after "year."
147. The co-ordinate clause "and no one seems much the worse" does not fit with *with which*. It should therefore be changed to the absolute construction, " no one seeming much the worse."
148. Change *than* to "to what it was in."
149. Change *providing* to "provided." Say "with any one whom."
150. Change *but* to "than."
151. Insert *when* before "once."
152. Change *like* to "as."
153. Insert *when* before "once."
154. Change *equally* to "as." Or change *as* to "with."
155. Change *providing* to "provided."
156. Change *without* to "unless."
157. Insert *if* before "once."
158. Change *like* to "as" or "such as."

159. Insert *travellers are* after " when."

160. Change *immediately* to " as soon as."

161. Change *than* to " besides."

162. " Than " cannot be used after " prefer." Reconstruct thus : —" who prefer saying that their fathers came down in the world through their own follies to saying that they," etc.

163. Insert *if* before " once."

164. Change *but* to " when."

165. Change *like* to " as."

166. Change *but* to " than."

167. Change *except* to " unless." (The preposition *upon* should be changed to " with.")

168. Change *like* to " as." The word " like " may be retained as an adjective qualifying " systems " only on condition that " surviving " is inserted after " sea." Even then the construction is not so natural.

169. Cancel *other.*

170. Change *than* to " besides."

171. Change *like* to " as." (*Much* should be substituted for " very.")

172. Insert *as* after " old." Say, " are as old as tradition or even older."

173. Say, " In order to believe, even though I might be blind, that Saturn has a belt, I need only make," etc.

174. Change *that* to " whether " after " doubtful."

175. Change *than* to " when."

176. Change *than* to " besides."

177. Change *than* to " when." Or retain *than* and say, " No sooner had the vast successes," etc.

178. Insert some conjunctive adverb, as " why," after *reason.*

179. Change *like* to " as."

180. Change *like* to " as."

181. Change *but* to " than."

182. Change *because* to " that."

183. Cancel *that.* Or if *that* is to be retained, we might say, " he expressed a wish to his wife, who was at the time pregnant, that if she brought him a son, she should place," etc.

184. Cancel *other ;* or change *but* to " than."

185. Cancel *other ;* or change *except* to " than."

186. Say, " with eyes different from what they would have been had the history or the poem borne any other name."

187. Say, " no thicker than the finest needle, nor one-thousandth part so thick."

188. Say, " as to the absence of vehemence." Or cancel " so much," and leave " but rather " as it is.

189. Change *than* to " when."

190. Change *equally* to " as."

INDEX

The references are to pages.